MW00694705

The Bible and Catholic Theological Ethics

CATHOLIC THEOLOGICAL ETHICS IN THE WORLD CHURCH

James F. Keenan, Series Editor

Since theological ethics is so diffuse today, since practitioners and scholars are caught up in their own specific cultures, and since their interlocutors tend to be in other disciplines, there is the need for an international exchange of ideas in Catholic theological ethics.

Catholic Theological Ethics in the World Church (CTEWC) recognizes the need to appreciate the challenge of pluralism, to dialogue from and beyond local culture, and to interconnect within a world church not dominated solely by a northern paradigm. In this light, CTEWC is undertaking four areas of activity: fostering new scholars in theological ethics, sponsoring regional conferencing, supporting the exchange of ideas via our website (catholicethics.com), and publishing a book series.

The book series will pursue critical and emerging issues in theological ethics. It will proceed in a manner that reflects local cultures and engages in cross-cultural, interdisciplinary conversations motivated by mercy and care and shaped by shared visions of hope.

The Bible and Catholic Theological Ethics

Edited by

Yiu Sing Lúcás Chan

James F. Keenan

Ronaldo Zacharias

ORBIS BOOKS
Maryknoll, New York 10545

ORBIS BOOKS
Maryknoll, New York 10545

Founded in 1970, Orbis Books endeavors to publish works that enlighten the mind, nourish the spirit, and challenge the conscience. The publishing arm of the Maryknoll Fathers and Brothers, Orbis seeks to explore the global dimensions of the Christian faith and mission, to invite dialogue with diverse cultures and religious traditions, and to serve the cause of reconciliation and peace. The books published reflect the views of their authors and do not represent the official position of the Maryknoll Society. To learn more about Maryknoll and Orbis Books, please visit our website at www.maryknollsociety.org.

Copyright © 2017 by James F. Keenan

Published by Orbis Books, Maryknoll, New York 10545-0302.
Manufactured in the United States of America.

All rights reserved. No part of this publication may be reproduced or transmitted in any form or by any means, electronic or mechanical, including photocopying, recording or any information storage or retrieval system, without prior permission in writing from the publisher.

Queries regarding rights and permissions should be addressed to: Orbis Books, P.O. Box 302, Maryknoll, New York 10545-0302.

Library of Congress Cataloging-in-Publication Data

Names: Chan, Yiu Sing Lucas, 1968-2015, editor.
Title: The Bible and Catholic theological ethics / edited by Yiu Sing Lucas
    Chan, James F. Keenan, Ronaldo Zacharias.
Description: Maryknoll : Orbis Books, 2017. | Series: Catholic theological ethics in the
    world church series | Includes bibliographical references and index.
Identifiers: LCCN 2016048196 (print) | LCCN 2017007376 (ebook) |
    ISBN 9781626982185 (pbk.) | ISBN 9781608336838 (e-book)
Subjects: LCSH: Ethics in the Bible. | Catholic Church--Doctrines. |
    Christian ethics—Catholic authors.
Classification: LCC BS680.E84 B49 2017 (print) | LCC BS680.E84 (ebook) |
    DDC 241/.042--dc23
LC record available at https://lccn.loc.gov/2016048196

For Mr. Chan Yau & Mrs. Chan Cheng Chi-kin

and

For all others who teach young people how to read the Bible in love

CONTENTS

Part II: Perspectives

OLD TESTAMENT

NEW TESTAMENT

FEMINIST PERSPECTIVES

LIBERATION THEOLOGY

CONFUCIANISM

Part III: The Bible and Contemporary Ethical Issues

SOCIAL ISSUES

GENDER AND SEXUALITY ISSUES

Acknowledgments

We thank all the contributors for accepting our invitation not just to write for this volume but also to advocate for better dialogue and integration between the two disciplines of theological ethics and biblical theology.

We also thank those who have helped translate some of the essays: Thomas Brennan for the essay by José Manuel Caamaño López; Meg Guider for the essay by Maria Inês de Castro Millen and for her assistance with the essay by Ronaldo Zacharias; and Brian McNeil for the essays by Irmtraud Fischer, Wilfrid Okambawa, and Aristide Fumagalli.

A very particular word of thanks to Connor Murphy, our undergraduate research fellow, who helped edit and format this collection.

We are most grateful to the Planning Committee of Catholic Theological Ethics in the World Church (CTEWC) for their valuable insights. We extend our gratitude to the benefactors of CTEWC and our own universities for their support in various ways.

Finally, to James Keane, editor, and Robert Ellsberg, publisher of Orbis Books, our heartfelt gratitude for your interest in our book project and editorial support that makes this book possible.

May God bless all of you!

Introduction

Yiu Sing Lúcás Chan and James F. Keenan

The Background of This Collection

This volume is the fifth of the book series published by Catholic Theological Ethics in the World Church (CTEWC). James Keenan (United States), in the first volume, guided us to revisit the insights from the second international Catholic ethics conference (Trento Conference) in 2010.[1] In the second volume, Linda Hogan (Ireland) and Agbonkhianmeghe Orobator (Nigeria/Kenya) drew our attention to the role of women in engaging Catholic theological ethics from a global perspective.[2] Both the third and the fourth volumes then focused on specific and urgent global issues that are the signs of the times: Christiana Peppard (United States) and Andrea Vicini (Italy) turned to the issues of environmental degradation and called for the need of justice in any viable path to sustainability;[3] and Agnes Brazal (Philippines) and María Teresa Dávila (Puerto Rico) challenged us to look anew at the issue of migration.[4]

In this volume, we return to one of the "meta-ethical" questions in doing Catholic theological ethics, namely, the place of the Bible as a source of moral wisdom. This question is not new; since the 1980s some Christian ethicists from the English-speaking world have addressed this question and understood this engagement as part of the "theological" task.

Since the middle of the twentieth century, the Catholic Church's effort for a more biblical approach to the study of ethics was exemplified by the groundbreaking work of Bernhard Häring. Subsequently, Vatican II published *Optatam Totius*, which summoned us to attend to the role of the Bible in moral teaching. It was welcomed by biblical scholars and ethicists alike.

In simple terms, relating the Bible and morality points to the specific academic field of what is now being called "biblical ethics," which is in theory and in practice necessarily interdisciplinary, because it requires a certain integration between the disciplines of biblical studies and ethics.

Almost five decades have passed since the publication of *Optatam Totius*. What has happened in the field? Specifically, what were the attempts and developments in each discipline within the Catholic tradition? And what are the challenges and contributions of biblical ethics in the twenty-first century?

Taking the English-speaking North American world as an example, we observe that there were attempts in the 1970s and 1980s by individual scholars from both

1

disciplines and from both Catholic and Protestant traditions.[5] Within the Catholic circle, the ethicists Charles Curran and Richard McCormick and the biblical scholars Pheme Perkins and Sandra Schneiders were significant advocates.[6]

There have been further positive developments since the 1990s. Scholars from both disciplines recognized that such integration could help biblical studies from falling into irrelevancy with our Christian life, and could, in turn, enrich and enliven our discussion of morality.[7] Frank Matera, for instance, became an important contributor from the discipline of biblical studies. His works show us that the text of the Bible is important for doing biblical ethics, and hence we have to take the text seriously. He also points out the need to interpret the text's meaning for today.[8] The late William Spohn is likewise known by his Catholic colleagues as a key contributor from the discipline of ethics. He was applauded for engaging ethical reflection informed by the Bible and contemporary biblical studies.[9] Still, the collaborative works of the late Scripture scholar Daniel Harrington and the moral theologian James Keenan, though heuristic, were even more innovative.[10] They engaged in team-teaching and co-writing as an "interim" measure to engage biblical ethics that recognizes the equal importance of examining the biblical text and of interpreting its ethical meaning for today, this as a propaedeutic before a generation of double-competency Catholic scholars could be nurtured.

These attempts and developments are not limited to our North American colleagues. In 2008—more than four decades after the publication of *Optatam Totius*—the Pontifical Biblical Commission published a document that aims at restating the relationship, *The Bible and Morality: Biblical Roots of Christian Conduct*.[11] In Germany, a multivolume book project on relating a particular part of the Bible and ethics was launched shortly after that.[12] During the 2010 Trento conference, five professors from a single Roman institution, the Accademia Alfonsiana, also presented their findings on the 2008 church document.

Still, what are the views, developments, and initiatives by Scripture and ethics scholars in other parts of Europe, Asia-Oceania, Africa, and Latin America? We aim at offering a more systematic, comprehensive, and global perspective regarding the study of biblical ethics within the Catholic tradition in this volume.

In so doing, we have invited experienced scholars who engage in this field to share their insights. They come from different continents and from both the disciplines of biblical studies and theological ethics. Some discuss certain foundational issues in doing biblical ethics; others offer their views from specific perspectives and frameworks; still, one third of them demonstrate how the two disciplines are interplayed by addressing concrete contemporary ethical issues in light of selected scriptural texts.

Since this topic is interdisciplinary in nature and our contributors are from both disciplines, one scholar rightly comments that overlap in the content of the chapters in works like this is unavoidable. He claims that one would recognize that, "given the tortuous recent history of the relation between Scripture and ethics, articles with distinct starting or ending points will often cover some of the same ground along the way. In allowing for this, the editors have also anticipated that readers will typically not encounter these overlapping articles together."[13] Nevertheless, each contributor offers a unique voice grounded in the geographical, linguistic, and cultural context and from the specific theological perspective of that contributor.

* * *

Yiu Sing Lúcás Chan wrote the foregoing account a few days before his sudden death on May 19, 2015. He was the architect of this project. He recruited the Brazilian moral theologian Ronaldo Zacharias as his co-editor and solicited contributions from biblicists and ethicists around the world, guiding them in the drafting of their abstracts and eventually their submissions. In fact, the contributions were due only a few days after he died of sudden heart failure at the age of forty-six.

Chan was a major narrator and contributor to these developments. In *Biblical Ethics in the 21st Century: Developments, Emerging Consensus, and Future Directions*, he described the developments in the field of biblical ethics since the second edition of Spohn's *What Are They Saying about Scripture and Ethics?* Therein he completes what Spohn started, an account of the genesis and the shape of a new form of theological investigation in the Catholic Church, biblical ethics. But Chan was not a simple bystander. His account was critical and prescriptive. Throughout his book, he argued that biblicists need to attend to the hermeneutical work of moral theologians and moral theologians need to found their hermeneutical work on the exegetical work of biblicists.[14]

More important, he was the Catholic pioneer who embodied the integrated approach of exegesis and ethics in his biblical ethical work following in the footsteps of the Protestants Allen Verhey[15] and Richard Burridge.[16] Besides his essays on Boaz in the book of Ruth,[17] his *The Ten Commandments and the Beatitudes: Biblical Studies and Ethics for Real Life* provided the exegetical background on each of the Ten Commandments and the eight macarisms, as well as a virtue-ethics application, highlighting particular virtues and their practices, as well as exemplars and guidance in the social living-out of the virtue underlying each of the particular biblical utterances.[18] Harrington called his work "a manifesto for the double competencies of a biblically based ethics,"[19] and Alain Thomasset called the work a "tour de force" and predicted that "without doubt this work will become a classic."[20]

The Parts and Chapters of the Collection

Such diversity and complexity in content demands certain organization. For clarity's sake this volume is divided into three parts. Part 1 deals with certain foundational issues in doing biblical ethics. The first subpart concerns developments and challenges of biblical ethics for the global church. In the first chapter **Yiu Sing Lúcás Chan** provides a critical account of the development of recent scholarship by both biblical and moral theologians in highlighting how through three dimensions the field of biblical ethics has finally arrived at the end of its first generation. Chan suggests that the first dimension of this development is to be seen in the singular attempts by either biblicists or ethicists to integrate the two tasks of exegesis and ethical application; the second dimension comprises the collaborative projects in teaching, writing, and editing that make the years since 1998 a time of building in an interdisciplinary way a significant foundation; and the third is the ongoing innovation that helps us see how more recent work connects biblical ethics to other forms of contemporary research.

The French ethicist **Alain Thomasset** provides a complement and an example of Chan's claims as he looks to the concrete, urgent questions raised today by the issues of immigration and refugee movement through the virtue of hospitality. After investigating the hermeneutical challenges to biblical ethics today, he studies the virtuous example of Abraham at Mamre (Gen. 18:1–16) and the experience of Jesus as both host and guest at the house of the tax collector Zacchaeus (Luke 19:1–10). By offering an exegesis of these texts and reading them through a narrative hermeneutics employing virtue ethics, he shows how our individual and collective imaginations can be fed and make us a people who have a new capacity to respond to contemporary issues by going beyond elemental ethical principles.

These considerations naturally lead us to reflect on the meta-ethical question of the role of the Bible as a source for moral wisdom from both disciplines and for different social contexts. This is the second subpart of part 1. From Poland, moral theologian **Marian Machinek** explores how the Bible can be a source of moral wisdom for understanding the significant use of conscience in the Scriptures. Here mindful that contemporary Polish debates on the place and role of conscience today are charged with conflicting concepts, in particular between those emphasizing its subjective inviolability and those questioning its objective competency, Machinek demonstrates how the Bible can guide us to understand the agent's own source of moral wisdom, the conscience, and, in particular, he helps us see Paul's teaching on conscience within his ecclesiastical context.

The feminist ethicist **Lisa Sowle Cahill** from the United States discusses the practical, ecclesial, and political nature of biblical interpretation. In particular, she takes up the distinctive ways in which twentieth-century biblical interpretation in North America has advanced the cause of women's equality, as well as the limits of some of the earlier approaches. She also examines influential countercultures of women's biblical interpretations—especially from African American and Latina authors—that have presented new ethical agendas and critiques of "mainstream" (white, academic) feminist biblical interpretation in the United States.

In looking at the role of cultural context, which is the third subpart of part 1, the Old Testament scholar **Paul Béré** from Burkina Faso invites us to rethink the study of Old Testament ethics and the specific cultural context of the interpreter as well as the listening audience. He argues that the moral issues raised by Old Testament texts reveal a constant cultural conflict of interpretation. But the conflict is not simply one of interpretation but of the very scientific work of exegesis. He remarks, "We often take for granted that our reading of the text is free of any cultural bias, and we claim objectivity." He concludes with: "My contention has been that the exegesis of biblical ethics is deeply bound to the interpreter's cultural mind-set." To illustrate his point, he examines a few themes—truth, forbidden sexual relationships, and violence and peace—in order to delineate some methodological issues. In particular, he employs the narrative of Abram and Sarah in Genesis 12:10–20 to highlight the complexity of doing Old Testament ethics in diverse West African societies. He demonstrates that multiculturalism is a major parameter in formalizing the meaning of the biblical narratives.

Whereas Béré looks at the exegetical issues of context, the biblical theologian **Wilfrid Okambawa** from Benin is interested in the question of biblical and ethical interpretative hermeneutics. By turning to the problem of food offered to idols (1 Cor. 8:1–13), he offers an ethics of consideration to engage the text while employing a binary logic of hermeneutics that can be applied to other global issues through liberationist, feminist, and inculturationist interpretations. The author, in developing the ethical understanding of the claims of Saint Paul, cannot escape the exegetical work that his binary logic engages. The claims that Chan makes in the beginning of this first part are proven in the process of doing biblical ethics.

In the final subpart of part 1, in a rather beautiful essay, **Aristide Fumagalli** of Italy takes us from the connection between the Bible and ethics into the world of preaching. Here he introduces the biblical poetics that give birth to moral action. He invites, effectively, the biblicist and the ethicist to imagine the world of the preacher and asks, "In what way does the Word of God mold, by means of the Scripture, the moral conduct of the one who frequents it?" What do we need to hear the Scriptures? He answers, a good preacher, and reminds us that this is moral work: "Jesus' preaching was moral, not primarily because he dictated rules or condemned inconsistency, but because he activated the liberty of his hearers, urging them to take the initiative and be creative, in order that they might discover, under the patina of the obvious, of prejudices and of inertia, the secret of human life."

In part 2, our contributors look at biblical ethics from various perspectives. Their findings reaffirm that the Bible is not a fixed text but needs to be subject to the interpretation of the readers if the moral wisdom rooted in Scripture is to be relevant to our contemporary, diverse contexts.

An excellent way to begin the first subpart is to take the perspective of three scholars—a biblical theologian, a biblical theologian turned ethicist, and a moral theologian—who read the Scriptures through the Old Testament. So often Christians have read the Old Testament through the New Testament, but these three writers insist on the priority of the earlier one. Moreover, each brings a particular added perspective to the case.

The first Scripture scholar, **Gina Hens-Piazza** of the United States, argues that the tradition of feminism raises a suspicion about those who are ignored. She argues that how we read the Bible affects how we read the "text" of our world. An ability to read the sacred text truly and completely allows us to see and better understand the world as it is. She writes, "That the Bible, particularly the Old Testament, can be mined for a whole host of ethical positions suggests that critical approaches to doing ethics in tandem with the Bible are crucial." She wants, therefore, to take us in a very different direction from the one we are normally accustomed to. Rather than examine the virtues, principles, or values that the text might yield, she wants to ask whether we might learn to read the text justly. She writes that her "essay is less concerned with how the text of the Old Testament yields principles of justice or interpretations that inspire or challenge readers with such issues. Rather it considers how reading the Old Testament can be a praxis of justice itself." To illustrate her point, she attends to minor unnamed characters in the Old Testament, and from there she claims that the resulting interpretations often challenge our ethical categories and redefine who the minor characters in our world might be. She concludes by noting that "reading the Old Testament with an eye to the supporting cast emancipates the reader from the injustices of the narrative caste system where major characters are named, featured by narrators, and deemed the important ones of a story. . . . This in turn cultivates a new sensitivity toward our own context and a more equitable and justice-based assessment of those residing among us." But, always an Old Testament scholar, Hens-Piazza takes us to the New Testament and wonders whether Jesus read his Scriptures with an eye for the least and, within a stunningly relevant conclusion, notes that after all, "Jesus had a penchant for the so-called supporting cast of his society."

From Costa Rica, **María Cristina Ventura Campusano** provides an excellent read of *hesed* (often translated as mercy, kindness, and love) in the Old Testament. She invites us first to consider the pervasiveness of *hesed* in the Hebrew Bible and then to read it through the eyes of someone in Costa Rica, where many who have migrated into the country find themselves most in need of hospitality and inclusion. Ventura insists that we see how *hesed*, whether as practiced by Lot or by Ruth, is transformative of the relationships that it involves. In particular, she uses the context of the desert in Numbers 14 when God's *hesed* curbs the people's complaint so as to bring the people to the Promised Land. Ventura uses the "desert" as a location where *hesed* is encountered and where the recipients begin to understand that *hesed* can literally lead them to a world of new possibilities. The message of *hesed* for Costa Ricans, then, is not simply a message that responds but transforms them and the world of relationships in which they live.

Yiu Sing Lúcás Chan noted in his essay the extraordinary contemporary interest in the Ten Commandments, and so he invited the Spanish ethicist **José Manuel Caamaño López** to reflect on that text. He sees the ethical contents of the Ten Commandments through a particular moral perspective, namely, the relationship between humankind and God in the form of partnership. From there he argues that the Decalogue points to a journey toward interiority rather than external prohibitions and prescriptions. For him therefore there is an inseparability of the two sides of the commandments. Morality is thus framed in the Decalogue, within the religious perspective, as two inseparable dimensions where, therefore, the division of faith and morality is impossible. This is something that encompasses the whole biblical world. In a way, an element that will be essential in the New Testament is foreshadowed here, namely the link between loving God and loving neighbor, which appears also in Leviticus 19:18–34, although not to the radical extent to which Jesus will extend this mandate to the love of enemies. Citing Pierre Grelot, Caamaño writes that "the most important aspect of the Old Testament is not the contents of the moral Law, but 'the structure of the relationship between God and men, a normal framework in which the content of the moral law will be progressively revealed.'"[21] In this way he leads us to see that further inquiries into the moral wisdom of the Scriptures are yielded not only by how we read the Scriptures but also by the relationships the Scriptures reveal precisely in order to read it rightly.

As Caamaño offers us a foundational text for his Old Testament perspective, North American Pauline expert **Thomas Stegman** takes a pivotal New Testament claim, "the new creation," as a hermeneutical key for mining scriptural ethics. In a way, Caamaño and Stegman develop fundamental perspectives from the opposite ends of the Christian Bible's arc from the Decalogue all the way to the emerging promise. From his point of departure, Stegman begins with Pauline anthropological issues: the empowerment and freedom to live after the manner of Jesus, the new Adam, the "image of God" par excellence. He then describes life in the new creation under two aspects: the proper attitudes and stances for Christians in "the sharing of goods as an enactment of the divine plan of *isotēs* ("equality" or "fairness") and in their relationship to the nonhuman-created order, especially the environment. He concludes with reconciliation and some implications of "our heavenly citizenship" (Phil. 3:20).

In his design of this collection, Chan wanted us to see what Caamaño and Stegman demonstrate: that although each of us has cultural perspectives with which we read the Scriptures, often enough each of us chooses a fundamental scriptural lens, providing, but also limiting us to, another perspective for understanding the moral wisdom of the sacred text.

The Australian New Testament scholar **Francis Moloney** reflects on the biblical foundations of Christians' view on the issues of marriage and wealth by turning to one of the deliberately constructed narratives of the Gospel of Mark (10:1–31). Yet he does so not simply with an Anglo-Saxon Australian voice but, more important, from an ecumenical perspective that seeks common ground among Catholics, Protestants, and other Christians looking for the scriptural moral wisdom in marital and economic ethics. Moloney helps us see that distinctive, selective Catholic and Protestant readings of Scripture might not allow us to see what other Christians see; the bridge-building between biblical and moral theologians must therefore by extension be a bridge-building between Protestants and Catholics in either field. An ecumenical perspective effectively emerges as normative in Moloney's insightful investigation.

The biblical scholar **Chantal Nsongisa Kimesa** from the Democratic Republic of Congo offers a feminist reading of two Pauline passages (1 Cor. 11:2–16 and Gal. 3:23–28) that touch on moral issues regarding women, gender parity, and social expectations regarding their clothing in an African context. She investigates critically how it is possible to reconcile Paul's teaching on equality in Christ (Gal. 3:28; 1 Cor. 12:13; and Rom. 16:3–15) with the issue of a wife's head-covering (1 Cor. 11:2–16). As she arrives at her answer, mindful of the Greco-Roman cultural context of Paul's day, she turns to the topic of dress for women in Africa and in particular religious women there. By her own investigations she demonstrates the diversity of what Lisa Sowle Cahill highlighted in her essay, that feminist readers from the Global South have their own specific cultural perspectives, reminding us that the feminist perspective is not a singularly reducible one but a highly variegated one with shared presuppositions and concerns.

We then turn to another very different feminist perspective. For the past few decades there has been a long-standing discussion about the Gospel of John and theological ethics. Some have pointedly asked: Is there any ethics in the fourth Gospel? More recently there has been a variety of new approaches to the question by asking the prior question, What is the ethics that we are looking for in the Gospel of John?[22] The Scripture scholar **Rekha M. Chennattu, RA,** offers a fresh and compelling Indian feminist reading of John's Gospel. She proposes an ethic of giving life in abundance as a hermeneutical key for interpreting John; such a premise presupposes a principle of combined radical equality and inclusiveness and a process of dialogue at all levels. Within the essay she highlights that doing the will of God, loving one another, fostering communion, laying down one's life for the common good, working for economic and social justice, being inclusive, promoting gender equality, entering into a process of discernment, and caring for creation are all imperatives for every disciple of Jesus. Reading her contribution in light of Stegman's, we see on the one hand the distinctiveness of the Pauline and Johannine fundamental claims, but on the other we recognize how from different sets of perspectives (scriptural, ideological, and cultural) bridges can be built precisely if we honor the specificity of these perspectives.

The Peruvian ethicist **Jaime Vidaurrázaga** takes us to a Latin American perspective. He proposes "a narrative showing how a morally motivated renewal of the praxis and organization of the postconciliar Latin American church led to the discovery of the Bible as 'memory of the poor,' and that such a discovery and the corollaries that followed from it have shaped the way in which theological ethics has developed in the continent over the last five decades." Analogous to Hens-Piazza's interest in reading Scripture, Vidaurrázaga narrates the way the Bible was read in Latin America by giving special attention to the emergence of both ecclesial base communities (CEBs) and liberation theology. Regarding both as the fruits of a moral choice taken by the church to stand on the side of the poor and vulnerable, he turns to the "see, judge, and act" methodology popular among Latin Americans, a method more in tune with the experience of the people than any particular teaching. Herein we find the discovery in theological ethics of the biblically evident "preferential option for the poor." He writes: "As the CEBs engaged the biblical text in their life of faith, they discovered that the story of the Bible is their story too."

From South Africa, the ethicist **Anthony Egan** also turns to the historical effectiveness of the social reading of the Bible. He begins his original and compelling essay by noting that "there has never been a strong tradition of Catholic biblical ethics in South Africa, or a strong tradition of Catholic biblical scholarship, or even a strong Catholic theological tradition." He goes on to say, however, that he will argue that "in the context of the anti-apartheid struggle there emerged at every level a moral discourse of resistance that drew—particularly at the grassroots level—on the (almost inevitably selective) use of the Bible as a resource." He attributes these developments to a combination of ecumenism and liberation theology that was used by grassroots Catholic organizations, supported by a core group of activist clergy and theologians who served as the "organic intellectuals" of these movements. He notes that when democracy in South Africa was achieved in 1994 the entire movement collapsed, in part because of a lack of sustained theological sophistication. He concludes nonetheless that this theology of biblical mining has provided the foundations for limited theological ethical reflections in post-apartheid South Africa today.

We conclude this part with another Asian perspective, Confucianism. After Lúcás Chan's death, we asked his colleague from the Jesuit province of China, the Canadian Jesuit moral theologian **Louis Gendron**, to give us an essay that might capture a Confucian perspective in biblical ethics. Chan, who had spent his years pioneering biblical ethics, had likewise paved new roads in Asian theological ethics,[23] and Gendron was once Chan's provincial who commissioned him to doctoral studies. Gendron provided a study of the biblical scholarship of ninety-year-old Mark Fang Chih-jung, SJ. Through Fang's work, Gendron classically notes the comparability between the values that emerge from the sacred texts of both religious traditions, Christianity and Confucianism, but then Gendron argues that the biblical texts take us to transcendent and ultimate grounds of meaning that go beyond the cultural and religious claims of Confucianism, without, though, compromising the latter.

In part 3 we see how biblical scholars and theological ethicists alike turn to the Bible for concrete insights in dealing with contemporary moral issues identified in their particular contexts. The Indian ethicist **Mathew Illathuparampil** seeks to explore the role of the Bible in addressing multifaceted ethical issues in his widely religiously diverse country by looking for fundamental or general biblical values rather than specific, concrete solutions. After first raising a variety of methodological issues that make even the search for biblical values a difficult task, he specifically looks at classic Indian social ethical issues: poverty, the caste system, and religious pluralism. In each instance by providing fundamental background he shows how each is an ethical challenge in contemporary Indian culture[24] and then highlights corresponding biblical values that inevitably emerge. These values, human dignity, equality, and integral liberation, emerge as he reads the Bible through the lens of the experience of those who are oppressed. He warns us, however, that we cannot continue this type of work of using biblical values, that it will eventually be "truncated," unless we agree on the methodological issues raised both at the beginning of this essay and of this book.

The president of the Brazilian Society of Moral Theology, **Maria Inês de Castro Millen**, similarly is interested in exploring how the Bible can address complex social and ethical issues in her own context. This foundational essay lays the groundwork for demonstrating how the Bible illuminates our lives so that we can see not only our present condition but also alternative pathways from the usual compromises that keep us in darkness. She recognizes the Brazilian context and these social issues as chronic, resulting from a socioeconomic and cultural and political dislocation that has brought the Brazilian population to a state of weakness and poverty. She turns to the Prophets and the person of Jesus for insights based on the belief that they both denounce the system that leads to the present situation and defend the rights and dignity of the poor as they bring the kingdom of God into this world.

As Maria Inês de Castro Millen provides the foundations of Scripture to confront contemporary Brazilian society, the New Testament scholar **John Donahue** uses Jesus' proclamation of the kingdom of God as a direct challenge to the contemporary culture of the United States. Donahue, the Catholic forerunner in biblical studies who brought out the cry for justice from the Scriptures to theological and ministerial communities throughout the United States, examines each of the synoptic Gospels to uncover the kingdom of God as a clarion call for contemporary America. From Mark he highlights how the proclamation subverts our national narcissistic fascination with power and prestige; from Matthew we hear how the kingdom's summons to become a community of mercy and justice stands as a contradiction to American individualism and fractionalism; and from Luke we find a repudiation of greed, marginalization, and the growing economic gap. This powerful social critique leaves us with the question: "The kingdom proclamation of Jesus opens many doors for Catholic ethics in the twenty-first century; who will enter?"

After three chapters on the Bible and social ethics, the Austrian Old Testament scholar **Irmtraud Fischer** invites us to turn to the subject of gender and sexuality. Convinced of the evident need for hermeneutics, she asserts that "both ethicists and biblical scholars agree today that one cannot simply translate 'what is in the Bible' into ethical principles." Faced with the normativity of heterosexuality in the creation texts and its societal context, she asks what the Bible can bring to contemporary gender-democracies. Mindful that "what must be explained today is not the patriarchy, but rather the equality of the genders," she writes that it "seems clear that we should begin with the creation texts, which see an equal partnership of the two genders as willed by God." As she looks for the possibility of an adequate hermeneutics to build bridges between the sacred texts and contemporary life building regarding gender and sexuality, she notes that looking for gender equity is not enough and instead turns to questions regarding intersectionality. She writes:

> Using the criteria applied today to the phenomenon of intersectionality, it has defined patriarchy as a social-hierarchical societal form in which female members of one social stratum are lower in rank than the men who belong to the same social stratum. But the most serious societally effective difference between persons in the Ancient East was not their gender, but rather the citizenship status of the free and the unfree, since this was the criterion on which the decisive question depended: Did someone have the rights of a person, or did these rights belong among the property rights of the slave owners?

Like others in this volume, she is concerned with the question of who the readers of the Bible are, what their reception of the texts is, and who will divine and proclaim the values and virtues of particular texts. She concludes: "We must struggle on equal terms, in a variety of forms of living, to arrive at ethical decisions that make a good life possible for everyone, not only older, Christian, healthy, and mostly white, free men."

The moral theologian **Christopher Vogt** raises concern about the recent phenomenon in the United States in which church employees have been fired for being openly gay. He introduces the concept of scandal as the call to avoid leading others into confusion regarding faith and morals, a position that we find in Paul's argument over idol meat (1 Cor. 8:1–13) as well as in the synoptic Gospels. Scandal functions in another, often overlooked way in the New Testament. Vogt writes:

> Although there are passages in the New Testament that speak to the issue of scandal in the sense of some Christians causing others to falter by their behavior (Matt. 18:6; Mark 9:42; Rom. 14:13; 1 Cor. 8:9), it is more typical to read of Jesus' teaching or the cross or Jesus Christ himself as scandal (Matt. 13:57; Mark 6:3; 1 Cor. 1:23; Gal. 5:11; 1 Pet. 2:8; Rom. 9:32–33). His life, his preaching, and his humiliating death on a cross all upset expectations, offended sensibilities, and challenged everyone, including his disciples.

Here Vogt focuses on the unsettling actions of Jesus to show that this more pervasive notion is not only overlooked in the church's tradition, but even when it is recognized, it is not fully appreciated: "To say that Jesus Christ caused scandal is to say more than that he put forward a challenging call or message; it is to say that Jesus and his disciples engaged in behavior that many people regarded as morally offensive and wrong." Referring to Jesus' associations with prostitutes, sinners, and tax collectors, Vogt writes, "Jesus became an offense or scandal by challenging individuals' most cherished beliefs and violating their assumptions about the way the world should be." He concludes by asking if we as a church know how to distinguish whether scandal should change how we see the world.

The final chapter is by the Brazilian ethicist **Ronaldo Zacharias**, who, with Yiu Sing Lúcás Chan, designed this entire collection. Their essays rightly serve as the collection's bookends. Zacharias provides a foundational essay on the resources of the Bible for providing moral wisdom with regard to human sexuality. Such a task is not easy. He offers us a general account of how the Bible shapes our lives even in the field of sexuality. Noting that the patriarchs of Israel convey to us a God who is male, a Father and even a husband, but knows no sex, and since sex does not belong to the divine person, nor, therefore, to the cultic, he argues that sex is relegated to being directed and controlled by the Law; in the Law we find the extensive concerns and anxieties that Israel has for sexuality. In the New Testament, sexuality is treated in much the same way.

As an alternative approach to the Law, Zacharias steps back, if you will, to provide a biblical anthropological vision. He argues that our imitation of God comes through an imitation of Christ, who through the Spirit allows us to realize that all of the Scriptures call us to respond to the divine initiatives. Our response is therefore deeply relational, and our understanding of God's will for our responsiveness is not only in the text but in the community of faith that today receives revelation.

Zacharias's essay is filled with hope and promise. Like the collection itself, it centers on the foundational claims about how the Scriptures can and are being received. Many of these essays are about fundamental biblical claims such as *hesed*, the Decalogue, the kingdom of God, or the new creation, whereas others are about fundamental methods for bridging the texts, providing hermeneutics through virtues, narratives, and values, or through feminism and liberation theology. Others are instructive in reflecting on how we preach the Scriptures or how we read and receive them.

Finally, in every instance, the contributors are mindful of their own social location and of their own attempts at bridging their reception with others', and, in this sense, the essays and this collection itself are deeply Catholic, without compromising their ecumenical instincts.

Before beginning this project, Chan reminded those of us committed to biblical ethics that we in ethics must learn from those in biblical theology and they in turn must engage us. Therein he recognized that a consensus in the field was reached: building that bridge of encounter between those two theological investigations is, in a word, indispensable for biblical ethics. For this international collection, he took us a step further. He asked his contributors to participate in a three-dimensional work made up of foundations, perspectives, and descents into the particular. In this, the collection itself models the ways we must proceed to face the tasks that lie before us as we move into the next generation of biblical ethics.

Notes

1. James F. Keenan, SJ, ed., *Catholic Theological Ethics, Past, Present, and Future: The Trento Conference* (Maryknoll, NY: Orbis Books, 2011).

2. Linda Hogan and Agbonkhianmeghe Orobator, eds., *Feminist Catholic Theological Ethics: Conversations in Our World Church* (Maryknoll, NY: Orbis Books, 2014).

3. Christiana Z. Peppard and Andrea Vicini, eds., *Just Sustainability: Technology, Ecology, and Resource Extraction* (Maryknoll, NY: Orbis Books, 2015).

4. Agnes Brazal and María Teresa Dávila, eds., *Catholic Theological Ethics on the Migrations of Peoples: Living with(out) Borders* (Maryknoll, NY: Orbis Books, 2016).

5. Charles Curran and Richard McCormick identified four major aspects of using Scripture in ethics: (1) The determination of the meaning of the particular scriptural text; (2) the meaning of the text for today's diverse historical, cultural, and sociological reality; (3) the different approaches within Christian ethics itself; and (4) the relationship between Scripture and other sources of moral theology. See Charles E. Curran and Richard A. McCormick, SJ, eds., *The Use of Scripture in Moral Theology Readings in Moral Theology No. 4* (New York: Paulist Press, 1984), vii–viii. Kenneth Himes similarly enunciated four separate and yet related tasks in using Scripture in ethics—namely, exegetical, hermeneutical, methodological, and theological tasks. See Kenneth Himes, "Scripture and Ethics: A Review Essay," *Biblical Theology Bulletin* 15, no. 2 (1985): 65–73. See also William C. Spohn, "The Use of Scripture in Moral Theology," *Theological Studies* 47, no. 1 (1986): 88–102. Correspondingly, within the discipline of biblical studies, scholars likewise talk about the moral (or topological) sense of Scripture—one of the four senses whose origin can be traced back to Saint Gregory the Great.

6. See Curran and McCormick, *Use of Scripture in Moral Theology*; Pheme Perkins, "New Testament Ethics: Questions and Contexts," *Religious Studies Review* 10 (1984): 321–27; Sandra M. Schneiders, "From Exegesis to Hermeneutics: The Problem of the Contemporary Meaning of Scripture," *Horizons* 8 (1981): 23–39.

7. Daniel J. Harrington, SJ, and James F. Keenan, SJ, *Jesus and Virtue Ethics: Building Bridges between New Testament Studies and Moral Theology* (Lanham, MD: Sheed and Ward, 2002), 13.

8. See Frank J. Matera, *New Testament Ethics: The Legacies of Jesus and Paul* (Louisville, KY: Westminster John Knox, 1996).

9. See William C. Spohn, *What Are They Saying about Scripture and Ethics?* rev. and exp. ed. (New York: Paulist, 1996); *Go and Do Likewise: Jesus and Ethics* (New York: Continuum, 1999).

10. See Harrington and Keenan, *Jesus and Virtue Ethics*; Daniel J. Harrington, SJ, and James F. Keenan, SJ, *Paul and Virtue Ethics: Building Bridges between New Testament Studies and Moral Theology* (Lanham, MD: Rowman and Littlefield, 2010).

11. Pontifical Biblical Commission, *The Bible and Morality: Biblical Roots of Christian Conduct* (Vatican: Vatican Library, 2008).

12. Friedrich Wilhelm Horn and Ruben Zimmermann, eds., *Jenseits von Indikativ und Imperativ: Kontexte und normen neutestamentlicher Ethik/Contexts and Norms of New Testament Ethics*, vol. 1 (Tübingen: Mohr Siebeck, 2009).

13. Tommy Givens, review of *Dictionary of Scripture and Ethics*, ed. Joel Green, *Journal of Theological Interpretation* 6, no. 2 (2012): 309.

14. Yiu Sing Lúcás Chan, *Biblical Ethics in the 21st Century: Developments, Emerging Consensus, and Future Directions* (New York: Paulist Press, 2013).

15. Allen Verhey, *The Great Reversal: Ethics and the New Testament* (Grand Rapids, MI: Eerdmans, 1986); *Remembering Jesus: Christian Community, Scripture, and the Moral Life* (Grand Rapids, MI: Eerdmans, 2002); "Scripture as Script and as Scripted: The Beatitudes," in *Character Ethics and the New Testament: Moral Dimensions of Scripture*, ed. Robert L. Brawley (Louisville: Westminster John Knox, 2007), 19–34.

16. Richard A. Burridge, *Imitating Jesus: An Inclusive Approach to New Testament Ethics* (Grand Rapids, MI: Eerdmans, 2007).

17. Yiu Sing Lúcás Chan, "A Model of Hospitality for Our Times," *Budhi: A Journal of Ideas and Culture* 10, no. 1 (2006): 1–30; "The Hebrew Bible and the Discourse on Migration: A Reflection on the Virtue of Hospitality in the Book of Ruth," *Asian Horizons* 8, no. 4 (December 2014): 665–79.

18. Yiu Sing Lúcás Chan, *The Ten Commandments and the Beatitudes: Biblical Studies and Ethics for Real Life* (Lanham, MD: Rowman and Littlefield, 2012).

19. Daniel J. Harrington, SJ, Foreword to Chan, *Ten Commandments and the Beatitudes*, xi.

20. "Nul doute que ce livre deviendra un des classiques de cette question."Alain Thomasset, "Bulletin de Théologie morale," *Recherches de Science Religieuse* 101, no. 2 (2013): 302, 304.

21. Pierre Grelot, *Problèmes de morale fondamentale: Un éclairage biblique* (Paris: Editions du Cerf, 1982), 19.

22. See, for instance, Michael Labahn, "'It's Only Love—Is That All? Limits and Potentials of Johannine 'Ethic'—A Critical Evaluation of Research," in *Rethinking the Ethics of John: "Implicit Ethics" in the Johannine Writings,* ed. J. G. van der Watt and R. Zimmermann (Tübingen: Mohr Siebeck, 2012), 3–43.

23. Yiu Sing Lúcás Chan with James Keenan, "Bridging Christian Ethics and Confucianism through Virtue Ethics," *Chinese Cross Currents* 5, no. 3 (July 2008): 74–85; "Bridging Christian and Confucian Ethics: Is the Bridge Adequately Catholic and Asian?" *Asian Christian Review* 5, no. 1 (Summer 2011): 49–73; "As West Meets East: Reading Xunzi's 'A Discussion of Rites'—Through the Lens of Contemporary Western Ritual Theories," in *'Ahme nach, was du vollziehst': Positionsbestimmungen zum Verhältnis von Liturgie und Ethik*, ed. Martin Stuflesser and Stephan Winter(Regensburg, Germany: Friedrich Pustet KG, 2009), 101–20; "Catholic Theological Ethics: Some Reflections on the Asian Scenario," in *Moral Theology in India Today*, ed. Shaji George Kochuthara (Bangalore: Dharmaram Publications, 2013), 101–21; and, edited with James F. Keenan and Shaji George Kochuthara, *Doing Catholic Theological Ethics in a Cross-Cultural and Interreligious Asian Context* (Bangalore: Dharmaram Publications, 2016).

24. In Illathuparampil's essay, "religious pluralism" describes a negative phenomenon, one that suggests that religious diversity is unsettling and threatening to another's faith and that as a result it becomes an object of intolerance. As he notes, "Religious pluralism gives way to religious fanaticism."

Part I

Foundational Concerns

DEVELOPMENTS AND CHALLENGES OF BIBLICAL ETHICS FOR THE GLOBAL CHURCH

BIBLICAL ETHICS: 3D

Yiu Sing Lúcás Chan, SJ

Two questions need to be raised at the outset: What is biblical ethics, and what does "3D" in the title stand for? The first question is better rephrased as "What is happening in the field of biblical ethics?"[1] Although for centuries using Scripture as the sole authority for Christian ethics has distinguished Protestant from Catholic methodology, biblical ethics is not a new area of research within the Roman Catholic tradition. Between the Council of Trent and Vatican II, for example, Catholic manualists often drew proof texts from the Scriptures.[2] During the seventeenth and eighteenth centuries, Catholic scholars called for a more biblical approach to moral theology.[3] In the middle of the twentieth century, the Catholic moral theologian Bernhard Häring demonstrated that Scripture itself should furnish our moral thinking. A decade later Vatican II's *Optatam Totius*, the Decree on Priestly Training, called for emphasizing the biblical-theological foundations of Catholic moral theology; this affected, and was welcomed by, Catholic Scripture scholars and moral theologians.[4] In 2008, more than four decades after Vatican II, the Pontifical Biblical Commission published a document that aims at situating "Christian morality within the larger sphere of anthropology and of biblical theologies . . . [and demonstrating that] the Bible does provide some methodological criteria for progress along this road."[5]

The second question may lead readers to associate "3D" with popular three-dimensional movies. Rightly so. I propose a three-dimensional analysis of the field of biblical ethics, looking at integration, collaboration, and innovation and beyond, through which a more realistic and comprehensive response to the first question can be suggested.

First Dimension: Integration

The late Daniel Harrington observed that, despite the welcoming attitude by both Scripture scholars and moral theologians toward Vatican II's statement, the two branches "continue to operate separately without much cooperation, and that the integration of Scripture and theological ethics is far from satisfactory: moral theologians do not read much of what biblical scholars write, while few biblical scholars have interest in conversing with moral theologians."[6] Besides the lack of interest, the growing complexity of the two fields, the related issue of professional training and developing competencies, and the lack of communication between the two disciplines are notable obstacles.[7]

Nevertheless, attempts to advance the integration were continued in the 1970s and 1980s by scholars such as the Christian ethicists James Gustafson and Thomas Ogletree, and the Catholic moral theologians Charles Curran and Richard McCormick.[8] In the field of New Testament studies, Pheme Perkins and Sandra Schneiders were also important Catholic advocates.[9]

Since the 1990s we have seen further developments advanced by scholars. They recognize that integration "can help rescue biblical exegesis from falling into anti-quarianism and irrelevancy, and can at the same time help to enrich and enliven moral theology precisely as a Christian theological discipline."[10] Biblical scholars began to go beyond the exegetical task to engage in interpretive hermeneutics; theological ethicists similarly started to pay attention to their use of Scripture in ethical reflection. Within the North American English-speaking context, the Methodist Richard Hays and the Roman Catholic Frank Matera are two important contributors from the discipline of New Testament studies in the 1990s.

Efforts by Scripture Scholars

In *The Moral Vision of the New Testament* Richard Hays seeks to identify the "moral vision" of the New Testament and demonstrates how the values and practices of today's Christian community ought to be shaped.[11] He elaborates on the fourfold task of New Testament Ethics (NTE) that he developed earlier:[12] (1) an exegetical survey of the writings; (2) a discussion of the likelihood of a coherent and normative NTE; (3) an examination of contemporary hermeneutical proposals; and (4) an application of these methodological frameworks to certain ethical issues.

Moral Vision is recognized for its comprehensiveness. As far as the methodology is concerned, Hays's approach goes beyond what conventional NTE scholars have done, by taking on the entire task from the descriptive to the normative, and from theory to practice.

Since Frank Matera's major work on NTE, *New Testament Ethics: The Legacies of Jesus and Paul*, was published in the same year, the two studies were often compared.[13] Matera is concerned that traditional methods used in NTE are inadequate for disclosing the diverse ethical principles applied in the biblical texts. Thus, hoping to offer a systematic presentation of NTE, he presents an approach different from Hays's, one that examines the moral teaching ascribed to Jesus and Paul.

Both moral theologians and biblical scholars have commented on Matera's work and consider it a good supplement or alternative to that of Hays. Its methodological orientation is encouraging despite concerns raised that the ethical teachings identified by Matera do not satisfy an ethicist's expectations. In short, the works of Hays and Matera show us that biblical ethics is alive and well. The two authors also point out the need for a hermeneutics concerned with the text's meaning for today. Their efforts, however, also disclose some limitations: (1) inadequate and even inconsistent ethical claims; (2) the lack of reference to or consultation of the works of ethicists; and (3) the failure to ground their claims in any major ethical framework, like virtue and duties. Simply put, they still stress the importance of the text more than the need for an ethical hermeneutics on a normative level.

A significant development occurs with Richard Burridge's *Imitating Jesus: An Inclusive Approach to New Testament Ethics*.[14] Burridge offers an alternative approach to NTE, grounded in the hypothesis that the genre of the four Gospels is one of ancient Greco-Roman biography.[15] Specifically, he claims that the literary genre is crucial to the interpretation of the text. Subsequently, he emphasizes the need to focus on the subject in the text, the inseparability between the subject's words and deeds as presented in the text, and the turn to the subject's character that invites us to imitate the subject and appropriate the subject's virtues. These claims present important implications: a biographical approach to interpreting the text is not simply a method/genre within biblical studies; it is also a solid platform for ethical analysis: its emphasis on imitation, the subject's character, and virtues is characteristic of virtue ethics.[16] In other words, Burridge implicitly employs a virtue framework for interpretation.

Burridge also engages literature normally employed by ethicists. From the perspective of biblical scholarship, his work hints at how biblical ethics can be advanced: a strategy that embraces the importance of ethical hermeneutics while attending to the importance of the biblical text, especially through building our findings on a sound platform of ethical analysis or ethical theory.

Efforts by Christian Ethicists

Rosemary Radford Ruether and the late William Spohn are known by their colleagues as pioneers in integrating Scripture and ethics. Spohn surveyed the different models of using Scripture in ethics in *What Are They Saying about Scripture and Ethics?*[17] Later, in *Go and Do Likewise*, he engaged Scripture with ethics by first focusing on biblical narratives.[18] He claimed that narrative theology "can support a broader definition of ethics that recognizes the normative guidance that symbolic material brings to disposition and character."[19] He also employed analogical imagination to bridge the gap between the Bible's world and our own.

Finally, Spohn advocated the use of virtue ethics as a hermeneutical tool. Scholars applauded him for engaging ethical reflection informed by the Bible and contemporary biblical studies.

Although Ruether is not an ethicist in a strict sense, her use of the Bible in carrying out the task of feminist interpretation sheds light on our discussion.[20] First, Ruether appeals to several biblical traditions (e.g., the Lukan Marian tradition) that emerge from selected texts to depict a liberating prophetic Christian faith that helps interpret ethical responsibilities, demonstrating the advantages of employing a specific means for interpretation.[21] Second, Ruether's turn to the expertise of Scripture scholars for insights needs to be acknowledged. It highlights the importance of the ethicist's need for exegetical assistance.

Both Spohn and Ruether demonstrate the need to engage in both exegetical and ethical hermeneutics. They also confirm the gradual shift from concern with principles and norms to Scripture's role in forming values and practices.

Their efforts, however, like those of Hays and Matera, reveal certain limitations: (1) a rather selective use of Scripture and (2) the less-than-satisfactory exegesis and interaction with biblical scholarship. They are still concerned more with interpreting the text's meaning for the contemporary world than with first examining its original meaning to see whether the text can be rightly employed.

If Burridge helped improve the works of Scripture scholars, the late Allen Verhey, former president of the Society of Christian Ethics, demonstrated an impressive command of biblical materials and exegetical skill and was, in fact, recognized as a New Testament scholar.[22] Verhey developed an approach to NTE that stresses the need to remember Jesus, the role of the community, and the significance of practices.[23] Methodologically speaking, his work is built upon a hermeneutic of remembering and an ethical model that bears the traits of virtue theory.

Verhey's competency and engagement in the Bible reminds us that, even as ethicists, we have to attend to the original meanings of biblical texts before applying them to postbiblical situations. Verhey also shows that such a task is possible. Furthermore, his construal of the Bible as "scripted script" is very helpful in summarizing our progress toward integration in biblical ethics.[24] The text as "scripted" refers to what was written at a particular time in the past and needs to be studied in that context. The text is understood as a "script," like the script of a play, and so needs to be performed, that is, interpreted. The tasks of exegesis and interpretation are thus almost inseparable in doing biblical ethics.

Reception

A growing body of literature tries, with varying degrees of success, to engage integration between ethics and Scripture.[25] Since 2004 at least seven books on the Ten Commandments have been published by biblical scholars, Christian ethicists, and rabbis offering (direct or indirect) guidance for contemporary moral living.[26]

Besides the publications on the Decalogue, other studies have appeared that employ the Bible or just the New Testament to address concrete ethical issues. An outstanding example is Lisa Sowle Cahill's 2013 work on global justice. It contends that "the Christological commitments enshrined in the New Testament" are crucial for our ethical response.[27] Cahill turns to certain New Testament writings for understanding the Word and Spirit Christologies and frequently invokes renowned biblical scholars and their works to clarify and support her arguments.[28]

Other scholars reflect persuasively on the foundational questions in biblical ethics. Kyle Fedler, for example, not only explores the ways the Bible can be employed in Christian ethics but also how the Bible can be used responsibly, especially by asking whether it should be employed as a rule book.[29] David Jones, on a different track, claims that biblical ethics is all about the application of moral law as it is revealed in the Bible.[30]

Some of these scholars attempt to bridge the two fields not only in their writings but also in their teaching. John Donahue, for instance, offered a course in which he "examine[s] and discuss[es] select biblical themes and texts which help to provide a foundation for ethical and theological thought on social justice."[31] John Collins created a course that "examine[s] what the Bible has to say about several issues that are controversial in the modern world . . . and discuss[es] biblical attitudes to family values, ecology, gender, and sexuality . . . and other issues."[32] While teachers of biblical studies offer many of these courses, they demonstrate the strong interest in integrating the two fields as a way to make sense of the Bible for the contemporary world.

Before moving to the second dimension of my 3D approach, it is worth noting that among the advances surveyed so far, several (e.g., those of Burridge, Verhey, and Spohn) have turned directly or indirectly to character and virtues in carrying out their hermeneutical task. For instance, Robert Brawley and I follow this approach.[33] This consensus is worth reflecting on, for many agree that the concept of virtue is found in the Bible, either explicitly or implicitly. John Collins, for example, calls for speaking of values (and virtues) rather than laws in the Bible.[34] In fact, Scripture not only discloses virtues, values, and vision, it actually promotes them.

Several dimensions of virtue ethics make it effective for interpreting Scripture.[35] The first is its turn to dispositions and character formation. Scripture orients believers around certain values and virtues that reflect God's self-revelation in Christ, shaping character and identity in a distinctively Christian way.[36] The second is the role of the exemplar. The Bible contains many "characters" who model for us distinctive Christian moral characters and virtues. The third is the shaping of the community and communal identity. Since character is "a process of communal formation of individual identity," the Bible, as originating in and from a community or communities, is relevant to the formation of the characters and identity of the community as well.[37] In fact, Scripture "forms community as much as community informs the reading of Scripture."[38] Moreover, the Bible forms a particular spiritual and moral community in the sense that it "render[s] a community capable of ordering its existence [in a way] appropriate to such stories."[39] These strengths of virtue ethics complement well the texts of Scripture themselves.

Second Dimension: Collaboration

Some scholars have taken the challenge a step further and work hand in hand with colleagues of the other discipline. In the early 1970s, the biblical scholar Bruce Birch and the Christian ethicist Larry Rasmussen coauthored a book in which they attempt to "bridge the gap between biblical studies and Christian ethics,"[40] but very few coauthored books like this appeared in the following decade. One collaborative work of that period was *Christian Biblical Ethics,* edited by Robert Daly, who noted that the contributors, mainly biblical scholars, were well aware of "the theologically interdisciplinary nature" of their task in which "biblical exegesis . . . and Christian ethics are the central skills involved"; they therefore invited Charles Curran to offer his views as a theological ethicist during their preproduction discussion.[41] Despite this early contribution, not until the 1990s do we find collaborative authorship emerging in force.

Collaborative Teaching

David Hollenbach, the late William Spohn, and John Donahue pioneered in bringing collaboration to a higher level. As early as 1981, with the New Testament scholar Jerome Neyrey, Hollenbach structured a graduate course around selected major themes (e.g., the Kingdom of God motif).[42] Two years later, he team-taught with the Hebrew Scripture scholar Richard Clifford on the Old Testament and social ethics.[43] In both courses biblical perspectives on selected topics/themes were first presented, followed by ethical reflections and analyses with a focus on Christian social justice (e.g., just-war theory).

Spohn and Donahue also started team-teaching New Testament and Christian ethics in the '80s with a particular approach, starting with a description of the ethics of the New Testament and then discussing the various interpretive methods employed by contemporary theologians.[44] These pioneers, however, did not engage in demonstrating how biblical scholarship and ethical reflection interact in concrete situations.

Starting in 1996 Harrington and James Keenan team-taught courses titled "Jesus and Virtue Ethics" and "Paul and Virtue Ethics." They also offered a course on "John and Virtue Ethics."[45] Their approach was quite different from that of Spohn and Donahue in that they tried to accommodate what is heard from each other, dialogically, into their own framework and reflection. They also applied their findings to contemporary situations.

Their joint effort, though remaining experimental, encouraged other teachers of both disciplines to take up this model. Between 2003 and 2012, Richard Clifford and the social ethicist Thomas Massaro team-taught a course that "interpret[s] the social message of the Bible in a way that illustrates contemporary issues of social justice."[46] However, they focused on the use of Scripture and, despite regularly turning to certain official church documents on Catholic social thought, they did not adopt any particular ethical framework.

In 2010, the Hebrew Scripture scholar Carolyn Sharp and the Christian ethicist Willis Jenkins also team-taught "an interdisciplinary seminar that addresses the relation of scriptural interpretation and Christian responses to poverty."[47] They read and interpreted selected biblical texts related to poverty by employing various social ethics models, such as Social Gospel, Catholic social teaching, and liberation theology.

A year later, the Catholic ethicist Stephen Pope and the biblicist David Vanderhooft offered a course that examines some major Hebrew texts on selected moral issues, such as war, stealing, and lying.[48] Vanderhooft first analyzed Scripture texts exegetically; Pope then lectured on their use throughout the history of Christian ethics and offered ethical reflection on certain general ethical themes such as covenant, law, and virtues.

These team-taught courses and their respective approaches differ from one another. Though Sharp and Jenkins's approach is close to that of Clifford and Massaro in concentrating on a particular ethical issue, none of the teachers employed a specific hermeneutical tool. In contrast, Pope and Vanderhooft, as Harrington and Keenan before them, took up first the task of exegesis and only afterward its ethical implications. Still, these experiments confirm the value of collaboration in doing biblical ethics prior to the generation of scholars formed with double competency.

Collaborative Writings

In their two coauthored books, *Jesus and Virtue Ethics* and *Paul and Virtue Ethics*, Harrington and Keenan set out a common framework built on certain ethical themes, and employ virtue ethics as their methodological approach. They acknowledge that their work is a heuristic effort "at stimulating discovery and dialogue," hoping to "provide material for further and deeper conversations about the relationship between Scripture and moral theology."[49] Despite the absence of an ideal, seamless integration ("interaction between the authors") that would make their work a truly remarkable success as some reviewers commented, many praised them for modeling and inviting further collaborative and interdisciplinary work.[50]

Protestant authors also contributed to the field. The New Testament professor Andreas Köstenberger and the Christian ethicist David Jones coauthored an integrative treatment of marriage issues and the Bible.[51] They first treat the nature of marriage and family from biblical perspectives, then discuss corresponding ethical issues in the context of the church community.

As for methodology, Köstenberger and Jones each produce chapters written from their own perspectives, as do Harrington and Keenan, but by contrast they do not integrate the biblical texts into their discussions through a particular lens.

As a whole, their project is seen by some as a useful "handbook that brings together biblical data and scholarly literature" on important contemporary ethical matters, but they do not provide a common foundational framework.[52]

However, the *Dictionary of Scripture and Ethics*, a recent groundbreaking project, has brought together many experts from the two disciplines.[53] The volume's core editorial team is composed of renowned Scripture scholars and Christian ethicists who for a long time have been relating the Bible and Christian ethics in their own research and writings: Bruce Birch, Charles Cosgrove, Joel Green, and Allen Verhey. In addition, more than 230 contributors from various traditions and disciplines (mainly biblical studies and Christian ethics) have provided nearly 500 entries on a broad spectrum of biblical and ethical topics.

According to Green, the project is aimed at providing a reference tool that "will survey the literature and provide an introduction to the ethics of Scripture . . . survey the relation of Scripture and ethics . . . [and] provide an account of particular features of the other discipline that are especially relevant to the conversation between disciplines."[54] Despite the labyrinthine task of bridging the two disciplines, Green hopes to "provide a map that will locate and orient conversations about the relation of Scripture and ethics . . . and [cast] a little light on the path."[55]

I agree with most reviewers that this landmark work is an excellent resource and serves the purpose of filling the niche and "a void in the arena of theological reference, [and] bringing topics of ethical importance into a single volume."[56] Some rightly point out that certain entries in ethics lack a strong scriptural component or that textual critical analysis or entries on biblical books do not really focus enough on their ethical relevance.[57] However, this mass collaborative work opens up and encourages further dialogue and interaction between the two disciplines.[58]

Third Dimension: Innovation and Beyond

The bridging between biblical studies and Christian ethics is by no means limited to North America. In Europe, the British moralist Brian Brock, for example, seeks to reframe the whole discussion of relating Scripture and ethics in terms of the role the Bible plays in God's regeneration of a holy people and their participation in that regeneration. He rightly argues that engagement in the exegetical tradition is central to theology and ethics.[59]

In his latest book, the Italian ethicist Giuseppe de Virgilio analyzes the relationship between the Bible and moral theology in the context of interdisciplinary dialogue and the formation of believers' biblical morality.[60] He first addresses the foundation issue on which the relationship between the Bible and moral theology builds—that is, its theological and epistemological bases. He then analyzes various models of relating the two based on the role the text plays in the elaboration of moral theology. The book is recognized for its richness in both quality and content.

Collaborative Writing

Colleagues in Europe have been actively engaged in collaborative writing for almost a decade now. The Italian moral theologian Aristide Fumagalli and the prolific biblical scholar Franco Manzi coauthored a volume on biblical hermeneutics and Christian ethics.[61] Fumagalli has written on various issues related to the field in the past, such as the perspectives of biblical ethics.[62] His work is praiseworthy, for it goes beyond the study of the ethics in Scripture to explore how greater attention to, and familiarity with, Scripture will affect ethical reflection. Moreover, Fumagalli's and Manzi's willingness to work collaboratively demonstrates the virtue of intellectual humility.

Beginning in 2009, German scholars launched a multivolume project titled *Kontexte und Normen neutestamentlicher Ethik*. In its second volume, the contributors focus on the interrelatedness of morality and its language in the New Testament.[63] They explicitly refer to analytical moral philosophy in order to address certain foundational questions. Although the bridge built here is with philosophy rather than theology, the volume affirms the need and benefit of consistent use of a particular ethical framework for interpretation. The fourth volume specifically engages biblical studies with Aristotelian virtue ethics.[64]

Besides this multivolume project by our German colleagues, the collection of essays in this volume that we have edited belongs to a book series published by an international Catholic ethics network that focuses on the world church. Our collection is distinctive in that, besides having a moral theologian or biblical scholar writing each essay, every contributor takes into account her or his specific cultural contexts.

Conferences

Several of the above-mentioned publications originated in academic conferences. Daly's *Christian Biblical Ethics* stems from a continuing seminar on NTE proposed and organized by the Catholic Biblical Association in 1975.[65] In recent decades, both the Society of Biblical Literature and the Society of Christian Ethics have set up units/interest groups in their annual conferences to provide platforms for conversations between the two fields with a view to subsequent publications.[66] The volume on moral language in the New Testament is likewise the result of a Humboldt-Kolleg conference held at the University of Pretoria, South Africa, in 2008.

These conferences provide another window for assessing advances in biblical ethics within national and international contexts. In 2004, a group of ethicists from Germany and Switzerland organized a symposium at the University of Bern on relating the Bible and ethics, "Die Ethik in der Bibel—die Bibel in der Ethik."

A few months after the Pontifical Biblical Commission's 2008 publication of *The Bible and Morality*, the Accademia Alfonsiana of Italy organized a full-day event to study and respond to this document.[67] Faculty members and students (of both disciplines) from institutions in Rome discussed the document from various perspectives.[68] Encouraging were the concluding words of Klemens Stock, the secretary of the Pontifical Biblical Commission. He said that while the commission had made a joint effort of listening, applying, and actualizing the integration of Scripture and morality, it is for the moralists to determine whether and to what extent this attempt was successful and useful to Christian moral reflection and action in our contemporary world. Some of the Alfonsiana professors have continued to examine the relationship between Scripture and morality, and they presented their research at the second international Catholic Theological Ethics in the World Church conference held in Trento in 2010.[69]

That same year, a four-day international conference on the Bible and justice was held at the University of Sheffield in Britain.[70] Although the specific objective was to explore how the Bible can play an active role in addressing contemporary social issues, the overarching purpose was to "promote bridges between the academic field of biblical studies and the various endeavors for a just world."[71]

In London, an international and interdisciplinary conference on the Ten Commandments was held in Trinity College of Oxford University in 2012.[72] Although the conference primarily examined this biblical text through the lenses of history and culture, some discussions engaged the ethics discipline directly, such as its role as moral charter for contemporary society. One contribution traced the Decalogue as the central organizing principle for moral teaching in the three centuries prior to Vatican II; another explored the medieval interpretation of the Ten Commandments in terms of natural law.[73]

Last but not least, in September 2014 in Berlin, an Italian group held a six-day seminar on the Bible and discrimination. Indeed, the choice of Berlin, a city where the memory of discrimination is fresh, highlighted the focus of the conference, which was to explore the theme of discrimination on the basis of religion (persecution of Jews and Christians), gender and sexual identity (homosexuality), and ethnicity (Romani). Scholars were challenged to reflect on the roles of the Bible in each ethical issue within the postbiblical period.[74]

Thinking Outside the Box

The development and future of biblical ethics need not be limited to integrating Scripture and ethics. Other inter- or multidisciplinary approaches are also proposed. As early as the mid-1990s, for example, the French theologian Louis-Marie Chauvet examined the individual relationships that sacramental theology has with the Bible and ethics.[75] For Chauvet, "They are not two isolated pairs of mutual relationships but . . . there exists integration (albeit tensions) among [the three]."[76] The integration of these disciplines forms the structure of Christian identity by providing a fundamental anthropological structure of cognition-recognition-praxis. In *Go and Do Likewise*, Spohn similarly argues that the New Testament, virtue ethics, and spirituality are interrelated as sources for reflection on Christian discipleship.

Cahill's *Global Justice, Christology, and Christian Ethics* further brings ethics, biblical studies, and systematic theology together. Cahill argues that "theology and biblical interpretation are already embedded in and indebted to ethical-political practices and choices."[77] Specifically, biblical narratives of Jesus contour Christian social ethics, while key Christological formulations provide its inspiration and reasoning.

The additional fields to be brought on board go beyond spirituality and other theological disciplines. For instance, Richard Hiers expands his research to bring biblical studies, social ethics, and legal theory together and stresses that the underlying values of justice and compassion integral to biblical law can serve as a base for matters of civil law.[78]

Finally, bridging biblical studies and Christian ethics inevitably considers ecumenism as the Italian theologian Placido Sgroi does. He convincingly argues that an ecumenical reading of Scripture could contribute to better ethical consensus among Christians.[79]

So far I have not explored any discrete innovations and initiatives from our colleagues in Asia, Latin America, and Africa.[80] However, Rasiah Sugirtharajah, a Sri Lankan professor of biblical hermeneutics, deserves mention. Although he does not write on biblical ethics as such, his advocacy for using a postcolonial and Asian/developing nations perspective in biblical interpretation can be illuminating for engaging biblical ethics in the Global South.[81] Sugirtharajah's approach raises serious methodological questions that challenge the entire biblical studies enterprise. This approach holds promise by providing a "location for other voices, histories, and experiences to be heard" so that new methodologies to biblical ethics may emerge.[82]

In a recently published volume based on a conference in Africa, two biblical scholars, Chantal Nsongisa and Paul Béré, reflect on the role of the Bible in doing African theology along the lines described above. Although neither author addresses African moral theology per se, their insights are still pertinent to my discussion here. For example, Nsongisa argues that an intrinsic link exists between exegesis and Christian experience (of faith), and insists that it is the task of exegetes to collaborate with other theological disciplines, especially in regard to "the hermeneutical task of understanding this experience."[83] Béré suggests that reconnecting exegesis and biblical theology can be helpful in understanding and dialoguing with theology, including moral theology. He further claims that "exegesis should be in tune with our cultural and social mind-set" if a Scripture-based African theology is to be worked out.[84]

The insights of Sugirtharajah, Nsongisa, and Béré point us to another innovation for advancing biblical ethics, namely, engaging in interfaith and cross-cultural dialogue.

Many major religions and traditions search their sacred texts for ethical guidance and teachings. In other words, their ethics are primarily the product of careful interpretation of these texts. Thus, greater attentiveness to the Bible on the part of

Christian ethicists and subsequently a more integrated biblical ethics will provide common ground that can make Christian ethics as such more understandable to other religious communities and more supportive of interfaith and cross-cultural dialogue on ethics. Developing an interfaith or cross-cultural ethics begins not with analogous generalities but with very specific texts, and needs to be both text-based and interpretive.

For example, Christian ethics is sometimes compared to Confucian ethics from a virtue ethics approach. Still, dialogue between the two (religious) ethical traditions will be more beneficial if our understanding of Christian virtues is grounded in biblical texts (like the Ten Commandments and the Beatitudes), just as Confucian virtues are extracted from their sacred texts (e.g., the Four Books and Five Classics). In this way, Christian virtues will be more explicable to their Confucian Chinese audience, as Louis Gendron illustrates in his essay in this collection.

A concrete example from a Gospel text and a Confucian text highlights the need for the virtue of humility. An exegetical and hermeneutical reading of the first beatitude in Matthew 5:3 ("Blessed are the poor in spirit, for theirs is the kingdom of heaven") calls for the virtue of humility toward God. A text from the *Analects* also calls for humility: the Master said, "Meng Chi-fan was not given to boasting. When the army was routed, he stayed in the rear. But on entering the gate, he goaded his horse on, saying, 'I did not lag behind out of presumption. It was simply that my horse refused to go forward.'"[85]

Biblical ethics has gone through significant developments since the 1990s. I hope that by creating a 3D experience, though artificial in its construction and small in scale, those interested in biblical ethics may be able to sense the depth (integration), length (collaboration), and width (innovation and beyond) of these developments so as to acquire a more enhanced, realistic, and comprehensive understanding of what is going on in the field worldwide, and to see where we need to go in the future.

Notes

1. This essay originally appeared as "Biblical Ethics: 3D," *Theological Studies* 76, no. 1 (2015): 112–28. It has been slightly adapted and updated for this collection, reprinted with permission of *Theological Studies*.

My survey focuses on developments in New Testament ethics since the 1990s. Though I write as a Catholic biblical ethicist, I consider both Catholic and Protestant contributions.

2. Charles E. Curran, *The Catholic Moral Tradition Today: A Synthesis* (Washington, DC: Georgetown University Press, 1999), 49.

3. Unfortunately, for various reasons the attempts failed. See Charles E. Curran, "The Role and Function of the Scriptures in Moral Theology," in *The Use of Scripture in Moral Theology*, Readings in Moral Theology 4., ed. Charles E. Curran and Richard A. McCormick (New York: Paulist Press, 1984), 180.

4. Daniel J. Harrington, SJ, and James F. Keenan, SJ, *Jesus and Virtue Ethics: Building Bridges between New Testament Studies and Moral Theology* (Latham, MD: Sheed and Ward, 2002), xiii.

5. Pontifical Biblical Commission, *The Bible and Morality: Biblical Roots of Christian Conduct* (Vatican City: Vatican Library, 2008), 12–13.

6. Yiu Sing Lúcás Chan, SJ, *Biblical Ethics in the 21st Century: Developments, Emerging Consensus, and Future Directions* (New York: Paulist Press, 2013), 2. See also Harrington and Keenan, *Jesus and Virtue Ethics,* 13.

7. See Pheme Perkins, "A Note to the Reader," in *Love Commands in the New Testament* (New York: Paulist Press, 1982), preface.

8. See James M. Gustafson, "The Place of Scripture in Christian Ethics: A Methodological Study," *Interpretation* 24, no. 4 (October 1970): 430–55; Thomas W. Ogletree, *The Use of the Bible in Christian Ethics: A Constructive Essay* (Philadelphia: Fortress, 1983); Curran and McCormick, eds., *Use of Scripture in Moral Theology.*

9. See Pheme Perkins, "New Testament Ethics: Questions and Contexts," *Religious Studies Review* 10 (1984): 321–27; Sandra M. Schneiders, "From Exegesis to Hermeneutics: The Problem of the Contemporary Meaning of Scripture," *Horizons* 8 (1981): 23–39.

10. Harrington and Keenan, *Jesus and Virtue Ethics,* 13.

11. Richard B. Hays, *The Moral Vision of the New Testament* (San Francisco: HarperCollins, 1996).

12. See Richard B. Hays, "Scripture-Shaped Community: The Problem of Method in New Testament Ethics," *Interpretation* 44 (1990): 42–55; and "New Testament Ethics: A Theological Task," *Annual of the Society of Christian Ethics* (1995): 97–120.

13. Frank J. Matera, *New Testament Ethics: The Legacies of Jesus and Paul* (Louisville, KY: Westminster John Knox, 1996).

14. Richard A. Burridge, *Imitating Jesus: An Inclusive Approach to New Testament Ethics* (Grand Rapids, MI: Eerdmans, 2007).

15. See Richard A. Burridge, *What Are the Gospels? A Comparison with Graeco-Roman Biography*, foreword by Graham Stanton, 2nd ed. (Grand Rapids, MI: Eerdmans, 2004).

16. I have written before on Burridge; see Chan, *Biblical Ethics,* 52–62.

17. William C. Spohn, *What Are They Saying about Scripture and Ethics?*, rev. and exp. ed. (New York: Paulist Press, 1996).

18. William C. Spohn, *Go and Do Likewise: Jesus and Ethics* (New York: Continuum, 1999).

19. William C. Spohn, "Parable and Narrative in Christian Ethics," *Theological Studies* 51 (1990): 113.

20. A detailed work by Ruether that searches for an ethics of ecojustice is *Gaia and God: An Ecofeminist Theology of Earth Healing* (San Francisco: HarperSanFrancisco, 1992).

21. See Jeffrey S. Siker, *Scripture and Ethics: Twentieth-Century Portraits* (New York: Oxford University Press, 1997), 178–98.

22. See James H. Burtness, review of *The Great Reversal: Ethics and the New Testament*, by Allen Verhey, *Christian Century* 102, no. 19 (May 29, 1985): 563; Michael J. Gorman, review of *Remembering Jesus: Christian Community, Scripture, and the Moral Life*, by Allen Verhey, *Interpretation* 57 (2003): 434.

23. See Allen Verhey, *Remembering Jesus: Christian Community, Scripture, and the Moral Life* (Grand Rapids, MI: Eerdmans, 2002).

24. Allen Verhey, "Scripture as Script and as Scripted: The Beatitudes," in *Character Ethics and the New Testament: Moral Dimensions of Scripture*, ed. Robert L. Brawley (Louisville, KY: Westminster John Knox, 2007), 19–34.

25. See James T. Bretzke, SJ, *Bibliography on Scripture and Christian Ethics*, rev. and exp. electronic ed. (Lewiston, NY: Edwin Mellen, 2014).

26. William P. Brown, ed., *The Ten Commandments: The Reciprocity of Faithfulness* (Louisville, KY: Westminster John Knox, 2004); Henning Graf Reventlow and Yair Hoffman, eds., *The Decalogue in Jewish and Christian Tradition* (New York: Continuum, 2010); Mark F. Rooker, *The Ten Commandments: Ethics for the Twenty-first Century* (Nashville, TN: Broadman and Holman, 2010); Yiu Sing Lúcás Chan, *The Ten Commandments and the Beatitudes: Biblical Studies and Ethics for Real Life*, foreword by Daniel J. Harrington, SJ, and James F. Keenan, SJ (Lanham, MD: Rowman and Littlefield, 2012); Dominik Markl, ed., *The Decalogue and Its Cultural Influence* (Sheffield, UK: Sheffield Phoenix, 2013); Robertson McQuilkin and Paul Copan, *An Introduction to Biblical Ethics: Walking in the Way of Wisdom*, 3rd ed. (Wheaton, IL: IVP Academic, 2014); and Rifat Sonsino, *And God Spoke: Ten Commandments and Contemporary Ethics* (New York: URJ Press, 2014).

27. Lisa Sowle Cahill, *Global Justice, Christology, and Christian Ethics* (New York: Cambridge University Press, 2013), xi.

28. For example, in the chapter "Kingdom of God," Cahill cites almost one hundred biblical texts and regularly refers to the works of Séan Freyne, Elisabeth Schüssler Fiorenza, E. P. Sanders, James Dunn, Gerd Theissen, Annette Merz, Daniel Harrington, and John Meier.

29. See Kyle D. Fedler, *Exploring Christian Ethics: Biblical Foundations for Morality* (Louisville, KY: Westminster John Knox, 2006).

30. See David W. Jones, *An Introduction to Biblical Ethics* (Nashville, TN: B&H Academic, 2013).

31. John R. Donahue, "Biblical Foundations of Social Justice" (BSCE 2260 syllabus, Jesuit School of Theology, Berkeley, CA, Spring 2011) The syllabi have been removed from their server. However, course descriptions are still available: wiz.gtu.edu. I too offered a graduate course on biblical ethics in the same year: Lúcás Chan, "Doing Biblical Ethics" (BSCE 4405 syllabus, Jesuit School of Theology, Berkeley, CA, Spring 2011), also available at wiz. gtu.edu.

32. John J. Collins, "What Are Biblical Values?" (REL 562b syllabus, Yale Divinity School, New Haven, CT, Spring 2014); the syllabus is inaccessible to non-Yale users.

33. See Robert Brawley, ed., *Character Ethics and the New Testament: Moral Dimensions of Scripture* (Louisville, KY: Westminster John Knox, 2007); Chan, *Biblical Ethics*.

34. John J. Collins, "What Are Biblical Values?" in *Scripture and Justice: The Bible in Contemporary Struggles for Social Justice; Essays in Honor of John R. Donahue, SJ*, ed. Gregory E. Sterling and Anathea Portier-Young, forthcoming.

35. For a detailed discussion on relating Scripture and virtue ethics, see Chan, *Biblical Ethics*, 78–112.

36. Lisa Sowle Cahill, "Christian Character, Biblical Community, and Human Values," in *Character and Scripture: Moral Formation, Community, and Biblical Interpretation*, ed. William Brown (Grand Rapids, MI: Eerdmans, 2002), 10.

37. Ibid.

38. William P. Brown, ed., *Character and Scripture: Moral Formation, Community, and Biblical Interpretation* (Grand Rapids, MI: Eerdmans, 2002), xi.

39. Stanley Hauerwas, *A Community of Character: Toward a Constructive Christian Social Ethic* (Notre Dame, IN: University of Notre Dame Press, 1981), 67.

40. Bruce C. Birch and Larry L. Rasmussen, *Bible and Ethics in Christian Life*, rev. ed. (Minneapolis: Augsburg, 1989), 7–8.

41. Robert J. Daly et al., *Christian Biblical Ethics: From Biblical Revelation to Contemporary Christian Praxis* (New York: Paulist Press, 1984), 9–10.

42. David Hollenbach, SJ, and Jerome Neyrey, SJ, "Faith and Justice: New Testament Perspective" (NT/MT 214, former Weston Jesuit School of Theology, Spring 1981).

43. David Hollenbach, SJ, and Richard Clifford, SJ, "The Old Testament and Social Ethics" (OT/MT 326, former Weston Jesuit School of Theology, Spring 1983). In 1990, they offered the same course with additional topics, such as economic justice and preferential option for the poor ("Social Justice in the Bible," OT/MT 354, former Weston Jesuit School of Theology, Spring 1990).

44. John R. Donahue, SJ, and William C. Spohn, SJ, "The New Testament and Christian Ethics" (NTCE 4301 syllabus, Jesuit School of Theology at Berkeley, Spring 1990). See also William C. Spohn, "Teaching Scripture and Ethics," *Annual of the Society of Christian Ethics* (1990): 277.

45. Daniel J. Harrington, SJ, and James F. Keenan, SJ, "New Testament and Ethics" (NT/MT 333 syllabus, former Weston Jesuit School of Theology, Fall 1996, 1998, 2000); "Paul and Virtue Ethics" (NT 330/334/TH 650/TM 713 syllabus, former Weston Jesuit School of Theology, Fall 2005, 2008, Spring 2011); and "John and Virtue Ethics" (TH 712/TM 762 syllabus, Boston College, Spring 2013). The syllabi are not available online. It was the last wish of Harrington that New Testament professor Thomas Stegman co-teach these courses with James Keenan in the future.

46. Richard Clifford, SJ, and Thomas Massaro, SJ, "Social Ethics and the Bible" (OT/MT 353 syllabus, former Weston Jesuit School of Theology, Fall 2003, 2006).

47. Carolyn Sharp and Willis Jenkins, "Scripture and Social Ethics" (REL 564 syllabus, Yale Divinity School, Fall 2010).

48. Stephen Pope and David Vanderhooft, "God and Morality: The Ethical Legacy of the Hebrew Bible" (TH 465 syllabus, Boston College, Spring 2011).

49. Daniel J. Harrington, SJ, and James F. Keenan, SJ, *Paul and Virtue Ethics: Building Bridges between New Testament Studies and Moral Theology* (Latham, MD: Rowman and Littlefield, 2010), xii.

50. See George M. Smiga, review of *Jesus and Virtue Ethics: Building Bridges between New Testament Studies and Moral Theology*, by Daniel J. Harrington, SJ, and James F. Keenan, SJ, *Catholic Biblical Quarterly* 65 (2003): 637.

51. Andreas J. Köstenberger with David W. Jones, *God, Marriage, and Family: Rebuilding the Biblical Foundation* (2004; Wheaton, IL: Crossway, 2010); their *Marriage and Family: Biblical Essentials* (Wheaton, IL: Crossway, 2012) is an abridgment of their 2004 text.

52. David W. Loy, review of *God, Marriage, and Family: Rebuilding the Biblical Foundation*, by Andreas J. Köstenberger with David W. Jones, *Concordia Journal* 33 (2007): 412.

53. Joel Green, ed., *Dictionary of Scripture and Ethics* (Grand Rapids, MI: Baker, 2011).

54. Ibid., 1.

55. Ibid., 2–3.

56. Dennis M. Swanson, review of *Dictionary of Scripture and Ethics*, ed. Joel Green, *Master's Seminary Journal* 23 (2012): 140. See also Robert J. Turner, review of *Dictionary of Scripture and Ethics*, ed. Joel Green, *Stone-Campbell Journal* 16 (2013): 106.

57. See Craig L. Blomberg, review of *Dictionary of Scripture and Ethics*, ed. Joel Green, *Bulletin for Biblical Research* 22 (2012): 459.

58. Aaron Perry, review of *Dictionary of Scripture and Ethics*, ed. Joel Green, *Wesleyan Theological Journal* 47 (2012): 233.

59. See Brian Brock, *Singing the Ethos of God: On the Place of Christian Ethics in Scripture* (Cambridge, UK: Eerdmans, 2007); his biblical focus is on the Psalms.

60. Giuseppe de Virgilio, *Bibbia e teologia morale: Paradigmi ermeneutici per il dialogo interdisciplinare* (Rome: Pontifical University of the Holy Cross, 2014).

61. Aristide Fumagalli and Franco Manzi, *Attirerò tutti a me: Ermeneutica biblica ed etica Cristiana* (Bologna: Dehoniane, 2005).

62. For articles and books written on the Bible and ethics, see Fumagalli's bibliography at www.teologiamilano.it.

63. Ruben Zimmermann and Jan van der Watt, with Susanne Luther, eds., *Moral Language in the New Testament: The Interrelatedness of Language and Ethics in Early Christian Writings* (Tübingen: Mohr Siebeck, 2010).

64. Friedrich W. Horn, Ulrich Volp, and Ruben Zimmermann, with Esther Verwold, eds., *Ethische Normen des frühen Christentums: Gut—Leben—Leib—Tugend* (Tübingen: Mohr Siebeck, 2013). In 2010, a group of German-speaking ethicists published a collected work on the role of the Bible in Christian theological ethics. However, they simply examined certain biblical motifs and surveyed commonly employed biblical traditions, but they did not engage in conversation directly with their biblical colleagues. See Marco Hofheinz, Frank Mathwig, and Matthias Zeindler, eds., *Wie kommt die Bibel in die Ethik? Beiträge zu einer Grundfrage theologischer Ethik* (Zurich: Theologischer Verlag, 2011).

65. Daly et al., *Christian Biblical Ethics*, 3.

66. These presentations were published in their respective journals. See http://web.ebscohost.com.

67. For more details, see www.alfonsiana.org.

68. The conference papers were published as *Parola di Dio e morale, Studia morala supplemento* 4 (Rome: Alphonsianum, 2009).

69. Their papers were later compiled and published: Vincenzo Viva and Gabriel Witaszek, eds., *Etica teologica nelle correnti della storia: Contributi dall'Accademia alfonsiana al secondo Congresso mondiale dei teologi morali cattolici* (Vatican City: Lateran University, 2011).

70. The conference papers were published in *Bible and Justice: Ancient Texts, Modern Challenges*, ed. Matthew J. Coomber (London: Equinox, 2011).

71. James Crossley, "The Bible and Justice Conference," *Earliest Christian History* (blog), earliestchristianhistory.blogspot.com/2007.

72. For details on the conference titled "The Influence of the Decalogue: Historical, Theological and Cultural Perspectives," see www.crhb.org.

73. See James F. Keenan, "The Decalogue and the Moral Manual Tradition: From Trent to Vatican II," in *Decalogue and Its Cultural Influence*, ed. Markl, 216–31; Randall B. Smith, "Thomas Aquinas on the Ten Commandments and the Natural Law," ibid., 148–68.

74. For details of *Abitare la memoria: Bibbia e discriminazioni* conference, see http://www.biblia.org.

75. See Louis-Marie Chauvet, *Symbol and Sacrament: A Sacramental Reinterpretation of Christian Existence*, trans. Patrick Madigan and Madeleine Beaumont (Collegeville, MN: Liturgical, 1995), 159–316. See also E. Byron Anderson, and Bruce T. Morrill, eds., *Liturgy and the Moral Self: Humanity at Full Stretch before God: Essays in Honor of Don E. Saliers* (Collegeville, MN: Liturgical, 1998).

76. Quoted in Chan, *Biblical Ethics,* 116.

77. Cahill, "General Editor's Preface," in *Global Justice,* xi.

78. Richard Hiers, *Justice and Compassion in Biblical Law* (New York: Continuum, 2009).

79. Placido Sgroi, "Etica e Scrittura: Una prospettiva ecumenica," *Fondamenti biblici dell'etica cristiana: Prospettive ecumeniche, Quaderni di studi ecumenici* 16 (2007): 13–78. See also Sgroi, *In cammino verso la comunione morale: La riflessione sui problemi etici nel dialogo ecumenico* (Tricase: Youcanprint, 2010).

80. In this volume, thirteen scholars from Africa, Asia, and Latin America write from their specific ethnic and cultural contexts. Australian biblical scholar Francis Moloney also writes on the Bible and ethics in the context of ecumenism in this volume.

81. See Rasiah Sugirtharajah, *Asian Biblical Hermeneutics and Postcolonialism: Contesting the Interpretations* (Sheffield, UK: Sheffield Academic, 1999); *Postcolonial Criticism and Biblical Interpretation* (New York: Oxford University Press, 2002).

82. Rasiah Sugirtharajah, *The Bible and the Third World: The Precolonial, Colonial, and Postcolonial Encounters* (New York: Cambridge University Press, 2001), 272.

83. Chantal Nsongisa, "The Role of the Scriptures: The New Testament in African Theology," in *Theological Reimagination: Conversations on Church, Religion, and Society in Africa*, ed. Agbonkhianmeghe Orobator (Nairobi: Paulines, 2014), 73.

84. Paul Béré, "Scripture Studies and African Theology: A Critical Overview from an OT Perspective," in *Theological Reimagination*, ed. Orobator (Nairobi: Paulines, 2014), 69.

85. Confucius, *The Analects*, trans. D. C. Lau (Middlesex, UK: Penguin Classics, 1979), 6:15.

THE VIRTUE OF HOSPITALITY ACCORDING TO THE BIBLE AND THE CHALLENGE OF MIGRATION

In memoriam Yiu Sing Lúcás Chan, SJ

Alain Thomasset, SJ

The question of migrants has become prominent in Europe. Wars and political turmoil in the Middle East, Syria, Libya, Iraq, Afghanistan; the terrorist threat in Mali, Nigeria, Cameroon; the widespread poverty in many African countries—all these have provoked many people to migrate, first within their own continents[1] and then to Europe. Fleeing from disaster, several hundreds of thousands of refugees have tried to cross the Mediterranean Sea. Thousands have died, victims not only of unscrupulous smugglers chartering unseaworthy boats, but also of the indifference or even hostility of the governments and populations of Europe. Faced with this tremendous problem, public opinion in different countries lurches between fear of "invasion" and compassion toward people so desperate that they are ready to risk their lives. In this political and social climate, rational arguments struggle to find a hearing. Judgment and policy are easily driven by passion and by collective fantasies. How can we react as Christians?

Catholic Social Teaching is quite clear on the right of migrants to seek a better life, and on the duty of persons and societies to be generous and welcoming toward them. But a mere invocation of the principles of Catholic social thought is not sufficient to address the questions that arise when migrants come to our shores, because conflicts about immigration often have their roots in our social representations. Faced with the foreigner, how are we going to react—with hostility or with hospitality? It is striking that these two terms have the same Latin root; the two realities are disquietingly close.[2] Our social and political relationships are mediated by our social imagination, our inner attitudes, and our shared fantasies, ideologies, and utopias.[3] These mediations affect decisively our images of humanity and its possibilities. The purpose of this essay is to show how the Bible can help shape in us a virtuous attitude of hospitality toward foreigners. In the field of Christian ethics, the Bible's major contribution may well be as a means of forming our characters and of nourishing particular virtues that predispose our action in the world. Reading the Bible is no substitute for moral argumentation and reasoning, but it does help us orient our minds and hearts in a right direction.

34

Challenges to Biblical Ethics

Before entering the discussion about biblical hospitality, let us note the challenges involved when we seek to use the Bible in Christian ethics.[4]

The first challenge is that of finding the right way of using the Bible. What are we looking for when we examine the biblical text in order to face our ethical problems? We might be tempted to seek moral norms and direct ethical answers to our questions. However, though the Bible speaks very often of right human behavior toward God and other people, its primary aim is not to give moral indications. The Bible is not a book of moral rules, but rather a discourse about who God is and how God acts in the world. Its focus is theological and not directly about morality. As the Pontifical Biblical Commission says,

> The God of the Bible reveals not primarily a code of conduct but "Himself" in his mystery and "the mystery of his will." . . . Morality is secondary to God's founding initiative, which we express theologically in terms of gift. In the biblical perspective morality is rooted in the prior gift of life, of intellect and of free will (creation), and above all in the entirely unmerited offer of a privileged, intimate relationship between human beings and God (covenant).[5]

It would be erroneous and even dangerous to try to read off moral norms directly from the biblical text. Morality is a consequence of revelation; it represents an answer to God's gift. But it can be discerned only in connection with revelation and with authentic worship of God.

Furthermore, the biblical text presents obvious difficulties of interpretation for the moralist. It is not just that the Bible was written in distant epochs and cultures, in which life conditions and cultural context were very different from those of today; the Bible itself is marked by an internal moral development. We can no longer accept as valid the commandments to exterminate all the enemies in the sacred wars that we find in the books of Samuel or the indications on slavery or divorce in the book of Deuteronomy. We need an interpretation. And in ethical contexts, the issues of interpretation are particularly difficult. The Bible is a source less of precise normative indications than of deep moral themes and attitudes running through the whole text. Welcoming the stranger is one of these.

Asking the right question depends on the use of the right method of interpretation. For a long time, Christians have used the Bible as a quarry from which to extract neat proof texts in order to support a demonstration based primarily on philosophical arguments. This method is obviously inadequate, because it separates the text from its literary and historical contexts, and reduces the Bible to a tool within another type of thinking altogether. The historical-critical methods, which seek to understand the meaning of a text on the basis of its original setting, are much more adequate. For their part, synchronic methods of analysis illuminate the interpretation of the text by unveiling the literary structures and the forms or styles of writing. But neither of these more enlightened approaches can tell us what impact the revealed text should have on our lives.

We need a hermeneutical model that treats the text as an autonomous reality, to be interpreted in a living dialogue between the text and the reader, but remaining under the control of the text. Our focus is then not so much on the intention of the author hidden behind the text (though we still need a sense of the original historical setting), or on the meanings implicit in the text's internal structures (necessary though they are), but on "the world of the text," the way of living in the world displayed "in front of the text" and that the reader can appropriate. In this task, if we have to go through the different methods (the "explanation"), the aim is to find the contemporary "meaning" for us. To consider the text in its "poetic" dimension is to unveil its active power on its reader. Moreover, this "world of the text," this reality that can be grasped through a careful analysis, is primarily addressed not to the reader's will, but to his or her imagination. Imagination is the mediation between the world of the text and the reader's appropriation.[6] Hence, in what follows, special attention will be given to the power of the biblical text to transform the ways in which its readers imagine reality and live in the world.

The Biblical Tradition on Hospitality

There are many biblical texts on hospitality and right relationships with the stranger or foreigner.[7] For reasons of space, I shall deal with just two significant passages, one from each Testament.

The Example of Abraham

In an essay on welcoming strangers, one can hardly overlook the example of Abraham at Mamre (Gen. 18:1–33). This text served as a reference for many writers and became a historical tradition which can illuminate many passages of the Bible. My intention here is not to make a full exegetical analysis of this passage, but rather to offer a style of biblical hermeneutics that may help us understand hospitality as an ethical virtue and thus enrich our moral imagination.

The story of Abraham at Mamre is a striking example of hospitality, which has many layers of meaning. Usually this narrative is divided into three parts: (1) verse 1: Abraham is sitting at the entrance of his tent when God pays him a visit; (2) verses 2–15: Three men arrive, and Abraham drops everything so as to welcome them in a very sensitive and generous manner, and offers them food. They announce that Sarah will have a child. Sarah laughs, but God reassures Abraham; (3) verses 16–33: The men travel toward Sodom, and there is a dialogue between God and Abraham on the fate of the city.

From the second part of the story onward, God as such seems to disappear, and it is the wayfarers who play a central role.[8] Why this shift from a visit from God to a visit from three wayfarers?

The former UK chief rabbi, Jonathan Sacks, has a helpful suggestion here. Sacks suggests that Abraham lets God wait while he entertains some tired nomads. The third verse (My Lord, do not pass by . . .) is enigmatic and can be interpreted in two different ways, depending on which vowel is supplied to the noun *Adonai*: it can mean either "my lords" or "my Lord." If we read "my lords," then Abraham is speaking to the wayfarers, asking them not to leave but rather to stay so as to enjoy his hospitality. If we read "my Lord," Abraham is talking to God, asking God to be patient while he looks after the strangers. Sacks chooses the second interpretation. Abraham has God wait while he takes care of the three strangers. And God seems not in the least disturbed by this decision. Thus the story teaches that "hospitality takes precedence over the spiritual enjoyment of an intimate encounter with God."[9] The Talmud confirms this order of priorities. Moreover, the story tells us that the ethical virtue of hospitality has a theological bearing: God reveals Godself in the face of the other. God shows and conceals Godself in the stranger, and we discover later that we have met God incognito. "Where one makes room for the other, one resides in God's presence." And Sacks says: *Greater is the person who sees God in the face of the stranger than one who sees God in a vision of transcendence*, for the Jewish task since the days of Abraham is not to ascend to heaven but to bring heaven down to earth in simple deeds of kindness and hospitality."[10] After Abraham has attended to the three visitors, God continues where the discussion left off and reveals God's plans for Sodom. Abraham then challenges God boldly in the name of justice, and God agrees to enter this moral debate. "In welcoming the foreigners and in standing against God, Abraham shows himself to be a man who incarnates the virtue of kind justice."[11] It is by resisting both the temptation to ignore the stranger, and the idea of injustice toward the people of Sodom and Gomorrah, that Abraham realizes his true vocation. He exemplifies mercy and kindness to all.

Yet the biblical narrative surprises us. The story does not correspond to our normal expectations. Our imagination is shaken. Twice Abraham challenges God, and God seems not to be offended by the confrontation. It is as though the narrative is correcting a conventional image of God. One of the themes in this passage is the relationship between universality and particularity, the tension between the openness to all and the defense of identity. This tension comes into play in any relationship of hospitality. How are we going to behave in the presence of a stranger who could be an enemy or a threat to our group's cultic purity?

It is worth recalling that Abraham in Genesis 18 is recovering precisely from his circumcision, done only a few days before—the sign of his new participation in God's covenant (Gen. 17). The challenge represented by the strangers' arrival comes as he is beginning to work out what circumcision means. Will he understand the covenant in terms of a closed symbolic community? Will God become another tribal god?[12] Genesis 18 makes it clear that the answer to those questions is no.

Abraham's election is not exclusive; it involves a responsibility for all humanity. In pain, "in the heat of the day," and with God waiting for him, Abraham nevertheless does not hesitate to run toward the three visitors and welcome them.

The story illustrates well how Israel's election is not a charter for tribalism; rather, it implies a responsibility for other peoples. Moreover, if to welcome the stranger is to welcome God's own self (the three visitors reveal themselves as messengers of God), this says something about who God is and about God's ultimate design. The call of Abraham in Genesis 12 was already pointing toward all the nations: "by you all the families of the earth shall bless themselves" (Gen. 12:3). Abraham's election is for the whole world, and this openness to a wider future is expressed within the covenant itself, as the Apostle Paul will later highlight: "Behold, my covenant is with you, and you shall be the father of a multitude of nations" (Gen. 17:4). If God loves and chooses Abraham and Israel, it is in order to show his love for all the nations.[13] The virtue of hospitality is deeply related to friendship with the true God, the One who reveals himself in the encounter with the stranger. By contrast, the story of Lot and Sodom (Gen. 19), which immediately follows the story of Abraham at Mamre, involves a violent breaking of hospitality. This is considered an offense to God and leads to the destruction of Sodom.

Welcoming the stranger is an expression of faith, an act of worship. Furthermore, hospitality anticipates the eschatological communion and the time of ultimate peace. "When the stranger is seen as a guest and, instead of being held in execration, is invested with the conspicuous dignity of the brother in humanity—on such a day, one can say that something has changed in the world."[14]

Jesus as a Host and Guest

In the Gospels, the ministry of Jesus includes numerous references to meals and feasts, which are an expression of his living according to the coming of the kingdom. In particular, Jesus shares meals in a way that challenges the exclusivism at table officially sanctioned or accepted as normal. Jesus' links with marginal people known as tax collectors and sinners are subversive (Mark 2:15–16 and parallels; Luke 19:1–10, 7:36–50, 14:1–2). These meals are signs of God's kingdom and its impending presence. In Jesus' view, Israel's true vocation was life in communion with God. It thus needed to move beyond isolation, and encounter God's abundance—an abundance offered in Jesus' ministry through the central metaphor of a banquet (e.g., Mark 2:19; Matt. 22:1–10; Luke 14:16–24; Mark 14:25).

From the numerous passages illustrating this theme, I have chosen the one which best shows the reversals of perspective that arise from the interaction between guest and host: the episode in which Jesus is hosted at the house of a tax collector named Zacchaeus (Luke 19:1–10), a narrative that also makes a reference to the example of Abraham. The story takes place in Jericho, which is the last stop of Jesus' long journey before his arrival to Jerusalem. He is drawing near to the goal of his "visitation," the holy city, but Jesus will experience in Jericho a hospitality which he will not receive from the leaders of Jerusalem. After the third announcement of his passion according to the Scriptures (18:31–34), and the healing of a blind beggar (18:35–43) on his way into the city, Jesus meets Zacchaeus as he is passing through (19:1–10). This man suffers exclusion for two reasons. As a "chief tax collector" and a "rich man," he was considered a collaborator of the occupying power of Rome, one who took advantage of his position to exploit the people. Second, his short size prevents him from seeing over the crowd and serves to symbolize his socioreligious exclusion. But in an extravagant and audacious gesture, Zacchaeus overcomes his physical handicap by running and climbing a sycamore tree (v. 4). As in the preceding episode of the blind beggar (and many others, such as the woman suffering from hemorrhages, Luke 8:40–48), a marginalized person breaks with social convention in order to meet Jesus. Running and climbing a tree do not fit the image of a dignified rich man of affairs; they are more like the behavior of a child. But this audacity gives Zacchaeus access to Jesus. And Jesus, arriving at the spot and seeing him, asks Zacchaeus to allow him to stay in his home (v. 5).

Let us pause a moment. The biblical text says that Jesus "looked up" at him. Maybe for this man of short stature, it was the first time that somebody had ever looked up at him. But once again, the point can also be understood symbolically. This man who was despised by the others ("looked down upon") was now seen as a friend and a host to Jesus, a Jesus who was looking at him from below. What Jesus says is: "Zacchaeus, hurry and come down, for I must stay at your house today" (v. 5). Jesus here uses the Greek impersonal *dei*—"it is necessary that I come"—a usage suggesting the divine purpose that drives all the mission of Jesus and shapes its direction.[15] This encounter is very significant for the mission of Jesus.

At the same time, Zacchaeus's actions may remind us of Abraham in Genesis 18. Zacchaeus moves quickly and receives Jesus joyfully just as Abraham moved quickly and received his guests with joy, as it is reported in many texts of antiquity. Since Abraham was noted for hospitality in Luke's day, Zacchaeus's hospitable actions may be a further indication that he is a "son of Abraham."[16]

As on many occasions in Luke's Gospel, there are third parties present who resist the need for conversion. The bystanders all begin to murmur and say: "He has gone to be a guest of one who is a sinner" (v. 7). Luke insists on the scandal provoked by Jesus' behavior. But Zacchaeus "stood there," which we can see as a sign of recovered dignity and freedom, and said to Jesus: "Look, Lord, half of my possessions I (will) give to the poor; and if I have defrauded anyone of anything I (will) pay him back four times as much" (v. 8). Jesus accepts his statement, and something changes in Zacchaeus's situation, because the Lord says to him: "Today salvation has come to this house because he too is a son of Abraham" (v. 9). This solemn declaration, which echoes the inaugural "today" heard in the synagogue of Nazareth (4:21) as Jesus proclaimed the fulfillment of Isaiah's messianic prophecy, recognizes Zacchaeus as a member of the community of salvation. The one who was excluded is now reintegrated; Jesus brings him from the margins to the center.

What happens to Zacchaeus exemplifies vividly the "salvation" that Jesus brings today. Salvation begins here and now as Jesus incorporates within the community the excluded and the lost, the poor and the rich. "For the Son of Man came to seek out and to save the lost" (v. 10). This is the main purpose of the whole mission of Jesus. As with other instances of this kind in Luke, we are not told the final reaction of the listeners. We know what the answer of the leaders in Jerusalem will be. But what will be the answer of the reader?

It is worth quoting the conclusion of Brendan Byrne's analysis:

> The episode with Zacchaeus, along with that of the woman who anointed Jesus in the house of Simon, offers a perfect paradigm of Luke's sense of the hospitality of God. Zacchaeus, one of the marginalized despite his wealth, provides hospitality to Jesus and finds in return the hospitality of God: a welcome into the community of salvation, his dignity and decency defended. At the same time, the exchange of hospitality that occurs between himself and Jesus enlarges the sphere of God's hospitality. It challenges the community to become more effectively a beachhead of the kingdom, where lost human beings can find welcome and new life in the grasp of a hospitable God.[17]

This episode of Zacchaeus's hospitality illustrates what the whole mission of Jesus is about and what is at stake when we are asked to receive the God who visits us. The entire Gospel of Luke, in a sense, describes the different human responses to this "visitation of God": how some welcome this visitor and are converted, and others reject him. Against such a background, the practices of visiting and hospitality take on a particular symbolic meaning. The community of believers, following its master, has the mission to seek out and find the excluded and the lost, welcoming them into the community. Hospitality is an *imitatio Dei*; in the encounters of hospitality, the mission of announcing the good news is at stake. Hospitality is an expression of the salvation already given by the welcoming God. The point carries over into the celebration of the Eucharist. Believers have received an "invitation to the banquet" of life in the Eucharist, and they celebrate the hospitality of God. Even while they consider themselves unworthy to receive Jesus "under their roof," they welcome this grace as a prefiguration of the final hospitality of the kingdom. Furthermore, we have a sign of whether the sacrament is being celebrated authentically: Can the community practice hospitality as part of its diaconal service?

The Shaping of the Virtue of Hospitality

How can the biblical imagination contribute to shaping our attitude of hospitality? How can hospitality be seen as a virtue enabling us to see the world with different eyes?

First, the history of ancient Israel as well as the texts of the New Testament insist on the fact that the best hosts are those who know that they were once themselves strangers and aliens, or those who have experienced in their lives lack of either status or power. "You shall love the alien as yourself, for you were aliens in the land of Egypt" (Lev. 19:34) is the motto of the Hebrews once they arrive in the Promised Land. Abraham, Isaac, and Jacob lived as sojourners in the land of Canaan. Jesus himself experienced exile and was not welcome in his own country. Zacchaeus was considered as an outcast, like the woman who anointed the feet of Jesus in Simon the Pharisee's house. Cornelius was a foreigner to the Jews, and yet Peter accepted his hospitality. In the same way, Christians are also aliens and exiles in this world (1 Pet. 2:11–12). They claim an inner freedom, a critical distance, from the institutions and values of the world, even as they remain deeply concerned for it. This recognition of a sense that one is never at home helps open us up to welcome the foreigner. Because our identity is rooted in the love of God and not in a special culture or land, we should be able to overcome the fear of being threatened by the strangeness of the other's culture or way of living. Because we have experienced vulnerability we can be attentive to the weaknesses and needs of the others.

Second, our ability to accept and welcome the other fundamentally depends on our own sense of having been welcomed ourselves in our vulnerability. Our hospitality is based on the hospitality of God toward us. Abraham and all the people of Israel have experienced the gracious initiative of God in the offer of the Covenant. They remember that they were a pilgrim people saved by God; that is why they can share with the stranger in their midst. The entire Gospel of Luke, and especially the story of Zacchaeus, expresses the "visitation" of God to Israel and to the world. Jesus the guest brings to those who receive him a wider experience of the "hospitality of God." In the encounter between Peter and Cornelius in Acts 10–11, God extends hospitality to the Gentiles and invites the Christian community to do the same. If we can be host, it is because we were guest from the beginning. Our hospitality is the reflection of God's hospitality. We are like Zacchaeus or the woman anointing Jesus' feet. Rescued and welcomed by Jesus, we can show in our turn justice and love to others. In a sense our hospitality enables God's hospitality to spread in the world: "Who was I that I could withstand God?" (Acts 11:17).

This leads to the third characteristic of Christian hospitality. In the welcoming of the stranger, our relationship with God is at stake. Hebrews, alluding to Abraham, speaks of some "who have entertained angels unawares" (Heb. 13:2). In the stories of Zacchaeus and of Peter with Cornelius hospitality becomes the vehicle of salvation for both sinners and gentiles: a merciful action enabling us to discover the true God who forgives and welcomes all nations and humans in God's love. Furthermore, Jesus himself identifies with the foreigners to whom we minister: "as you did it to one of the least of these my brethren, you did it to me" (Matt. 25:41). The welcoming of the stranger is a sign that the two great commandments are being observed: the love of God and the love of one's neighbor as oneself. With Abraham, we saw that even the value of hospitality to strangers overrides the concerns of hospitality to God. It is because there is no contradiction: "Where one makes room for the other, one resides in God's presence."

Fourth, hospitality is an occasion of conversion at various levels. When Abraham is visited by the strangers or when Peter encounters Cornelius, their images of God are challenged, and the ways they look at the world are transformed. Meeting foreigners changes their own sense of identity within God's covenant. The narratives show God inviting them to understand their election or salvation not as an expression of a closed symbolic community, but as engendering a responsibility for, and openness to, all humanity. The God of the Bible is not another exclusive tribal god, who reserves God's favors for the elect and the good, but rather the God who loves and tends all human beings, offering forgiveness to sinners, as the Zacchaeus story shows us, and healing to the sick. If our image of God changes, so our judgments upon "others" change. Abraham presses the claims of justice for the people of Sodom; Zacchaeus is reintegrated into the community; and Peter is obliged to revise his point of view about purity rules and commensality with Gentiles. Hospitality does not leave us untransformed, and we are often invited to become the guest of our guest. The host must understand the perspective of the alien. When we receive the stranger in our home, we receive also the precious "gift of his difference."

This leads us to the last characteristic: hospitality guides us to reciprocity and friendship. Hospitality is more than giving food and shelter. Hospitality opens us up to receive in turn the surprising gifts our guests might give us. Abraham received the gift of a son; Zacchaeus received salvation and became the friend of Jesus; Peter and Cornelius initiated a new and cordial relationship between Gentiles and Jews in the Christian community. This sharing pattern is particularly important when dealing with people who are poor and marginalized. When we show our concern by welcoming them, we may receive in turn a better understanding of their situation, the causes of their plight, and their own unique experience. And then the movement reverses again: the recognition we can give becomes a new gift, deeper than that of food or shelter. Hospitality to the stranger, the needy, and the poor gives us a direct emotional contact, which deepens our understanding of the social changes that are necessary and inspires actions of solidarity that can lead to global transformation. When we welcome the stranger, we are helped to discover other worlds. Initial animosity becomes fruitful friendship. What may have been an asymmetrical relationship at the beginning can become both respectful and reciprocal.

Hospitality is not merely a personal virtue, inviting us as individuals to show a generous welcome toward strangers. It is also a social and political virtue. How do we regard the foreigners already in our countries? What room are we making for refugees and migrants? The attitude of hospitality, shaped by biblical imagination, can nourish the spirit of public laws and guide their interpretation. Of course, any state has the right to regulate the immigration process in order to preserve social order or to foster the common good of its existing population. But this right is not unconditional. It needs to be set alongside other rights and priorities, such as respect for human dignity, or a wider version of the common good. The virtue of hospitality challenges a narrow conception of rights and justice that does not take into account the order of necessities. Catholic Social Teaching recognizes a person's right to change nationality for social and economic as well as political reasons, as a way of seeking conditions of life worthy of their common humanity. It is a well-established principle that those whose basic rights are most imperiled have the strongest claim.

The way we "see" the situation, "hear" the claims of the needy, and "judge" or implement the law is shaped by the moral metaphors invoked in the narratives we choose to inspire our lives. If we are guided by the examples of Abraham, Jesus, and Peter, our perceptions may change in a way that fosters new public policies and structures. We will be reminded of our own history of migration, and of the vulnerability that is part of our common humanity. We may sense an invitation to work for public policies that protect the rights of refugees and migrants as our neighbors and brothers and sisters in humanity. It is in this kind of way that biblical ethics can shape not only theological ethics but also public debate, reminding us of our past and pointing prophetically to what might be. The Bible invites us to imagine that in showing hospitality to strangers we can be "hosting Angels without knowing it" (Heb. 13:2). It should inculcate a basic stance of generosity in migration policy and encourage us to move, as Pope Francis urges us, from a "throwaway culture" to a "culture of encounter."

Notes

1. Lebanon, for example, has received more than one million Syrian refugees into a population of 4.5 million. The vast majority of migrants and refugee movements in the world are South-South.

2. Greek too had one word—*xenos*—that denoted both the enemy/stranger and the guest. See Richard Kearney and Kasha Semonovith, eds., *Phenomenology of the Stranger: Between Hostility and Hospitality* (New York: Fordham University Press, New York, 2011).

3. See Paul Ricoeur, *Lectures on Ideology and Utopia,* ed. G. H. Taylor (New York: Columbia University Press, 1986).

4. See also Lúcás Chan, SJ, *Biblical Ethics in the 21st Century* (New York: Paulist Press, 2013).

5. Pontifical Biblical Commission, *The Bible and Morality: Biblical Roots of Christian Conduct*, no. 4 (Vatican City: Libreria Editrice Vaticana, 2008).

6. See Alain Thomasset, "L'imagination dans la pensée de Paul Ricoeur: Fonction poétique du language et transformations du sujet," *Études Théologiques et Religieuses* 80 (2005/4): 525–41.

7. See, for example, John Koenig, *New Testament Hospitality: Partnership with Strangers as Promise and Mission* (Philadelphia: Fortress, 1985); Andrew Arterbury, *Entertaining Angels: Early Christian Hospitality in Its Mediterranean Setting*, New Testament Monographs, 8 (Sheffield: Sheffield Phoenix Press, 2005); Christine Pohl, *Making Room:*

Recovering Hospitality as a Christian Tradition (Grand Rapids, MI: Eerdmans, 1999); Alain Thomasset, *Les vertus sociales: Justice, solidarité, compassion, hospitalité, espérance* (Namur: Lessius, 2015).

8. For this analysis I rely on Marianne Moyaert, "Biblical, Ethical and Hermeneutical Reflections on Narrative Hospitality," in *Hosting the Stranger: Between Religions,* ed. Richard Kearney and James Taylor (New York: Continuum, 2011), 95–108.

9. Ibid., 98.

10. Jonathan Sacks, "Abraham and the Three Visitors," *Covenant and Conversation* 11 (November 2006), quoted by Moyaert, "Biblical," 98–99 (underlined by Sacks).

11. Moyaert, "Biblical," 99.

12. Cf. ibid., 100.

13. See Paul Beauchamp, *L'un et l'autre testament: Essai de lecture* (Paris: Seuil, 1981).

14. Jean Daniélou, "Pour une théologie de l'hospitalité," *La Vie Spirituelle* 85 (1951): 39–347, 340, quoted by Moyaert, "Biblical," 101n21.

15. Cf. Luke 2:49, 4:43, 9:22, 13:33, 17:25, 22:37, 24:7. See Brendan Byrne, *The Hospitality of God: A Reading of Luke's Gospel* (Collegeville, MN: Liturgical Press, 2000), 150.

16. See Andrew Arterbury, "Abraham's Hospitality among Jewish and Early Christian Writers: A Tradition History of Genesis 18:1–18 and Its Relevance for the Study of the New Testament," *Perspectives in Religious Studies* 30 (2003): 374.

17. Byrne, *Hospitality of God,* 152.

THE BIBLE AS SOURCE
OF MORAL WISDOM

PAULINE INSPIRATIONS FOR THE THEOLOGICAL AND ETHICAL DISCOURSE ON CONSCIENCE TODAY

Marian Machinek, MSF

A theological analysis of a biblical text calls for the employment of proper modern methods of historical-critical exegesis and biblical theology. It does not follow, however, that only professional exegetes and Bible scholars are entitled to take on such a task. After all, the Bible is the source of inspiration for all theological disciplines, including moral theology, represented by the author of this article.

The objective of the article is to examine those passages from the letters of Saint Paul about conscience that can be utilized in the moral and theological discourse on conscience today. Of course, one has to analyze Paul's texts very carefully first, taking notice of their meaning and placement within other New Testament writings, and within the Bible at large. Conclusions from the analysis are treated in a thorough way in the context of contemporary theological and moral reflections on conscience.

Biblical Understanding of Conscience

The moral value of human acts was of great interest to biblical authors. It is apparent already in the oldest texts, where the problem of good versus evil is a recurring theme in various stories and admonitions. The idea of conscience, however, which is so central to Christian ethical reflections today, seems to have occupied the minds of the ancient authors much less than we would expect.

Most ancient writers did not know the *concept* of conscience. There is no Hebrew equivalent of the word in the Old Testament. The main reason for this was that the Old Testament writers entertained different anthropological convictions from their Greco-Roman, and later Hellenistic, counterparts, who were focused on reason and self-awareness. Their reflection was radically theocentric, concentrated on the covenant with Yahweh and Yahweh's most important gift to Yahweh's people, which governed their lives and defined their entire moral universe: the Torah. Today, the idea of law invokes an image of a written codex, a rigid prescription of behavior. But for a faithful Israelite it was something vastly more than a code; it was one's "home," an environment where one breathed and was nourished, a signpost giving direction to the true life. Every member of God's chosen people was supposed to listen to the Torah attentively and be obedient to it. In doing so, everyone could be put in a direct relationship with the Creator. Thus the Torah, in a way, replaced the role of the conscience as the mediator.[1]

Nonetheless, the *phenomenon* of conscience was not entirely unknown. Many protagonists of the prehistoric biblical stories feel ashamed of the bad things they have done (Gen. 3:7), experience painful consequences of their sins (Gen. 42:21), are "repulsed" by the thought of having transgressed God's command (1 Sam. 42:6, 25:31), and feel anxiety for having done wrong (2 Sam. 24:10). Very important in this context is the concept of the heart (Hebr. *lēb*), which appears no less than 858 times.[2] Heart is the center of the person, where all dimensions of human existence are brought together. It is the source of the intellectual, emotional, and volitional spheres of the person. Modern readers of the Bible will probably relate the Old Testament phrases, describing the state of the human heart in the context of human acts, to the states of conscience. For instance, a hardened heart, a rebuking heart, a throbbing heart, a broken heart, and so on. It is evident also in the Septuagint, where phrases such as *katara kardia* (a pure heart) or *agathe kardia* (a good heart) seem to contain certain elements of the Hellenistic philosophy. The classical idea of conscience, *syneidēsis*, appears three times in the Septuagint (Wis. 17:10; Eccles. 10:20; Sir. 42:18), where it has a moral connotation, on the one hand, and indicates knowledge about a certain fact, on the other.[3] In classical Greek, the word *synoida* implied a shared knowledge, in the sense of possessing knowledge about something as an eyewitness to it, along with other witnesses, as well as a self-knowledge. Self-awareness of one's decisions and acts usually involves not only remembering—which is one of the faculties of the human spirit—but indicates the presence of a certain assessing element. It clearly implies a moral dimension.[4]

That out of the thirty places in the New Testament in which the term *syneidēsis* appears[5] it is fourteen times in the letters of Saint Paul (only in Rom. and 1 and 2 Cor.) clearly indicates that it was Paul who introduced it into the Christian theological reflection.[6] Because it makes an especially prominent appearance in the context of the disagreement in the First Letter to the Corinthians over eating meat sacrificed to idols, some scholars conclude that it must have existed in Corinth prior to Paul's arrival, who later only referred to it in his correspondence with the Corinthian community.[7] More likely, however, he borrowed it from the popular Hellenistic philosophy, because neither during the Corinthian dispute, nor on any other occasions, did he consider it necessary to explain this concept to his readers, probably assuming their familiarity with it.[8]

Strangely enough, the term *syneidēsis* never once appears in the canonical Gospels, except for the later version of the story about the adulteress (John 8:9). Authors of many manuscripts introduce it to explain the motive of her accusers to drop the charge, after they had been challenged by Jesus to go ahead with the stoning on condition of their being absolutely convinced of their own sinlessness. They left the place of the would-be execution "accused by their conscience" (*hypo tēs syneidēseōs elegchomenoi*). This commentary, though thoroughly proper, does not appear in authoritative manuscripts. That is why it did not make its way into the canonical text.[9] It seems that it presupposes a more mature, later reflection on conscience.

Despite the absence of the concept of conscience in the Gospels, it would be difficult to deny that they describe experiences relating to conscience by invoking the classical (also for the Old Testament) idea of the heart (*kardia*). For the authors of the synoptic Gospels, it concerns not only emotions, but thoughts and motives, too. Jesus blesses the pure in heart (Matt. 5:8, 6:21) because only they are able to experience God's presence. At the same time, he warns that heart may be a source of serious sins and may lead to constraining oneself to worldly affairs and away from God (Mark 7:21).[10] Jesus' description of the human heart growing coarse (*sklero-kardia*), known already in the Septuagint, is a warning that one can become so used to the rejection of God's inspirations that he is no longer able to tell good from wrong (Matt. 13:15, 19:1–9). Protagonists of Jesus' stories experience states that today are classified as the voices of conscience. The prodigal son comes to his senses so that he can return to his father, even if initially his motives were influenced by considerations of personal advantage (Luke 15:17).

The concept of conscience was also used in some later New Testament texts, when the expected Second Coming did not materialize and Christians needed clear norms of behavior in the pagan world. In the Acts of the Apostles, it appears in the speeches of Saint Paul, when he argues for his honesty (Acts 23:1, 24:16). In the pastoral letters it is usually clarified by an adjective (1 Tim. 1:19; 2 Tim. 1:3; Titus 1:15; 1 Pet. 3:16). It can be good and clean, or bad and stained.[11] In the Letter to the Hebrews, conscience is strictly connected to the cult and faith. Only the one whose conscience has been purified from dead actions by the blood of Christ is able to render a proper homage to God (Heb. 9:14, 13:18). In his polemics with the cult practices of the Old Covenant, the author of the letter states that: "None of the gifts and sacrifices offered under these regulations can possibly bring any worshipper to perfection in his conscience" (Heb. 9:9). Only the knowledge of Christ's sacrifice enables the faithful to approach God, sincere in heart and filled with faith, their hearts "free from any trace of bad conscience [*apo syneidēseōs ponēras*]" and their bodies "washed with pure water" (Heb. 10:22).

All these subtle shades of meaning in the texts of the New Testament differ from Paul's understanding of *syneidēsis*, which is chronologically first.

References to Conscience in the Letters of Saint Paul

Even though the concept of conscience does not occupy a central place in Paul's anthropology, it can nevertheless be safely said that he inherited it from popular Hellenistic ethics and molded it into an unmistakably Christian one. Conscience, besides allowing its owner an access to a shared knowledge (about an event or state, along with others), enables one to recognize the moral value of one's own acts.

"The secrets of human hearts" (Rom. 2:16)

Paul connects the inner workings and decisions of conscience with the depths of a person's innermost being, unknown to all others (*ta krypta tōn anthrōpōn*), which will be revealed and ultimately judged by God (Rom. 2:16). This is the key passage in Paul's thought on conscience, because it brings together the above-mentioned biblical concepts about the human's moral actions and anthropological terms originating in popular Hellenistic philosophy: law, nature, heart, thoughts, and conscience. Exegetes maintain that one cannot recognize in it a fully developed concept of conscience, or a theology of the natural law. They argue that it should be viewed in the context of the leading theme of this particular part of the letter, that is, the dispute over the salvific value of the Torah. Some even think that Paul did not mean all pagans in general, but only those who fulfill the demands of the Torah.[12] But it would be hard to deny that Paul describes a phenomenon that concerns all, not only believers. He does it using the terms known to Hellenistic philosophy.[13] Pagans too invoke the "voice" of conscience in their struggles to reach good decisions. Conscience is connected with "various considerations [*logismoi*], some of which accuse them, while others provide them with a defense" (Rom. 2:15b).[14] In this way, conscience participates in bearing witness (*symmartyrein*) to a person's deeds; it is incorruptible; it can discover and reveal the moral truth about one's good or evil deeds (what Paul calls: "the secrets of human hearts"), whether one wishes it or not. It works in this way: it enables a person to make a correct assessment of any given situation, on the one hand, and informs one about the requirements of the Torah, on the other, the content of which is engraved on all human hearts, including those of the pagans. Paul supports his reasoning with a well-known Greco-Roman ethical premise that human-made law (*thesis*) should comply with certain unalterable norms, engraved on human nature (*physis*).[15] The knowledge of the requirements of the Torah, according to Paul, is invoked precisely by conscience, which then applies it to a concrete situation.[16]

The connection between the workings of conscience and cognitive processes (*logismoi*) is not a mere logical statement of facts. Knowing right from wrong urges one to act according to that knowledge.[17] Paul appeals to testifying qualities of conscience again in Romans 8:16 and in 9:1, where he employs it in defense of his truthfulness. He is proud of his conscientious conviction, which, like an impartial judge, confirms his words (2 Cor. 1:12). The universal applicability of conscience is demonstrated in Paul's appeal to the judgment of consciences of other members of community (cf. 2 Cor. 5:11) and his readiness to commend himself to "every human being with a conscience" (2 Cor. 4:12).[18]

Generally speaking, conscience reacts to what has already been done. Classical moral theology calls it *conscientia consequens*. In this, Paul faithfully renders the then-popular meaning of conscience in Hellenistic moral philosophy, where he actually borrowed it from in the first place. Nevertheless, it seems that he expands it toward *conscientia antecedens*, that is, anticipative-predictive capabilities of conscience, which binds and urges future acts.[19] Conscience ought to be a guarantor of Christians' loyalty to the rightfully established authorities. This admonition refers also to future attitudes toward the state (cf. Rom. 13:5–6).[20]

"Conscience in the Holy Spirit" (Rom. 9:1)

Notwithstanding the universal applicability of conscience, Paul never doubts that the decisive factor for its proper performance is the faith. Even though he did not elaborate on it as much as many authors after him, he clearly did have it in mind. When he invokes his conscience, he is fully aware of its close association with the Holy Spirit (Rom. 9:1). Only the connection of *syneidēsis* with *pneuma hagion* provides conscience with ultimate credibility.[21]

The admonition that "every action which does not spring from faith is sin" (Rom. 14:23), which sounds like a generalized moral rule, should be viewed in this context. Though Paul does not use the concept of conscience here, that is what he means. In the later exegesis of the Letter to the Romans, this sentence evolved into a maxim according to which every action contrary to the firm judgment of conscience is sin. The fact that Paul uses here the word *pistis* indicates that he does not mean a strong conviction in general, but a conviction grounded in faith, cleansed by faith and ensured by faith. In order to arrive at such a conviction, Paul insists on the need to examine oneself (*dokimazein* or *peirazein*), that is, in the modern parlance, examination of conscience (Gal. 6:4; 2 Cor. 13:5). He makes it clear that the aim of such an examination is to see if one remains steadfast in faith.[22]

Though Paul lays great stress on the theological aspects of conscience, he is clear that it is not simply "God's voice" in us. He is remarkably realistic about the potential influence of external factors on concrete judgments of conscience. Despite its testifying qualities, conscience is not the highest court of justice. This prerogative belongs to God alone, when all will be revealed: "It is true that my conscience does not reproach me, but that is not enough to justify me. It is the Lord who is my judge" (1 Cor. 4:4). Paul seems to perceive here a very important truth, which the theology of later centuries will develop into the concept of the misguided conscience.

"For conscience's sake" (1 Cor. 10:25; Rom. 13:5)

The phrase *dia tēn syneidēsin* has no equivalent in other texts of the New Testament. Paul, however, uses it on several occasions in—as it seems—a fixed form. It usually refers to the relationship between believers within community, as well as their attitude toward nonbelievers—for instance, civil authorities. It stands for a general sense of moral responsibility for one's actions. Paul encourages his listeners to stay loyal to the state authority, which comes from God and, if it is just, rewards the good and punishes the wicked on behalf of God (Rom. 13:1–4). They must be obedient to it not only because of fear of punishment, but also for conscience's sake, that is, out of a sense of responsibility. The term "for conscience's sake" denotes not only an external obedience, but also an internal obligation. Remarkably, conscience judges not only the deeds done, but anticipates future, everyday activities like paying taxes.[23]

The term *dia tēn syneidēsin* occupies a special place in the context of the disagreement over eating meat sacrificed to idols (1 Cor. 8:7–13, 10:23–30). Paul expands his array of adjectives by saying that conscience can be "weak" or "strong." The "strong ones" are those Corinthians who, acting on their knowledge (*gnōsis*) grounded in faith, are convinced that the gods, whom the sacrifice has been offered to, do not exist; therefore, they think that they are allowed (they possess *exousia*) to eat the food offered to them, whether found in a market or distributed at a banquet. The "weak ones" are those who are afraid that eating such food amounts to idolatry. Perhaps they are driven by fear of the pagan cults in which they may have participated.[24]

On the one hand, Paul takes the side of the "strong ones." The witness of their own conscience is enough; they should follow it and the rest of the community should not condemn them (1 Cor. 10:29). But the witness of the conscience of the "weak ones" is also binding on them, even if unaware that it is misguided. Acting against it would be sinful (1 Cor. 8:7, 10:12). Paul qualifies his advice with a serious admonition that the solution to this conflict should be governed by sibling love. Love must overrule everything, even one's rights derived from his or her freedom in Christ, lest they cause their sibling's downfall. The "strong ones" should be guided more by sibling love (*agapē*) than their knowledge (*gnōsis*) grounded in faith. If one hurts one's sibling in the name of the freedom of one's conscience, that one sins against Christ himself (1 Cor. 8:12).[25]

Inspirations for Modern Theological and Moral Reflections

Two thousand years after Saint Paul, readers of his letters may have a hard time deciphering his message about conscience, as they attach quite a different importance to it than he did. For one thing, the concept of conscience was never at the foreground of Paul's teaching on morality, whereas today it occupies quite a central place in moral theology. Development and better understanding of the concept of conscience, especially during the process of greater recognition of the autonomy of the subject, triggered by the Enlightenment, justified appeals to individual conscience as expressions of personal and inalienable moral responsibility. It also made it synonymous with personal independence. Totalitarian systems in the twentieth century demonstrated that nobody can shed or reduce personal responsibility for one's acts. Modern democracies respect it, too. However, demands of respect for the judgments of individual conscience have, in fact, reduced its pronouncements to mere personal opinions and convictions, with no reference to objective moral values. If conscience is sometimes respected by society, it is rather as a personal fancy than anything else. Instead of a greater appreciation of the role of conscience, one can often hear it branded as a long, historical burden that should be discarded.

It seems that two particular elements of Paul's concept of conscience may significantly enhance and inspire various opinions on the matter within contemporary moral theology.

Personal Relationship with Christ

The first of these is a close connection between conscience and faith. Even though Paul admits that unbelievers too enjoy the capability to know the moral law in their conscience, he never wavers from his conviction that the content of that moral law is God's Law: the Torah. If one wanted to refer modern moral concepts of conscience to that of Paul, he would certainly have to describe it as the theonomic one. Neither the concept of ideal autonomy, nor that of social heteronomy, does full justice to the Christian vision of conscience. Though Paul stresses the universal nature of conscience, his letters do not lend support to the view that conscience can be appealed to as the highest judging authority, independent of faith.[26] Conscience is the unquestioned center of the person; it is the person's "heart," where one is confronted with the truth about one's outward deeds and hidden motives and intents.[27] Hence, if one acts against the clear judgment of one's conscience, one acts against one's own moral integrity. Having said that, however, it must be remembered that conscience is not infallible. It is an extremely sensitive property of the human spirit, which must be nourished and developed. For the Christian, the key element in this development is one's faith in Christ and relationship with him. Only as the person redeemed is one able to accept the requirements of the Torah in full, just as Jesus explained them in his ultimate, messianic interpretations of God's commandments (cf. Matt. 5:17–20). In this sense, conscience remains the obligatory norm of conduct for Christians.

Faith nourishes good deeds and influences moral obligations. It relieves Christians of unnecessary burdens (cf. disagreement in Corinth over eating of meat sacrificed to idols) and sharpens their moral sensitivity "in knowledge and depth of insight, so that you may be able to discern what is best" (Phil. 1:9–10). "Strong conscience"—to recall what has been said above—does not mean a liberal conscience, but one enlightened by faith. Using the dispute over eating sacrificial food as an example, Paul demonstrates a strict connection between conscience and knowledge grounded in faith, and between conscience and a sense of responsibility before God for one's conduct toward one's neighbors.[28] Paul illustrates this new, faith-based sensitivity with a criticism of the popular Corinthian saying "Everything is permissible" (*panta exestin*). Paul advises his readers that instead of using this as an excuse for indulging in their old vices, they better discern whether what is permissible builds other people up and does not bring about their spiritual enslavement (cf. 1 Cor. 6:12, 10:23).[29]

The criterion of the living faith constitutes a significant supplement to the contemporary concept of autonomous conscience. It challenges this particular interpretation of moral autonomy that grants it total freedom from all external instructions and neglects the need for self-improvement. Christian morality is not dramatically different from the universal sense of morality. But the mere universality of the models of behavior cannot be hailed as the moral norm until tried by the requirements of the Gospel. It is telling that in many important spheres of life today one can hardly discern any difference between Christians and non-Christians. Of course, one can assume—optimistically—that universally used moral norms and evaluations comply with the Gospel standards. Another, more likely explanation is that Christians have already uncritically accepted and internalized moral standards that are alien to the Gospel; perhaps their consciences have grown so accustomed to making various accommodations that they no longer see any discrepancy between their behavior and the requirements of the Gospel.

The Role of the Ecclesial Community

Although Paul says that faith, as a close, intimate relationship with Christ, is a very *personal* matter, he nevertheless makes it crystal clear that it is not a *private* matter. It is not a *private* faith, but faith in the community of believers. Paul knows that there are such things as personal inspirations, and knowledge of one's own motives, and one's own spirituality; he knows that they manifest themselves precisely in one's own conscience and enable each one to formulate one's own opinions (cf. 1 Cor. 10:29). But he also knows that there is such a thing as *typos didachēs* (cf. Rom. 6:17), the form of teaching, providing a pattern of conduct in accordance with the faith in the Good News about the liberating and transforming power of God. And he knows how to remind those who transgress it. He does so by recalling the very words of Jesus on a given subject (if he knows them), whose authority is unquestionable and beyond dispute (e.g., on divorce: 1 Cor. 7:10), or referring to his own apostolic authority, by virtue of which he can prescribe and appeal to the consciences of the believers (1 Cor. 7:25).

It does not mean a heteronomy, in the sense of a total obedience to an external court. It rather means that one must seek God's will always. The possibility of going astray means that no decision of individual conscience may be accepted as "self-sufficient, absolute, or definitive" (cf. 1 Cor. 4:4).[30] The importance of conscience's capacities for making critical assessments and issuing recommendations in no way diminishes God's commandments, or the importance of the community of believers.

Today, in the midst of ethical individualism, consultation with the ecclesial context—to which, according to Catholic moral theology, belongs the entire tradition and the teaching authority of the Church—is very important. Processes of globalization in the world lead to a globalization of morality too, and a wide dissemination of certain moral standards. Christians should not withdraw to their own communities and separate themselves from external influences. God acts outside the visible church too. Common moral awareness and common moral standards may become a sort of *locus theologicus* for Christian ethical reflection. Nevertheless, the primary and fundamental environment of the believers is the community of people living out their faith. Only there can Christians know for sure if the urgings of their consciences agree with the requirements of the Gospel. Only there can they learn how to respect the personal, conscientious responsibility of others. Paul's insistence on the role of the community in the search for answers to moral challenges is extremely relevant even today.[31]

Notes

1. Eberhard Schockenhoff, *Wie gewiss ist das Gewissen? Eine ethische Orientierung* (Freiburg: Herder, 2003), 73–76.

2. Hans Walter Wolff, *Anthropologie des Alten Testament*, 6th ed. (Gütersloh: Gütersloher Verlagshaus, 1994), 68.

3. Cf. H. Ch. Hahn and Martin Karrer, "Gewissen," in *Theologisches Begriffslexikon zum Neuen Testament*, ed. Lothar Coenen and Klaus Haacker (Wuppertal: Neukirchen, 1997), 1:775; S. Szymik, "Starotestamentowe: Judaistyczne i grecko-rzymskie pojęcie sumienia," *Forum Teologiczne* 15 (2014): 8–12.

4. Cf. Hahn and Karrer, "Gewissen," 774.

5. The verb *synoida* appears in the New Testament only two times (1 Cor. 4:4; Acts 5:2). The term *syneidos* does not appear at all. Cf. H. Ch. Hahn, M. Karrer, "Gewissen," 775.

6. G. Lüdemann, "Syneidesis," in *Exegetisches Wörterbuch zum Neuen Testament*, ed. Horst Balz and Gerhard Schneider, vol. 3, 2nd ed. (Stuttgart: Kohlhammer, 1992), 721.

7. Michael Wolter, "Gewissen II: Neues Testament," in *Theologische Realenzyklopädie: Studienausgabe*, part 1 (Berlin: Walter de Gruyter, 1993), 214.

8. Ceslas Spicq, "Gewissen," in *Bibeltheologisches Wörterbuch*, ed. J. B. Bauer (Graz: Styria, 1962), 509–10. For more examples of *syneidēsis* in the non-Christian ancient literature see Gerhard Pfeiffer, *Das Gewissen in geistesgeschichtlicher Sicht* (Daader: Saarbrücken, 1990), 9–11.

9. Cf. Andrew T. Lincoln, *The Gospel according to Saint John* (London: Continuum, 2005), 533. Cf. Rudolf Schnackenburg, *Das Johannesevangelium* (Freiburg: Herder, 1971), 2:230.

10. Volker Stolle, "Herz," in *Theologisches Begriffslexikon zum Neuen Testament*, ed. Lothar Coenen and Klaus Haacker, 1:950–51.

11. G. Lüdemann, "Syneidesis," col. 724. Cf. Wolter, "Gewissen II: Neues Testament," 217.

12. Wolter, "Gewissen II: Neues Testament," 216.

13. Cf. Hans-Joachim Eckstein, *Der Begriff Syneidesis bei Paulus* (Tubingen: J. C. B. Mohr, 1983), 156–58.

14. Cf. Walter Klaiber, *Der Römerbrief* (Neukirchen: Neukirchener Verlag, 2009), 38–39; Heinrich Schlier, *Der Römerbrief* (Freiburg: Herder, 1977), 79–80; Robert Jewett,

Romans (Minneapolis: Fortress, 2007), 215–17. To some authors, the struggle between the thoughts accusing or defending is tantamount to the very mode of conscience's working (cf. Eduard Lohse, "Die Berufung auf das Gewissen in der paulinischen Ethik," in *Neues Testament und Ethik*, ed. Helmut Merklein [Freiburg: Herder, 1989], 212; Michael Wolter, *Der Brief an die Römer*, part 1 [Neukirchen: Neukirchener Verlag, 2014], 187). Other scholars understand it as an additional, confirming authority, along with the righteous deeds, demanded by the Law, and the witness of conscience (cf. Colin G. Kruse, *Paul's Letter to the Romans* (Grand Rapids, MI: Eerdmans, 2012), 132–33; James D. G. Dunn, *Romans 1–8* (Dallas: Word, 1988), 105.

15. Ulrich Wilckens, *Der Brief an die Römer*, 4th ed. (Neukirchen: Neukirchener Verlag, 2008), 133–35. For more on Paul's appeal to nature see also Kruse, *Paul's Letter to the Romans*, 135–36.

16. Cf. Hahn and Karrer, "Gewissen," 776.

17. Spicq, "Gewissen," 510.

18. Cf. Lohse, "Die Berufung auf das Gewissen," 213.

19. Spicq, "Gewissen," 510–11. For more on the relationship between *conscientia antecedens* and *conscientia consequens* in Paul's letters see Eckstein, *Der Begriff Syneidesis bei Paulus*, 172–73.

20. Margaret Thrall, "The Pauline Use of Syneidesis," *New Testament Studies* 14 (1967–68): 124.

21. Schockenhoff, "Wie gewiss ist das Gewissen?" 83; Joseph A. Fitzmyer, *Romans* (New Haven, CT: Yale University Press, 1993), 543–44.

22. The practice of daily examination of one's conduct was known to the popular Hellenistic ethics, as well as to Judaism influenced by it; the latter employed it as means of comparing one's conduct with the requirements of the Torah. Cf. Michael Theobald, *Römerbrief: Kapitel 1–11* (Stuttgart: Katholisches Bibelwerk, 1992), 77–78.

23. Cf. Schockenhoff, "Wie gewiss ist das Gewissen?" 87–88.

24. Roy E. Ciampa and Brian S. Rosner, *The First Letter to the Corinthians* (Grand Rapids, MI: Eerdmans, 2010), 390–94; Lohse, "Die Berufung auf das Gewissen," 216.

25. Wolter, "Gewissen II: Neues Testament," 214–15.

26. Cf. Hahn and Karrer, "Gewissen," 776–77.

27. Cf. Theobald, *Römerbrief*, 58–60.

28. Cf. Schockenhoff, "Wie gewiss ist das Gewissen?" 88–89.

29. Hans-Josef Klauck, *1. Korintherbrief* (Wurzburg: Echter Verlag, 1984), 75–76; Lohse, "Die Berufung auf das Gewissen," 217.

30. Cf. Wolfgang Schrage, *Ethik des Neuen Testamentes* (Göttingen: Vandenhoeck & Ruprecht, 1982), 185.

31. Ibid., 188. See also Rudolf Schnackenburg, *Die sittliche Botschaft des Neuen Testaments*, vol. 2: *Die urchristlichen Verkündiger* (Freiburg: Herder, 1988), 58.

Bible, Ethics, and the Global Church

A Feminist View from North America

Lisa Sowle Cahill

North American Christian feminism today expands beyond the needs and interests of North American women, to include the situation of women globally as part of the North American feminist conversation. At the same time, all theology, even an intentionally global theology, always begins from its own context. This context highly influences the questions identified as important, the answers envisioned, and the audience to which the theology will appeal. Therefore, North American feminist theologies must learn from their global conversation partners, adapt and correct their own perspectives, and work toward shared perceptions of the ethical-political relevance of the Bible in the struggle for gender equality.

This essay first discusses the practical, ecclesial, and political nature of all biblical interpretation. It then takes up the distinctive ways in which twentieth-century biblical interpretation in North America has advanced the cause of women's equality, as well as the limits of some of the earlier approaches. The discussion includes influential "countercultures" of women's biblical interpretations—especially from African American and Latina authors—that have presented new ethical agendas and critiques of "mainstream" (white, academic) feminist biblical interpretation in the United States. The emphasis in this chapter is primarily, though not exclusively, on Catholic women. We must recognize, however, that Catholic and Protestant biblical hermeneutics are interdependent, and that male proponents and allies of feminism in North America are numerous. It is also important to realize that feminist biblical interpretation, feminist theology, and feminist ethics are not easy to separate. All Christian feminist theology and ethics refer to Scripture as a constituent authority, and all feminist biblical hermeneutics and theology have a constitutive political agenda. Hence they converge with ethics at the practical level.

Some of the characteristic contributions of North American feminist theological ethics are a commitment to equality in all spheres of life, a healthy suspicion of the idea that women are "equal but complementary" to men,[1] confidence that progress in church and society are politically possible, confrontation with biblical "texts of terror" as revealing oppressive elements in Scripture itself, and a cultural experience of women's growing social participation and legal rights. Women's biblical hermeneutics, theologies, and ethics from the "two-thirds world" expand the North American perspective in crucial ways, many already foreshadowed by countercultural biblical-theological feminisms within North America. For example, the radical nature of evil must be confronted, while hope for a different future grows from solidarity and shared practices of resistance.

The Bible's Meaning for Ethics:
Text, Interpretation, and Action

One reason that the Bible is a potent source of ethical and political formation is that it is a highly symbolic and fluid narrative, not a purely factual history or a philosophical treatise. The Bible pulls readers into its world of meaning, even as readers transform that meaning by bringing the Bible into dialogue with their own experiences, values, and questions. The Bible is a conduit and an occasion of the continual "remaking" of the Christian community as the Gospel is received and lived by peoples around the world. Several decades ago, the biblical scholar Phyllis A. Bird aptly titled a work *The Bible as the Church's Book*.[2] The canonical collection of writings that we call "Scripture" has meaning and authority only if, when, and because it is the formative narrative around which the community's life coheres and through which the community experiences God's presence.

As the biblical scholar Sandra Schneiders expresses it, "The integral interpretation of any biblical text is the process of engaging it in such a way that it can function as a locus and mediator of transformative encounter with the living God."[3] Lúcás Chan agrees: the exegesis of a text is interdependent with its interpretation, if and because description of the text's meaning engages a community trying to "perform" that meaning faithfully today.[4] In fact, "meaning" in its most complete sense "should be considered as an event that perdures in and through transformative appropriation."[5] The dynamic creation and re-creation of meaning is the process by which the Bible is handed on from one generation to the next, and in which it is claimed as what Schneiders terms "the revelatory text."[6] Without the church, there would be no Scripture.

But although the Bible is always received and interpreted in a specific context, and while its meaning also has context-specific reference points, it is also true that local meanings fit within general parameters of the Gospel message as discerned and tested by the universal community of the church over time. A distinctively Catholic point of biblical hermeneutics is that "the tradition," with its "rule of faith," has a certain authority over the meaning of the Bible, even though the Bible is more fundamental than tradition, is the condition of the possibility of tradition, and always challenges tradition. As Schneiders points out, any particular interpretation of the Bible must conform to what is known about God on the basis of other biblical teachings, on the basis of the Bible as a whole, in accord with the affirmation of Jesus Christ's full humanity and divinity (for the Western church, at Nicaea and Chalcedon), and in conformity to the ongoing practices of existential faith.

Robert Schreiter uses the term "global theological flows" to refer to a dynamic process of biblically based and participatory resistances to violence and social exclusion. He names four examples: liberationist, human rights–based, feminist, and ecological. Global theological flows are "not uniform or systemic," because of their "commitment to specific cultural and social settings." But they do "represent a series of linked, mutually intelligible discourses that address the contradictions or failures of global systems." These discourses are generated by a biblically inspired vision of spirituality, compassion, and justice.[7]

North American Biblical Feminist Interpretation

Early Biblical Feminism

From almost the beginning, feminist biblical interpretation in North America has taken a historically critical approach, made possible by the pioneering work of turn-of-the-century European scholars such as F. C. Baur, C. H. Dodd, Albert Schweitzer, Johannes Weiss, and William Wrede. Some of these critics ended in rejecting the divine and salvific meaning of Jesus as the Christ—a conclusion by no means shared by most Catholic feminist theologians. Nevertheless, historical criticism positively offers feminist biblical interpretation the possibility of seeing Jesus, his first followers, and the authors who recorded and collected the biblical narratives (both of the Hebrew Bible and the New Testament) as living historical figures. They spoke in and for specific contexts, contexts that shaped their viewpoints and social expectations. Therefore, for feminist biblical ethicists, understanding the social settings of various parts of Scripture is an important tool both to gain appreciation of the likely "message" of the text, given its original audience, and to interrogate whether that message should be authoritative, or remain so today. North American feminists also use another general method of biblical interpretation shared in other regions, known as literary, narrative, or rhetorical criticism: carefully examining the interplay of aspects of a text or story to uncover possible meanings that lie hidden or suppressed in standard readings.

*   *   *

At this moment, 3:45 pm, May 19, 2015, while composing this page, I have received news of the sudden death this morning of my friend, former student, and colleague, Lúcás Chan. Thank you Lúcás, with Ronaldo, for giving us the opportunity to reflect more deeply on all the ways the Scriptures shape the Christian life. You have lived that life; may you rest in peace, even as you continue to inspire our work.

*   *   *

Feminist biblical interpretation and ethics has as its raison d'etre the creation of Christian communities that more faithfully embody the Gospel. The context of feminist biblical interpretation is the life stories of women, unfolding within communities, cultures, and churches that see their status as second-class. Elizabeth Cady Stanton (1815–1902) was a notable early advocate of a critical, woman-oriented rereading of the Bible. She was also a leader of the movement to grant women in the United States the right to vote. She and her associates were white, middle-class, educated Protestants. Restrictions on women's education at the time meant that Cady Stanton had few of the theological or linguistic tools necessary for sophisticated biblical interpretation. Common sense and Christian faith, however, told her that biblical passages that are demeaning to women, even condoning violence against women, cannot and do not have the full weight of divine authority. Elizabeth Cady Stanton and seven colleagues produced *The Woman's Bible*, a version in which offending passages were identified and followed by commentaries contesting their meaning and authority.[8] *The Woman's Bible* was extremely controversial in its day, yet its popularity is attested by the fact that it was translated into several languages. In honor of its 100th anniversary, teams led by US feminist biblical scholars produced *The Women's Bible Commentary* and *Searching the Scriptures*, collections that represent a more religiously and culturally diverse set of contributors, as well as the high scholarly standards which today's feminist interpreters have attained.[9]

Elisabeth Schüssler Fiorenza

The most prolific and well-known feminist biblical interpreter in the United States in recent decades is the German-born New Testament scholar, Elisabeth Schüssler Fiorenza. Like all feminist theology, her hermeneutics is explicitly ethical and political. Schüssler Fiorenza defines her target as "kyriarchy," which she defines as "a complex pyramidal system of intersecting multiplicative social structures of superordination and subordination, of ruling and oppression," in which "elite, educated, propertied men" hold power over women and less elite men.[10]

Her most well-known and influential book is *In Memory of Her: A Feminist Theological Reconstruction of Christian Origins*.[11] Schüssler Fiorenza titles the book from a story in Mark's Gospel, in which an unnamed woman anoints Jesus, an event that looks ahead symbolically to his passion and death. Jesus declares, "And truly I say to you, wherever the Gospel is preached in the whole world, what she has done will be told in memory of her" (14:9). Ironically, however, this woman's prophetic action did not become part of evangelization, and even the name of this faithful disciple is lost to us—because she is a woman.[12] This fact should inspire contemporary women and men to uncover past injustices and root out their entrenched consequences in today's church.

Schüssler Fiorenza depicts the ministry of Jesus as offering an alternative to patriarchy, and, more broadly, kyriarchy. Although its radical nature lessened as the Christian movement grew and became acculturated, the early community formed around Jesus represented a "discipleship of equals," at least as an ideal, a standard, and a goal, if not always as a historical reality. "In the discipleship of equals, the role of women is not peripheral or trivial, but at the center."[13] The Bible presents equal discipleship as a historical possibility and ongoing task for the church. Schüssler Fiorenza does not see the New Testament as an unchanging archetype for later Christian practice and politics—it is not a timeless pattern to which all future embodiments of church must be molded. Rather it is more like a prototype—an "original" that is open to the possibility of its own transformation through the creation of recognizably similar but substantially different future versions.[14]

Because of the church's differing historical circumstances, and also because certain biblical texts reflect the kyriarchal culture of their own era, biblical examples or models of discipleship must have a provisional character. Only those that "critically break through patriarchal culture" have the authority of revelation. On the one hand, it is undeniable that the Bible privileges the male as normative and sees women's subjection to men as willed by God. The Bible also depicts God primarily in male terms.[15] On the other hand, the Jesus movement was a Jewish initiative to renew Israel and thus resisted oppressive and patriarchal/kyriarchal Roman rule. Its most basic themes and claims have to do with liberation from oppression as made possible by God's action in the person and work of Jesus Christ. This is a resource for women's liberation specifically.[16]

Rosemary Radford Ruether

Rosemary Radford Ruether is one of the first Catholic ethicists to develop a feminist perspective. Ruether realizes, with Schüssler Fiorenza, that all biblical texts were composed in patriarchal cultures. Some biblical narratives function to uphold a patriarchal ideology. Patriarchal premises and worldviews within the Bible obstruct its potentially liberating character. These must be subjected to a thorough feminist critique.[17] The feminist ethical norm of all theology and biblical interpretation is "the full humanity of women." Whatever does not reflect women's full humanity cannot be an authentic revelation of the divine.[18]

Ruether finds liberation particularly within the prophetic traditions. The prophets portray God as a liberating sovereign, image God with both male and female imagery, and prohibit idolatry.[19] All three themes are fruitful for feminist biblical ethics. Ruether may be insufficiently critical of the patriarchal dimensions even of the prophets, such as Hosea, who compares Israel to an adulterous wife, and God to a patient husband, and she may be insufficiently attentive to other biblical themes and narratives such as covenant.[20] However, Ruether does usefully show the possibility of recognizing some of the Bible's historical, religious, and ethical limits, while still treating it as "sacred Scripture" on the basis of its ageless message of salvation and liberation.

Biblical Resources for Feminist Ethics Today

One of the key themes and resources for feminist theology is Jesus' ministry of the reign of God, including what has come to be known in liberation theology and in recent papal encyclicals as the preferential option for the poor. Jesus was not a social reformer in the sense of an advocate for change in Roman imperial policy, or for "social justice" for those living under Roman rule. Jews in the Roman Empire were a protected group, allowed to worship in the Jerusalem Temple. But they were still a minority, forced to pay tribute to the emperor and his local representatives.

Because of periodic Jewish revolts and uprisings, the Romans constantly subjected Jews to threats of violence, and occasionally employed it. Two examples are the execution of Jesus and the destruction of the Temple in about 70 CE.

Jesus, as a Jewish teacher, was not in a position to influence imperial laws and policies, nor did he envision it as his mission. In fact, his prophetic gathering of a community of dangerous riffraff was among the causes of his death at imperial hands. Nevertheless, these very acts of reaching out to the poor, to the socially unacceptable, and to women have quite radical implications for later Christian social ethics. Where Christians are no longer a persecuted minority, or even attain elite status, their obligation to seek social change grows proportionately.

As Jesus announces at the beginning of his ministry, "The time is fulfilled and the kingdom of God has come near" (Mark 1:15). Jesus' healings, exorcisms, and "nature miracles" show that in Jesus, God's kingdom is already invading the realm of Satan. Matthew's and Luke's Gospels display the concrete ethical contents of this new experience of God's power in history. Those who follow Christ must love their neighbors in the same way the Good Samaritan had compassion for the Jew left for dead by robbers (Luke 10). They must give more than they are asked, renounce violence against evil, and love even their enemies (Matt. 5:38–48). They must meet the basic needs of the least powerful for food, clothing, shelter, and solidarity (Matt. 25). To be righteous in God's eyes and to enter the kingdom of heaven require a moral conversion and social commitment. The kingdom or reign of God is a corporate metaphor for salvation that involves the formation of a community and looks forward politically to changed ways of doing things in the world.[21]

Just as God's Spirit empowers Jesus (Luke 4:18–19), the Spirit sent by the risen Jesus shares resurrection life with his followers (Acts 2:1–13). In the Gospel of John, Jesus promises to send the Comforter or Advocate to strengthen the bonds of love in the community after his death (John 15). Union with God in love, through union with Jesus Christ as the incarnate Word, is the premise and precondition of the power of disciples to exercise a preferential option for the poor in a way that has genuine transformative power.

Many North American feminist biblical scholars have used narratives about women in the Bible to revive the discipleship of equals in today's church and to challenge restrictive roles that have evolved historically. Such narratives shape feminist faith and action with a critical, transformative edge. They include the Genesis creation stories, where the first man and woman are created in the image of God;[22] Jesus' remarkable ministry to and among women, with women disciples;[23] the role of Mary Magdalene as the first witness to the resurrection (John 20);[24] and the respect Paul shows women leaders in his churches, including Junia, who in Romans 16 Paul calls (with her husband Andronicus) "outstanding among the apostles."[25]

It is undeniable that even the New Testament contains texts with oppressive implications for women, the most obvious of which are the "household codes" commanding women to be obedient to their husbands, fathers, and masters (Eph. 5:22–6:9; Col. 3:18–4:1; 1 Pet. 2:13–3:7); and the views of Paul (or a later editor) and of the author of 1 Timothy that women should not speak up in the Christian assembly, or teach with authority, but must remain quiet and seek wisdom from their husbands (1 Cor. 14; 1 Tim. 2:11–12). Yet feminist theologians see these instructions as in tension with, and as of secondary authority (or no authority) in comparison to, the Gospel of redemption for people in Jesus Christ. The model of the restored divine-human relation is Jesus' inclusive table fellowship and ministry of the reign of God, as well as Paul's new family of sisters and brothers in the body of Christ (cf. Gal. 3:28).

Just as they were not modern social reformers, neither were Jesus, Paul, or the evangelists "feminists" in today's sense of the word. "Jesus and his first followers were people of their particular time and place. To act otherwise would have marked Jesus as a social deviant. Nevertheless . . . Jesus was remarkably open to the participation of women in his movement."[26] This openness became an irrepressible dimension of Christianity, a thread visible in the Gospels to which later interpreters return again and again for inspiration and courage.

The most noted North American Catholic feminist ethicist, Margaret A. Farley (who has built theological and practical bridges to women in Africa), notes that the commands of Jesus focus the moral life on love of God and neighbor. Specific biblical statements about sex and gender must be placed in their first-century context and judged by the standard of neighbor-love. Moreover, love relationships must be structured by justice, especially where disparities of power are involved.[27]

Counter-Cultural Alternatives to "Feminist" Biblical Ethics

Up until the middle of the twentieth century, most Christian feminists interpreting the Bible in North America were white academics. The nature of women, women's needs and rights, and the goals of women's liberation were all constructed from the perspective of white women. Feminist goals such as political equality of women, equal respect and roles for women in the church, equal pay for equal work, and the right to determine for oneself whether to engage in sex, whether and whom to marry, and whether to have children, might be fairly uncontroversial in and of themselves. Yet what early white feminism sorely lacked was an awareness that the different ethnic, racial, and class identities of women overlap to expand and intensify oppressions. This is called "intersectionality."[28] In fact, women "of color" were rarely envisioned to be necessary and full partners in "mainstream" debates about feminist biblical ethics at all.

Yet as more African American, Latina, and Asian American women, as well as more lesbians and gender-queer women, embraced a theological vocation, and rose to significance in church and academy, this situation began to change. Women once considered "minorities" in the larger US culture now interpret the Bible and write theologically from their own experience. Kwok Pui-lan, born in Hong Kong but teaching in the United States, describes women's theology from the Global South in a way that also applies to the difference between the biblical ethics of white feminists and that of women of color in the United States. The struggle of the latter

> has not been defined by the liberal politics of the women's suffrage movement, women's rights, and the demand for equal access to opportunities and privileges enjoyed by men. [They] do not have the luxury of attending to gender oppression alone, without simultaneously taking into consideration class, racial, colonial, and religious oppression. Their political theology takes many forms, including the option for solidarity with the poor, the critique of cultural alienation and racial oppression, the challenge of a globalized economy, and activism for ecojustice and protection of nature.[29]

María Pilar Aquino describes herself as "a Latina Catholic woman born in Mexico of grassroot migrant farmworker parents, with many years of experience and involvement with various feminist movements throughout the Americas." She believes that culturally different women share many personal and political goals with white feminists, but their voices offer more than simply copies of white feminism. She defines her own approach as "a mestizo theory, method, spirituality, and praxis" that is reflective of the "daily life experiences of grassroot working-class Latina women."[30] Similarly, Ada María Isasi-Díaz (originally from Cuba) locates her theology and ethics in *lo cotidiano* (the everyday). She places theology within the struggle (Lucha) of "Latinas' daily life where the norm is *hacer lo que se puede aunque no sea siempre lo mejor*, to do what one is able to do even if it is not the best thing to do, in order to survive."[31]

African American women approach biblical ethics from the standpoint of a heritage of enslavement and the subsequent denial of social, political, and economic rights. From the starting point of the Black experience in America, they advocate a theology and biblical hermeneutics of gender and racial equality. Suffering and struggle are part of their daily existence in a racist society. Many prefer the identifier "womanist" over feminist, a term invented and defined by the novelist Alice Walker: "Womanist is to feminist as purple is to lavender."[32]

The most prominent womanist theological ethicist is the Protestant Katie Cannon. She relates growing up in a Black church community where her grandmother taught her of God's universal parenthood and love for all. This led her to ask, "How could Christians who were white refuse to treat as fellow human beings, flatly and openly, Christians who had African ancestry?"[33] Cannon also identifies a problem shared by Latina theologians: the men in their cultural and faith communities fail to recognize the triple oppressions of gender, race-ethnicity, and class suffered by women, and thus fail to prioritize the liberation of women within their "liberation" theologies.[34] Her biblical-theological solution is to lift up the image of God for women, drawing on the theology of the African American theologian Howard Thurman:

> Being created in the image of God means . . . that within each individual there is the presence and power of the divine. Only in the concreteness of God's revealed love does each person recognize her worth, purpose and power. . . . This built-in sense of the creator provides oppressed people with ultimate meaning and the ability to transform circumstances.[35]

Women from racial-ethnic North American cultures that run counter to the "white mainstream" often draw on their community's experiences and traditions to nurture religious identity, build solidarity, and inspire collective action. One prominent example is the popular Latina representation of Mary the mother of Jesus as Our Lady of Guadalupe, who according to legend appeared to a sixteenth-century Mexican peasant in garb reminiscent of the indigenous Aztec goddess Tonantzin.[36] Another is the slave history of Black American women, captured powerfully by spirituals in which a captive people lamented their plight and cried to God for solace, redemption, and release. Although the Christianity of their masters was used to promote an ethos of obedience, the true liberating message of the biblical texts was not lost on the slaves, who stole away to conduct their own worship unheard and unseen by their vicious overseers.[37]

Evil and Redemption

The Cross

Many feminists and womanists in North America and elsewhere have problematized the image of Jesus dying on the cross for human sins. Christ-like sacrificial love has too often been used to validate a self-destructive and uncomplaining role of subservience for women. Worse, the idea that Christ takes the punishment for human sinfulness implies an unmerciful God who demands and takes pleasure in the death of an innocent man.[38] Instead, many feminists see the meaning of the cross as God's solidarity with human suffering, and as the divine presence to and in human suffering, a presence that heals and redeems. Biblically, the cross is salvific because it is joined to resurrection and the sending of the Spirit.

Delores Williams, a womanist theologian, believes that atonement theologies of redemption through the cross must be repudiated.[39] However, Shawn Copeland, another African American, and Isasi-Díaz, from a Latina point of view, offer examples from the piety of ordinary women caught in cycles of adversity and violence who see Christ's death on the cross as meaningful and redemptive for them.[40] These hermeneutical and theological-political differences reveal that the Bible is a rich but often perplexing source for feminist ethics. Its meaning must be appropriated contextually. The test of any interpretation is transformative action for justice, especially (for feminist ethics) justice for women. Does it overcome acquiescence to patriarchy and other forms of violence, and empower the oppressed?

"Texts of Terror"

A particular challenge for feminist ethicists is the glaring presence of biblical narratives that Phyllis Trible deems "texts of terror."[41] Not only does the Bible contain stories of violence toward women, but the male "heroes" and the biblical narrators seem to pass over these events with complacence if not approval. Trible's examples are Hagar, the slave or concubine of Abraham and Sarah, who is forced to become the mother of Abraham's son Ishmael, then cast out by the couple; Tamar, who is cheated out of the opportunity to bear sons by her father-in-law Judah; a Levite's concubine who is raped to death and dismembered; and the daughter of an Israelite general, Jephthah, who is foolishly promised as a human sacrifice if her father wins a battle (Hagar, Gen. 16:1–16, 21:9–21; Tamar, 2 Sam. 13:1–22; an unnamed concubine, Judg. 19:1–30; and the daughter of Jephthah, Judg. 11:29–40).

In one case, that of Hagar, God does not liberate the exploited woman, but does assist her survival. Thus, in a womanist interpretation, Hagar's "wilderness experience" can be a model for enslaved African women, and their daughters today, who are forced to have sex with their masters, then left "in the wilderness" to "make a way out of no way" with their children.[42] After everything she has endured, God at least saves Hagar's life, and promises that her son's heirs will be "a great nation" (Gen. 17:20).

But some texts do not permit any sort of positive recovery. The rape and murder of the concubine is particularly shocking, but in numerous troublesome texts, the rapes of Dinah and Bathsheba among them, the woman's perspective seems completely subordinate to the interests and careers of the stories' male "heroes." It is easy to recognize in these biblical women the plight of women across the ages who are raped, tortured, and murdered as acts of war, or who endure life-long abuse with never a gesture of kindness to alleviate their despair.

Such situations occur everywhere, but they are more common and more readily tolerated or condoned in societies that suffer endemic poverty and ongoing violence of many sorts. Writing from post-apartheid South Africa, the Protestant biblical theologian Sarojini Nadar unveils a sinister backdrop of institutionalized child rape in the colorful saga of Queen Esther. The Bible recounts how Esther, a beautiful Jew, is chosen to be the wife of the Persian King Ahasuerus after an empire-wide search: "the king loved Esther and she found favor beyond all the other virgins" (Esther 2:17). This puts her in a position later to save her people from a genocide planned by the king's evil adviser Haman. Nadar notes, however, a detail of the story that is usually overlooked: each of the girls competing for the honor of marriage to the king is kept in a harem for a year until it is her turn to spend one night in the king's palace. In the morning, she is taken to a second harem where she awaits the king's decision. The king is sequentially raping young girls until selecting a bride. Yet this process is concealed and normalized by the focus of the narrator on the honor bestowed on Queen Esther. Thus, "unless these texts are read and exposed, they will continue to hurt women in our courts, cities, townships, rural areas, and . . . the church as well."[43]

What can be said about such accounts and their presence in Christians' "holy Scriptures"? Yes, they can be subordinated to larger narrative themes having to do with God's relation to Israel, its leaders, its enemies, and its history. But this does not explain why they are not reported with a suggestion of negative judgment. A similar issue exists with the household codes, which some view as adaptations to Greco-Roman culture that were necessary for survival. Even so, these texts are symptomatic of structural sin in the communities that passed on the texts, and in their theologies (including white feminist theologies). Such narratives and instructions embody a huge challenge confronting liberationist and political theologies. Although the Gospel of Jesus Christ inspires us to resist and transform inequality and violence, our formative texts tacitly mediate these very same sins and structural evils.

What this shows is that even Christianity's sacred traditions and time-honored practices must be subjected to an unwavering hermeneutic of suspicion. But the presence of these texts is also, paradoxically, a reason for hope. First, they remind us that abused and abandoned women are already a part of our reality and must be given a place at our table. Second, they remind us that even though the church and its members are sinful, they are also graced by God's presence, and called to repentance and redemption. Despite terrible betrayals of God's invitation to salvation, Christianity has mediated the presence of God across the ages, and can continue to do so today. Finally, the fact that there are distortions even within Scripture forbids any kind of complacency about the ultimate triumph of liberation, and inspires Christian feminists to work all the harder to eradicate evil in church and society.

Christina Astorga is a Filipina feminist theological ethicist who has for many years lived and taught in the United States. She dedicates a substantial chapter to a feminist biblical ethics in her 2014 book *Catholic Moral Theology and Social Ethics*. Because of her cross-cultural and interracial experience, she is a good spokesperson for feminist theological ethicists in North America who understand Christian feminism as pluralistic, see their own identities as open-ended, and join cause with counterparts in other cultural settings. According to Astorga, the key to a feminist, liberationist, global ethics is the building of community in light of the eschatological promise of transformation and new life.[44] The community of faith and liberation affirms our common humanity and common destiny, without renouncing particularity. "The church must emerge from within the diversity of people, cultures, and religions and assume a plurality of faces—an African face, a Latin American face, an Asian face."[45]

For Astorga (paralleling Schneiders and Chan), the meaning of any particular biblical text must always be determined through the encounter of "flesh-and-blood readers," embedded in their own highly contextual social locations, and seeking the meaning of "abundant life" for them (John 10:10). This encounter may be interreligious and is receptive to the divine presence in non-Christian traditions.

Liberation and salvation are the guides through "an explosion of possible readings." "The priority of the contemporary reader as the subject of the revelatory event, the hermeneutical privilege of the oppressed as the locus of the scripture's meaning, and the life-giving call of John 10:10 as the basic interpretive lens are the principles that must guide the reading and interpretation of Scripture."[46]

Other essays in this volume take up the specific contributions of feminist theological ethics and of biblical hermeneutics in a variety of global settings. Yet in conclusion here, some points on our common trajectory can be named. First, the Gospel of Jesus Christ proclaims an inclusive community in which the poor and the "least of these" (Matt. 25) have a special place and claim. Membership in this community is diverse, but it is united in its search for "abundant life" for all. Second, this community is not merely an eschatological ideal; it is a present reality, whose historical growth by the grace of God must be embraced and defended. Community inaugurating the basileia of God is the source and criterion of authentic biblical interpretation, authentic Christian ethics, and authentic Christian feminism. This requires Christian feminist biblical ethics to be engaged, positive, and constructive, yet not naive.

Third, love may be stronger than death (Rom. 8:38–39), but evil is often stronger than human life, and should never be underestimated. Christians in the two-thirds world, and those living at the margins of "privileged" societies, know this only too well. Fourth, interreligious cooperation for social change is a reality and a necessity in global Christian social ethics, including the struggle for greater equality of women in the face of entrenched and worldwide institutions of violence against women.

Therefore, a justice-oriented hermeneutics of the Gospel of Jesus Christ must be open to resonances and expansions of meaning found in the encounter with other faiths. Finally, hope comes from solidaristic action, centered on practical and communal commemoration of biblical events, and of the life and teaching of Jesus. Hope thrives in communities centered on transformative action against injustice, inspired and empowered by God's Spirit.

Notes

1. See Christine E. Gudorf, "Woman as Other: The Papacy on Women," *Social Compass* (Louvain) 36, no. 3 (1989): 295–310.

2. Phyllis A. Bird, *The Bible as the Church's Book* (Philadelphia: Westminster, 1982).

3. Sandra M. Schneiders, *The Revelatory Text: Interpreting the New Testament as Sacred Scripture* (San Francisco: HarperSanFrancisco, 1991), 197.

4. Yiu Sing Lúcás Chan, SJ, *Biblical Ethics in the 21st Century: Developments, Emerging Consensus, and Future Directions* (New York: Paulist Press, 2013), 7.

5. Schneiders, *Revelatory Text*, 161.

6. Ibid., 193.

7. Robert J. Schreiter, *The New Catholicity: Theology between the Global and the Local* (Maryknoll, NY: Orbis Books, 1998), 16.

8. Elizabeth Cady Stanton, *The Woman's Bible* (The Project Gutenberg eBook of The Woman's Bible, by Elizabeth Cady Stanton, 2006).

9. Carol A. Newsome and Sharon H. Ringe, eds., *The Women's Bible Commentary* (London: SPCK Westminster/ John Knox, 1992); and Elisabeth Schüssler Fiorenza et al., eds., *Searching the Scriptures* (New York: Crossroad, 2001).

10. Elisabeth Schüssler Fiorenza, *Wisdom Ways: Introducing Feminist Biblical Interpretation* (Maryknoll, NY: Orbis Books, 2001), 211.

11. Elisabeth Schüssler Fiorenza, *In Memory of Her: A Feminist Theological Reconstruction of Christian Origins* (New York: Crossroad, 1983).

12. Ibid., xiii.

13. Ibid., 152.

14. Ibid., 35.

15. Sandra M. Schneiders, "The Bible and Feminism," in *Freeing Theology: The Essentials of Theology in Feminist Perspective*, ed. Catherine Mowry LaCugna (New York: HarperCollins, 1993), 34–35.

16. Bonnie Thurston, *Women in the New Testament: Questions and Commentary* (New York: Crossroad, 1998), 4–5; citing Luise Schottroff, *Lydia's Impatient Sisters: A Feminist Social History of Early Christianity* (Louisville, KY: Westminster John Knox Press, 1995).

17. Rosemary Radford Ruether, *Sexism and God-Talk* (London: SCM Press, 1983), 24.

18. Ibid., 19.

19. Ibid., 61–68.

20. Schüssler Fiorenza, *In Memory of Her,* 19.

21. Frank J. Matera, *New Testament Theology: Exploring Diversity and Unity* (Louisville, KY: Westminster John Knox, 2007), 11–15, 30–36, 84–88.

22. The Protestant biblical scholar Phyllis Trible (*God and the Rhetoric of Sexuality* [Minneapolis: Fortress, 1986]) cleverly rereads the creation stories to show that the subordination of Eve to Adam is completely belied by the texts, in which, for example, the woman is made from the rib of the first human to show they are of the same nature; whereas the first was made from a lower material, the dust of the ground (Gen. 2:27)! See also Mary Catherine Hilkert, OP, *"Imago Dei:* Does the Symbol Have a Future?" Santa Clara Lectures 8/3 (2002), Santa Clara University.

23. See, for example, Thurston, *Women in the New Testament;* and see the work of Elaine Wainwright.

24. Bernard of Clairvaux and John Paul II called Mary Magdalene the "apostle to the apostles." See *Mulieris Dignitatem* (1988), no. 16. She is an apostle by the same criteria applied to St. Paul: she saw the risen Jesus and was sent by him to preach the Gospel.

25. Over the centuries, Junia's name was repeatedly rendered in the male form "Junias" by translators (even though such a name for men did not exist in first-century Roman culture), because they could not believe that Paul would recognize women as having a status comparable to his own.

26. Daniel J. Harrington, SJ, *Jesus: A Historical Portrait* (Cincinnati, OH: St. Anthony Messenger, 2007), 53.

27. Margaret A. Farley, *Just Love: A Framework for Christian Sexual Ethics* (New York: Continuum, 2006), 38, 215–32.

28. Kimberle Crenshaw, "Mapping the Margins: Intersectionality, Identity Politics, and Violence against Women of Color," *Stanford Law Review* 43, no. 6 (1991): 1241–99.

29. Kwok Pui-lan, "Feminist Theology, Southern," in *The Blackwell Companion to Political Theology*, ed. Peter Scott and William T. Cavanaugh (Malden, MA: Blackwell, 2004), 206–7.

30. María Pilar Aquinas, "Latina Feminist Theology," in *A Reader in Latina Feminist Theology: Religion and Justice*, ed. María Pilar Aquino, Daisy L. Machado, and Jeannette Rodriguez (Austin: University of Texas Press, 2002), 136. *"Mestiza"* means a woman of mixed race, especially the offspring of a Spaniard and an American Indian. In the context of Latin America liberation theology and ethics, *mestizajo* can connote a mixed heritage of indigenous religions from Latin America and the Christianity introduced by the colonizers.

31. Ada María Isasi-Díaz, *En la Lucha/ In the Struggle: Elaborating a Mujerista Theology* (Minneapolis: Augsburg Fortress, 1993), 172.

32. Alice Walker, *In Search of Our Mothers' Gardens: Womanist Prose* (New York: Harcourt, 1983), xi.

33. Katie G. Cannon, *Black Womanist Ethics* (Atlanta, GA: Scholars, 1998), 1.

34. Ibid., 174; see María Pilar Aquino, "Evil and Hope: A Response to Jon Sobrino," *CTSA Proceedings* 50 (1995): 91.

35. Cannon, *Black Womanist Ethics*, 160.

36. Jeanette Rodriguez, *Our Lady of Guadalupe: Faith and Empowerment among Mexican-American Women* (Austin: University of Texas Press, 1994); D. A. Brading, *Mexican Phoenix: Our Lady of Guadalupe: Image and Tradition across Five Centuries* (Cambridge: Cambridge University Press, 2001).

37. M. Shawn Copeland, "To Follow Jesus: Slave Narratives and Spirituals Retell the Story of the Suffering Jesus," *America* 196, no. 7 (2007); Dwight N. Hopkins and George C. L. Cummings, eds., *Cut Loose Your Stammering Tongue: Black Theology in the Slave Narratives,* rev. and exp. ed. (Louisville, KY: Westminster John Knox, 2003).

38. Rita Nakashima Brock and Rebecca Ann Parker, *Proverbs of Ashes: Violence, Redemptive Suffering and the Search for What Saves Us* (Boston: Beacon Press, 2002).

39. Delores S. Williams, *Sisters in the Wilderness: The Challenge of Womanist God-Talk* (Maryknoll, NY: Orbis Books, 1995), 166.

40. M. Shawn Copeland, "Wading through Many Sorrows: Toward a Theology of Suffering in Womanist Perspective," in *A Troubling in My Soul: Womanist Perspectives on Evil*

and Suffering, ed. Emilie M. Townes (Maryknoll, NY: Orbis Books, 1993), 111–29; Ada María Isasi-Díaz, *La Lucha Continues: Mujerista Theology* (Maryknoll, NY: Orbis Books, 2001), 260–61. See also an interpretation by the Asian American Protestant, Wonhee Anne Joh, *Heart of the Cross: A Postcolonial Christology* (Louisville, KY: Westminster John Knox Press, 2006).

41. Phyllis A. Trible, *Texts of Terror: Literary-Feminist Readings of Biblical Narratives* (Philadelphia: Fortress Press, 1984).

42. Williams, *Sisters in the Wilderness,* 3–6, 159–61.

43. Sarojini Nadar, "'Texts of Terror': The Conspiracy of Rape in the Bible, Church and Society: The Case of Esther 2:1–18," in *African Women, Religion and Health: Essays in Honor of Mercy Amba Ewudziwa Oduyoye*, ed. Isabel Apawo Phiri and Sarojini Nadar (Maryknoll, NY: Orbis Books, 2006), 90.

44. Christina A. Astorga, *Catholic Moral Theology and Social Ethics: A New Method* (Maryknoll, NY: Orbis Books, 2014), 233.

45. Ibid., 227.

46. Ibid., 167.

THE ROLE OF CULTURAL CONTEXT

Is There Any Faithful Exegete?
Old Testament Ethics in a West African Cultural Context

Paul Béré, SJ

The Celestial Church of Christ in West Africa, the largest of its kind,[1] uses biblical quotations to back up its ethical demands,[2] while the Catholic Church proposes an elaborate ethical system inherited from Western philosophy and theology. By and large, African Christians seem to find in the African Initiated Churches an ethical system that is closer to their traditional norms, principles, and rules. And the Catholic Church, since Vatican II, invites theology to live by Scripture studies. Teaching biblical ethics in a West African context faces the challenge first of deciphering the affinity between the ethical world of the Bible and that of traditional West Africa, on the one hand, and the fundamental difference, on the other. Second, it has to heighten the awareness of the interplay between three cultural matrixes: the audience (say, the students); the interpreter's matrix, in the event that it is different from that of the audience; and the Bible. How do I then handle moral issues raised by the Bible with my West African audience?[3]

I contend that moral issues raised by OT texts reveal a constant cultural conflict of interpretation between the above-mentioned worlds. They do share the basic values that make up what it means to be a human being, but the way the concepts are formulated in narratives, proverbs, poetry, laws, social structures, and so on does not always yield consent. We often take for granted that our reading of the text is free of any cultural bias, and we claim objectivity. To overcome such a bias, I suggest that we use an intercultural approach, which means in the present context that we look for the best in culture that might provide the best tools to help unpack the meaning of a given text. Such an approach would render possible the unpacking of the ethical values enclosed in the text. The notion of faithfulness to the text—a moral value!—becomes possible by selecting the best cultural code to communicate the message.

Otherwise, the interpretive process recedes into an imposition of one's cultural value system upon the Bible. We may even assume that to collect data either from the biblical texts or from the extrabiblical sources would lead to an accurate rendering of what the text has to say.

In this essay, I would like to point out a few biblical instances (OT in particular) that account for the above-stated position. The best place to highlight the conflictual aspect, often unconscious, of our interpretations can easily come to the fore in the realm of ethics. I thus look at key issues such as truth and forbidden sexual relationships, then consider violence and peace, and finally suggest some methodological considerations flowing out of the preceding analysis.

Truth and Forbidden Sexual Relationships

> Please say that you are my sister so that it may go well with me because of you, and that I may live on account of you. (Gen. 12:13)

Genesis 12:10–20 tells the story of Abraham[4] traveling to Egypt with Sara, for "there was a famine in the land" (v. 10). When they were about to enter into Egypt, Abraham said to Sara, "When the Egyptians see you, they will say, 'This is his wife'; and they will kill me, but they will let you live. Please say you are my sister so that it may go well with me because of you, and that I may live on account of you" (vv. 12–13). Abraham's proposal stirred a lot of ink, because, by "our" standards, the patriarch lied, and invited Sara his wife to do likewise.

I have written "our" (by "our" standards) with quotation marks, but this personal pronoun needs some specification. The reception of this biblical narrative was not smooth for my West African audience, which is culturally diverse. In the Fulani culture, for instance, for a particular group called Wodaabe (in Niger), marriage between patrilineal cousins was the norm. A French anthropologist who studied the matrimonial system of the group says that for a young adult who wants to get married,

> the daughter of the paternal uncle has a marked preference: first choice wife, when it results impossible to find one near, then one seeks a *biddo bappanyon* ["daughter of the little father"], a classificatory daughter of the father's male cousin; cross cousins, male or female, come only next. Contrariwise, the maternal aunt's daughter is subject to an extremely rigorous prohibition; to marry her would be a shameful incest, and this fact extends to the daughters of the classificatory maternal aunts, the mother's paternal and maternal cousins.[5]

From a reception critical point of view, a Wodaabe audience of the Genesis 12:10–20 narrative would feel at home with what Abraham says, whereas the Bambara (in Mali, West Africa) would feel some discomfort because in the Bambara culture (a patrilineal society) the woman moves instead to the husband's house. The quotation above witnesses therefore to the consonance or dissonance problem our ethical reception might generate. One might doubt that such a system exists as a reference in the OT, based on the dominant model that the church has borrowed from the Western tradition and enforced in its own canonical dispositions. To return to our initial question, shall we agree that Abraham's advice to Sara, wife and sister, is not a lie but a shrewd way to avoid the worst? Some have rightly argued that Abraham nevertheless puts Sara's life at risk to shield his own.[6] The discussion here might be interesting, but it will take us away from the moral judgment that exegetes make on Abraham's advice. I contend that we are not judging the text within its own value system, but against our own cultural values.

To sharpen the point I want to make, I refer to King David's mesmerizing family in 2 Samuel, where an affair happened between Amnon and Tamar, respectively King David's son and daughter. Their mothers are different. Amnon fell in love with his half sister Tamar. Overcome by his passion, he wanted to force her to have sex. Then she responded saying:

> No, my brother, do not violate me, for such a thing is not done in Israel; do not do this disgraceful thing! As for me, where could I get rid of my reproach? And as for you, you will be like one of the fools in Israel. *Now therefore, please speak to the king, for he will not withhold me from you.* (2 Sam. 13:12–13)

I have italicized the advice she is giving to her brother, son of her own father (not her uncle!). The king would not rule out a marriage between his son and his daughter. The moral code understood here does forbid sexual misconduct. Tamar suggests the right path to an ethically accepted intimate relation.[7]

We have thus shown that the ethical appreciation of Abraham's declaration amounts to a culturally bound appraisal. The characterization of the kinship has not been false in its substance. Sara is Abraham's "wife" and "sister."[8] As is well known, the term "sister" covers a whole range of references that we have clarified with Tamar and Amnon's example. That which could sound as a dissonance resonated as a consonance in an African community. It therefore reveals that any exegesis should begin with a critical awareness of the cultural "bias," as it were, that one imposes on the cultural product (e.g., a text) of another people. That said, should we say that Abraham's statement is a half-truth and therefore that he lied to his audience?

From a cultural point of view, Abraham's attitude is seen as shrewdness. In the Acts of the Apostles, we have a similar case. Taken to the Sanhedrin to be judged on religious matters,

> Paul was aware that some [in the audience] were Sadducees and some Pharisees, so he called out before the Sanhedrin, "My brothers, I am a Pharisee, the son of Pharisees; I am on trial for hope in the resurrection of the dead." When he said this, a dispute broke out between the Pharisees

and Sadducees, and the group became divided. For the Sadducees say that
there is no resurrection or angels or spirits, while the Pharisees acknowledge all three. (Acts 23:6–8)

The recurrent use of what we consider a lie must have had a particular purpose in
social dealings. There is even worse than Paul's intelligent move to get his case
supported by part of the audience. "Elisha's willingness to lie to Ben Hadad, even
to facilitate divine purposes, raises questions as to whether or not statements made
by the prophet may be taken as true (see Deut. 18:9–22; 1 Kings 13, 22). Ultimately, such a strategy suggests that even YHWH might be questioned (see 1
Kings 22; cf. Job)."[9]

To uphold social values, African and biblical ethics tend to share some
common ground. Life supersedes any other form of value, except God's will. Human
life can be sacrificed to comply with divine demands. The life of the community
takes precedence over that of an individual, for "it is better that one dies so that the
community lives." One can therefore consider divine will as the supreme good. In
this latter case, African ethics differ as the ground lies not in the divine, but in the
human: The "African moral system originates from human welfare and interests,
not from divine pronouncements," says Kwame Gyekye.[10]

Violence and Peace

Love and truth will meet; justice and peace will kiss. (Psalm 85:11)

Another place where ethical behavior can be considered a point of convergence is the experience of "violence and peace." A particular social category plays
an important role here: women, who indeed are generally associated with life in
West Africa. They are not associated with death, or with causing suffering, for they
cannot be both givers of life and killers. As a case in point, the famous wise decision
made by King Solomon to discover the real mother worked, as "the woman whose
child *was* the living one spoke to the king, for she was deeply stirred over her son
and said, 'Oh, my lord, give her the living child, and by no means kill him.' But
the other said, 'He shall be neither mine nor yours; divide *him*!'" (1 Kings 3:26).
The opposing women are types of human characters, illustrating virtues of folly and
wisdom at their respective "best" (see Prov. 9). They are two extremes that stand as a
merismus for the whole range in between. The wise king made a divine decision by
siding with the "mother of life" (see Exod. 1:15–17). Cases of women "fighting" to
protect life in the Bible are many. Beyond the surface, women characters can refer
to the inner dimension of any human being, both male and female.

As a matter of fact, two African paintings representing the Good Samaritan
(Luke 10:29–37)[11] and the Prodigal Son (Luke 15:11–32)[12] have expressed the
compassionate dimension toward a near-to-death victim and a son who nearly died
with a female character in both cases. In the first painting, Luke 10, the character

that bends toward the victim is female and stands before the Samaritan. One could interpret the female personage as the feminine side (anima) of the Samaritan. In the representation of Luke 15, the father does not run alone to meet his son. The mother is also in the painting with the father. Both embrace the prodigal son. These artistic interpretations of the biblical texts do not misread the Bible. They rather disclose its deepest meaning. They confirm the cultural association of women with that which brings life, such as compassion and wholeness.

The Hebrew word "shalom," very dear to the ethical world of the Bible, refers to that wholeness of life. Usually translated as "peace," the connotations are not properly captured. It also speaks deeply to the soul of African society. The way people greet one another whenever they meet expresses the very concern for a harmonious totality as sign of peace/wholeness, which in turn means being in a good health. Thus the individual person cannot be in good health when his or her "social body" (society), and the physical environment (cosmos) are suffering.

In the biblical social setting, the notion of a person seen as a network of relations both within the human and material realm is better illustrated in the case of sin. Take for instance the case of Achan in Joshua 7. His sin wreaked havoc in the Israelite society as it was striving under Joshua's leadership to make its way into the Land of Canaan, according to the biblical narrative. To bring back peace within the national community, Achan deserved punishment. Not only was he sentenced to death "with the silver, the mantle, and the bar of gold" he stole, but "with his sons and daughters, his ox, his donkey and his sheep, his tent, and all his possessions" (Josh. 7:24). The material and human relations are all part of Achan's identity.

This uprooting of a social element that constitutes a threat to the social body, because of disobedience to the national God, does not resonate with the African soul. As Gyekye rightly points out, African ethics does not depend on religion. It is meant to shape harmonious social relationships, and to ensure human individual and social welfare.[13] And yet the "African lives in a religious universe: all actions and thoughts have a religious meaning and are inspired or influenced by a religious point of view."[14] I believe that African Christians are still wrestling with these two poles of morality, and their respective grounds: the Bible, on the one hand, where ethical actions are meant to conform to divine will, and society, on the other hand, where they are oriented to human well-being and interests. Bringing the two together in the interpretive process raises a hermeneutical problem yet to be solved. As it appeared to me in the course of my teaching, we have to address the issue of a faithful interpretation of the Bible. The key problem in the end seems to be methodological.

Methodological Issues

The foregoing analysis may have given the impression that African cultural contexts are homogeneous. Reality tells another story, as noted above in the first section. Sexual and family moral issues, for instance, are usually conflicting as patrilineal and matrilineal social systems coexist in almost all sub-Saharan countries, unlike in the West. The interpreter of the biblical text applies in his or her reading the mental frame of the social structure to which he or she belongs. Correlating the Bible and ethics creates therefore a multi- and/or intercultural encounter in a context like ours, West Africa. Each group tends to blame the other for lack of morality, judged by its own standards. The exegetes' unawareness of the ingrained culturally molded ethics forces upon the biblical text a heterogeneous value system. Scholars of hermeneutics have insisted on "presuppositions" we all live by.

The first step in encountering the biblical text therefore must be the work on our own preconceptions. It will then pave the way to finding a new and sound intercultural interaction with the OT texts. Such a move requires that we work out an intercultural code of communication that would then allow for the transfer of meaning from one system to the other, as suggested by the African ethicist Mathieu Ndomba.[15]

The Pontifical Biblical Commission's document on Bible and Morality tried to give some orientations in terms of principles and guidelines. The West African context, namely African ethics, commands a double assessment. First, the exegetical production on biblical ethics should be reviewed in light of the cultural and social structure background of the interpreters. Second, the social structure of West African societies that are made up of either mother or father focused should be carefully studied as one embarks in deciphering the ethics of the Bible. As noted above, African traditional ethics are not moored to the divine being.[16] It is fundamentally human-centered. The response of Catholic moral teaching in the African context has been to encourage inculturation.[17] As matter of fact, most African ethicists[18] or moral theologians seem to agree on the centrality of life.[19] A challenge remains that I would like to formulate as a question: How do we integrate laying down one's life for others as Jesus did into the fabric of African ethics?

African ethics is character-centered, as already noted above. In fact, our traditional proverbs, myths, maxims, and so on portray characters whose behavior is in the end evaluated as ethically right or wrong. The biblical world seems to share the same communicative process. This can be considered an asset for teaching ethics or moral theology in a way that elaborates more on the Scripture characters than on its conceptualizations or its pronouncements. The basic reason for the sensitivity to characters rather than ideas, or better, characters as embodiment of ideas, could be the oral/aural process in communication. By focusing on the characters, one hopes to reshape the African ethical world through the biblical figures such as the first disciples of Jesus in the Acts of the Apostles:[20] Peter, Paul, Philip, and others.

This essay has set out to look at the hermeneutical experience of translating biblical ethics in the West African context. My contention has been that the exegesis of biblical ethics is deeply bound to the interpreter's cultural mind-set. To illustrate my point, I have chosen to examine a few themes—truth, forbidden sexual relationships, and violence and peace—in order to delineate some methodological issues. Interculturality and aural criticism[21] proved to be one of the most relevant approaches to unpack first and foremost the ethical content of a given text.

The results have been, first of all, that in the African context, matrilineal and patrilineal societies do not handle sexual ethics the same way. The interpreter has to be aware of the ethical system of his or her cultural origin. On the other hand, one must carefully identify the particular system at stake. On the theme of violence and peace, we have noted that female characters, physical or symbolic, are associated with the idea of a harmonious life in society and cosmos. The notion of peace, as wholeness, proves to be a meeting space between the biblical and the African worlds. Teaching, therefore, the Bible and ethics in West Africa challenges our traditional exegetical methods and calls for the use of interculturality to first deconstruct our culturally preconditioned mind-sets before one can unpack the ethical message of the Bible for the African audience.

Notes

1. See T. Oduro, "Theological Education," in *Handbook of Theological Education in Africa*, ed. Isabel Apawo Phiri and Dietrich Werner (Pietermaritzburg: Cluster Publications, 2013), 423n3. The author mentions the countries where the CCC has been established: Nigeria, USA, Canada, United Kingdom, France, Italy, Spain, Austria, Netherlands, India, Ireland, Ghana, Guinea, Togo, South Africa, etc.

2. "Biblical Justification for Celestial Church of Christ," June 2015, www.celestial-church.com.

3. Such an enterprise would have required a study of ethics of both Israelite and West African societies. Luckily, John Barton has provided a well-read study showing that the ethics of Israel is made up of several models of thinking about ethics. See Dominik Markl, ed., *The Decalogue and Its Cultural Influence* (Sheffield: Sheffield Phoenix, 2013); J. Barton, *Ethics in Ancient Israel* (Oxford: Oxford University Press, 2014).

4. In the biblical text, the name of the Patriarch is "Abram." For the sake of the reader, we have adopted the usual spelling.

5. Margverite Dupire, *Peules nomades* (Paris: Institut L'Ethnologic, 1962), 268: "la fille de l'oncle paternel jouit d'une préférence marquée: épouse d'élection, lorsqu'on n'en peut trouver une proche, on recherche une *biddo bappanyon* ['fille du petit père'] classificatoire, fille d'un cousin du père; les cousines croisées, paternelle ou maternelle, ne viennent qu'ensuite. Par contre la fille de la tante maternelle est l'objet d'un interdit extrêmement rigoureux; l'épouser serait un inceste honteux et ce caractère s'étend aux filles des tantes maternelles classificatoires, cousines paternelles et maternelles de la mère." The author even emphasizes what we see in the Bible: the traditional marriage *koobgaal* is celebrated with the paternal uncle's daughter ("le mariage traditionnel *koobgal* [se fait avec] la fille vraie du frère du père" [273]).

6. Matthieu Arnold, Gilbert Dahan, and Annie Noblesse-Rocher, eds., *La sœur-épouse (Genèse 12, 10–20)* Lectio Divina 237 (Paris: Cerf, 2010).

7. The exegetical synthesis of moral issues should include the historical parameter as in Barton, *Ethics in Ancient Israel*. Texts such as Deuternony 27:22, Levitcus 18:9,11, 20:7, and so on are in contradiction with the ones we have analyzed. See R. de Vaux, *Les institutions de l'Ancien Testament* (Paris: Cerf, 1960), 52–56.

8. "The limits of my language mean the limits of my world . . . the limits of language (of that language which alone I understand) mean the limits of my world," as affirmed by Ludwig Wittgenstein, *Tractatus Logico-Philosophicus*, 5.6, 5.62.

9. Marvin A. Sweeney, *I & II Kings*, Old Testament Library (Louisville, KY: Westminster John Knox Press, 2007), 318.

10. Kwame Gyekye, "African Ethics," in *The Stanford Encyclopedia of Philosophy*, ed. Edward N. Zalta (Fall 2011 ed.).

11. In the chapel of the Loyola Jesuit College in Abuja, Nigeria.

12. Jesus Mafa, in Cameroon.

13. See Gyekye, "African Ethics."

14. See Kwame Gyekye, *African Cultural Values: An Introduction* (Accra: Sankofa Publishing, 1996), 3.

15. Mathieu Ndomba, "Droits humains et tabous africains: De la métaphorisation à la re-description africaine du langage des droits humains" *Kanien* 1, no. 2 (2014): 53–79.

16. Even this statement should be qualified. In *moore* (a language in Burkina Faso), when someone uses violence against an animal, people would say: "*A Wênd na n zabame!*" meaning "Its God will blame you!" It means the God of the animal will defend the defenseless creature. God is not completely absent from the moral world.

17. See Bénézet Bujo, *Foundations of an African Ethic: Beyond the Universal Claims of Western Morality* (New York: Crossroad, 2001).

18. See Bujo, *Foundations*; Nathanaël Yaovi Soede, *Sens et enjeux de l'éthique: Inculturation de l'éthique chrétienne* (Abidjan: Editions UCAO, 2005).

19. Soede, "Ethique et morale dans la pensée africaine," *Sens et enjeux*.

20. See, for instance, Odile Flichy, *La figure de Paul dans les Actes des apôtres*, Lectio Divina 214 (Paris: Cerf, 2007); Patrick Fabien, *Philippe "l'évangéliste" au tournant de la mission dans les Actes des Apôtres*, Lectio Divina 232 (Paris: Cerf, 2010).

21. "Aural Criticism" is an approach developed in exegesis with a cultural sensitivity to the hearers and not only to the readers of the biblical text. In that sense, "aural criticism" (different from "oral criticism") is a specific form of reception criticism.

The Ethics of Consideration as a Solution to the Problem of Food Offered to Idols (1 Corinthians 8:1–13)

Wilfrid Okambawa, SJ

In 1 Corinthians 8:1–13, Paul elaborates an ethics of consideration of the other person, and especially of the one who is weak, that takes priority over one's own interests and privileges—even when one's own position would in fact be correct. This ethics is so far-reaching that one renounces one's own rights in order to promote the well-being and the salvation of the other. It is regrettable that the originality of such an ethics has scarcely been recognized in the history of scholarship, probably because an atomistic interpretation of the Bible in the West has led to individualistic understandings of morality.[1] The inclusive interpretation of consideration of the other, with the aid of the Ifa hermeneutic (defined below in a later section) with its binary logic (like the Jewish divinatory system of Urim and Thummim) will help us grasp more precisely what the ethics of consideration means.

I shall not discuss the question of Gnosis here. I believe that those who claim to have "knowledge" are pre-gnostics with a Gentile background; the allegedly weak consciences also have a Gentile background.

What are the characteristics and the logic of this ethics of consideration? What is the relationship between the ethical question and the hermeneutical and gnoseological questions, on the one hand, and the soteriological, Christological, and ecclesiological questions, on the other?

This essay proceeds in four main steps:

1. The formulation of the problem of food offered to idols and of the interpretative method using the binary Ifa system;
2. The gnoseological and theological preparation of the reflection on the problem of the food offered to idols (1 Cor. 8:1–6);
3. Toward a solution of the problem of food offered to idols: the ethics of consideration (1 Cor. 8:7–13);
4. Theological reflections on the ethics of consideration.

The Formulation of the Problem of
Food Offered to Idols and of the
Interpretative Method Using the Binary Ifa System

The Formulation of the Problem of Food Offered to Idols

The problem of food offered to idols can be understood only in relation to the sociocultural context of the church in Corinth. The question its members would have asked Paul can be reformulated as follows: "Are we allowed to eat meat that has been sacrificed to idols? Yes or no?" This question, which has both economic and religious motivations, can be better understood in connection with the sociocultural context of the ancient Mediterranean world. There was little livestock farming, and meat was basically obtained by hunting. This meant that only those who were well-off could enjoy the privilege of eating meat.[2] Meat that had been offered in sacrifice to the idols was often resold in the town market. There were even laws in Greek cities that prescribed that all the meat sold in the market had to come from sacrifices.[3] As we shall see, therefore, this was an ethical question with ecclesiological, Christological, soteriological, and eschatological implications.

Besides this, the ancient Hellenistic world attached a high value to education and knowledge, and popular philosophers such as the Stoico-Cynics were greatly appreciated in a world that consisted mostly of illiterate persons. This creates a social tension between those who know and those who are ignorant, between the initiates and the non-initiates, between the strong and the weak.

Articulation of the Interpretative
Method Using the Binary Ifa System

Let me underline at the very outset that there are resemblances among the Ifa system, Jewish divination, and the Pauline halakah. They employ an approach that could be called "deliberative casuistry" in dealing with moral cases.[4] These resemblances allow me to elaborate a binary hermeneutic and to apply this in a relevant manner.

The Ifa system is a type of divination of the Yoruba people sustained by a worldview and commanded by a binary logic. It consists of a corpus of poems displaying legends and stories that are embellished historical facts or actions of the heroes. In fact, these lives have become paradigms that could help in increasing understanding of the present and the future. The corpus is subdivided into 256 figures, or chapters, called *Odus* (something big) or the "roads of Ifa." Each chapter contains nearly 800 verses called *Ese*. Each figure is named and interpreted in terms of its two halves: the right half is considered male and more powerful, while the left half is considered female, and the halves of a figure are called *Ese*.[5]

Since there was no writing as such among the Yoruba, although the figures drawn by the Ifa priest on a tray could be considered a way of writing, the Ifa priest has to memorize the whole corpus. The divination itself is performed by casting the divination chain made of sixteen palm nuts on the floor. Each time he is performing divination, he recites the Odu in a kind of singing psalmody.

> The whole of Ifà is a binary order of thinking and marking. It is still not clear, but I think when the Odu were coming, perhaps they come as individuals, instead of as twins. How they became coupled is probably a very important transformation in Yoruba thought and mythology. Eji Ogbe mentions something like that when he says, "I will bless or support people when they are coupled. I will no longer support people when they stand as individuals."[6]

In Jewish divination, the two words *Urim* and *Thummim* signify, respectively, "lights" and "perfections" (Exod. 28:30; Deut. 33:8; Neh. 7:65). This divinatory system can be compared to that of the Ifa, since both are instruments of divination or revelation[7] that are held to reply with a yes or a no to the questions that are put to them (hence the binary character of their logic). Both systems aim to grasp the truth using research methods, and both have mantic-religious, gnoseological, and ethical aspects. The Corinthians consult Paul, just as the kings in the past consulted Urim and Thummim and the prophets.

We find a similar opposition in the Odu Obara Iwori of the Ifa system. Iwori means introspection and obara, contemplation.[8] The Obara Iwori teaches the import of collection, intuition, and memory.[9] As consciousness, the Yoruba concept of Iwori in the binary Ifa logic converges with the Pauline understanding of *syneidēsis*, which means etymologically "knowing with."[10] Consequently, there is no consciousness without otherness, and there could be no ethics without otherness, even in the case of Robinson Crusoe in Daniel Defoe's novel. The story of the "obara iwori" stresses so much the duty of the consideration of the other that it extends it to nature, to the whole creation.[11]

The Odu Obara Iwori of the Ifa system looks like this:

II   I
I   II
I   II
II   II

This Odu is uttered as follows: "Be aware of your weakness; you will find the strength to find a remedy for it," and it is accompanied by the explicatory aphorism: "You, human being! Hasten to go and give strength to your dead father, then be courageous and have no more fear." Since the bull was shrewder than the other animals, it asked the Creator for the gift of physical size. It received this, together with the advice that it should be careful about its snout, and make a moderate use of it, for otherwise it would suffer calamity. In order to ward off every possible evil, the bull would have to offer sacrifices. The bull receives a huge body, and the servants who look after it give it great consideration. But since it did not offer any sacrifice and grazed on everything along its path, the Creator stripped it of its privileges.[12]

This story teaches us, first, that if one is to receive consideration, one must show consideration to the other person by renouncing privileges, and second, that there must be strong persons who show consideration to the weak. These two levels are in accord with the teaching of Paul in 1 Corinthians 8:1–13.

This method is based on the model of "problem, question, solution, answer," as in cases of divinatory consultation, and indeed of medical consultation. This method could be applied to the case that is taken up in our passage, 1 Corinthians 8:1–13, by examining the following five questions:

1.   Who is the "other" of the person, or of the concept, who is shown consideration?
2.   How does the subject who is shown consideration relate to his "other" in the text, in the past and in the future?
3.   Is the relationship between the subject and his "other" conflictual or harmonious? Do they complement each other as equals, or is it a relationship of inequality and dependence?
4.   How were similar conflicts resolved in the past? How will these conflicts be resolved in the perspective of promises and their fulfillment?
5.   What ethical behavior and/or sacrifices are necessary in order to resolve the problem that has been posed?

The binary and holistic hermeneutic is the opposite of the atomistic hermeneutic that associates pairs that are in tension, such as:

- knowledge—ignorance
- love—knowledge
- to build up—to puff up
- to encourage/to build up—to destroy, to cause to perish
- the strong—the weak
- to eat—to abstain
- God—idols
- true—false
- life—death

In most divinatory and hermeneutic systems, the aim of the investigation is to arrive at the knowledge of one's own self (anthropology), of the cosmos (cosmology/cosmogony), and of God (theology).

The Gnoseological and Theological Preparation of the Reflection on the Problem of the Food Offered to Idols (1 Corinthians 8:1–6)

Gnoseological Preparation of the Reflection on the Problem of Food Offered to Idols (1 Corinthians 8:1–6)

Paul begins by formulating, or better, by *reformulating* the problem that the Corinthians themselves had submitted to him: "Now concerning food sacrificed to idols, we know that all of us possess knowledge" (1 Cor. 8:1b).

The pronoun "all" designates all the members of the Christian community of Corinth. Its use here in a general sense is an argument in favor of the view I take, namely, that *gnôsis* at this historical stage does not mean the system of Gnosticism that appeared later in the early church between the end of the first century and the beginning of the second century of the Common Era, where it became the mark of a sectarian movement. Nevertheless, one part of the community is certainly beginning to mark itself off and to identify itself by means of this concept, in order to assert its own education and its affinity to Greek philosophical culture, unlike the uneducated, the weak. Paul takes up the position of his pre-gnostic adversaries as if he agreed with them, but he does so in order to extend to all Christians the ability to have access to knowledge, whereas the pre-gnostics appeared to be reducing it exclusively to the members of their group. It is as if Paul was affirming that the capacity for knowledge—or, in other terms, common sense—is the most widespread thing in the world.

The first refutation: Even if knowledge *can* be a value, this is not obviously the case, since: "Knowledge puffs up, but love builds up" (1 Cor. 8:1c). The verb "to puff up," in its physical sense, means taking on excessive proportions vis-à-vis normal measurements. It therefore alludes to immoderation (*hubris*), which is the greatest moral problem. It is linked to the verb "to boast," to which Paul is so keenly attentive precisely because of his own strong inclination to pride, against which he has to wage a constant struggle. Paul presents and judges two modes of access to God. Knowledge is a relationship, a connection between the intelligence and a thing; but love is an existential relationship: Adam knew Eve (Gen. 4:1). It is through violence that the human being attained the knowledge of good and evil (Gen. 3:22), but it is through grace and *kenôsis* that the human being will receive the tree of life (Phil. 2:5–11).

The second refutation: Paul vigorously attacks impressions, illusory representations: "Anyone who claims to know something does not yet have the necessary knowledge; but anyone who loves God is known by him" (1 Cor. 8:2–3). The imagination is the seat of fantasies and illusions, of opinions (*doxa*) and errors. There is the knowledge that one believes one possesses, and there is the knowledge that one truly possesses: subjective knowledge and objective knowledge. There is illusion, and there is reality. This means that there exist several types of knowledge. Paul disqualifies that of the pre-gnostics, whose knowledge is based on the intellect and on philosophical-religious reflection, and he promotes the mode of knowledge that is based on love and on discernment in prayer. It is as if Paul advocates an apodictic knowledge that is the outcome of sure and tested judgments. It is more important to be known by God than to know God. It is more important to love God than to know God.

Theological Preparation of the Reflection on the Problem of Food Offered to Idols (1 Cor. 8:4–6)

Paul once again asks the central question: "May one therefore eat meat that has been sacrificed to idols?" (1 Cor. 8:4a). This question demonstrates that the entire passage is a moral deliberation.[13] The question awaits a positive or a negative answer. The deliberative genre is often used in a law court and in political forums where important decisions about the life of the city are to be taken. But it is also found frequently in the prophetic tradition, especially at its origins, when a king consulted a diviner to know whether or not he should begin a war.

The first attempt at an answer: "We know that no idol in the world really exists, and that there is no God but one" (1 Cor. 8:4b–c). The formulation is based on that of the monotheistic faith of Israel (Deut. 6:4, 32:39). If the idols possess no reality, the meat consecrated to them has, in principle, no effect.

The second attempt at an answer (reinforcing the first): Paul compares the position of the Christians on the question of the gods with that of the pagans: "Indeed, even though there may be so-called gods in heaven or on earth—as in fact there are many gods and many lords—yet for us there is one God, the Father, from whom are all things and for whom we exist, and one Lord, Jesus Christ, through whom are all things and through whom we exist" (1 Cor. 8:5–6). In reality, Paul's position with regard to the idols is ambiguous: Do they exist or not? Even the Old Testament bears witness to this ambiguity, especially in the book of Wisdom (chaps. 12–15). If the idols do not exist, one could eat the meat that has been offered to them. But one must take heed not give scandal to the weak.

Toward a Solution of the Problem of Food Offered to Idols: The Ethics of Consideration (1 Corinthians 8:7–13)

The Limits of the Gnôsis of the Weak and of the Strong: Nourishment Is Morally Indifferent in One's Relationship to God (1 Corinthians 8:7–8)

Paul had affirmed in 1 Corinthians 8:1 that everyone has knowledge, but now he passes to an antithesis: "It is not everyone, however, who has this knowledge" (1 Cor. 8:7a). Paul is attacking here the position of the pre-gnostics, who claimed an exclusive possession of knowledge. He insinuates that they do not possess the appropriate knowledge, because they do not consider the situation of the weak and their salvation.

Examination of the past: "Since some have become so accustomed to idols until now, they still think of the food they eat as food offered to an idol, and their consciousness, being weak, is defiled" (1 Cor. 8:7b–c). These persons who are accustomed to eat meat sacrificed to idols are probably Gentile Christians. The noun *sunêtheia* is missing from many Byzantine and Orthodox manuscripts, which read instead *suneidêsis* ("conscience"). The word *sunêtheia,* which is found only three times in the entire New Testament (here; 1 Cor. 11:16; 2 Thess. 2:15), is a composite noun formed of the prefix *sun* and the root *êthos*. It means "custom, habit."

The noun *suneidêsis* was probably used for the first time by Zeno, the father of Stoicism, to designate the moral ideas that are innate in every human being. According to its etymology, the word signifies knowing something together with someone else, agreeing with someone about something. This etymology shows that consciousness is more than self-knowledge, and that it is deeper and broader than the private experience of the individual.[14] Indeed, I would say that where the person is alone, there cannot exist consciousness; and that wherever there is consciousness, there are at least two persons. Consciousness always has three dimensions: the anthropological, the cosmic, and the theological. On the anthropological level, one can distinguish between the consciousness of another person and the consciousness of one's own self, consciousness per se, consciousness for oneself, consciousness of the world, and transcendental consciousness. What is the relationship between consciousness and knowledge?

Did Paul adopt the concept of conscience from his adversaries, who claimed to be enlightened when they ate meat offered to idols without any consideration for the weak?[15] According to Khiok-Khng Yeo, the weak (*asthenês*)[16] conscience is a conscience that is weak in rhetoric.[17] I disagree, because the problem in Corinth is not solely a question of rhetoric. Is the weak conscience a scrupulous conscience? Most commentators think that this is the case,[18] although there are others who dispute this. I believe that both the weak and the strong are Gentile Christians. The notion of defilement may have a Jewish background. The expression "as food offered to an idol" would imply a hypothetical-analogical morality. Since idols are regarded as realities, whoever eats the meat that has been sacrificed to them is genuinely sharing in the cup of the demons (1 Cor. 10:14–22).

First attempt at a solution: Does Paul have recourse here to the principle of indifference in order to resolve the problem of the meat offered to idols, when he writes: "Food will not bring us close to God. We are no worse off if we do not eat, and no better off if we do" (1 Cor. 8:8)? Alex Cheung believes that indifference has been projected into this text, thanks to the habitual interpretation of Romans 14, since it would be completely counterproductive for Paul to affirm the moral indifference of foodstuffs at this point in his argumentation, given his wish that the strong should abstain from eating meat offered to idols.[19]

The Ethics of Consideration of the Weak and the
Refutation of the Strong (1 Cor. 8:9–12)

A second attempt at a solution: In this section, Paul proceeds to a *refutatio,* after making a kind of *concessio:* "But take care that this liberty of yours does not somehow become a stumbling block to the weak" (1 Cor. 8:9). Four words are very important in this verse, which is the climax of the whole of chapter 8: *blepete, exousia, proskomma,* and *asthenês.* The Greek verb *blepein* means "to look at, to consider." Being on one's guard means paying attention, taking care of something, and not neglecting it. With an object in the accusative, it means "to consider" rather than "to pay attention to" (as in 1 Cor. 1:26).[20] The verb is an invitation to contemplation, to *theôria,* to insight or illumination. The imperative form of the verb could be interpreted as a categorical imperative.

Should *exousia* be translated as "right" or as "liberty"? It would be best to begin by understanding it as the power and the right to do something, without excluding the meaning of "liberty" that some translations present. One is free to do good, not to do evil. To put it in radical terms, we do not have rights, but only responsibilities.[21] It is in 1 Corinthians 9 that we can see most clearly the link between liberty (*eleutheria,* 1 Cor. 9:1) and right (*exousia,* 1 Cor. 9:4).

The word *proskomma* often means "scandal," not necessarily in the sense of something shocking, but in the sense of something that can cause a person to fall.[22]

First objection to a ruinous libertinism: "For if others see you, who possess knowledge, eating in the temple of an idol, might they not, since their conscience is weak, be encouraged to the point of eating food sacrificed to idols?" (1 Cor. 8:10). Far from offering an edifying spectacle, the "strong" one leads the weak one to sin. Strong and weak perform the same act; both eat meat that has been offered to idols. But the strong one sins, not because of having eaten, but because of encouraging the other one to eat. And the weak one sins because of having eaten while his conscience reproached him. No one, therefore, no matter how strong he or she may be, may impose upon the conscience of a weak person.

Second objection to a ruinous libertinism: "So by your knowledge the weak person perishes, the brother for whom Christ died" (1 Cor. 8:11). Paul derides the "knowledge" of those who have no consideration for the one who is weak. Ironically, it is precisely by eating something that is morally indifferent that the strong one becomes an agent of destruction, because of the link to idolatry.[23] Paul makes a preferential option here, in favor of solidarity with persons who are weak in societal terms.[24] Here, we see the truth of Rabelais's maxim: "Knowledge without conscience is nothing other than the ruin of the soul."

The third objection to a ruinous libertinism: "But when you thus sin against members of your family and wound their conscience when it is weak, you sin against Christ" (1 Cor. 8:12). Sin against one's brother or sister is a sin against Christ, because he or she is an *alter Christus,* an image of Christ. The weak person is *christophoros* (a bearer of Christ), precisely because he or she is *staurophoros* (a bearer of the cross). The other person's conscience, even if it is badly informed or erroneous, must be respected. It must never be violated. What is the relationship between the wounded conscience and the defiled conscience?

The Royal Road of Renunciation out of Consideration for the Weak (1 Cor. 8:13)

The definitive solution: voluntarily restricting one's liberty: "Therefore, if food is a cause of my brother's falling, I will never eat meat, so that I may not cause my brother to fall" (1 Cor. 8:13). The word "never" means that Paul does not simply renounce his right to eat meat for a certain period: he renounces it once and for all. We could also paraphrase his words as follows: "If one particular drink causes a brother or a sister to fall, I will forever refrain from consuming that drink," although I know that, in principle, there is nothing wrong with consuming it. But would not this involve the loss of a right? The answer is that the free and voluntary renunciation is the expression of a higher liberty.

Although liberty is good, it has limits: "'All things are lawful for me,' but not all things are beneficial. 'All things are lawful for me,' but I will not be dominated by anything" (1 Cor. 6:12). The ethics of consideration is not the ethics of a permissiveness that enslaves. It is the ethics of authentic freedom. The subject who freely restrains his freedom manifests a freedom that is superior to libertinism or to an unrestrained freedom. As far as I know, only Panayotis Coutsoumpos has touched on this ethics of consideration, when he affirms that the behavior of a Christian must be determined by positive considerations vis-à-vis one's neighbor, not by wicked actions.[25] However, he does not develop this intuition sufficiently.

Theological Reflections on the Ethics of Consideration

Strategy of the Ethics of Consideration: Negation of the Negation in Order to Affirm a Higher Freedom

Paul's strategy consists of renouncing a negative freedom in order to affirm a higher freedom. In order to do this, he makes himself free with regard to everyone, in order to serve and to win over the highest possible number of persons, adapting himself both to the Jews and to those without the Law: "To the weak I became weak, so that I might win the weak. I have become all things to all people, so that I might by all means save some. I do it all for the sake of the Gospel, so that I may share in its blessings" (1 Cor. 9:22–23).

Four observations will help us understand this passage. First of all, Paul bases his ethics on freedom, and he draws a distinction between two aspects: the negative aspect, expressed by the *genitive of separation,* which is a "freedom from," and the positive aspect, which is freedom for service. Second, Paul does not say that he endeavors to adapt the Gospel to the various cultural groups in his communities; rather, he adapts *himself* to them. Third, the verb "to win" is not to be understood solely in numerical terms. It has a soteriological significance here. Fourth, the goal of the adaptation is not to please human beings, nor to make the Gospel agreeable, but to win over the greatest possible number. Is Paul advocating a hypocritical morality, a morality of "as if"? Is it a casuistic morality? Is it a morality of adaption or of inculturation? At first sight, the approach may appear to be amoral or even cynical, but it leads in reality to a lofty ethics of respect or consideration, and of perfection.

Aspects of the Ethics of Consideration

Consideration of the weak is expressed concretely as compassion for the weak, as solidarity with them: to share in the Gospel means sharing in both the suffering and the glory of Christ.

On the basis of Paul's declaration that "knowledge puffs up, but love builds up" (1 Cor. 8:1c), we can infer that the ethics of consideration is an ethics of love. Love makes us see beyond that which is immediately perceptible to the senses. Love makes us see what is invisible.

The ethics of consideration is an ethics that goes beyond the law that is codified in terms of what is permitted and what is forbidden.

The ethics of consideration is the ethics of intuition and of illumination. Accordingly, it presupposes a *theôria,* a clear vision of the best thing that one ought to do, going beyond what is laid down by the law.

The ethics of consideration is also an ethics of vigilance. One must be awake, that is to say, *buddha* ("awake" in Sanskrit), in order to put this ethics into practice.

The ethics of consideration is an ethics of subtlety that does not simply move within the dialectic between good and evil, between the permitted and the forbidden, but carries out a discernment in the context of the problem of identifying the good and the better. It is thus an ethics of excellence.

From the perspective of Henri Bergson,[26] who draws a distinction between morality as a result of external pressure and the morality of aspiration, the ethics of consideration appears as an ethics of aspiration, a morality that is open rather than closed, a morality appropriate to societies that are open rather than closed. For closed ideologies are the enemies of the open society.[27]

The ethics of consideration is an ethics of specificity and of universality, because it considers the particular case without drowning it in general and empty considerations. It goes to the depths of the human experience and the experience of God, *subsuming* it in a universal that is concrete, not abstract.

Pastoral Application of the Ethics of Consideration, and Debates

In a context that is still strongly marked by the consumption of meat sacrificed to idols or to one's ancestors, the pastoral application is highly promising. The same applies to the milieus that are touched by industry: Am I allowed to use a Rolls

Royce in a poor quarter of Africa? Yes, I have the right to do so, and at first sight, this is not morally prohibited. But if driving such an automobile in such a context of poverty could lead weak consciences to sacrifice enormous resources in order to do what I am doing, it would be better to renounce my privilege of driving it.

The binary logic of the Ifa system has left such a deep mark on those who live in the Ifa region of West Africa that their spirit and their way of reasoning are influenced by it, even when they no longer practice it. This is the case with many of our Christians, who practice Christianity while continuing to operate, consciously or not, according to the Ifa binary logic. This means that a binary hermeneutic inspired by such a system would help many Africans understand the Bible better. Besides this, the Ifa system is always open to new possibilities, just like the Jewish hermeneutic. Christian dogmatism, with its conception of the closed revelation, risks becoming a closed and exclusivist system.

The verb "to consider" comes from Latin and means "to see, to observe, together." Consideration thus always implies at least two persons. It expresses a respect, a look back. Consideration has two advantages over respect. First of all, it does not imply any distance (as respect does). On the contrary, it implies a solidarity between the person who exercises consideration and the person who is given consideration. Second, consideration necessarily implies a judgment, whereas this is not demanded by respect. Respect contains a kind of fear, but consideration contains a love that makes the other person grow.

It is only through its consciousness of the other that self-consciousness grasps itself as what it is. This leads Jean-Paul Sartre to conclude: "The look of the other—which is a look that looks, not a look that is looked at—denies my distances from objects and unfolds its own distances. . . . I am deprived of my distanceless presence to my world, and I am supplied with a distance to other people."[28] The other's look thus breaks down my world, or at least it turns it upside-down by calling it into question. Besides this, the look of the other determines my objectivity, because it is enough for someone to look at me for me to be "what I am. Not for myself . . . but for the other. Once again, the annihilating evacuation of the 'for itself' is frozen, once again, the 'in itself' withdraws into the 'for itself.' . . . And thus I have stripped off my transcendence for the other."[29] Is then the transcendence of the "I" not an illusion? Sartre concludes that hell is the other person. Levinas protests against this, by affirming the priority of the other over the "I."

The ethics of consideration is an ethics of liberation, which guarantees not only the freedom of the other person but also, and necessarily, one's own freedom, which attains its summit thanks to its readiness to set limits to itself, to go beyond oneself in self-renunciation. The ethics of consideration can thus be seen to be the ethic of *yeyi,* that is to say, the ethics of delicacy, since it goes beyond the table of stone in order let the heart of flesh speak.

Although the binary hermeneutic is anchored in the specific systems of the Ifa and of the Jewish divination by means of Urim and Thummim, it accords with the universal of the spirit of every human being. Since computers function on a binary logic, can we say that one day, the computer will be able to offer us a good biblical hermeneutic? No, certainly not, because the computer is not a human subject, and will thus never be capable of empathetic consideration of the human other.[30]

Translated by Brian McNeil

Notes

1. Grant R. Osborne, *The Hermeneutical Spiral: A Comprehensive Introduction to Biblical Interpretation* (Downers Grove, IL: InterVarsity Press, 1991), 518.

2. Jack Barentsen, *Emerging Leadership in the Pauline Mission: A Social Identity Perspective on Local Leadership Development in Corinth and Ephesus* (Eugene, OR: Wipf and Stock, 2011), 82.

3. Marcel Detienne and Jean-Pierre Vernant, *The Cuisine of Sacrifice among the Greeks* (Chicago: University of Chicago Press, 1989), 11.

4. John Collins and Daniel Harrington, *First Corinthians* (Collegeville, MN: Liturgical Press, 1999), 383; Peter Tomson, *Paul and the Jewish Law: Halaka in the Letters of the Apostle of the Gentiles* (Assen, NL: Uitgeverij Van Gorcum, 1990), 298.

5. William R. Bascom, *Ifa Divination: Communication between Gods and Men in West Africa* (Bloomington: Indiana University Press, 1991), 40.

6. Wande Abimbola and Ivor Miller, *Ifá Will Mend Our Broken World: Thoughts on Yoruba Religion and Culture in Africa and Diaspora* (Roxbury, MA: Aim Books, 1997), 93.

7. Cornelis van Dam, *The Urim and Thummim: A Means of Revelation in Ancient Israel* (Winona Lake, IN: Eisenbrauns, 1997).

8. Velma E. Love, "The Blue Cat Scholar: Answering the Call for a New Critical Orientation to the Study of Scripture," in *Refractions of the Scriptural: Critical Orientation as Transgression*, ed. Vincent Wimbush (London: Routledge, 2016), 40.

9. Claude Assabe, *Vivre et savoir en Afrique: Essai sur l'éducation orale en Yoruba* (Paris: L'Harmattan, 2000), 120.

10. For more information see Michel Coune, "Le problème des idolothytes et l'éducation de la syneidèsis," in Jacques Dupont, "Synéidèsis: Aux origines de la notion chrétienne de conscience morale," in *Studia Hellenistica*, ed. Willy Peremans et al. (Louvain: Maisonneuve, 1948), 119–53; Margaret E. Thrall, "Pauline Use of Syneidèsis," *New Testament Studies* 14 (1967): 118–25.

11. Mahougnon Sinsin, *Vie et plénitude: Chemins de la sagesse Ifa*, book 1, Paris (Raleigh: ReckSeba Academy, 2013), 71.

12. Basile Adjou-Moumouni, *Le code du primitif: Sagesse africaine selon Ifá* (Cotonou, BJ: Éditions Ruisseaux d'Afrique, 2007), 2:163–65.

13. Cheryl Anderson, *Ancient Laws and Contemporary Controversies: The Need for Inclusive Biblical Interpretation* (Oxford: Oxford University Press, 2009), 103.

14. Robert Solomon, *The Conscience: Rediscovering the Inner Compass* (Singapore: Genesis Books, 2010), 14. [Translator's note: The French noun "conscience" means both "consciousness" and "conscience."]

15. Panayotis Coutsoumpos, *Community, Conflict, and the Eucharist in Roman Corinth: The Social Setting of Paul's Letter* (Eugene, OR: Wipf and Stock, 2015), 79.

16. David Alan Black, *Paul, Apostle of Weakness: Astheneia and Its Cognates in the Pauline Literature* (Eugene, OR: Pickwick, 2012).

17. Khiok-Khng Yeo, *Rhetorical Interaction in 1 Corinthians 8 and 10: A Formal Analysis with Preliminary Suggestions for a Chinese, Cross-Cultural Hermeneutic* (Leiden, NL: Brill, 1995), 208.

18. R. C. H. Lenski, *Interpretation of I Corinthians* (Minneapolis: Augsburg Press, 2008).

19. Alex Cheung, *Idol Food: Jewish Background, Pauline Legacy* (Sheffield, UK: Sheffield Academic, 1999), 134.

20. Ben Witherington, *Paul's Letter to the Philippians: A Socio-Rhetorical Commentary* (Grand Rapids, MI: Eerdmans, 2011), 188.

21. Bill Oswalt, *Help I'm Hurting: Finding Meaning, Hope and Happiness in the Words of Jesus* (Bloomington, IN: Cross Books, 2011), 61.

22. George Montague, *First Corinthians* (Grand Rapids, MI: Baker Academic, 2011), 146.

23. Roberto Savino Overtile, *Impossible Reading: Idolatry and Diversity in Literature* (Aurora, CO: Davies Group, 2008), 60.

24. Jae Won Lee, *Paul and the Politics of Difference: A Contextual Study of the Jewish-Gentile Difference in Galatians and Romans* (Oxford, UK: Casemate, 2015), 193; Neil Elliot, *Liberating Paul: The Justice of God and the Politics of the Apostle* (Minneapolis: Fortress Press, 2006), 87; Michael Gorman, *Cruciformity: Paul's Narrative Spirituality of the Cross* (Grand Rapids, MI: Eerdmans, 2001), 303.

25. Coutsoumpos, *Community, Conflict, and the Eucharist in Roman Corinth*, 79.

26. Henri Bergson, *Les deux sources de la religion et de la morale* (Paris: Payot, 1938).

27. Karl Popper, *The Open Society and its Enemies* (Princeton, NJ: Princeton University Press, 1966).

28. Jean-Paul Sartre, *L'être et le néant* (Paris: Gallimard, 1943), 309.

29. Ibid., 301–2.

30. Most scriptural texts are taken from the New Revised Standard Version, but occasionally a more literal translation from the Greek is given.

RELATING THE BIBLE, ETHICS, AND OTHER DISCIPLINES

BIBLICAL ETHICS AND THE PROCLAMATION OF THE GOSPEL

Aristide Fumagalli

The contribution of biblical ethics to the church's proclamation of the Gospel, which is the subject of the present essay, will be illustrated primarily by proposing a specific conception of the relationship between sacred Scripture and moral conduct and then by showing its significance for the church's preaching of the Gospel.

Sacred Scripture and Moral Conduct

Acknowledging the validity of the biblical renewal making great progress in that period, the Second Vatican Council urged moral theology to be "*S. Scripturae magis nutrita*."[1] The papal magisterium subsequently followed up this appeal by the council and often repeated the importance of Scripture, going so far as to define it as "the living and fruitful source of the Church's moral doctrine."[2]

The biblical renewal of moral theology in the aftermath of the council can be divided into three successive stages.[3] In the first period, the *phase of juxtaposition,* all that was done was to prefix a brief biblical introduction to the manuals of moral theology. After this came the *phase of integration,* with the attempt to structure moral reflection on the basis of the principles and directives that can be found in the Bible. The biblical integration, however, brought to light the difficulty and the complexity of this undertaking. This paved the way for the *phase of interdisciplinarity,* in which moral theology opens the door to a close collaboration with the biblical sciences.[4]

If this collaboration were envisaged as the transfer from one discipline to another of that which each discipline has elaborated on its own, we would not get beyond bi-disciplinarity. The object studied by moral theology—the relationship between human action and divine action[5]—would be merely complemented by the data or the perspectives drawn from the object studied by the biblical sciences, namely, the text of sacred Scripture. Authentic interdisciplinarity overcomes this methodological extrinsicism, redefining the object that is to be studied jointly. In the case of an interdisciplinary biblical ethics, the object of study is now the relevance of sacred Scripture in the relationship between human action and divine action. How does the action of God that is operative in sacred Scripture cause moral action in the human being? What human response is generated by hearing the divine Word that is contained in sacred Scripture?

As the wind produces the sound by passing across the folds of the musical instrument, so the Spirit pronounces the word of God, breathing in the varied passages of Scripture. Reading the Scripture, or hearing it read, is thus the condition that makes it possible for the human being to hear the word of God—a necessary but not sufficient condition, because hearing the word of God means allowing the Spirit to resound in the Scripture without shutting God up in the literal meaning of the text. When this happens, the creative power of the word of God means that it gives new life to the one who hears the word, transforming his or her moral conduct.

When we propose the Scripture as the instrument through which the Spirit speaks of God and reaches and molds the moral personality of the hearer, we must at least point out that it is not the only instrument in the orchestra of the Spirit. Without claiming to limit the unforeseeable creativity of the Spirit—for the paths of the Lord are infinitely numerous—we must nevertheless indicate at least two other outstanding instruments: the celebration of the sacraments and the life of the hierarchically structured community. Together with Scripture, the sacraments and the community constitute the church, which is the community of those who listen to the Word and participate in the sacramental acts of Christ. The present essay will not discuss the varied actions of the Spirit in the church, but the simple mention of the church is important, in order to make it clear that when we concentrate on sacred Scripture, we certainly do not intend to maintain that Christian moral conduct is adequately described in reference to the Word *alone,* or that the Scripture can be adequately understood if one prescinds from the faith of the church, which is brought to us by the tradition and is authoritatively confirmed by the magisterium.[6]

The Biblical Po-etica

Much still remains to be done in order to elaborate a theory of the relationship between sacred Scripture and human conduct.[7] But recent biblical hermeneutics offers valuable pointers, suggesting a theological way of looking at Scripture, which, as the word of God, inspires and makes demands of moral conduct.[8] The development of this perspective finds a valuable reference point in the work of Paul Ricoeur. To put it very simply, the link that the French philosopher proposes between sacred Scripture and moral conduct can be defined as the intersection of "poetics" and "ethics."[9] The biblical poetics reveals the world of the possibilities of existence and of action that are revealed by Scripture. If these are appropriated by the subject, they are then translated into a lived ethics.[10]

The Biblical Poetics

Ricoeur distances himself both from a "Romantic" reading that looks for the meaning beyond the text and from a "structuralist" reading that encloses the meaning within the structures of the text. He maintains that the interpretation must "unfold the possibility of existence that the text indicates,"[11] because every text carries out a poetic function that can be described with recourse to the category of the "world of the text," or "the way of being in the world that is unfolded in front of the text . . . a world in which it can take up its dwelling in order to sketch there one of the possibilities that are more proper to it."[12]

The poetic function of a text stands out particularly strongly in its metaphors and narratives, which are capable of producing the "semantic innovation."[13] In the case of metaphor, the semantic novelty comes about through an attribution that is per se inappropriate (for example, "nature is a temple," "the moon is a golden sickle in a field of stars"). In the case of narrative, the novelty arises from the creation of an intrigue that depicts facts, causes, instances, and circumstances as elements of the unfolding of one and the same action.

The poetic function that is proper to every text can also be observed in the Bible in an emblematic manner, in the parables (e.g., "The kingdom of heaven is like . . ."). The Bible presents itself to us as Scripture (lit., "writing"), and this prevents biblical hermeneutics from looking too quickly for the divine Word without bearing in mind its inscription in human letters.

The biblical text, to an even greater degree than any other individual literary work, presents itself in a plurality of structured forms. Accordingly, biblical hermeneutics cannot shirk the patient analysis of the various forms (narrative, prophetic, sapiential, parabolic, and so on) that structure the discourse. It must highlight the relationship that, in various ways, each one of these forms has with the world of the text.

The concept of "the world of the text" allows us to avoid the antithetical reefs of the objectivism of Scripture and the subjectivism of the reader. Although it is an insuperable mediation, the text opens up a world that protrudes beyond the Scripture. Its meaning is not objectified by the Scripture; the Scripture allows its meaning to appear in order that it may be appropriated by the subject who reads it. The world of the text, which extends beyond the Scripture, also prevents the reduction of the text to the meaning of the text (understood in a subjectivist manner). The insuperability of the textual mediation means that the world that it opens up has an objective validation that functions as a regulative criterion for the activity of the interpreter and as a canonical norm for his or her interpretations.

The world opened up by the biblical text is that of the covenant between God and human beings, the new world of the revelation in Christ, and the correlative new way of existing and of acting that belongs to the Christian faith. The primary task of hermeneutics, therefore, will not be to prompt an untimely operative decision, but to allow the world of the biblical text to open up in such a way that it makes an appeal to the freedom of the interpreter. This world is not restricted to the exclusive relationship between the human being and God. It also embraces the global horizon within which this relationship is situated, and hence nature, culture, history, and, in a special manner within these, the entire spectrum of human relationships.

The new world opened up by the text does not present itself to the reader as an inert spectacle. It addresses the reader and leads him or her to appropriate the new possibilities of living that it holds out. The biblical poetics gives birth to moral action. The biblical revelation of God prompts the action of the human being. The question of appropriation constitutes the nodal point between the poetics and the ethics of the Bible.

With regard to the world of the text, the appropriation concerns neither the intention of the author that stands at the origin of the text (Romanticism), nor the structure that now carries the text (structuralism), but rather the new possibilities of being and of acting that the biblical text holds out. Appropriating a text means appropriating a new identity, entering into something that is "more proper" to one's own self. Since the appropriation of oneself takes place through the mediation of the text, this process implies a moment at which the "self" does not yet coincide completely with one's own self, but is at a distance from it. The appropriation implies an expropriation that takes the form of a critique of the subjective prejudices that keep the "self" far away from the possibilities of being that the text opens up, and hence far away from one's own self. The hermeneutic of the text integrates a hermeneutic of "suspicion" that lets us glimpse a link to the criticism of religion that was carried out, in particular, by the "masters of suspicion": Marx, Nietzsche, and Freud.

The new existential potentialities opened up by the biblical text demand a personal appropriation. In what way does the Word of God mold, by means of the Scripture, the moral conduct of the one who frequents it?[14] To find the answer to this question, we must go back to the point of impact between the biblical text and the responsibility of the one who hears it.[15]

Biblical Ethics

Above all, the Scripture is heard. Hearing, even before acceptance, requires a certain attention on the part of the hearer: just as the ear hears the voice, so too the attention must be directed toward what it hears. Accordingly, before the hearer decides whether to appropriate the possibilities that are held out by Scripture, he must already grant it an audience; he must make room for it. The reading of Scripture, attracting the attention of the hearer, already makes its mark on his or her moral conduct by enabling and obliging him or her to make a response.[16] The reading of the Bible makes demands of the responsibility of the hearer.

The simple contact with Scripture, inviting the hearer to go beyond the literal dimension of the text, gives an essential dialogical status to the ethics that derives from this contact. Since it derives from hearing the word of God that is pronounced by means of Scripture, biblical ethics is distinctly a priori from "the ethics of natural morality, essentially founded on reason."[17] It also differs from the model of autonomy of an atheist or laicist ethics of the modern contemporary West. The originating and essential reference to the Word of God identifies biblical ethics as responsorial and religious.

What I have said up to this point indicates that reading the Bible influences the conscience of the hearer, but without as yet saying how this happens. How does the Scripture in its multitudinous forms give orientation to the moral conduct of the hearer? How does the varied biblical poetics inspire her or his ethics? Along what path does the Spirit of God, who breathes in the biblical letter, address the one who hears God?

The "analogical imagination" plays a decisive, though not exclusive, role in this process.[18] If we define analogy as "an explicit statement of how one thing may be understood in relation to another,"[19] we could define the analogical imagination as the reflexive activity of the reader who hears the biblical narratives and elaborates an image of how he himself or she herself could act. The obvious subjective and objective differences between the praxis narrated in Scripture and the circumstances of the reader's life prevent one from thinking of an identical copy, for example, by miming Jesus' washing the feet of his disciples (cf. John 13:1–20). However, the command that Jesus gives his disciples to do "like" him also excludes an arbitrary invention of the action that is to be carried out. With regard to the actions narrated in the Bible, the action that is imagined must be simultaneously identical and different, or analogical: that is, "faithful and creative at the same time."[20]

Unlike deductive logic, which would apply to the specific cases a general principle that is already explicit in the biblical text or that is inferred from the text by abstraction, the analogical imagination proposes a new action on the basis of a concrete model. Overcoming the rigidity of rational logic in order to immerse itself in the complexity of existential praxis, the analogical imagination admits a flexibility that cannot be tied down in precise rules about how it ought to function—although it must work within the normative framework that is traced by the imperatives that the Scripture does not fail to inculcate. The legitimate use of the analogical imagination cannot be extended beyond the limits within which the differentness of the biblical model of action prevents one from discerning any similarity. The skill in using it consists in avoiding the two antithetical reefs of a univocal repetition and an equivocal invention.

The analogical imagination is not an exclusively cognitive process. It is also affective, because the imagination of the new possibilities of being does not act on its own, but in an osmosis with emotions and sentiments, which give it an affective clothing.[21] The feelings are not simple states or changes within a person. From the moment they arise, they form intentional relationships with external reality, which thus resound in the intimate sphere of the person.

The relationship suggested here between poetics and ethics is particularly suited to bring out the specific relationship that, in the morality revealed by

Scripture, exists between the divine gift and the human response. In the biblical ethics, "the acceptance of God's gracious gift precedes and orientates the human response":[22] "God's founding initiative" comes first, while morality, without being secondary, is logically second.[23] The binomial "divine gift and human response"— or better, the pattern of "appeal and response" that is characteristic of some of the manuals that were renewed after the Second Vatican Council[24]—expresses the fact that the initiative of God, before being a moral demand enjoined upon the human being, is the offer of the potentiality to accomplish this demand.

The primacy of the gratuitous initiative of God in shaping the moral conduct of the human person is the essential truth that the church is called to rediscover in the proclamation of the Gospel to today's world. It is in relation to this challenge of evangelization that a poetical conception of the Bible, such as that illustrated above, appears particularly appropriate.

The Proclamation of the Gospel and Moral Preaching

"The time is fulfilled and the kingdom of God is near; repent and believe in the Good News" (Mark 1:15): from the very start, Jesus' preaching links and coordinates the gratuitous event of God's drawing near and the demand that human beings get ready to welcome him. The grace of the God who is near at hand demands "the obedience of faith (Rom. 16:26; cf. Rom. 1:5; 2 Cor. 10:5–6) by which man commits his whole self freely to God."[25] The proclamation of the Gospel is above all the proclamation of a grace, that is to say, of the act whereby God freely draws close. It is only at a second stage that this proclamation takes on the moral tone, urging men and women to live freely in accordance with grace.

The essential reference to the event of grace from which Christian morality derives its origin has been recently affirmed by Pope Francis, in harmony with his immediate predecessor: "I never tire of repeating those words of Benedict XVI which take us to the very heart of the Gospel: 'Being a Christian is not the result of an ethical choice or a lofty idea, but the encounter with an event, a person, which gives life a new horizon and a decisive direction' (*Deus Caritas Est,* no. 1)." Pope Francis's exhortation is a decisive and heartfelt appeal: the morality taught by the church must be authentically and effectively Christian, allowing every person and all persons to draw from the fountain of "the infinite love of God, who has revealed himself to us in Jesus Christ."[26]

At the heart of the Gospel there "shines forth the beauty of the saving love of God made manifest in Jesus Christ."[27] Its proclamation "invites us to respond to the God of love who saves us." If the Christian morality that is proclaimed as a "response of love" to the prevenient and gratuitous love of God was *not* the truth at the center of the moral teaching of the church, this teaching would be reduced to "a house of cards." The Gospel would be deprived of its "freshness" and "fragrance."[28]

This central truth of Christian morality must guide the church in the "new missionary 'going forth'"[29] that is demanded by its perennial evangelizing mission.

The Gospel, the Good News that the church proclaims with its own message, is that "God takes the initiative, that 'he has loved us first' (1 John 4:19) and that 'he alone gives the growth' (1 Cor. 3:7)."[30] In keeping with the "principle of the *primacy of grace*,"[31] the morality taught by the church, which is an integral part of the proclamation of the Gospel, is "not a form of stoicism, or self-denial, or merely a practical philosophy or a catalogue of sins and faults."[32] But instruction about the good life, while coming second in relation to the proclamation of the Good News of the Gospel, is not secondary. The proclamation of the event of grace is inseparably linked to the preaching of the moral demand.

Evangelization and Postmodern Culture

The church's moral preaching today is one aspect of the challenge of "the new evangelization, especially in those nations where the Gospel has been forgotten or meets with indifference as a result of widespread secularism."[33] Although it is "new in its ardor, methods, and expression,"[34] today's evangelization is, in fact, only fulfilling anew the task that is assigned to the church in every age: "the inculturation of the Gospel" based on the conviction "that the Word of God is inherently capable of speaking to all human persons in the context of their own culture."[35]

The culture to which the "new evangelization" is addressed is, above all, the Western postmodern culture for which the Christian kerygma seems simply empty of meaning and relevance. Although today's postmodern culture has its roots in the Hellenistic culture that the Christian culture encountered in an outstanding manner, and in the Latin culture in which it found its primary expression, it follows after the modern culture in which the kerygma was frequently challenged.

In today's Western societies, the postmodern culture imposes the notion of an "emancipated liberty" from any kind of tie that might enchain it—all the more so, if the enchainment would be definitive. Since the Christian faith is the link to Christ, who is acknowledged and welcomed as the absolute Truth, it is immediately perceived as killing individual liberty, and hence it is abandoned.

Although it seems that the postmodern culture is resistant to the proclamation of the Christian Gospel, we are nevertheless justified in discerning favorable elements in this culture.

It is easy to recognize in the contemporary process of emancipation from religion the ancient and constant temptation of Adam and Eve to make themselves autonomous vis-à-vis God, in the failed attempt to become like God (cf. Gen. 3:5). But it seems difficult to deny that one contributory element here is a faulty configuration of religion, lived by individuals in fear of a God who was ready to punish them, under the pressure of an ecclesiastical authority against which no appeal was possible, and moved by societal conventions that were taken for granted. With regard to such a religion, emancipation is a positive process of unburdening oneself of distorted images of the tie to God, of obedience to the church, and of belonging to society.

Another reason for discerning in the postmodern culture elements that are favorable to the proclamation of the Christian Gospel is the acknowledgment of the value of personal freedom. Without denying, here too, the temptation to deify freedom and detach it from every tie that could limit it, we must recognize that freedom is the essential precondition, if the Christian truth, which coincides with the person of Jesus Christ, is to be recognized and welcomed. The following that he proposes—as the Way, the Truth, and the Life (cf. John 14:6)—is always an appeal to freedom: "If you wish ..." (Matt. 19:17,21). Authentic Christian faith does not understand human freedom as detached from the truth of Christ; but at the same time, it does not reflect on the Christian truth in abstraction from human freedom: "Truth and freedom either go together hand in hand or together they perish in misery."[36]

Emancipation from religious distortions and the appreciation of personal liberty are elements that invite us to refrain from condemning in toto today's postmodern culture. We must acknowledge its good qualities, even in the midst of its defects.

The notion of "emancipated liberty," which deserves to be valued more highly than a condition of undue submission, nevertheless reveals all its inadequacy if we look at its claim to an absolute independence and a total autonomy. If it is cut adrift from every tie, especially from the tie to God and to one's neighbor, liberty loses its foundation and its orientation. The emancipated liberty is a liberty that has lost its way. The proof of this diagnosis, which is also widely present in academic literature, can easily be seen in the widespread uncertainty about personal identity, in the instability of interpersonal relationships, and in the fragmentation of the network of society. Without a shared truth, each one lays claim to his or her own truth. In that case, it is the truth of the one who is strongest that imposes itself on the truth of the weak person, and the truths of those who are equal, if they manage to refrain from conflict, achieve nothing more than a negotiation of their survival.

The present-day crisis of the liberty that is emancipated and has lost its way, a liberty that is both passionate and depressed, is a symptom of a culture—the postmodern culture—and even more, of a civilization—that of the West—that are gravely ill. But it is also true that when the illness gets worse, the sick person is more disposed to seek a cure. The present day, even more than past ages, seems to be the time prophesied by Amos: "Behold, the days are coming, says the Lord God, when I will send a famine on the land; not a famine of bread, nor a thirst for water, but of hearing the words of the Lord" (8:11).

Evangelization and Moral Preaching

Today's cultural circumstances demand a fine-tuning of moral preaching that, without renouncing the truth of the Gospel, makes contact with the liberty of the postmodern person in his or her specific situation. The truth of the Gospel envisages the tie—first of all, the religious tie to God, and, inseparably from this, the social tie to one's neighbor—as the essential condition for human life. The postmodern contingency invites us to envisage the religious and societal tie first and foremost as an opportunity that is offered to personal liberty, before being a norm to be observed and a task to be taken on. If we take account of this double demand, the privileged register of today's moral preaching ought to be poetical, rather than normative or paraenetic.[37]

Normative preaching is concerned with teaching the norms of behavior, endeavoring to demonstrate their reasonableness. With its starting point in arguments of faith and of reason, normative preaching defines the boundary between consistent and inconsistent behavior. Its axis is the law in its objective truth, which is enjoined on liberty, in order that liberty may regulate itself on the basis of the law.

Paraenetic preaching is in a different register. It takes the objective law for granted and is concerned to appeal to the subjective liberty, in order that it may adapt to the law. The strategy adopted is not to explain why one must act in one particular way, but to move the person to do so by appealing to the will and the feelings rather than to the reason. Paraenesis addresses its exhortation to a person's goodwill, making use of emotion. It summons liberty to do its duty.

Moral predication that is normative or paraenetic is not erroneous per se, because it involves dimensions of Christian morality that are indispensable, such as the objective aspect of the truth, an aspect formulated by the law, and the subjective aspect of liberty, which is called to let itself be tied to the truth through the observance of the law. The normative and paraenetic registers of moral predication are valid in a Christianized society, but they are less suitable for evangelization today. Today's proclamation of the Gospel is located within the "conflict of the convictions,"[38] and this means it is not primarily a question of insisting (in the normative register) on the norms of behavior that allow us to measure the coherence with regard to a Christian truth in which the person believes; nor is it a question (in the paraenetic register) of appealing to people to act with respect to a truth that is held to be already present. The new generations are born and grow up in a world that is ever more distant from the standard of a Christianized society, and this means that their perception is not that of a world that is progressively moving away from the Christian faith and from the moral values, but of a world that perceives faith and Christian morality as distant. In view of this new societal situation, the diagnosis of a culpable estrangement and the therapy of a recalling to the religious and moral principles of the past are ineffective.

The inefficacy of this relationship to the world leads to two opposite attitudes in those who are engaged in pastoral work, especially in priests. Some grow rigid in a preaching of principles and norms, attempting to prevent the world from slipping farther away; others, instead, avoid tackling the moral questions and leave them up to the personal conscience. Two styles of preaching, which Cardinal Martini called "occasionalist" and "schoolmasterly," correspond to these two attitudes. In the first case, "the recourse to the biblical texts provides an occasion of talking about many, many things, even things that are important and relevant, but which are tackled in accordance with the urgency and the weight of circumstances, without reaching the radically new perspective that is opened up only by a more original and organic approach to the Scriptures." In the second case, one approaches the biblical text "almost as if one were reading good literature, attentive to the fine points of the pages of Scripture—but this reading is abstract and self-contained. This attitude is based on a somewhat simplistic idea of the efficacy of the Word of God: namely, that it suffices to make the Word present in its naked objectivity, in order that the very power of God may make itself present."[39]

If moral preaching is not to descend into a moralist "occasionalism" or a biblical "schoolmastering," a fruitful encounter is needed between the proclamation of the Christian truth and the welcoming of human liberty. The best way to pursue this goal will be for moral preaching to take the poetic register, inspired by Jesus, who preferred to speak to everyone in parables. The parable—whether it concerns the elementary experiences of life (cf. Luke 7:41–43), the paradoxes of life (cf. Matt. 20:1–16), or the laws of life's evolution (cf. Mark 4:3–9)—demands the activation of the hearers to a greater degree than in other literary genres. The hearers must guess the "moral" that is hidden in the parable. At any rate, it elicits a reaction, which may be of interest, as when the disciples ask Jesus for explanations (cf. Matt. 13:36, 15:15), or disregard, as in those "who see but do not see, and hear but do not hear and do not understand" (Matt. 13:13). Communication in parables activates the addressee and establishes a dialogic style that better corresponds to the dialogue with the world that the Second Vatican Council has indicated as the style of the church's mission for the third millennium of the Christian era.[40]

Jesus' preaching was moral, not primarily because he dictated rules or condemned inconsistency, but because he activated the liberty of his hearers, urging them to take the initiative and be creative, in order that they might discover, under the patina of the obvious, of prejudices and of inertia, the secret of human life. Today, it appears particularly opportune to illustrate how the Christian truth allows one to discover an unsuspected and surprising meaning in human existence, in all its aspects, in being born and in dying, in loving and in suffering, and so on.

This form of preaching is not primarily the product of a technique: it is the fruit of a praxis. This means that when we rethink preaching, we are sent back to the fertile encounter between the Word of God and human hearing that biblical ethics is called to investigate. The development of the biblical poetics that I have sketched in the present article can make a valuable contribution to this task, as would an elaboration of biblical ethics carried out by the biblical sciences and by moral theology in a genuinely interdisciplinary way.

Pope Francis, appreciating and encouraging theological investigation, recommends that theologians "must always remember that the Church and theology exist to evangelize, and not be content with a desk-bound theology."[41]

In the light of this admonition, the moral theologian and the exegete are invited to personalize the Word. The same invitation is addressed to every preacher, who "ought first of all to develop a great personal familiarity with the Word of God. Knowledge of its linguistic or exegetical aspects, though certainly necessary, is not enough. He needs to approach the Word with a docile and prayerful heart so that it may deeply penetrate his thoughts and feelings and bring about a new outlook in him"[42]—namely, "the mind of Christ" (1 Cor. 2:16).

Translated by Brian McNeil

Notes

1. Paul VI, *Optatam Totius*, no. 16.

2. John Paul II, *Veritatis Splendor*, no. 28. On this, see S. Pinckaers, "L'uso della Scrittura in teologia morale," *Nova & Vetera* 1, no. 2 (1999): 11–25.

3. Édouard Hamel, "Écriture et théologie morale, un bilan (1940–1980)," *Studia Moralia* 20 (1982): 177–93. For an almost complete bibliography of the relationship between sacred Scripture and ethics in the epoch after the Second Vatican Council, see James T. Bretzke, *Bibliography on Scripture and Christian Ethics, Studies in Religion and Society* 39 (Lewiston, NY: Edwin Mellen Press, 1997).

4. Guiseppe De Virgilio, "Bibbia e teologia morale: Paradigmi ermeneutici per il dialogo interdisciplinare," *Studi di teologia* 17 (Rome: EDUSC, 2013).

5. "The collaboration of human action and of divine action in the full realization of the human being: it is precisely this that is the problem underlying the whole of Christian morality" (J. Ratzinger, *La via della fede: Le ragioni dell'etica nell'epoca presente* [Milan: Ares, 1996], 96).

6. R. Maiolini, "'Il credente legge e interpreta la Scrittura nella fede della Chiesa' (EB, n. 1468). Una questione teologico-fondamentale prima che ermeneutica," in *Interpretare la Scrittura* (= Quaderni Teologici del Seminario di Brescia 18) (Morcelliana: Brescia, 2008), 77–105.

7. The present essay is written against the background of A. Fumagalli and F. Manzi, *Attirerò tutti a me: Ermeneutica biblica ed etica Cristiana* (= Trattati di etica teologica) (Bologna: EDB, 2005).

8. P. Grech, "Ermeneutica," in *Nuovo Dizionario di Teologia Biblica*, ed. P. Rossano, G. Ravasi, and A. Girlanda, Cinisello Balsamo (Milan: Edizioni Paoline, 1988), 464–89.

9. [Translator's note: "po-etica" in the subhead represents an untranslatable play on the words poetica (poetics) and etica (ethics).] For this synthesis of Paul Ricoeur's thinking, see Alain Thomasset, *Paul Ricoeur: Une poétique de la morale: Aux fondements d'une éthique herméneutique et narrative dans une perspective chrétienne* (Louvain: Presses Universitaires de Louvain 1996), 227–319.

10. The term "poetics," etymologically derived from the Greek verb *poiein* (to produce, to create, to do) and with a philosophical reference to Aristotle, emphasizes the point that the relationship between sacred Scripture and ethics is to be understood as a creative action of the former on the latter. The broad horizon opened up by these reflections can be appreciated if one reads the dossier *Fides ex auditu: Scrittura, ascolto, fede*, published in the theological periodical of the Archdiocesan Seminary in Milan: *La Scuola Cattolica* 129, no. 1 (2001), especially the essay by D. D'Alessio, "Il racconto e la vita: Lectio biblica come avventura della mente e del cuore," 103–44.

11. Paul Ricoeur, *Ermeneutica filosofica ed ermeneutica biblica*, 2nd ed. (Brescia: Paideia, 1983), 39.

12. Ibid., 73–74.

13. Paul Ricoeur has elaborated the theme of semantic innovation especially in *La métaphore vive* (Paris: Le Seuil, 1975) (English translation: *The Rule of Metaphor* [London: Routledge and Kegan Paul, 1978]), and in the trilogy *Temps et récit*, vol. 1: *L'intrigue et le récit historique* (Paris: Le Seuil, 1983); vol. 2: *La configuration dans le récit de fiction* (Paris: Le Seuil, 1984); vol. 3: *Le temps raconté* (Paris: Le Seuil, 1985) (English translation: *Time and Narrative*, 3 vols. [Chicago: University of Chicago Press, 1984, 1985, 1988]).

14. S. Fausti, *Per una lettura laica della Bibbia* (Milan: EDB – Ancora, 2008), 9.

15. Paul Ricoeur, "La Parole, instauratrice de liberté," *Cahiers universitaires catholiques* 10 (1966): 493–507.

16. This is the central thesis in W. P. Brown, ed., *Character and Scripture: Moral Formation, Community and Biblical Interpretation* (Grand Rapids, MI: Eerdmans 2002).

17. Pontifical Biblical Commission, *The Bible and Morality* (Vatican City, 2008), no. 156.

18. We borrow this concept from William C. Spohn, *Go and Do Likewise: Jesus and Ethics* (New York: Continuum, 1999), 50–71, who in turn borrows it from David Tracy, *The Analogical Imagination: Christian Theology and the Culture of Pluralism* (New York: Crossroad, 1981).

19. Spohn, *Go and Do Likewise*, 54.

20. Ibid., 56. The contemporary relevance of this challenge can count on resources that are present in the patrimony of moral theology. The casuistry of the past, which is attracting renewed attention today after some decades of harsh criticism, made the comparison between individual cases a distinctive characteristic of its method of argumentation.

21. The interweaving of the cognitive and affective dimensions in the metaphorical process is investigated in Paul Ricoeur, "The Metaphorical Process as Cognition, Imagination, and Feeling," in *On Metaphor*, ed. S. Sacks (Chicago: University of Chicago Press, 1978–79), 141–57.

22. Pontifical Biblical Commission, *The Bible and Morality*, no. 156.

23. See ibid., no. 4.

24. The pattern of appeal and response already structured the manual that, more than any other, prepared the change at the council: Bernhard Häring, *Das Gesetz Christi* (Freiburg i.Br.: Herder, 1954). English translation: *The Law of Christ* (Cork: Mercier Press, 1961). Later manuals chose to indicate this pattern already in their title: A. Günthör, *Anruf und Antwort* (Vallendar: Patris Verlag, 1974); H. Weber, *Allgemeine Moraltheologie: Ruf und Antwort* (Graz: Styria, 1991).

25. Second Vatican Council, *Dei Verbum*, no. 5.

26. Pope Francis, *Evangelii Gaudium*, no. 7.

27. Ibid., no. 36.

28. Ibid., no. 39.

29. Ibid., no. 20.

30. Ibid., no. 12.

31. Ibid., no. 112.

32. Ibid., no. 39.

33. Benedict XVI, *Verbum Domini*, no. 122.

34. John Paul II, *Veritatis Splendor*, no. 106; these words are a quotation from his address to the bishops of CELAM on March 9, 1983.

35. Benedict XVI, *Verbum Domini*, no. 114.

36. John Paul II, *Fides et Ratio*, no. 90.

37. See C. Theobald, *Il cristianesimo come stile: Un modo di fare teologia nella postmodernità*, 2 (= Nuovi Saggi Teologici 79), (Bologna: EDB, 2009), 832–34.

38. A. Lob-Hüdepohl, ed., *Ethik im Konflikt der Überzeugungen* (= Studien zur theologischen Ethik 105) (Freiburg i.Br.: Herder, 2004).

39. C.M. Martini, "In principio la Parola. Lettera al clero e ai fedeli per l'anno pastorale 1981/82," in idem, *Programmi pastorali diocesani* 1980–1990 (Bologna: EDB, 1990), 55–56.

40. John Paul II, *Novo Millennio Ineunte*, nos. 54–56.

41. *Evangelii Gaudium*, no. 133.

42. Ibid., no. 149, quoting John Paul II, *Pastores Dabo Vobis*, no. 26.

Part II

Perspectives

OLD TESTAMENT

Supporting Cast versus Supporting Caste

Reading the Old Testament as Praxis of Justice

Gina Hens-Piazza

The Bible qualifies as a powerful force in our contemporary culture. By both direct and subtle means, the Bible continues to inspire, entertain, converse with readers and listeners, and remain present in both expected and unexpected ways. Certainly across Jewish and Christian communities, the Bible participates as a formative player, a partner of doctrine and ethics alike. But also in various other sectors of our culture and before people who have never opened its covers, the Bible manifests its cultural import in a host of influential representations ranging from the sublime to the absurd. From Caravaggio's *Sacrifice of Isaac* to Michelangelo's Sistine Chapel, the Bible as subject for art has been unsurpassed. Works such as Handel's *Messiah* suggest the Bible's influence on musical scores. Whether as intertextual partner in Dostoyevsky's work, subject of imagery in Gerard Manley Hopkins's poetry, or as analogue for popular fiction like *The Red Tent*, the story and the themes of the Bible frequently echo across literary works. Then there are those absurd commodifications of the biblical texts—from chocolate bars stamped with the Ten Commandments and board games such as Bible Trivia to jello molds in the shape of Noah's ark and all the animals to accompany the journey. The Bible etches itself in the mundane and the absurd. And how could anyone forget Hollywood's many articulations, whether in the form of Disney's *The Prince of Egypt*, Cecil B. DeMille's *David and Bathsheba*, Mel Gibson's *The Passion of the Christ*, or more recently Russell Crowe's role in *Noah*? Without a doubt, the Bible remains embedded in a whole variety of cultural manifestations suggesting the "here to stay" status of "this old book."

On a more serious note, critical readers are keenly aware, for better or for worse, of the Bible's authoritative intonements on matters of justice. It has been mined to authorize distorted notions of the sacred as a punitive force to explain why some people suffer. It continues to be selectively quoted to justify politicians' positions on moral matters. It is enlisted to support nations in their imperialistic land-grabbing escapades. And it is called on to underwrite the liberation campaigns aimed at overturning such colonizing overtures. Even today, the controversy over territory that has kept some people hostage and others at war or living in fear stems from a biblical tradition about land and to whom it was bequeathed. Whether used critically or uncritically, the Bible has been assigned significant authority on matters of social justice that, even in this twenty-first century, makes it a powerful cultural force. All this should serve as warning. Failing to recognize or at least grant the Bible its influence in culture today will not curtail the Bible's influence.

That the Bible, particularly the Old Testament, can be mined for a whole host of ethical positions suggests that critical approaches to doing ethics in tandem with the Bible are crucial. Over the years, Catholic and Protestant scholars working in the fields of ethics and moral theology have established sound theoretical grounding for the systematic use of Scripture in these matters.[1] Such scholarship not only wrestles with fundamental methodological questions, it also provides helpful guidelines that challenge and help derail idiosyncratic, selective, or literal interpretations of Scripture, especially in matters of social justice. However, this essay is less concerned with how the text of the Old Testament yields principles of justice or interpretations that inspire or challenge readers with such issues. Rather, it considers how reading the Old Testament can be a praxis of justice itself.[2]

The matter of justice is a significant and central theme throughout the Bible, with its earliest articulations echoing in the Old Testament.[3] The summons for people to live justly resounds across all these texts. They are founded on God's own activity as revealed in the first testament, which precedes, fashions, and ultimately forms the basis of Christianity's origin and self-understanding. In the Old Testament, the practice of justice constitutes the very character of God. But the nature of God eclipses the Old Testament, not confining itself to any era, covenant, or dispensation.[4] For the Old Testament itself gives testimony to an understanding of God that precedes, succeeds, and transcends both Israelite and Christian constructions. In the Old Testament, God is grasped as the Lord of the universe (Ps. 99:1–4) who "does justice for *all* who are oppressed" (Ps. 103:6) and establishes "justice for all" the oppressed of the earth (Ps. 76:9; Jer. 9:24). Thus, this is the God who not only attends to the oppressed Israelites or persecuted Christians but also works one justice for *all* people and for *all* time. God's justice becomes a model for human justice and provides a path for fulfilling the great commandment to love one another. As God expresses divine love through acts of justice, so too living justly becomes a channel by which we love. "Sow for yourselves justice, reap the fruit of steadfast love" (Hosea 10:12, 2:19, 10:12; Jer. 9:24; Mic. 6:8; etc.).

A Shift in Our Reading Practice

The significance and intrigue of characters of the Old Testament are well known. So enormous is their impact that the heroic persons of the biblical writings frequently burst off the page and as already noted become subjects for colossal sculpture, steamy novels, massive paintings, magical operas, and Hollywood block-busters. This essay explores the impact of our reading practices when it comes to characters in the ancient stories of the Old Testament. However, it is not interested in the reading practices surrounding the "big" characters or major players that typically command our attention, or even the secondary characters, often referred to as antagonists or contrasting characters. The characters on whom this essay dwells are those making up the supporting cast. There are passing references to "the maidens," "the servant," "the quarrymen," "the crowd," who are typically understood as the minor characters. Ordinarily they are thought to fill in the scenery, inhabit a story's background, or serve as literary props. In literary categories, they are referred to as a "type" or "agent" and are never regarded for the story they might tell.[5] Often interpreted in the service of the major character, they shoulder the burden of a story that is never theirs. However, this investigation of their status is not confined merely to their functioning in the literary realm. Rather, the cultural yield and ethical import resulting from more democratized reading practices when it comes to members of the supporting cast is at the heart of this proposal. Moreover, if the cultural yield is great and the ethical implications are significant, failure to give the supporting cast its just due may inadvertently cultivate injustice. Moreover, failure to pay attention to the supporting cast may deprive readers of important insights as well as enlist their unintended support for the caste system of the narrative.

The Anatomy of the Supporting Cast

Who are these members of the supporting cast? Fleetingly referenced, some are "the maidens dancing in Shiloh" who are kidnapped and taken for the Benjaminites as wives (Judg. 21:15–26). They are the remaining "inhabitants of Gath, Gaza, and Ashod" after Joshua's bloody campaign against the Anakim (Josh. 11:21–23). Among their quiet ranks list the "the prostitute of Gaza" visited by Samson in his exploits of the Philistines (Judg. 16:1–3) and the two children of a widowed mother about to be handed over as slaves to a creditor (2 Kings 4:1–7). They are the friends of Jephthah's daughter, fleetingly referenced in the text, accompanying her to the hills to mourn her unfulfilled life, and they are the implied peasants whose subsistence farming is taxed beyond what they can endure under the reign of Jeroboam II. Entered into the story with the most economic description, their identity is rarely personalized. Often they are ensconced in a social category—"widow," "child," "foreigner," "servant," and so on. Their individual identity may be even further obscured by a collective reference to their presence in the tale—"villagers," "peasants," "enemy," "captives." Accorded only a few words or often remaining completely silent, they are frequently understood as narrative fixtures or agents enhancing or advancing the action of a story that obscures them. Located somewhere in the junction between implied person and narrative form, they exist only in the margins of the story, often facilitating a story that is never theirs. Yet literary theorists have recognized that every story speaks of many stories and that narratives tell more than one tale at a time. Do current practices urge us to read past these characters and support the caste system of the narrative? What would be the consequences if we entertained the other stories that the supporting cast would tell? Might shifting our attention away from the so-called major characters and attending to the numerous members of the supporting cast in biblical stories heighten our sensitivity to the unnoticed or frequently taken-for-granted peoples in our own world? Further, could how we read this important cultural and religious text have ethical implications for how we read the text of our world?

Theoretical Orientation

Since the 1980s, a group of theorists known as New Historicists argue for a more dynamic understanding of what happens in the reading process.[6] Reading and interpreting literary works such as the Bible is understood as a mutual process of self-fashioning. Texts and their interpretation not only reflect life and make it possible for readers to understand what they read, but life, society, culture, and readers themselves are shaped by texts and what they inscribe. This is a process of mutual fashioning of society and literature simultaneously. How texts are read and interpreted mirrors how society is read and interpreted. Those we attend to in texts, those we analyze, what we emphasize in our scrutiny and what we ignore mirror and shape those same tendencies in our approach to our society.

In her monumental work *A Poetics of Postmodernism*, Linda Hutcheon summarizes it best. She writes, "How we read is not unrelated to how we see at least from the point of view of subjectivity."[7] In other words, how we read and interpret texts, especially important cultural or religious texts like the Bible, has a great deal of influence on how we read and interpret the text of our world. "Who we attend to, who we ask questions about, or who we study in depth in texts cultivates a similar interest in terms of who we see, who we inquire about, and who we seek to better understand in our own surroundings." In addition, New Historicists have demonstrated that our interest in texts, even ancient texts, is always directly or indirectly tied to the present and our interests in the present. The questions we ask about the past are inevitably tied to the questions we ask ourselves about the present. And the questions we ask about characters in stories are yoked to or grow out of questions we ask or need to ask ourselves about people in life.

Second, in addition to this theoretical orientation, a study of the supporting cast rests on its own underlying sociopolitical commitment to justice. It aims to reverse the order of how we read and interpret texts. It endeavors to overturn the scale of reading priorities and practices. Focusing on the supporting cast helps redress the disproportionate amount of attention on the so-called major players, the protagonists, often identified as the heroes of biblical narrative. The focus on the supporting cast intends to tell the story and to give voice to those characters who qualify as the subaltern of these biblical tales. The change in focus is not for its own sake but on the grounds that every effort to encourage recognition of and sensitivity toward every human person contributes to a more equitable and just world.

Attention to previously disregarded literary subjects could grant access to a multiplicity of stories and a multiplicity of yet unrecognized voices in the narrative. It could urge readers to abandon social constructions of the story world that are singular and even reciprocal, and instead entertain those that are multiple and incommensurable. Readers would then be in better positions to abandon the social classism and establishments of a narrative that occlude their visions of all the unheeded voices that are quietly speaking there.

In the process, reading and interpreting biblical texts would become more than an exercise in literary analysis, especially when the supporting cast is included. Accessing the multiple stories present there might reinforce or challenge the definitions and assumptions by which we understand people in our world. Becoming a practitioner of "stories from below" may counter or undercut the dominant story of the victor (typically deemed main or major character) with that of the vanquished or virtuous (the supporting cast). Attending to the supporting cast may disclose the way a society is. Or a consideration of their placement or silence in a story may prompt consideration of how a society ought to be. With a focus on the supporting cast, issues that are divisive in our own world—matters of class, capital, labor, race, gender, and so on—come into bold relief. What constitutes a hero, who really is virtuous, and where subtle but nevertheless real violence rears its head—all invite scrutiny with this narrative population. And if shifting our attention to unnamed or previously unnoticed characters in important texts like the Bible can potentially nudge us toward recognizing and then dismantling the unjust and excluding structures of our world, then we ignore the supporting cast at our own peril.

The Supporting Cast: Four Categories

No character is without complexity, purpose, or importance, whether they appear briefly, assist as part of the narrative scenery, number among members of the "watching crowd," or participate as the implied occupants (men, women, and children) of "the town destroyed by the enemy." All members of the supporting cast contribute to the story either explicitly or subtly and indirectly. Without each of them, the story would be less of a tale, a different tale, or perhaps not exist at all. All members qualify to be considered as characters who, in different ways, participate in the makeup of the narrative. Moreover, their importance is determined not solely by the narrative but also as the result of the reader who contributes to their fashioning. In other words, they exist, derive recognition, and are deemed worthy of attention only insofar as a reader grants them recognition. It is also true of their counterparts in our world. They are visible and deemed worthy of recognition and importance only insofar as each of us cultivates a vision to see and acknowledge the significance of such persons in our surroundings.

Who constitutes a real character or carries significance has little to do with how much of a role they play in the narrative. Character is as much the product of readers as it is of the texts. Scholars of the tricontinental world, along with feminist interpreters, have long demonstrated that some of the members of the supporting cast are far more significant in the story than their minimal role or abbreviated appearance suggests.

Like the immense variety of individuals who make up our world, members of the supporting cast manifest a great variety in these stories. Borrowing a few terms from drama, four designations of character are offered here as an attempt to encourage a more comprehensive and inclusive roster of all the members of the supporting cast. The four categories include complementary role, bit part, cameo appearance, and implied presence. Although the groups reflect a quantitative relegation of characters' participation in the narrative, the four designations do not signify any qualitative difference between the groups. Thus, they allow for the major importance of any one character in any of the categories to emerge.

Complementary Roles

Characters who might be designated members of the complementary role group are most common in the narrative. Despite their less-than-front-and-center roles, they have staying power in the story. They often even receive a detailed introduction or have their own tale to tell. They wield a healthy hand in the story, often being responsible for a good amount of direct discourse. They directly influence plot, theme, and outcomes of the high drama unfolding there. They frequently prompt the dialogue and actions of other characters and even form a contrast to some of these players in the story. Typically, the narrative provides a good deal of information about them either directly in the form of a detailed description or indirectly by virtue of their direct speech and action.

In a story often titled "Joab Negotiates the Return of Absalom," a wise woman of Tekoa (2 Sam. 14:1–24) qualifies as a member of the supporting cast playing a complementary role. Though unnamed, she plays a key role in prompting David to assume his authority as king. Assuming the part of a widow, she nudges David to act on behalf of his exiled son Absalom. She has her own (fictitious) story and commands a great deal of the dialogue, initiating every exchange between the king and herself. Though the narrative seems not to be about her, she looms large and is essential to the unfolding of the plot. The unnamed woman's speech directly affects King David and steers the story forward. The exchanges between David and this woman enable him to act on behalf of his son as well as to begin functioning in his role as king. On close scrutiny of her character, the woman's role is not minor or even secondary. She complements the narrative as well as demonstrates that the social distance and difference often assumed between such social categories as common woman and royal king are not what they appear. The woman shows herself wise in her ability to keep up her disguise. Though presumed the inferior, she boldly confronts the king, her superior. She skillfully employs idioms, patterns of speech, and tactics that were characteristic of folk wisdom. She manifests supreme forensic skill. In the story, she changed the course of events, and she even changed the heart of a king. But her goal was not limited to the fate of Absalom. The concerns voiced by the woman eclipse her story and show her to be an "active trident of covenant values" (land and inheritance).[8] In the end, David's decision to bring Absalom back acknowledged her authority. Hence, the authority, instruction, and insight of this wise woman induced the king to rule wisely.[9] Labeling her a minor character seems inaccurate. In her significant role, the wise woman of Tekoa makes the story and its outcome possible. Who are her counterparts in our world? Who are the individuals that by their skill and wisdom cause others to flourish and act wisely? How does the wise woman of Tekoa challenge the social hierarchies of the story and the social hierarchies of our world as mere facades? What persons does she make us see in our own surroundings who make possible the accomplishments, successes, and maturation of others but go unnoticed themselves?

Bit Parts

Other members of the supporting cast have bit parts, the second category of designation. Characters with bit parts have a few sentences about them or minimal description concerning their background, social standing, or role in the society implied in the story world. Their appearance is often brief and erroneously reduced in character studies to a mere function. But when those assumptions are sidelined, and their place in the narrative given a prolonged analysis, their importance and significance often exceed their short narrative appearance. They frequently have a sentence or a question to speak. Often they appear and disappear quickly. And although their narrative involvement in the story is much more abbreviated than characters like the Tekoite woman, they have the same potential. They can change the course of the story, and they can even change the course of history. The major difference between them and other characters is a matter of the diminished narrative space they are afforded. They too play significant and instructive roles despite their abbreviated appearance.

In 2 Kings 4:1–7, a brief tale relates the crisis of a widow who is in danger of losing her two children. She tells her story to the prophet Elisha. The two children are members of the supporting cast. They receive little description other than that they are about to be taken by a creditor as slaves to satisfy the widow's dead husband's debt. No names, ages, or other information is provided about these two youngsters. They enter the story again briefly when the widow, following the prophet's instruction, is pouring oil into jars in her house. "They pass her the jars and she keeps on pouring" (2 Kings 4:5). This time the two children are referred to collectively as "they." Finally, when the widow asks for another jar, it falls to one of the children (we don't know which one) to announce, "There are no more" (2 Kings 4:6). The recognition and announcement that the miracle is complete falls to one of the children. One of the two children with only a bit part assumes responsibility for announcing the achievement of the divine intervention. This child becomes the witness to the fulfillment of the promise to the widow as well as to the salvation that lies ahead for all three of them in the tale. The children enter the story one more time as a reference in the prophet's speech to the widow after she conveys the results. He tells her to go and sell the oil and then pay off her deceased husband's debts. The prophet adds that both she and her children can live off the money that is left over. Though only members of the supporting cast, the children undergo a transformed existence. In the opening of the story their widowed mother defines the threat to their existence, saying, "A creditor has come now to take my two children and make them his slaves" (2 Kings 4:1). In the conclusion of the tale the prophet assures the widow that they will have a secure existence with provisions. "Go and sell the oil and redeem your pledge; you and your children can live on the remainder" (2 Kings 4:7). Though members of the supporting cast, the children are at the heart of the crisis that reaches resolution. Their secured existence is evidence of the scope of the miracle's effect. Though lacking the depth and narrative space of some of the other characters, the children are just as integral to the story both for the construction of the plot and for the role they actually play. Their restored well-being bears witness to the scope of divine intervention. To miss or ignore them risks missing those less-visible persons in our own world whose transformed lives also bear witness to God's presence in our surroundings. Who are their counterparts in our age? Who are these individuals who discover abundance and well-being in life despite limited resources? Do we see them? And do we allow their faith amid the most challenging of life's circumstances to challenge the fallacy that we are in charge of our own destiny?

Cameo Appearances

The third group of supporting cast members, cameo appearances, registers the largest. These characters emerge from a mere name or job function and have no speaking part. Their identification in the story may be individual or collective. They might arise from an isolated look or a passing statement. They are "the laborers," "the quarrymen," "the spinners," "the soldiers," "the foreigners," "the slaves," and so on, who, when taken seriously, suggest the archaeology of the society embedded in the story world. It has long been assumed that these characters are simply meant as background. At best, they are thought to be literary props scaffolding the scenery. Yet some of the most interesting examinations of these characters begin where other studies stop for apparent lack of extrapolative base.

In the book of Ruth, "the reapers" are mentioned in passing several times (Ruth 2:3, 6, 14) in the account of the first encounter between Ruth and Boaz in his fields (Ruth 2:2–17). They say nothing and receive no description. These workers could be easily dismissed as scenery that helps establish Boaz as someone with property and wealth. Thus their presence in the story is qualified only as a means to amplify

Boaz's authority over a large constituency of employees. They appear in verse 2:3 and disappear in verse 2:17. But the reapers' implied activity and implied response to Ruth assure her safety in a hostile environment even before Boaz comes on the scene. "So she went out and gleaned in the field after the reapers" (Ruth 2:3). Though not narrated, their respectful response to her in the field is implied here. Later, though never described or detailed, evidence of their obedient response to Boaz's orders via his foreman that they should pull out the sheaves so she can glean materializes in the story. At the end of the day, Ruth returns home to Naomi with "an ephah of barley," suggesting the virtue of these workers. The implied action of the reapers on behalf of Ruth enables both Ruth and Naomi to flourish. And because Ruth is enlivened rather than threatened by them and their actions, her eventual offspring not only restores life to the widowed Naomi, it also paves the way for the Davidic line in Israel. Hence this unnamed collective, "reapers," have a hand in a very large project of divine design, that is, the continuance of Israel. Who are their counterparts in our world? Who makes up the hosts of individuals that contribute to the abundances of our lives but go unrecognized for the expenditure of their talents and labor? Failure to recognize their contributions cultivates a failure to recognize their person. Their behind-the-scenes work, contributions, and gifts become taken for granted. The virtue accompanying their steadfast labors gets missed, and we all become impoverished by such oversights.

Implied Presence

The last group of the supporting cast in biblical narrative is made up of characters implied in the text, or what is being called here those with implied presence. One might ask what is the smallest amount of information that the text can provide out of which a reader can perceive a character. Since a character need not even be named to exist, any passing reference, or indirect statement, or a phrase, or even an allusion establishes a point of reference. "Towns being destroyed" indicates slaughtered people. "Cheating in the marketplaces" implies cunning merchants. "Stones being quarried" suggests hard-working laborers. Stanley Fish would argue the scope of the experiential base that a reader brings to this reference determines the image of the character that develops.[10]

In this group of implied supporting cast members, the character that emerges is least able to lend itself to a general analysis, as so much here rests on the reader's sensitivity and experience. Even the identification of these implied presences is reader-dependent. For example, a group of students may read the account of Josiah's religious reform (2 Kings 21–22), in which this king tore down all the local shrines, closed houses of prostitution, and shut down the houses where women were weaving clothes for Asherah. However, one reader among the group with an experiential base of living in the Alta Plano of Bolivia may wonder about all the peasants who lost their jobs as a result of Josiah's reform. The implied presences would be, therefore, the unemployed peasants who previously ran the local shrines, wove clothes for Asherah, or worked in the houses of prostitution. In another familiar story of the two women before Solomon (1 Kings 3:15–28), another character emerges via implied presence. The king gives the order for a sword to be brought before him to solve the dispute as to which woman is the real mother of the living child. The text reports, "And a sword was brought before the king" (1 Kings 3:24). The implied presence here is the sword bearer whom many readers report visualizing when they hear the text. Depending on the experiential base of the reader, this supporting cast character not only is recognized but may be granted added complexity. Was the implied character of the sword bearer in crisis bringing forth the sword, or was he utterly complicit with the king's order to "divide the child in two, giving half to one and half to the other" (1 Kings 3:24)? Did this character struggle with his own fear of the king or with the anxiety that he would actually have to witness or even carry out the slaying of an innocent infant? Readers of this text who themselves have had to struggle with a crisis of conscience when it comes to warfare might be particularly sensitive and sympathetic to what may have been a terrible dilemma for this invisible individual. In the process, the implied presence becomes a real character whose importance allows readers to contemplate the struggles that others in warfare or strife must wrestle with.

Reading with attention to the supporting cast aims for a more egalitarian reading where all characters receive a hearing. But the thesis motivating such interest eclipses mere literary intrigue. It presumes an intrinsic relationship between the critical eye trained to survey such important religious and cultural texts as the Bible and that same critical eye's attention to the presence and importance of the supporting cast in our own world. Grappling with the broadest range of characters grants us urgently needed insights into the many and different "others" who make up our world. It challenges and redefines who among us are assigned to categories of privilege and power in our private and communal schemes of reality. It gives us pause before those whose importance we might otherwise have missed or looked past. And at this juncture in the life of our vast and ever-shrinking global village, the value of such knowledge and understanding needs little defense or explanation.

Moreover, reading the Old Testament with an eye to the supporting cast emancipates the reader from the injustices of the narrative caste system where major characters are named, featured by narrators, and deemed the important ones of a story. It encourages us to engender alternative reading practices that might result in a more equitable and just assessment of the characters present there. This in turn cultivates a new sensitivity toward our own context and a more equitable and justice-based assessment of those residing among us. How we read important texts like the Bible affects and influences how we read and interpret the "text" of our world. A reading practice that refuses to read past the supporting cast and, instead, even privileges it does more. It qualifies our reading as a praxis of justice.

Ironically, such a practice also resoundingly echoes the message and priorities of a well-known teacher from years ago who counted himself as a servant and likely studied these texts. Jesus had a penchant for the so-called supporting cast of his society. He considered most blessed the unnamed meek, the poor in spirit, and persons persecuted for justice's sake. He encouraged attention to the multitude of his world and ours who suffered hunger, thirst, or imprisonment. He called to be his followers not the upper echelons of society but common fishermen and tax collectors. He healed nameless lepers, unidentified blind men, and unknown persons afflicted with unclean spirits. And he spent more time with the anonymous masses and crowds than with reputable or popular high officials. And when asked who is the greatest in the kingdom, Jesus said, "Whoever wishes to become great among you must be your servant" (Matt. 20:26). If how we read important texts such as the Bible influences how we read and thus participate in our world, then we might conclude that perhaps Jesus himself read his scriptures with an eye to the supporting cast.

Notes

1. See, for example, William Spohn, *What Are They Saying about Scripture and Ethics?* (New York: Paulist Press, 1983); James Gustafson, *Protestant and Roman Catholic Ethics: Prospects for Rapprochement* (Chicago: University of Chicago Press, 1978); Charles E. Curran and Richard A. McCormick, SJ, eds., *Readings in Moral Theology, No. 4: The Use of Scripture in Moral Theology* (New York: Paulist Press, 1984); Daniel J. Harrington, SJ, and James F. Keenan, SJ, *Jesus and Virtue Ethics: Building Bridges between New Testament Studies and Moral Theology* (Lanham, MD: Sheed & Ward, 2002); Lúcás Chan, *Biblical Ethics in the 21st Century* (New York: Paulist Press, 2013).

2. Many virtue ethicists point out praxis as the path to forming character. See James F. Keenan, SJ, who notes that "virtue ethics . . . sees every moment as the possibility for acquiring or developing a virtue" ("Virtue Ethics," in *Christian Ethics: An Introduction,* ed. Bernard Hoose [Collegeville: Liturgical Press, 1998], 89). Similarly, Lisa Fullam writes, "Since character and habits are formed in the usual everyday events of our lives, it is the daily cultivation of small good habits that counts chiefly. The opportunities for small acts of kindness, of generosity, of justice . . . are found in abundance in daily living." Lisa Fullam, "Virtue Ethics: An Introduction," *Journal of Lutheran Ethics* 6, no. 12 (December 2006).

3. Of the Hebrew words for justice, *ṣᵉdāqāh* has the sense of a gift, of abundance, and generosity and *mišpāṭ* communicates relief, release, and deliverance.

4. Stephen Charles Mott, *Biblical Ethics and Social Change* (Oxford: Oxford University Press, 1982), 61.

5. Adele Berlin, *Poetics and Interpretation of Biblical Narrative* (Winona Lake, IN: Eisenbrauns, 1994), 31–32.

6. Stephen Greenblatt, *Renaissance Self-Fashioning: From More to Shakespeare* (Chicago: University of Chicago Press, 1980); *Shakespearean Negotiations: The Circulation of Social Energy in Renaissance England* (Berkeley: University of California Press, 1988); *Learning to Curse: Essays in Early Modern Culture* (New York: Routledge, 1990); and Catherine Gallagher and Stephen Greenblatt, *Practicing New Historicism* (Chicago: University of Chicago Press, 2000). For the appropriation of New Historicism in biblical studies, see Gina Hens-Piazza, *What Is New Historicism? Guides to Biblical Scholarship* (Minneapolis:

Fortress, 2001); Stephen Moore, ed., *New Historicism: Biblical Interpretation* 5 (Leiden: Brill, 1997); and Daniel Boyarin, *Carnal Israel: Reading Sex in Talmudic Culture*, The New Historicism: Studies in Cultural Poetics 25 (Berkeley: University of California Press, 1993).

7. Linda Hutcheon, *A Poetics of Postmodernism* (New York: Routledge Press, 1988), 168.

8. See Claudia Camp, "The Female Sage in Ancient Israel and the Biblical Wisdom Literature," in *The Sage in Israel and the Ancient Near East*, ed. John G. Gammie and Leo G. Perdue (Winona Lake, IN: Eisenbrauns, 1990), 189. On this point, Camp proceeds to caution against any arbitrary division between "so-called secular wisdom tradition and religious Yahwism" (189).

9. For an extended study of her character, see Gina Hens-Piazza, *Of Methods, Monarchs, and Meanings: A Socio-Rhetorical Approach to Exegesis* (Macon, GA: Macon Press, 1996), 77–121.

10. Stanley Fish, *Is There a Text in This Class? The Authority of Interpretative Communities* (Cambridge, MA: Harvard University Press, 1980), 34.

A Look into *Hesed* in the Old Testament

From the Present Sociocultural Situation of Costa Rica

María Cristina Ventura Campusano

This essay is based on some biblical texts where the term *hesed* is present, and it is written from the perspective of contemporary social-cultural events in Costa Rica. I am conscious of the impossibility of addressing everything about either issue, without forgetting that the focus is on a wider dynamic context, while the aspects selected are just a detail. Moreover, for biblical studies to provide knowledge, we must take complex approaches that allow us to discover internal interactions within the texts.

To better understand this complex approach, the term *hesed* is presented and investigated. Then some data are provided about the context from which the reflection takes place. Here I try to bridge some texts in which the term appears in today's context and try to establish a dialogue with the world of the biblical texts. At the end, I present some reflections and ideas that hopefully weave together the main threads.

Hesed

Hesed has a central place in the Old Testament. The first investigation gave light to the use and meaning of this "rich, old, covenant word."[1] It is being translated as mercy, kindness, and love, among others. The Septuagint uses *oleos*—mercy. From the first known studies, the use of *hesed* is related to the behavior of the persons and their relations among one another.

In the second place, the behavior of the persons is related to God. And in the third place, the behavior of God is related to the people or the theological meaning of *hesed*.[2]

The studies on this term are seen as related to but not limited by other terms such as *berit* (covenant), *mispat* (right), and *sedaqat* (justice). It is also related to *rahamin* (mercy). In this sense, *hesed* is linked to the moral responsibilities, not legal ones, which places the term separate from a contract or an agreement.[3]

To Katharine Sakenfeld, *hesed* is one of the six roots used in situations where two persons or a group of people participate. Some of these roots refer to the adopted attitude for one person next to another or to the relevant attributes to establish interpersonal relations. The roots are: *hesed* (friendly, loving, merciful), *rahan* (beloved, pious, kind, have mercy), *hanan* (kind, benignant, merciful), *aman* (faithful, caring), *ahab* and *shen*; these last two contrast with the others because they are disregarding, negating attitudes. Thus the author shows that *hesed* should be understood linked to other words and always in relation to two persons or parts of a group or community.

In recent works,[4] *hesed* has been studied for its sociocultural importance in the book of Ruth. It is a call to pay attention to sociocultural context and not only to the etymology. Thus it is necessary to take into account the linguistic and sociocultural context where it functions. In the book of Ruth, *hesed* appears three times (Ruth 1:8, 2:20, 3:10), always related to the following characters: Ruth, Boaz, and Yahweh, each as an acting subject. The book may be considered as a story of *hesed* and represents the essence of the alliance between Yahweh and Yahweh's people.

Though there are those who claim that *hesed* is rarely used as a pattern between God and God's people, but rather within families and clans,[5] nevertheless, to speak of *hesed* is to think about relations and interrelations. *Hesed* does not exist without the idea of relationality, which has been confirmed among human beings, or with God in relation to human beings. *Hesed* describes the appropriate behavior between participants when they enter into a relationship that demands mutual duties. For this reason the context of the relationship is important.

Annotations of the Sociocultural Context of Costa Rica in the Present

Costa Rica has been historically a land of great social changes. However, in the present capitalist culture, which is hegemonic in the area, the commodity-memory is commercialized under lots of forms of fetishism. The one that calls for my attention, although it looks normal, is the repetition of expressions assumed popularly but without any critical analysis. "Pura vida" is one of the most popular expressions of the second half of the last century and is part of the identity of the Costa Rican people.[6] It is an expression used by the dominant ideology to make people think that a large number of Costa Ricans believe that the life imposed is good. However, at the beginning of the twenty-first century, some leaders, in the interest of solidarity, thought otherwise and sought to promote social benefits that included the majority of the people.

For the majority, the experience was of inequality, and equity dreams were just prohibited dreams for a great majority of the people.[7] To the people who were poor, marginalized, discriminated against, and excluded from the dream of an equitable society, there remained only "pura vida." This was a "pura vida": empty of solidarity, loyalty, and mercy and, mainly, empty of any social critique, leaving people with nothing but an expression that animates resignation.[8]

To give an example, in the country of "pura vida," 18.7 percent of the African descendants in the population do not have social security; 34.1 percent of the same population do not have their basic needs met; 30 percent of the indigenous population lives in poor conditions and 10 percent in extreme poverty.[9] Besides all of this, the territory of the eight Indigenous peoples is recognized constitutionally, though 43 percent of this territory is occupied by non-Indigenous people. This tells us that the original peoples in Costa Rica have been displaced from their lands and sent to live in low levels of poverty and exclusion.

The Committee of the United Nations for the Elimination of Racial Discrimination (CERD), for example, has expressed regularly its deep concern for the illegal occupation of indigenous lands in Costa Rica since 1999. The social contradictions are present in everyday life. "The conditions of life in Costa Rica have improved in the last fifteen years. But inequality persists as one of the main challenges that affect the country, as a difference between urban and rural counties."[10]

For whom have conditions improved? This is a relevant question. Conditions have not improved for the people living in the rural areas. Results show that the human development index has improved in most of the areas of the Costa Rican territory, but the best qualifications belong to the Grand Metropolitan Area, that is, the central urban area of the country. Costa Rica is one of the countries where inequality has grown more in the last years, at a rate of 0.507.[11]

Other numbers highlight the social contradictions experienced in Costa Rica: the growing number of murders of women as a result of violence[12] and the use of the highest level of pesticides in agriculture (18.2 kilograms per acre), the highest in the world, exposing Costa Ricans constantly to increasing damage to the environment and humankind.[13] Finally, it is impossible not to mention that Costa Rica is the land that receives people coming from different countries from the Caribbean and the Central American region, and from other Latin American countries. At the same time, as it occurs elsewhere, Costa Rica is marked by xenophobia and prejudice, and in many cases these lead to the criminalization of migrants.[14]

The situation described above demands an attentive look into *hesed*, specifically to discover what this biblical *hesed* has to tell us in light of the present concrete situations in Costa Rica. It is worthwhile to remember that the use of a word is conditioned by its meaning and that the meaning could be inferred by the way the word is used in context.[15] Moreover, it can be affirmed that the word is re-created in its senses in a specific context.

Hesed in Dialogue with Everyday Situations: Inside and Outside the Bible

My suggestion is to go back to different biblical texts where the word *hesed* appears and then listen, perceive, and feel what the social place tells us in the encounter. For this, I highlight that *hesed* in its more frequent translations is understood as goodness, kindness, loving goodness, loyalty, and mercy. *Hesed* is pervasive through a great number of texts, from narrative, lyric, wisdom, to prophetic texts. In the Psalms the term appears 131 times.

The Home as a Place of Mercy, Genesis 19

Genesis 19 belongs to the second part of the book, which is divided into two parts: Genesis 1–11 (creation and order of the world) and 12–50 (the story of the fathers and mothers of the people of Israel).[16] Here we focus only on some verses:

"You have already shown favor to your servant, doing me the great mercy of saving my life. But I cannot flee to the hills, or the disaster will overtake and kill me." (Gen. 19:19)

As can be observed in this text, the term *hesed* is translated as "mercy," and it is related to a life that has been protected. This protection has come from God (through two angels in verse 1). This text refers to Lot, who was saved from the destruction of the city. Following the text, it is found that there is no protection in the mountains.

However, there is a small "place" that can be a refuge: "Look, this town ahead is near enough to escape to. It is only a small place. Let me flee there—is it not a small place?—to save my life" (v. 20). I also highlight that the term *napash*, "refuge," in the sense of preserving life, is also part of the context to which *hesed* relates. We do not know why the mountain provides no security. It can be inferred that it is an uninhabited place or that it does not does not belong to Yahweh, or that this place is the place of other gods. In any event, it is found in the text that the place for protecting life is a small village, far away from the city: there Lot can be saved.

The city seems to be a place of danger. There hospitality is denied and the foreigner is at risk (Gen. 19:5) as are the "virgin women" (vv. 6–8). Then, mercy is revealed and produced through the reciprocal and vital relations of the family, exactly what a village can offer. Another aspect of importance in the text cited is the sense of reciprocity that involves *hesed* as both divine quality (as it can be found in Exod. 20:6, 34:6–7; Deut. 7:12) and human quality (Gen. 21:23). In this case, it moves between divine and human.

Interaction is reciprocity, mutual assistance, where there is not only the responsibility to reciprocate, but also to give or to receive. Lot gives refuge; he is hospitable; and this quality allows him to be hosted in order to save his life. But nothing can deny in Genesis 19:5 that there is threat against the young women. This gives us the chance to remember the situation of sexual harassment[17] and the threat that young women undergo, especially in Costa Rica and in other countries of Latin America, as well as the Caribbean and the entire world. It is a case where a woman's body is seen as a sexual object. In those contexts, there is violence, and women and their bodies are under threat.

Having the possibility to observe what is happening to women in the text allows us to confirm that where there is no mercy there is no solidarity, brotherly or sisterly. Then, it is urgent to protect life as well as the life of the planet. The hospitality of Lot in Genesis 19:2–3—"He said, 'Please, my lords, come aside into your servant's house for the night, and bathe your feet; you can get up early to continue your journey.' He prepared a banquet for them, baking unleavened bread, and they dined."—shows that hospitality and mercy are related. Lot, despite being a *gur* ("foreigner, stranger"), is open to weave a relationship where mercy reigns, because he is able to "give shelter," "receive," and "feed" people. It is an action that goes beyond the norms and provokes those who do not agree with this kind of attitude: "'Stand back! This man,' they said, 'came here as a resident alien, and now he dares to give orders! We will treat you worse than them!'" (v. 9).

Moreover, it is interesting to pay attention to the paradox that can be revealed when you choose to act from or with mercy in a context ruled by norms that impede relationships with those who are different—as it is in the text under study. Lot's merciful action threatens his daughters' life and his. However, acting with mercy is related to an ethic that gives priority to life and, at the same time, restores those old practices that pertain to the identity of the people.

This argument cannot ignore that patriarchal societies relativize norms when the lives of women or those of any other human group are threatened by violence. In this sense, the urgency of mercy by both God with humans and by humans among one another needs to stop violence. But mercy must also stop taking away the land from indigenous peoples. The land is what gives people a sense of identity. Appealing to divine mercy, from the concrete issue of the possession of land, is to appeal for justice and the right that the original peoples have. This is an example of how justice and mercy come together.[18]

Another important element has to deal with the threats to big cities. Thus, the big city in the text is destroyed: "God made a fire rain over Sodom and Gomorrah" (vv. 24–25). But before this happened, the text narrator made sure to explain that the destruction was due to the way the inhabitants lived (Gen. 18:20). It could be inferred that "place" is important when talking about mercy; such a place must receive another person (a foreigner), where the life of a woman or man, of any human being, is protected. And, mainly, where there persist threats (oppression, marginalization, dominance), the action of mercy ought to not only reveal those situations, but also obstruct their emergence or their success. So, insisting on *hesed* (mercy) concerns not only an attitude from God, but also provides an impulse for humans to develop new relations in everyday life.

The Mercy of God as an Impulse to Build a New Relationship, Numbers 14:19

Let us analyze Numbers 14:19, where *hesed* is the mercy of God with the people who protest for having had to pass through the desert: "Pardon, then, the iniquity of this people in keeping with your great kindness, even as you have forgiven them from Egypt until now." In the text, God in anger threatens to eliminate the people for their protest over the conditions in the desert. Life in the desert is hard because of the dangers that exist there. These could contribute to the failure of the project of having a new life, for the land represents a different life condition.

People can learn to live differently, in other types of relations. However, it is difficult to adapt to a new way of living.[19] It is necessary to have Yahweh's mercy in order to acquire that learning, and to keep the reconstruction of the history where God is always present. In this sense, God's annoyance with the people's complaint is not so much a negation of their resistance but an appeal for them to advance to the new, that is, to enter the Promised Land. This makes possible the restoration of God with God's people.

What happens to the people in the desert leads me to reflect on the situation of many migrants in Costa Rica. Their resistance must be focused on building new relations that allow them to live with dignity. That these people must migrate from their original land shows a lack of opportunities and the inequality they have lived. God wants the people to discover the importance of crossing the desert, that "the land in the middle or the land that does not belong to anyone" can be understood as the land that gives them the opportunity to restore their dignity. It is not right, then, to resist having this opportunity.[20] In this context, *hesed* is the impulse to continue the search.

The Mercy of Women: An Impulse to Attain Abundant Life, Ruth 3:10

Ruth is a text often present in the studies and readings about women and men in our communities: friendship, mercy, the power of women among women and men; these can be some of the emphatic ways of reading the text in various contexts. There is an emphasis on migrant families, widows, and, among all, the presence of mercy manifesting solidarity and the fulfillment of a law that protects them; "the book of Ruth speaks of food, fullness, merciful love."[21]

We should grasp the importance of the desert in revealing mercy. In this sense, Ruth 3:10 calls my attention: "Boaz said, 'May the Lord bless you, my daughter! You have been even more loyal now than before in not going after the young men, whether poor or rich.'" We should observe that in Ruth, mercy does not first come from God, but from a woman (Ruth) favoring another woman (Naomi). Still we should note that the mercy of Ruth is backed by the mercy of God, granted that it is through the law of the right of redemption (2:20–21). Ruth's responsibility, in the middle of a chaos prompted by death, is recognized in her decision to carry out the project that also includes Naomi.[22]

Naomi recognized that Ruth as well as Orfá (her other daughter-in-law) acted with *hesed* toward her and her dead sons. This suggests the mercy of the women toward women and men goes beyond the expected. Acting with mercy guarantees descendants (4:13). But it also allows the revelation of the power of a foreign woman to protect the life of another woman and to be recognized by other women (4:14). Mercy breaks through border barriers and opens to the celebration of the life of the people!

This celebration is part of the memory of the faithfulness of God with God's people. It is important to remember that *hesed* is related to *berit* (alliance, pact, agreement, or contract). As it has been said elsewhere in this essay, it is not only bequeathed in the covenant but is found wherever mutual efforts are expressed. Still, God's covenant is based on remembering that mutual aid: "Now, if you obey me completely and keep my covenant, you will be my treasured possession among all peoples, though all the earth is mine" (Exod. 19:5).

From there, the Law affirms: "You shall not oppress or afflict a resident alien. You shall not wrong any widow or orphan. If ever you wrong them and they cry out to me, I will surely listen to their cry" (Exod. 22:20–22). This command from God is manifested in Ruth and in her merciful relationship with her mother-in-law, Naomi, and the recognition as a foreigner by Boaz and the village women. Mercy, loyalty, and fidelity demand a pact and, at the same time, are born from one.

The text of Ruth not only makes us remember the Covenant with God, but it is important to show that the term *hesed* is a synonym of *raham* (to have mercy, merciful, love, and compassion, pity). It comes from the same root that *rehem* does (womb, maternal womb). That is why we find women having sensitivity to feel it and to act with mercy.

It is true that times and contexts are different and that many centuries separate us from biblical times. I recognize that the life-and-death experiences of women today resonate with those of women from the past, especially when they have had to invent or create possibilities for solidarity to take place. For instance, Ruth's idea is to give mercy to other women and to the community. Without mercy life is wasteful. Today motherhood is not always the way to celebrate life, especially when the possibility of conceiving can be trapped by violence and death. In this sense, the text of Ruth gives us the chance to go out and create proposals opposed to violence and against the death of young girls, women, and men.

These life proposals, according to the prophets, are continuously motivated and guided by God. So, it is interesting that the prophet attributes the terms *raham/ rehem* and *hesed* to the relational qualities of God (Mic. 7:18–20), and to the just and merciful ways of acting that God expects from God's people (Mic. 6:8; Hosea 12:7).

We can affirm at this point that *hesed* in the Old Testament opens a world of possibilities for us to think of life in and out of these texts. As it has been said through the essay, there are many texts that have mercy as a central message; the texts chosen are samples and an invitation to continue studying the topic deeply.

My reflection comes to the following conclusions:

- Mercy is both a human and a divine attitude that reveals the brotherly and sisterly face of the other. It leads to community building.
- Mercy overcomes the challenges and dangers of the "deserts" of life, allowing instead the realization of individual and collective dreams.

- Mercy is the expression of family relations and of reciprocity: there is no mercy where there is indifference, as in the "city" (Lot's text); as a contrary, it is expressed in the "village," that is, where family relations are evident.
- Mercy is based on the mutual acceptance between persons, as a necessary condition to overcome the sense of the foreign and to generate the familiar.
- Mercy leads to fruitfulness, transforming a situation of death into one of life, as in the case of Ruth.
- God's mercy awaits the mercy and justice of God's people.

And finally, mercy is the way both to peace and to building a new world. Jesus tells us in Luke 6:36, "Be merciful, as your heavenly Father is merciful." This means that mercy is the concrete translation of the way God specifically acts. To be merciful is to be like God, projecting and unifying the human and the divine. And this is the way to build the kingdom of God.

Notes

1. Gordon R. Clark, "The Word '*Hesed*' in the Hebrew Bible," *Journal for the Study of the Old Testament,* Supplement 157 (Sheffield: JSOT Press, 1993), 17.

2. Ibid., 18, referring to Nelson Glueck, *Hesed in the Bible* (New York: KTAV, 1968).

3. Ibid., 22, referring to Katharine D. Sakenfeld, *The Meaning of Hesed in the Hebrew Bible: A New Inquiry* (Eugene: Wipf and Stock, 1978).

4. Justin Manuel Alfredo, *The Book of Ruth from a Lomwe Perspective: Ḥesed and Ikharari* (Bamberg: University of Bamberg Press, 2013).

5. Ibid., 24, referring to H. J. Stoebe, "*Hesed*," in *Theological Lexicon of the Old Testament,* ed. Ernst Jenni and Claus Westermann (Peabody, MA: Hendrickson, 1997), 2:449–64.

6. "Pura vida" is from the 1956 Mexican film *Pura Vida,* directed by Gilberto Martínez Solares. The expression began to be used in Costa Rica in the 1950s. In 1990 it was incorporated into the Costarriqueñismos dictionary. See www.informador.com.

7. In 1942 a constitutional reform, with social guarantees and a Labour Code, was achieved. Throughout the second half of the twentieth century, there was growth in different cultural contexts, for example, in education. These achievements have been lost with the consolidation of the state, led by the agro-export oligarchy of "coffee producers," which began to dominate the entire nation. See Arnoldo Mora, *Historia del pensamiento costarricense* (San José, Costa Rica: EUNED, 1992).

8. Álvaro José Martínez. "Costa Rica ¡Pura Vida!" See http://revista-amauta.org.

9. X National Census of Population and VI National Census of Homes, 2011.

10. José Pablo Román, "Desigualdad entre hombres y mujeres afecta desarrollo cantonal: Cantones del centro del país tienen mayor Índice de Desarrollo Humano," in *Semanario Universidad* (San José, Costa Rica: UCR, 2016), http://semanariouniversidad.ucr.cr.

11. See the April 2015 report from the Economic Commission for Latin America and the Caribbean.

12. Between January 2011 to June 2015, 119 women were killed by domestic violence in a country of 4.5 million people that professes to be one of the most consolidated democ-

racies in Latin America. Costa Rica abolished its army with the Constitution of 1949. It is the third safest country in the Americas, after Chile and Uruguay, according to the Global Peace Index, and the American country with the greatest press freedom (nineteenth position worldwide), according to Reporters without Borders. It is also the first Latin American state to abolish sport hunting by a Popular Initiative Law. See www.feminicidio.net; www.nacion.com.

13. Vinicio Chacon, "Ambientalistas y gobierno en polémica por reglamento de plaguicidas," in *Semanario Universidad* (San José, Costa Rica: UCR, 2016). See semanariouniversidad.ucr.cr.

14. Carlos Sandoval García, ed., *El mito roto inmigración y emigración en costa rica* (San José, Costa Rica: Editorial UCR, 2007).

15. Robert Henry Robins, *Lingüística general: Estudio introductorio*, 4th ed., trans. Pilar Gómez Bedate and Eva Mendieta-Lombardo (Madrid: Gredos, 1995).

16. There is consensus among scholars on the division of Genesis into two major parts. See Susan Niditch, "Genesis," in *Women's Bible Commentary*, ed. Carol A. Newsom and Sharon H. Ringe (Louisville, KY: Westminster John Knox Press, 1998); Walter Brueggemann, *An Introduction to the Old Testament* (Louisville, KY: Westminster John Knox Press, 2003).

17. See Law 7476—against sexual harassment in Costa Rica.

18. Faced with this reality, we can remember the call of Pope Francis, standing with indigenous peoples, to unite our voices so that these peoples, threatened in their identity and their own existence, will be respected (Pope Francis, message July 2016).

19. There is consensus among some scholars that the book of Numbers is a text of the Priestly tradition, which begins in Exodus 25 and continues through Leviticus. Chapter 14 is part of the second block of the book, which reflects in an imaginary way on the crisis that the people encounter in the desert, by their inability to adapt to the new situation of displacement, caused by the exile of the sixth century. See Brueggemann, *Introduction to the Old Testament*, 75–83.

20. This is an invitation to leave the static, what always is and what never has an exit. It is a call to value the chaos (order-disorder). This leads me to consider not only the creation, from the religious point of view, but also in dialogue with the sciences; we can understand the universe itself not as static, when the apparent order is disorder, and we can move away from the balance in its evolutionary movement. "The universe changes over time, and has evolved from a simple condition to a more complex condition." For further reading, see John Brockman, *La tercera cultura—más allá de la revolución científica*, 2nd ed., trans. Ambrosio García (Barcelona: Tusquets Editores, 2000), 29.

21. Amy-Jill Levine, "Ruth," in *Women's Bible Commentary,* ed. Carol A. Newsom and Sharon H. Ringe (Louisville, KY: Westminster John Knox Press, 1998), 84.

22. Tirsa Ventura, "Salidas, muertes y regresos: Desde la sutileza del caos al resurgir de las historias de mujeres en Rut," *Pasos* 140 (San José: Costa Rica: DEI, 2008): 22–29.

THE MEANING OF THE DECALOGUE FOR CONTEMPORARY MORAL THEOLOGY

José Manuel Caamaño López

Hugh of Saint Victor wrote, "The whole sacred Scripture is one book and this book is Christ."[1] This statement, made by a Saxon theologian of the twelfth century, reflects, in a way, the same conclusion that the moral theology of the twentieth century has arrived at as the core of all the attempts at renewal that continue to this date—namely, that moral theology has to be nourished more and more from the Scriptures without losing its eminently Christocentric character. This is something that had been underlined by Vatican II in its decree *Optatam Totius* (no. 16). With good reason, biblical theology has supported a move over the past few centuries to take Christian morality out of the dead-end street on which, due to the casuistry born from Trent, it had been located, when excessive focus was placed on the dispute of the "moral systems" around the Law, sin, and the role of conscience. This focus brought about its degradation into a minimalist morality rather than a call to perfection.

At the same time, we know that the uses of Scripture can be diverse. We can corroborate this, not only throughout the history of Christianity and of theology in general, but also, and in particular, in its use in the shaping of moral theology.[2] The advances made in exegesis and biblical hermeneutics have been so important and relevant. They have shown not only the shortcomings of literal interpretations of the sacred texts but also the richness of other interpretations that enable us to discern the fundamental message that such texts intend to offer and the light they can shed on the problems posed by each historic moment. Because of this, from the Catholic perspective, the document published by the Pontifical Biblical Commission in 1993 titled "The Interpretation of the Bible in the Church" is so important, because it urges, on the one hand, that exegetes prepare the ground for the moralists and, on the other hand, that they consider the moral evolution that has happened that views Scripture as leading to a "discernment that takes into account the necessary progress of the moral conscience."[3]

All of this has enabled us to arrive at the conclusion that Scripture is neither a handbook of morality, nor, as Bernhard Häring expressed it, a "catalog of norms,"[4] despite its being the primary source of Christian morality and of offering a specific sense to confront the problems that affect the human experience in each concrete context, from a faith perspective. This is how Clodovis Boff expressed it:

> The Scriptures do not offer us formulas that we can copy or techniques that we can apply. It can offer orientation, models, types, directives, prin-

ciples, inspirations, and ultimately, the elements that enable us to acquire for ourselves an *hermeneutical competence*, that allows us the possibility to judge for ourselves, according to the *sense of Christ* or *in accordance with his Spirit,* the new and unexpected situations that we face every day.[5]

We have to recognize, however, that there are specific biblical texts whose literalness has significantly marked the Christian tradition, particularly regarding morality. It is precisely here that we can find the relevance that the Decalogue has always had, in its different versions, that frequently disregarded the spirit that Saint Jerome expressed in his commentary on the Epistle to the Galatians: "The Gospel does not consist of words, but of their meaning; not on the surface, but on their essence; not on the pages of sermons but in the roots of reason."[6] In any case this is a very important text in the Scripture itself that, furthermore, has more or less configured—even more clearly than the beatitudes—Christian morality through the centuries, especially because believers, theologians, and pastors of the church have seen a normative synthesis of God's will concerning humanity reflected in its words, a will that Christians should abide by, with a spirit of obedience, in order to firmly walk along the road to salvation.[7] There is no wonder then that Scripture is described as the "Ten Words of YHWH," even though it was only in the Patristic era—probably with Clement of Alexandria and Irenaeus—that the Greek term "dekálogos"[8] was introduced.

In any case, it can be said that in the Decalogue one can find a late compilation of Israel's Law. At the same time it constitutes one of the more advanced expressions of the Covenant between God and the people of Israel, expressed through the binomial gift-Law.[9] It is appropriate to note the relevance of this, since if there is a key of the morality of the Old Testament it is, without a doubt, the category of "Covenant." This is in spite of all the problems that it contains, which have generated controversies in biblical theology beginning with the studies of Julius Wellhausen at the end of the nineteenth century,[10] later reflected in the different views of subsequent biblical scholars such as Werner Eichrodt, Martin Noth, Albrecht Alt, Gerhard von Rad, George Mendenhall, Dennis J. McCarthy, and Ernst Kutsch.

It is clear that here we are not interested in the issue of the historicity of the Covenant, but only in its theological meaning in light of Christian morality and concretely in its relation to the Decalogue. The scholar Klaus Koch had remarked that the originality of Israelite morality is not its content, but its foundation in the unexpected relationship between God and the people, so that "all the religious and moral life of Israel is based upon the Covenant, a mutual relationship of belonging, with rights and duties that are born of this solidarity. This key theme, that drives all the moral and religious life of the chosen people, serves as the foundation of the history of salvation and consequently of the whole structure of biblical morality."[11] Unfortunately, it is impossible in this brief space to provide an exhaustive analysis of the Decalogue, nor do I intend to. I will only delve into what I consider to be the main elements of this text, based on the spirit in which it was conceived, so that it can continue to be significant for current moral theology.

The Text of the Decalogue

The Decalogue is narrated twice in the Scripture. First, we find it in Exodus 20:2–17, which was included in the Elohist narrative of the revelation on Sinai, and the second is found in Deuteronomy 5:6–21 as part of the Deuteronomic Code. It is worth presenting the complete version of both here.[12]

Exodus 20:2–17	*Deuteronomy 5:6–21*
[2]I am the Lord your God, who brought you out of the land of Egypt, out of the house of slavery. [3]You shall have no other gods before me. [4]You shall not make for yourself a carved image, or any likeness of anything that is in heaven above, or that is in the earth beneath, or that is in the water under the earth. [5]You shall not bow down to them or serve them, for I the Lord your God am a jealous God, visiting the iniquity of the fathers on the children to the third and the fourth generation of those who hate me, [6]but showing steadfast love to thousands of those who love me and keep my commandments. [7]You shall not take the name of the Lord your God in vain, for the Lord will not hold him guiltless who takes his name in vain. [8]Remember the Sabbath day, to keep it holy. [9]Six days you shall labor, and do all your work, [10]but the seventh day is a Sabbath to the Lord your God. On it you shall not do any work, you, or your son, or your daughter, your male servant, or your female servant, or your livestock, or the sojourner who is within your gates. [11]For in six days the Lord made heaven and earth, the sea, and all that	[6]I am the Lord your God, who brought you out of the land of Egypt, out of the house of slavery. [7]You shall have no other gods before me. [8]You shall not make for yourself a carved image, or any likeness of anything that is in heaven above, or that is on the earth beneath, or that is in the water under the earth. [9]You shall not bow down to them or serve them; for I the Lord your God am a jealous God, visiting the iniquity of the fathers on the children to the third and fourth generation of those who hate me, [10]but showing steadfast love to thousands of those who love me and keep my commandments. [11]You shall not take the name of the Lord your God in vain, for the Lord will not hold him guiltless who takes his name in vain. [12]Observe the Sabbath day, to keep it holy, as the Lord your God commanded you. [13]Six days you shall labor and do all your work, [14]but the seventh day is a Sabbath to the Lord your God. On it you shall not do any work, you or your son or your daughter or your male servant or your female servant, or your ox or your donkey or any of your livestock, or the sojourner who is within your gates, that your

that is in them, and rested on the seventh day. Therefore the Lord blessed the Sabbath day and made it holy. [12]Honor your father and your mother, that your days may be long in the land that the Lord your God is giving you. [13]You shall not murder. [14]You shall not commit adultery. [15]You shall not steal. [16]You shall not bear false witness against your neighbor. [17]You shall not covet your neighbor's house; you shall not covet your neighbor's wife, or his male servant, or his female servant, or his ox, or his donkey, or anything that is your neighbor's.

male servant and your female servant may rest as well as you. [15]You shall remember that you were a slave in the land of Egypt, and the Lord your God brought you out from there with a mighty hand and an outstretched arm. Therefore the Lord your God commanded you to keep the Sabbath day. [16]Honor your father and your mother, as the Lord your God commanded you, that your days may be long, and that it may go well with you in the land that the Lord your God is giving you. [17]You shall not murder. [18]And you shall not commit adultery. [19]And you shall not steal. [20]And you shall not bear false witness against your neighbor. [21]And you shall not covet your neighbor's wife. And you shall not desire your neighbor's house, his field, or his male servant, or his female servant, his ox, or his donkey, or anything that is your neighbor's.

Beyond the problems that a literal critique of biblical theology faces,[13] it is clear that the Decalogue has had a fundamental importance in the religious and ethical conscience of Israel, something that has been transmitted over the centuries and that was assumed by Christianity from its beginnings to this day. In fact, numerous authors present Christian morality from the perspective of the Decalogue, including the *Catechism of the Catholic Church*, which uses it as the guiding text to present the fundamental part of morality (nos. 2052–57): "The ten commandments, in expressing the fundamental duties of humans towards God and neighbor, reveal in their essential content serious obligations. These are basically immutable and their obligation is valid always and everywhere. No one is exempt from them. The ten commandments are engraved in the heart of men" (no. 2072). Now we have to ask ourselves: What is the ultimate meaning of the Decalogue? What is its real effect in Christian life? To answer this, we have to point to some fundamental aspects that will enable an updated reading of the Decalogue, so that it may continue to be a significant text for current moral theology.

Fundamental Aspects of the
Decalogue for Moral Theology

It is a known fact that the Decalogue is not exceptional with respect to its concrete contents,[14] since we can find lists of prohibitions that precede Exodus and Deuteronomy, but rather to the extent that its precepts were identified with the contents of natural law. It is enough to mention, for example, the Hammurabi Code or the Egyptian Book of the Dead, among others. Thus, the novelty of the Decalogue, more than its concrete commandments, is the context in which it is found, as the summit of divine election and the Covenant of God with the people of Israel—that is to say, in the internal articulation it possesses, where the rational dimension is integrated with the theological perspective. Thus, in relation to the issues of interest to us, we can point to some elements for a significant and current understanding of the Ten Commandments, elements that we can only outline here.

The Decalogue as a Relational Framework

The first element to highlight is that the Decalogue is a text that presents the relationship between humans and God and their relationship with one another. This gives a normative character to the act of creation that, on the one hand, comprises the created beings in an original relation with God, and, on the other, also in relation to others, from an otherness that in a way counterbalances autonomy (individuality).[15] In other words, the Law is the consequence of the interrelationship that exists between different free subjects, and, as a consequence, it has a vertical dimension (with respect to God) and a horizontal dimension (with respect to others).

In fact, the commandments have traditionally been differentiated between the commandments of the first part (that refer to God) and those of the second part (that refer to our neighbor). In this sense, the Law derives from the complementarity that exists with respect to those like us and where we find the limit of the subject. For this reason, the Hebrew concept of justice (צֶדֶק) refers not only to a relationship with norms but also to the relationships between people, whose transgression will be the basis, for example, of prophetic denunciations.

The Law as the Answer to a Gift

The second relevant element of the Decalogue is that the Law is the direct consequence of a prior gift from God: "I am the Lord your God, who brought you out of the land of Egypt, out of the house of slavery" (Deut. 5:6). Thus, the grace precedes any other precept and the normative discourse does not begin with the statement of the imperatives, but with the reminder of a prior gift from God.[16]

Thus, it is also a reminder of liberation and of the path to follow to avoid becoming slaves again: "God acted first, the Israelite responded."[17] This means that the Law by itself has no meaning, but only when it is linked to the Covenant offered by YHWH. Thus Martin Noth remarks that "in the Old Testament's tradition the concepts of 'covenant' and 'law' appear closely linked, . . . What this tradition remarkably achieved was to express the objective relation between 'covenant' and 'law,' even if it was done by placing in a single act what had developed over time, and within the lasting organization that originated from this act."[18]

The New Horizon of the Decalogue

The third element to highlight refers to the norms themselves. As we had advanced earlier, their novelty is neither their number nor the prohibitions nor the concrete mandates contained in them (at least for those in the second part), which have an apodictic and extensive character anyway.[19] What is more significant is the link established in the Decalogue between the precepts and prohibitions of the first group with respect to the second, or better still, the introduction of the commandments that refer to our neighbor within the dynamics of the Covenant with YHWH.

Thus, the Decalogue has a unitary dimension that is lost when the two types of precepts are separated. In fact, some authors, such as J. R. Busto, maintain that

> contrary to our traditional representation, the precepts are not divided into two segments according to whether their content makes reference to the relation of men with God or with his neighbor. The reason why there are two groups is due to the fact that it is assumed that the context of the covenant is that it is a bilateral contract, and that two copies should be written for each party to the contract, so that each could keep a copy in their respective sanctuary.[20]

Morality is thus framed in the Decalogue, within the religious perspective, as two inseparable dimensions, where the division of faith and morality is impossible. This is something that encompasses the whole biblical world. In a way, an element that will be essential in the New Testament is foreshadowed here—the link between loving God and loving neighbor, which appears also in Leviticus 19:18–34, although not to the radical extent to which Jesus will extend this mandate to the love of enemies.

The Internalization of Morality in the Decalogue

The fourth element relates to the prohibitions that refer to other human beings. Both Exodus 20:13–16 and Deuteronomy 5:17–20 formulate brief prohibitions that intend to regulate human behavior in relation to external acts.[21] The last commandment in Exodus 20:13–16 and Deuteronomy 5:17–20, however, introduces a very relevant element for moral theology. We refer here to the verb "covet" or "desire" (*hamad* in Hebrew and *epithymeo* in the Septuagint)[22] that produces an interesting development with respect to the previous commandments, which had to do with observable behavior. Now the Decalogue enters also the scope of human interiority, in the deepest intention of the people. With this the normative limits exceed formal legality and reach to the heart, since mere external obedience is not sufficient, as Jesus stated regarding pharisaism. In other words, our relationship with others radically involves our human conscience.

What the Decalogue tells us is that it is not enough to obey the Law, but it is also key to properly sort out the intent of our acts. Thus, great importance is conceded to the interior dimension in the scope of morality, something that is always current, because not only does it advance to the root of the Law itself, but it confronts us with ourselves and with the always menacing dangers of false pretenses and moral hypocrisy.

This does not mean that the concepts of "covet" and "desire" refer to a mere internal and subjective feeling; they also imply the act to appropriate what we covet or desire, that is to say, that both the desire and the action are two faces of the same coin, something that Hebrew verbs that refer to feelings tend to express. For example, love is a feeling, but it is, at the same time, more than a feeling, in that it demands a practical verification of its authentic reality.[23] Even so, morality affects and is understood not only from external acts but from the whole of the acting person. It is so much so that Gerhard von Rad went so far as to say that this penetration of the divine Law into the heart is really a specific element of Israelite tradition that is not found in numerous existing codes in other traditions, something which is well expressed in Deuteronomy 30:14: "The word is very near you; it is in your mouth and in your heart so that you may obey it."[24]

The Decalogue's Reception in Jesus of Nazareth

This last statement is important because, even if we can only offer a brief indication here, it offers a key to understanding Jesus' attitude with respect to the Law. Let's remind ourselves what he himself would say: "Do not think that I have come to abolish the law or the Prophets; I have not come to abolish them but to fulfill them" (Matt. 5:17). And later on, in his answer to a rich young man regarding what he had to do to attain eternal life, he points out compliance with the commandments, but he adds: "If you want to be perfect, go, sell your possessions and give to the poor. . . . Then come, follow me" (Matt. 19:21). Thus, the commandments are introduced within the scope of God's kingdom, an authentic interpretative key of the morality of the New Testament whose point of entry is following Jesus.

Furthermore, as Jesus himself affirmed: "The law and the prophets were proclaimed until John. Since that time, the good news of the kingdom of God is being preached" (Luke 16:16). Thus, it cannot be said that the Law is erased or eliminated; it is placed in an appropriate place, since salvation is not attained primarily through compliance with norms but through the kingdom. This is well expressed in the Sermon on the Mount: "Unless your righteousness surpasses that of the Pharisees and the teachers of the law, you will certainly not enter the kingdom of heaven" (Matt. 5:20). We can state that Jesus' preaching on morality is not a protest against compliance with the Law and norms, but against a form of legalism that runs the risk of making the rule absolute when, instead, it should be subordinated to the kingdom and to the salvation of the person,[25] genuinely the supreme norm of the life of the church. That is why he confronts legalistic behaviors both in the scope of cultic and ritual practices and in moral life (Matt. 23:23ff.). His attitude regarding the Sabbath is perhaps one of the best-known examples.

Jesus' own rereading of the Decalogue in various places can be understood in the same way, something that is clearly expressed by his known antithetical statements "you have heard . . . but I tell you." Suffice it to quote two of those present in the Sermon on the Mount: "*You have heard* that it was said to your ancestors: You shall not kill; and whoever kills will be liable to judgment. *But I say to you*, whoever is angry with his brother will be liable to judgment"; "*You have heard* that it was said: You shall not commit adultery. *But I say to you*, everyone who looks at a woman with lust has already committed adultery with her in his heart" (Matt. 5:21–22, 27–28). With these words Jesus does not refute the Law, but he overcomes legalism to penetrate the core of morality itself, in the deepest part of the person, introducing, as the Decalogue had done before, concepts that affect human interiority such as "to be angry" and "adultery in the heart." The intention is to go to the root from which the acts flow and where the Law is but the external dimension of the fundamental option and the form of life marked by the internalization of the following of Jesus and his commitment to the Kingdom. In a way we can say that in Jesus, with his rereading of the Decalogue, we find what Benedict XVI called the "pedagogy of desire," which is never satisfied with what has been achieved but always moves beyond legal observance to seeking to be authentically moral: "I desire mercy, not sacrifice" (Matt. 9:13, 1:7).

It is clear that the Decalogue is a text that cannot be appropriately understood without taking into consideration the entire Old Testament as well as the preaching of Jesus. From what has been presented here, I have synthesized some fundamental aspects of Christian moral theology, fundamentally based as it is on the relationship between humanity and God and in the relationships among all people. This is why many of the prophetic contributions in the areas of justice, mercy, and justification are only summons to reestablish relations that for various reasons have been broken at any time, with God and others, given that, ultimately, from a Christian perspective, the relations with one are inseparable from the other. This has been well expressed in the text on the final judgment in Matthew 25:40: "What you did for the least of my brothers, you did for me."

The Law (the Torah) can only be understood from that Covenant (*berith*) previously offered by God to the people of Israel and to the whole of humanity.

Thus, the call to conversion or to solidarity, where morality is properly integrated within the dynamics of the faith and salvation, in the dynamics of the kingdom of God annunciated by Jesus: "You believe that God is one; you do well. Even the demons believe—and shudder." (James 2:19) or faith "if it has no works, is dead" (James 2:17). Thus, the author Pierre Grelot wrote that the most important aspect of the Old Testament is not the contents of the moral Law, but "the structure of the relationship between God and men, a normal framework in which the content of the moral law will be progressively revealed."[26]

Translated by Thomas Brennan, SDB

Notes

1. *De arca Noe*, II, 8 (PL 176, 642).
2. William Spohn, *What Are They Saying about Scripture and Ethics?* (New York: Paulist Press, 1995).
3. Pontificia Comisión Bíblica, *La interpretación de la Biblia en la Iglesia* (Madrid: PPC, 2000), 107. See also Julio Luis Martínez and José Manuel Caamaño, *Moral fundamental: Bases teológicas del discernimiento ético* (Santander: Sal Terrae, 2014), 92ff. (see Decalogue, 156–63).
4. Bernhard Häring, *Free and Faithful in Christ* (Seabury: New York, 1978), 7.
5. Clovis Boff, *Teología de lo político: Sus mediaciones* (Salamanca: Sígueme, 1980), 279.
6. San Jerónimo, Comentario a los Gálatas, 1, 11 (PL 26, 347).
7. For a hermeneutical approach see André Wénin, "Le décalogue, révélation de Dieu et chemin de Bonheur," *Revue théologique de Louvain* 25 (1994): 145–82. For a complete study from the moral theological perspective see Yiu Sing Lúcás Chan, *The Ten Commandments and the Beatitudes* (Lanham, MD: Rowman and Littlefield, 2012).
8. Giuseppe Barbaglio, "Decálogo (Teología moral)," in *Nuevo diccionario de Teología moral*, ed. Francesco Compagnoni, Giannino Piana, and Salvatore Privitera (Madrid: Paulinas, adapt. Esp. de M. Vidal, 1992), 310–26.
9. Jean-Louis Ska, *El camino y la casa: Itinerarios bíblicos* (Estella: Verbo Divino, 2005), 161–91. Additionally, one should consider the relationship of the indicative with the imperative (of great importance in the Decalogue): Andrés Torres Queiruga, *Recuperar la salvación* (Santander: Sal Terrae, 1995), 51–59.
10. Julius Wellhausen, *Prolegomena zur Geschichte Israels* (Berlin: Walter de Gruyter, 1983); Ernest W. Nicholson, *God and His People: Covenant and Theology in the Old Testament* (Oxford: Oxford University Press, 1986); Dennis J. McCarthy, "Covenant in the Old Testament: The Present State of Inquiry," *Catholic Biblical Quarterly* 27 (1965): 217–41.
11. Cited by Francisco Lage, "Ley y alianza: Autonomía de la ética en el pensamiento del Antiguo Testamento," in *Perspectivas de moral bíblica*, Instituto Superior de Ciencias Morales (Madrid: PS Editorial, 1984), 11. See also José Luis Sicre, *Introducción al Antiguo Testamento* (Estella: Verbo Divino, 2000), esp. chap. 7 on the Law and the Decalogue, 117ff.
12. See also Exod. 34:10–28, which presents the renewal of the Covenant with Moses. Another version is found in Lev. 19:3–4, 11–13.

13. Werner H. Schmidt, *Introducción al Antiguo Testamento* (Salamanca: Sígueme, 1990), 146–52. For a more extensive perspective, see A. González Lamadrid, *Las tradiciones históricas de Israel* (Estella: Verbo Divino, 2000), 23–65; Joseph Blenkinsopp, *El Pentateuco* (Estella: Verbo Divino, 1999), 266–70 (for a general perspective, 233–91); Felix García López, *El Pentateuco* (Estella: Verbo Divino, 2003), 191–97, 291ff.; idem, *El Decálogo* (Estella: Verbo Divino, 1994). G. Johannes Botterweck, "El decálogo: Estudio de su estructura e história literarias," *Concilium* 5 (1965): 62–87.

14. It is clearly stated: the commandments are not original to the Bible. See Gerhard von Rad, *Teología del Antiguo Testamento I. Teología de las tradiciones históricas de Israel* (Salamanca: Sígueme, 1972), 247ff.

15. See P. Fernández Castelao, "3. Antropología teológica," in *La lógica de la fe: Manual de Teología Dogmática*, ed. Angel Cordovilla (Madrid: Upcomillas, 2013), 187ff.; Juan Luis Ruiz de la Peña, *Imagen de Dios: Antropología teológica fundamental* (Cantabria: Sal Terrae, 1988), 47–53.

16. Enrique Sanz Giménez-Rico, *Ya en el principio* (Madrid: Universidad Pontificia Commillas, 2008), 87. Interestingly, an author like Meeks holds that the commandments "are more signs than laws": Wayne A. Meeks, *El mundo moral de los primeros cristianos* (Bilbao: Desclée de Brouwer, 1992), 110.

17. González Lamadrid, *Las tradiciones históricas de Israel*, 60. In fact, this is the pattern that many precepts of the OT follow. Jürgen Moltmann goes on to say that the commandments are the ethical face of the promise and obedience to them is the fruit of hope, which, rather than fixed rules, direct us toward future compliance (Jürgen Moltmann, *Teología de la esperanza* [Salamanca: Sígueme, 1969], 159–60).

18. Martin Noth, *Estudios sobre Antiguo Testamento* (Salamanca: Sígueme, 1985), 52.

19. This points to the now classic distinction between causuisty and apodictic laws, that is, between those concerning individual cases, and those that rise above cases becoming general and absolute principles. In the Decalogue the laws belong to this second type. See Garcia López, *El Decálogo*, 10ff. We must remember that although normally we speak of commandments, most of them are prohibitions.

20. José Ramón Busto, "Las obras en el Antiguo y en el Nuevo Testamento," in *Libertad de verdad. Sobre la "Veritatis splendor,"* ed. Juan Antonio Martínez Camino (Madrid: San Pablo, 1995), 139 (cf. 131–48).

21. Professor Bruna Costacurta has done a provocative analysis of this in her course on biblical anthropology at the Gregorian University in Rome.

22. García López, *El Decálogo*, 46–49. Evidently, the Greek concept used in the Septuagint does not have the same scope as the Hebrew, given that it refers only to interior concupiscence.

23. Ibid., 46–47.

24. von Rad, *Teología del Antiguo Testamento I*, 256.

25. This is an important idea for Rudolf Bultmann, *Teología del Nuevo Testamento* (Salamanca: Sígueme, 1981), 50.

26. Pierre Grelot, *Problèmes de morale fondamentale: Un éclairage biblique* (Paris: Editions du Cerf, 1982), 19.

NEW TESTAMENT

SOME ETHICAL IMPLICATIONS OF SAINT PAUL'S VISION OF THE "NEW CREATION"

Thomas D. Stegman, SJ

"New creation" is a crucially important theme in Paul's letters. Although the phrase occurs only twice—2 Corinthians 5:17 and Galatians 6:15—it generates and lies just beneath the surface of a number of topics that are germane for ethical reflection. In 2 Corinthians, for example, Paul links the new creation with the following: Jesus' love as a dynamic force that inspires and energizes those who receive with faith the Gospel proclamation; his death and resurrection as bringing about a new possibility for human existence, one lived for him (i.e., Christ)—and, by extension, for the sake of others; a new way of looking at and valuing other people; and God's work of reconciling people to Godself and giving to the church the ministry and message of reconciliation (2 Cor. 5:14–19).

In what follows, we set forth several features of Paul's teaching on the new creation. The first section deals with anthropological issues: the empowerment to live after the manner of Jesus, the new Adam, and "image of God" par excellence; and Paul's understanding of authentic freedom. The second section describes life in the new creation under two aspects: the sharing of goods as an enactment of the divine plan of *isotēs* ("equality" or "fairness"), and the proper attitude and stance of Christians vis-à-vis the nonhuman-created order (especially the environment). The third section then takes up the topic of reconciliation and some implications of "our heavenly citizenship" (Phil. 3:20).[1] Given the nature and parameters of the essays in this volume, I present Paul's appreciation of the new creation in broad brush strokes and suggest lines of ethical relevance.

Jesus the New Adam: Authentic Freedom

In Romans 5:15–19, Paul offers an extended comparison between Adam and Christ. In doing so, he portrays Jesus as the new Adam. A key feature of Paul's presentation of the new creation is that the death and resurrection of Jesus—with the subsequent outpouring of God's Spirit—has brought about a new way of being human. In order to understand this sense of newness, one must recognize how he characterizes human beings apart from Christ. Paul does so in Romans 7:7–25, where he portrays humanity as enslaved under the tyranny of the powers of sin and death. The catalyst for falling into this slavery is succumbing to "coveting" or "desire" (*epithymia*), to the impulse to grasp after life in ways that are not offered by God (Rom. 7:7–8). Such coveting—expressed in all manners of acquisitiveness, be it for possessions, pleasure, or power (see 2 Cor. 5:15: "living for themselves")— often relegates the "other" to being a competitor or, worse, an enemy.[2]

The primordial "grasper," for Paul, is Adam, who in disobedience to God sought to exalt himself by taking fruit from the forbidden tree (see Gen. 2:16–17, 3:1–6). This portrayal of Adam provides background for the depiction of Jesus' incarnation and obedient death in the first half of the famous Christ-hymn in Philippians 2:6–8. Rather than grasp, Jesus does not regard his equality with God as something to be exploited or taken advantage of. Rather than seek to exalt himself, Jesus lowers himself in humility—both by taking on flesh and, as a human being, by offering his life as a "slave" (*doulos*) in service of others. And rather than disobey God's will for him, Jesus was "obedient to the point of death, even death on a cross." In short, the Christ-hymn reveals Jesus as reversing the various dynamics of Adam's disobedience, which led to the unleashing of the powers of sin and death upon the world (Rom. 5:12–14).

Whereas the Christ-hymn functions primarily, in the context of Philippians, to set forth Jesus' humility,[3] elsewhere Paul focuses on Jesus' faithfulness-unto-death as the full expression of his *love* (esp. Gal. 2:20—Christ "loved me and gave himself up for me"). Because, as God's Son, he is the personal expression of God, and Jesus' self-giving love is a manifestation of God's love (Rom. 5:6–8). From the vantage of his human identity, Jesus' offering his life in love on the cross was the most dramatic expression of his faithfulness (cf. Rom. 3:22)[4] and obedience (Rom. 5:19) to God. He thus not only revealed something about God, but also what authentic human existence looks like. Created in the image and likeness of God (Gen. 1:26–27), human beings are to reflect God's glory through their way of life. Jesus is the "image of God" par excellence (2 Cor. 4:4). He is the new Adam whose life was a constant "Yes" to God's will (2 Cor. 1:20), expressed in selfless love and service of others.

To be sure, Paul holds that Jesus most fully manifests God's image as the new Adam in his resurrection glory (see 1 Cor. 15:21–22, 45–49). Nevertheless, he also insists that, through the power of God's Spirit, human beings are being transformed *in the present* "into his [Christ's] image from one degree of glory to another" (2 Cor. 3:18). Such present transformation by the Spirit entails enabling its recipients to walk in the way of Jesus' self-giving love. Moreover, the Spirit bestows the "mind of Christ" (1 Cor. 2:16), by which Paul means Jesus' attitude and way of looking at people and situations. Possessing God's love in their hearts through the gift of the Spirit (Rom. 5:5), Christians can mature and make progress in offering themselves in loving service of others. They know that true life consists in this—rather than in the old Adamic impetus towards selfishness, acquisition, and competition.[5]

A striking feature of Paul's letters is his exhortation to his communities to "become imitators of me, as I am of Christ" (1 Cor. 11:1; cf. Phil. 3:17). The imitation of Jesus is not some wooden or rote replication of his words and deeds; rather, it centers on the self-giving love of Christ as constituting "a principal moral paradigm."[6] Rather than live for oneself, Paul summons his charges to follow the path of Jesus, the new Adam, and live for the sake of others (see 2 Cor. 5:15). *Agapē*-love is the commitment always to think and act for the good of others. It involves being sensitized to and growing in concern to respond to their needs. It means bearing one another's burdens (Gal. 6:2). In a word, the *imitatio Christi* that the apostle espouses is an exercise of radical freedom.

Paul's teaching about freedom is extremely relevant for moral reflection today. In Galatians 5:1, he declares, "For freedom Christ has set us free." Notice that Paul refers to two aspects of freedom here. First, there is "freedom from"— in this case, he contends that, through the death and resurrection of Jesus, God has brought about redemption from the enslaving powers of sin and death. This notion of "freedom from" is how most people today tend to think about freedom. Much "rights" language has, at its root, the concern (valid, to be sure) to protect people *from* the encroachment of others. Debates in situations where people's rights come into conflict with one another, however, can easily devolve into turf wars over whose rights are more legitimate and important.

But Paul's understanding of freedom is much richer. In addition to "freedom from," he holds that there is "freedom for": the freedom to set aside one's own rights and privileges in order to love others and serve their needs. Paul reminds the Galatians that "you were called to freedom; only do not use your freedom for selfish purposes, but through love be slaves of one another" (Gal. 5:13). The verb *douleuō* here recalls the description of Jesus as *doulos* ("slave") in the Christ-hymn (Phil. 2:7). The imitation of Jesus involves taking on, more and more, his mode of living as one who came "not to be served but to serve" (Mark 10:45). Authentic freedom is the ability to transcend one's own self in order to love and serve others. It is no accident that, in the passage concerning the Spirit's transforming people into the likeness of Christ, the apostle states that "where the Spirit of the Lord is, there is freedom" (2 Cor. 3:17).

A classic application of "freedom for" is 1 Corinthians 8–10.[7] The situation involved a community that was divided over the propriety of eating meat that had been sacrificed to idols. While Paul agrees in principle with those who advocate that eating such meat is fine (since "an idol has no real existence"—1 Cor. 8:4), he exhorts the so-called "strong" members of the community to be sensitive to other members whose conscience calls the practice into question. More important than insisting on one's own rights—and more important than insisting that one's knowledge is "right"—is acting in love for the sake of others. Because some of the members are scandalized by the eating of idol meat, Paul takes the lead and holds himself up as an example: "If food is a cause of my brother's falling, I will never eat meat, lest I cause my brother to fall" (1 Cor. 8:13). Such self-sacrifice enacted freely for the sake of others is why he can conclude the entire section with the exhortation: "Become imitators of me, as I am of Christ" (1 Cor. 11:1).

One other feature of Paul's response to the Corinthian idol meat controversy is deserving of comment here. He warns the "strong" members not to be condescending toward others. They are not to look down at those whose conscience is delicate as "weak," but rather to view them as brothers and sisters—even more, as brothers and sisters "for whom Christ died" (1 Cor. 8:11). The way people perceive and regard others makes an enormous difference. Not only does Paul constantly remind his communities that they are now brothers and sisters in Christ. He also wants them to reflect on the way Jesus viewed and acted toward others: with a love that held nothing back (see John 15:12–13). Christ's love levels the playing field because *everyone* stands in need of his mercy. Derogatory, condescending labels never accomplish anything positive. A hallmark of the new creation is an epistemological transformation (cf. 2 Cor. 5:16), a new way of knowing and regarding others.[8]

The Divine Plan of Isotēs: Care for Creation

Paul's vision of new creation goes beyond anthropological considerations. It also touches on the world in which we live, including the distribution of resources and care for the created order. Concerning the former, 2 Corinthians 8:1–9:15—his exhortation to the church in Corinth to contribute generously to the relief fund he organized for the impoverished Jerusalem church—provides rich material for theological and ethical reflection.[9] Paul employs a number of rhetorical strategies to inspire the Corinthians to generosity. First and foremost, he raises the example of Jesus who, "though he was rich, became poor for your sake, in order that you might become rich by his poverty" (2 Cor. 8:9). This passage aptly summarizes the dynamics of the first half of the Christ-hymn in Philippians 2:6–8 treated above, although now with economic terminology that suits well the apostle's call for monetary generosity.

An underappreciated feature of Paul's teaching appears in 2 Corinthians 8:13–14, where he raises the topic of *isotēs*, "equality" or "fairness." He wants the Corinthians to grasp that "your abundance [in material goods] at the present time should supply their [the 'Jerusalemites'] want." But he also emphasizes that, someday, the tables may be turned, and they can then expect help from others. The crucial point is that Paul insists that this is all "a matter of *isotēs*." But such "fairness" is more than a question of charity and justice among Christian communities. Paul also suggests that it is part of the divine plan to be enacted in the new creation. He does so by citing a text from Scripture (cf. "as it is written"), understood as *God's* word. The text is Exodus 16:18—"The one who gathered much did not have surfeit, and the one who gathered little did not lack" (2 Cor. 8:15)—from the story of God's provision of manna to the Israelites in the wilderness.

To understand Paul's use of Scripture here, it is necessary to look at the broader context of the manna story (Exod. 16:1–36). God provided manna to Israel every morning (as well as quails in the evening). The people were to collect only what was needed for their household for the day. Moses warned them not to store up for future days (except for the Sabbath); indeed, those who disobeyed found that what they kept for the following day had rotted. This broader context strongly suggests two things. First, Paul wants to inculcate among the Corinthians the realization that God is the source of their gifts, including their abundant resources. They are to grow in gratitude for God's goodness and generosity, and learn to place their trust in God and not in themselves. Second, the detail about what happened to those who attempted to hoard God's gifts for themselves serves as a warning: selfish clinging results ultimately in ruin.[10]

Paul reiterates these points in 2 Corinthians 9:8–12, though he now raises the ante by suggesting that the Corinthians are called to imitate God's generosity. The citation of Psalm 112:9 in 2 Corinthians 9:9—"He scattered [seed], he gave to the poor; his righteousness endures forever"—raises the question: Who is the referent of "he"—God or the generous person? It seems that Paul is being purposely ambiguous here. Psalms 111–12[11] function like a diptych. Psalm 111 sings God's praise for his merciful love and beneficence; Psalm 112 recounts the person who fears God and is generous to others, especially the poor. Paul's point is that human generosity participates in God's righteousness, in God's impetus to reach out to restore his people and to make right what has gone wrong.[12] In fact, earlier in the same letter, Paul makes the astonishing statement that, through Christ, "we have *become* the righteousness of God [*dikaiosynē theou*]" (2 Cor. 5:21).

Paul's theological grounding of his call to generosity has application well beyond the collection project. In today's context, the gap between rich and poor widens with each passing year. The disparities of access to economic resources, quality health care, and education have reached scandalous proportions. Paul's exhortations, while certainly pertaining to intra-church dynamics, are a call for Christians to be active promoters of God's plan of *isotēs* beyond the walls of churches. Policy-making and legislation regarding tax revenues, minimum wages, employees' rights and working conditions, education resources, access to health care (to name but a few issues) provide concrete opportunities for Christians to be agents to promote and enact the new creation inaugurated by the Christ-event. Paul's teaching in 2 Corinthians 8–9 reveals a new "economy," one grounded in God's self-giving love as revealed by Jesus.

What about the created order? These days, environmental concerns have rightly become a top priority for many prominent theologians.[13] Do Paul's writings have anything to say in this connection? At first glance, the answer appears to be no. His primary focus is anthropological (i.e., how God has acted through Jesus and the sending of the Spirit to save and transform human beings). However, texts such as Romans 8:19–23 and Colossians 1:15–20[14] considerably broaden the horizons. In the former, Paul declares that "creation itself will be set free from its enslavement to decay"; and in the latter, the author states that, through Christ, God has reconciled "*all* things" (*ta panta*) to himself. Such texts provide a basis for extending Paul's concerns beyond anthropocentric ones, especially when read in light of today's ecological crisis.[15]

Let's take the text from Romans. Paul's words—"the whole creation has been groaning in travail" (Rom. 8:22)—are especially poignant in the context of the depletion of natural resources in service of "progress" and the severe human-induced damage to ecosystems. Paul asserts that creation eagerly anticipates the revelation of the children of God (8:19), when it will be set free from its bondage (8:21). A challenging feature of the passage is determining who is the implied referent of the agent behind the subjection of creation "to futility" (8:20). Paul's use of a passive voice verb (cf. "was subjected") has suggested to many commentators that God is the one who subjected creation (cf. Gen. 3:17–19). Even so, this subjection was the result of human (Adam's!) rebellion against God. Indeed, Paul links the "futility" that held sway over people in consequence of their ungodliness and injustice (Rom. 1:18–23) to the "futility" that creation has endured. Human sin and arrogance have deadly ramifications for the nonhuman creation as well.

Admittedly, Paul's vision of the full transformation of the *kosmos* awaits the future and *God's* definitive action. Nevertheless, his insistence on the present transformation of people (who receive with faith the Gospel message) into the likeness of Jesus, the new Adam, strongly implies that this future hope is also to be translated into commitment and action. That is, human beings are now empowered by the Spirit to enact the vocation that God gave to Adam: namely, to be caretakers and stewards—not overlords—of God's gifts of creation. Thus, an essential way to anticipate the fullness of the new creation is to participate presently in its transformation by acting vis-à-vis the environment in ways commensurate with that future.[16]

Paul's writings thereby offer much for ethical reflection on social and ecological justice. Both issues entail the extension of a principle contained in his employment of the body metaphor in his exhortation for unity among the members of the community in Corinth (1 Cor. 12:12–27). There, he insists that God overturns typical hierarchical expectations by giving greater honor to the less honorable parts; moreover, joys and sufferings are to be shared among all the members, who are the "body of Christ." It takes little imagination to extend this image to the "body" of the church as a whole (e.g., Corinthians sharing with Jerusalemites). It requires more imagination to extend such care and solidarity to the larger human community, and even more to extend them to the "cosmic community" (although Colossians does give some warrant for extending the notion of "body of Christ" to the reconciled *kosmos*). A sanguine reading of Paul, for whom solidarity and self-giving love are "central meta-norms," leads to the conclusion that these norms should be extended to the social and created orders.[17]

Reconciliation and "Our Heavenly Citizenship"

We have just seen that Colossians 1:20 employs the imagery of God reconciling all things to Godself through Christ. In addition, the above-mentioned collection for the church in Jerusalem was more than a relief effort for Paul (though it was certainly that). It also symbolized God's work of reconciliation among peoples, especially the reconciliation between Gentiles and Jews. Part of Paul's motivation in taking up funds from the churches he founded—communities made up largely of Gentiles—was to demonstrate to the Jerusalem church the efficacy of the mission to the Gentiles. In accepting the Gospel proclamation, the Gentile believers came to regard their Jewish counterparts in Jerusalem as brothers and sisters in Christ. And they concretely expressed this new relationship by their sharing of goods.[18]

The metaphor of reconciliation presumes a prior situation of enmity and the breakdown of relationships.[19] Paul's understanding of the human condition before the coming of Jesus was that all peoples, in recapitulating the disobedience of Adam, had become enemies of God (see Rom. 5:10). They rebelled against the creator and giver of life. Furthermore, human sinfulness—characterized (as we saw in the first section, "The New Adam") by covetousness, grasping, and competition—resulted in devastating hatred and divisions among peoples (cf., e.g., the vice list in Rom. 1:29–31). This was the context in which God acted so magnanimously to make right what had gone wrong. As Paul declares in 2 Corinthians 5:19: "God was, in Christ, reconciling the world to himself, not counting their trespasses against them." That is, God has brought about the possibility of restored covenant relationships—right relationship between God and people, as well as right relationships among peoples. It is no coincidence that Paul describes this reconciliation immediately after his reference to "new creation" in 2 Corinthians 5:17.

While one strand of interpretative tradition has long given "justification" the pride of place in Paul's theology, it can be argued that reconciliation is what is truly central for him.[20] A glance at the exhortations throughout his letters reveals that his primary concern is the building up of communities of faith. For Paul, the "living proof" of the efficacy of the Christ-event and the sending of the Spirit is the formation of cells of believers—Jews and Gentiles, rich and poor, free and slaves—who now treat one another as family, as brothers and sisters in the new creation. They bear witness to God's work of reconciliation by their mutual love and support, and by their solidarity-in-diversity. Ethnic, cultural, socioeconomic, and gender diversity, rather than serve as sources of division and barriers between peoples, can be brought together in enriching, life-giving ways (cf. Gal. 3:28; Eph. 2:11–22). What Paul condemns most fiercely are attitudes or behaviors that destroy unity and allow old divisions to rear their ugly heads.

God's gift of reconciliation becomes a mission and an imperative.[21] Paul makes this clear in 2 Corinthians 5:18–19. After setting forth God's act of reconciliation through Christ, he states that God has now given to the church the "ministry" and the "message of reconciliation." Although this mandate necessarily entails preaching the Gospel, verbal proclamation alone is not sufficient for carrying it out. Communities of believers, in addition to embodying the unity-in-diversity just discussed, are to be instruments through whom God works to bring about reconciliation between peoples, a process that entails restorative justice. Such enacted proclamation serves to extend the reign of God's kingdom on earth as it is in heaven (cf. the apostle's description of the kingdom in Romans 14:17).[22] It is also striking to observe that Paul echoes Jesus' challenging teachings about loving one's enemies and nonretaliation (Rom. 12:14–21). In doing so, he gives warrant to nonviolent peacemaking—with the commitment to justice that underlies it—as being an essential task of the church.[23]

The relevance of Paul's teaching about reconciliation for today cannot be overstated. Political, ethnic, and religious differences among peoples are becoming more polarized, with consequent violence—locally, nationally, internationally. The world desperately needs agents of nonviolent restorative justice and peace. Faith communities can be "places" where unity-in-diversity gains a foothold. But alas, even the Christian churches are not immune to the plague of divisiveness. Paul puts forth the challenging summons that the church should be, as it were, a sacrament of enacted reconciliation and *koinōnia* for all to see. As such, it can then have the moral authority to call and help others live together in peace in the new creation.

As the foregoing has shown, Paul's ethical teachings strongly suggest that Christians are to be engaged in concerns beyond their own faith communities. They are to be good citizens and to work for the common good. Nevertheless, he also makes clear that, while they are to be "in" the world (cf. 1 Cor. 5:10), they are not to be "of" the world. Christians are always to keep at the forefront of their minds "our heavenly citizenship" (Phil. 3:20). This citizenship calls for ultimate loyalty and can, at times, lead to a clash of values held by the dominant culture. In Paul's day, the dominant culture was the imperial order of Rome.

A hotly debated issue in Pauline studies concerns the question of Paul and the Roman Empire.[24] On the one hand, according to Acts, Paul was a Roman citizen (e.g., 16:37–38). In many respects, the infrastructure of the empire benefited his ministry. And there are passages (e.g., Rom. 13:1–7) that have been read as indicating his proclivity toward the empire. On the other hand, Paul's fundamental proclamation—"Jesus Christ is Lord [*kyrios*]!" (e.g., 2 Cor. 4:5)—means that Caesar is not "lord." Paul's Gospel announces that salvation—with its concomitant peace and security—is from God, a claim that challenges Roman propaganda (cf. 1 Thess. 5:3). Moreover, Paul's call for the formation of nonhierarchical communities of believers, wherein disparate peoples regard and treat one another as brothers and sisters, would have sounded strange, if not subversive, vis-à-vis the Roman *pater familias* household.

It is interesting to note that, in his extant letters, Paul never mentions his Roman citizenship. Is this one of the things that he once valued but now, in light of knowing Christ, he regards as "loss"? (cf. Phil. 3:7–8). Perhaps. We are on surer ground in positing that "heavenly citizenship" trumps everything for the apostle. Although Christians today are to be good citizens, they are to remember where their ultimate loyalty resides—in God. The Christ-event, along with the outpouring of God's Spirit, has inaugurated the new creation. This new creation includes a new way of being human, marked by self-giving love and special consideration for those regarded as "weak." It empowers a freedom best characterized as "freedom for" service of others. It entails people who are committed to social and ecological justice. And it enables the formation of communities of faith, characterized by unity-in-diversity, that are to be nonviolent agents of restorative justice, reconciliation, and peacemaking. Rarely are these the values and ways of empires, whether ancient or modern.

Notes

1. Rendering *hēmōn to politeuma en ouranois*. Translations of Scripture in this essay are my own.

2. See Luke Timothy Johnson, *Reading Romans: A Literary and Theological Commentary* (New York: Crossroad, 1997), 104–15.

3. See, e.g., Stephen E. Fowl, "Christology and Ethics in Philippians 2:5–11," in *Where Christology Began: Essays on Philippians 2*, ed. R. P. Martin and B. J. Dodd (Louisville, KY: Westminster John Knox, 1998), 140–53.

4. Interpreting the phrase *pistis Iēsou Christou* as a subjective genitive.

5. For love as a Pauline virtue, see Daniel J. Harrington and James F. Keenan, *Paul and Virtue Ethics: Building Bridges between New Testament Studies and Moral Theology* (Lanham, MD: Rowman & Littlefield, 2010), 92–93. For putting love into practice, see James W. Thompson, *Moral Formation according to Paul: The Context and Coherence of Pauline Ethics* (Grand Rapids, MI: Baker Academic, 2011), 157–80.

6. David G. Horrell, *Solidarity and Difference: A Contemporary Reading of Paul's Ethics* (London: T&T Clark, 2005), 27. For a succinct description of "the imitation of Jesus in Paul," see Richard A. Burridge, *Imitating Jesus: An Inclusive Approach to New Testament Ethics* (Grand Rapids, MI: Eerdmans, 2007), 138–53.

7. See, e.g., Frank J. Matera, *New Testament Ethics: The Legacies of Jesus and Paul* (Louisville, KY: Westminster John Knox, 1996), 148–51.

8. See J. Louis Martyn, "Epistemology at the Turn of the Ages," in *Theological Issues in the Letters of Paul* (Edinburgh: T&T Clark, 1997), 89–110.

9. For more on this relief effort, see, e.g., David J. Downs, *The Offering of the Gentiles: Paul's Collection for Jerusalem in Its Chronological, Cultural, and Cultic Contexts* (Tübingen: Mohr Siebeck, 2008).

10. See Richard B. Hays, *Echoes of Scripture in the Letters of Paul* (New Haven: Yale University Press, 1989), 88–91.

11. Paul cites the Greek text. Septuagint (LXX) Pss. 110–11 = Pss. 111–12 in English translations.

12. For more on Paul's reading of 2 Cor. 9:9, see Thomas D. Stegman, "Paul's Use of Scripture in the Collection Discourse (2 Corinthians 8–9)," in *Biblical Essays in Honor of Daniel J. Harrington, SJ, and Richard J. Clifford, SJ: Opportunity for No Little Instruction*, ed. C. G. Frechette, C. R. Matthews, and T. D. Stegman (Mahwah, NJ: Paulist Press, 2014), 162–66.

13. See, e.g., Elizabeth A. Johnson, *Ask the Beasts: Darwin and the God of Love* (London: Bloomsbury, 2014).

14. Commentators are divided over the question of whether Paul is the author of Colossians. Even if he is not, all agree that the letter is truly "Pauline."

15. See, e.g., Cherryl Hunt, "Beyond Anthropocentrism: Towards a Re-reading of Pauline Ethics," *Theology* 112 (2009): 190–98.

16. David G. Horrell, "A New Perspective on Paul? Rereading Paul in a Time of Ecological Crisis," *Journal for the Study of the New Testament* 33 (2010): 19–25. For more on reading Paul through an "ecotheological hermeneutic," see David G. Horrell, Cherryl Hunt, and Christopher Southgate, *Greening Paul: Rereading the Apostle in a Time of Ecological Crisis* (Waco, TX: Baylor University Press, 2010).

17. Horrell, "A New Perspective on Paul?" 21.

18. We know from Romans 15:26 that the Corinthians did in fact contribute.

19. For more on reconciliation, see Thomas D. Stegman, "What Does the New Testament Say about Reconciliation?" in *Healing God's People: Theological and Pastoral Approaches / A Reconciliation Reader*, ed. T. A. Kane (Mahwah, NJ: Paulist Press, 2013), 33–44.

20. The classic expression of the view that reconciliation is central for Paul is Ralph P. Martin, *Reconciliation: A Study of Paul's Theology* (Atlanta: John Knox, 1981).

21. For reconciliation as a "sign" of the new creation, see N. T. Wright, *Paul and the Faithfulness of God* (Minneapolis: Fortress, 2013), 1484–1516.

22. See, e.g., Michael J. Gorman, *Becoming the Gospel: Paul, Participation, and Mission* (Grand Rapids, MI: Eerdmans, 2015), 17.

23. See Willard M. Swartley, *Covenant of Peace: The Missing Peace in New Testament Theology and Ethics* (Grand Rapids, MI: Eerdmans, 2006), 189–253.

24. For a brief explanation, see Thomas D. Stegman, "'Run That You May Obtain the Prize': Using St. Paul as a Resource of the Spiritual Exercises," *Studies in the Spirituality of Jesuits* 44, no. 4 (2012): 23–26. For Paul's Gospel as challenging Roman imperial claims, see Neil Elliott, *The Arrogance of Nations: Reading Romans in the Shadow of Empire* (Minneapolis: Fortress, 2008). For a more cautious approach to the topic, see John M. G. Barclay, *Pauline Churches and Diaspora Jews* (Tübingen: Mohr Siebeck, 2011), 345–87.

Marriage and Wealth

A Study of Mark 10:1–31

Francis J. Moloney, SDB, AM, FAHA

The legal and prophetic traditions of what Christians call the Old Testament, the Jesus of the Gospels, and the recommendations of Paul and the other writers of the Christian New Testament have always been at the heart of the liturgical life and much of the preaching of the Christian churches. But a long tradition of systematic reflection on ethical or moral traditions, until recent times, has looked elsewhere for its inspiration and justification. Largely determined by medieval European history, a more biblically and sacramentally inspired tradition, nourished by the Fathers of the Church, faded into the background in the eleventh century, as papal authority struggled with the secular princes. A more juridical and less biblical, theological, and sacramental self-understanding of Christianity emerged.[1]

Outstanding theological contributions, inspired by biblical, patristic, and liturgical traditions, continued to appear, singularly represented by Thomas Aquinas (1225–74). But a more juridical tradition of ethical thought gradually emerged in the development of an area of Christian reflection that came to be known as moral theology. It had little to do with the Gospel roots of the Christian phenomenon, except to refer—uncritically, piecemeal, and in a proof-text fashion—to biblical passages that might be applied to one or other moral "case." The history of modern Catholic moral theology has sometimes been marred by bitter factional divisions that have led this theological discipline a long way from its biblical roots.

That era is thankfully behind us, as moral theologians and ethicists working in the Christian tradition have returned enthusiastically to a consideration of the role of the Word of God in their reflections and research. In the Catholic tradition, Vatican II stated unequivocally that Sacred Scripture must lie at the heart of all theology (see *Dei Verbum* 24; *Optatam Totius* 21). This essay is dedicated to a critical reading of a passage from the Gospel of Mark (10:1–31) in which one finds Jesus' teaching on marriage and wealth. Not surprisingly, the interpretation of this passage across different Christian traditions has led to contrasting ethical conclusions on marriage and divorce, and the role of evangelical poverty.

The Structure and Message of Mark 8:22–10:52

Scholarly commentary recognizes a literary frame of two cures of blindness around 8:22–10:52 (8:22–26, 10:46–52). The cure of a blind man at Bethsaida (8:22–26) creates a literary "overlap." It leads into the confession at Caesarea Philippi with the following section of the Gospel. Between the two miracles where Jesus heals blindness, he predicts his passion three times (8:31, 9:31, 10:32–34). The three passion predictions, framed by two stories of blindness transformed into sight, are directed to the disciples as they journey toward Jerusalem. Across 8:27–10:45, more than anywhere else in the Gospel of Mark, Jesus directs his attention and his teaching toward the disciples. The disciples are *always* at the center of the action. On only three occasions, other characters appear (9:14–27, 10:2–9, 10:17–22). The father in 9:14–29 is used as a narrative ploy to highlight the failure of the disciples. But the Pharisees (10:1–12) and the rich man (10:17–31) are active agents.

Determined by its literary frame (8:22–26, 10:46–52) and the three passion predictions (8:31, 9:31–32, 10:32–34), this section of the narrative unfolds in three stages: 8:27–9:29, 9:30–10:31, 10:32–45. At the center of this carefully designed narrative (9:30–10:31), Jesus instructs his disciples on a God-directed understanding of marriage (10:1–12) and wealth (10:17–31).

Mark 10:1–31:
Disciples, Marriage, Receptivity and Wealth

Jesus has instructed his disciples to take up their cross, to give their lives for his sake and for the Gospel (see 8:34–9:1), and on the necessity for receptivity and service (9:33–37). In 10:1–9, he debates with the Pharisees over divorce and then speaks to the disciples "in the house" in verses 10–12. After a passage where children are brought to Jesus (10:13–16), recalling the earlier message of receptivity (see 9:36–37), in 10:17–22 Jesus offers a wealthy man the possibility of eternal life and subsequently speaks to his disciples in verses 23–31 about wealth and possessions. Jesus' earlier instruction on the cross (see 8:34–9:1), service, and receptivity (see 9:35–50) operate *at the level of principle*, in secret discussions between Jesus and the disciples (see 9:30b). In 10:1–31, before moving to the final passion prediction (10:32–34), Jesus addresses the *lived experiences* of marriage and wealth in the life of a disciple. He draws *principle* into *everyday life*. In marriage and in the use of wealth the call to cross, service, and receptivity are at risk. Mark 10:1–31 is concerned with the *practice*, and not only the *theory*, of discipleship.

Marriage and Discipleship (vv. 1–12)

In 10:1, the scene is set for the encounter with the Pharisees. Its hostile nature is indicated by the fact that the Pharisees came to "test him" (v. 2a: *peira, zontej auvto, n*). They question him about the lawfulness of divorce (v. 2b). The Pharisees ask for a judgment from Jesus on whether divorce should be allowed (v. 2b). The question touches only upon *the rights of a man* to divorce his wife, but Jesus responds in a fashion that reflects the process of a rabbinic debate. He asks them about the command of Moses (v. 3).

They respond that according to Moses (see Deut. 24:1–4) it is lawful to write a certificate of divorce, and in this way put a wife out of the man's house (v. 4). The debate appears to be based on an awareness of Jesus' absolute prohibition of divorce. They have Moses on their side; how can Jesus take a different position? Jesus argues that Moses' teaching (v. 5) has crept into Jewish tradition, via Moses, *because of the hardness of the heart* of the Israel the Pharisees represent (v. 5). God's plan is found in his action "from the beginning of creation" (v. 6: *avpo. de. avrch/j kti,sewj*). Jesus comments on the Genesis passages: "So they are no longer two but one flesh" (v. 8b). A woman and a man have been joined together in a loving and sexual union, as God designed.

In this debate, Torah has been used against Torah. For Jesus, the legislation of Deuteronomy 24:1–4, established subsequent to creation as a concession to men who were unable to live as God had planned, was provisional.[2] *God has established* the union between a man and a woman (*o ' qe,oj sune,zixen*). *No man has the authority* to tear that union apart (*a;nqrwpoj mh. cwrize,tw*). The process used by Jesus has taken the Pharisees from an awareness of what was *commanded by Moses* (see v. 3) to what *God wills* (see vv. 6–9). Jesus' position is determined by *the design of God*.

The storyteller focuses on the disciples. For Mark, "the house" is the place for private teaching (see 3:20, 7:17–23, 9:28, 33). The disciples ask for further clarification on the debate they have just witnessed (v. 10). Jesus gives a God-directed motivation: men and women are equal and equally responsible for their marital oneness (vv. 11–12). It is often pointed out that there is a shift in the argument here. In verses 2–9, the issue was divorce, whereas in verses 11–12 Jesus speaks of the remarriage of the divorced as adultery.[3] There was long-standing and clear legislation against adultery (see Exod. 20:19; Deut. 4:10, 5:21; Lev. 20:10; Deut. 22:22). Jesus' words to his disciples thus show how disobedience to his interpretation of Torah leads to the breaking of Torah. No disciple of Jesus, called to the cross, humble service, and receptivity, can contemplate such action.

The most intimate of human experiences, the union between a woman and a man, calls for loving self-gift. Jesus' new law in a new situation of God-human relationships, where the original creative design of God is reestablished, can be costly. The teaching of Jesus on this matter is as idealistic, countercultural, and difficult today as it was in the time of Jesus, but Mark has taken this element from Jesus' teaching and used it to tell disciples that cross, service, and receptivity are not simple *theory*. They come into play in one of the fundamental structures of their day-to-day lives: in man-woman relationships.

The response of the Western Christian churches to this teaching is fundamentally twofold.[4] In the first place, it is widely accepted that Jesus of Nazareth was not married, and that he prohibited divorce. This tradition is continued in the early church. As well as Mark 10:5–9, an absolute prohibition of divorce is found in Q (Matt. 5:32; Luke 16:18), and in 1 Corinthians 7:10–11, Paul speaks of the prohibition of divorce as "a word of the Lord."[5] The Roman Catholic Church has adhered strictly to this teaching, prohibiting divorce among validly married Catholics, allowing a so-called "annulment" when a case can be made for the lack of preparation, and unconditional consent prior to the marriage contract.[6] This situation has led to a great deal of pain in unhappy and unsuccessful Catholic marriages. There is a widespread call for better pastoral care for these sometimes dramatic cases.

Protestant churches looked to the "exception clause" in Matthew 5:32 and 19:9: there is to be no divorce, "except in the case of unchastity [*pornei,a*]." The Greek word *pornei,a* can refer to a number of sexual misdemeanors.[7] The Protestant tradition has looked to the Matthean "dominical word" as offering the possibility of divorce for moral failure. Paul also allows for divorce within mixed marriages (see 1 Cor. 7:12–16). Above all, the Protestant tradition insists upon "Jesus' spirit of unlimited forgiveness."[8] Ulrich Luz can even suggest "that the Catholic divorce law, close as it is to the substance of Matthew's position, does not do justice to the New Testament at an essential point."[9] Taking seriously today's social and psychological situation, and the increasing irrelevance of "established tradition" in a secularized postmodern world, the issue of divorce, remarriage, and ongoing participation in a Christian communion are urgent issues facing the churches.

This New Testament reflection cannot enter the complex pastoral issues raised by the "Gospel message" in contemporary society. It must be said, however, that Mark presents Jesus' teaching as the reconstitution of God's original design (see Mark 10:6).[10] That reconstitution has been fully present only in the person of Jesus; it is otherwise "in process." The "ideal" of God's original creative plan is not present in the ambiguity of the human story. But much church legislation presupposes that it is—from the first moment of the long journey of marriage. This is to confuse the "ideal" and the "real," with consequent complex results in the lives of "imperfect" people, striving (and sometimes failing) in their Christian lives.[11]

Receiving the Children (vv. 13–16)

Jesus and the disciples are still "in the house" (see v. 10), on the other side of the Jordan (see v. 1) as unidentified people bring children to Jesus, that he might touch them.[12] The choice of the expression *paidi,a* (rather than *te,kna*) for "children," indicates that they are past infancy, but still dependent. Strategically located between Jesus' instructions on marriage (vv. 1–12) and possessions (vv. 17–31), the passage plays the same role as 9:35–37 within the larger context of 9:32–10:31. As 9:35–37 established the theoretical basis for Jesus' teaching on service and receptivity in 9:32–50, so does 10:13–16 within 10:1–31: discipleship is to be marked by service and receptivity.

The disciples rebuke (v. 13: *evpeti,mhsan*) those who led the children to Jesus, as Peter rebuked Jesus in his misunderstanding of the first passion prediction (8:32). As with Peter in 8:32, the disciples in 10:13 refuse to accept or understand Jesus' teaching on the way to Jerusalem. The disciples appear to have no recollection of Jesus' earlier words to them that had focused on children (9:35–37). He asks that the children be allowed to come to him, "for the Kingdom of God belongs to such as these." The gift of the kingdom of God calls for receptivity. "The kingdom belongs to such as these because they receive it as a gift."[13] Much is being offered to the disciples, but they are loath to accept it (v. 15).

Jesus takes the children in his arms, blessing them and laying his hands upon them. This action recalls what he offered the Twelve in 3:14. He appointed them so that they might be "with him." It is the children who are used as a model of the true disciple—with Jesus and blessed by him. Taking the lowly and dependent (*paidi,a*) in his arms, Jesus shows that the kingdom of God reverses expected cultural absolutes (10:16. See 9:32–34).[14] Mark will not allow the reader to forget the principles that should determine the disciple's performance. "He has used a story which is linked to his basic theme of the meaning of discipleship."[15]

Possessions and Discipleship (vv. 17–31)

Jesus moves away from his location in the region beyond the Jordan (10:1), setting out on "the way" (*o 'do,n*) to Jerusalem (v. 17a). An unnamed man "runs" to Jesus and takes up the unusual position of kneeling before him. Addressing Jesus as "good teacher" (*dida,skale avgaqe,*), he asks what he must do (*ti, poih,sw*) to inherit eternal life (v. 17b). "What must *I* do?" is the wrong question. Jesus establishes that only God is good (see Deut. 6:1–4), and points to a selection of the Decalogue as the way to eternal life (vv. 18–19). In affirming the goodness of God, Jesus provides the basis for his instructions to the man that he is to follow God's commandments, already known to him (v. 19). Jesus makes a selection of the commandments from the Decalogue (see Exod. 20:12–16; Deut. 5:16–20). Those chosen might be called social commandments, as they deal with a person's treatment of his neighbor: adultery, theft, false witness, defrauding, and respect for parents (v. 19),[16] commandments that a rich man might be prone to offend. Ritual obligations toward God may be in place (see Exod. 20:2–10; Deut. 5:6–15), as one's weaker neighbor is dealt with sinfully. The man replies that he has always lived according to these commandments (v. 20). At this point Jesus' attitude toward the man changes. He has shown Israel's way to God. The man who ran up to him and knelt before him (v. 17b) has dealt justly with his neighbor all his life (v. 20). He senses that Jesus has something more to offer for eternal life (v. 17c).[17] His problem lies in his belief that he can attain this "something more" *by his own efforts* (see v. 17b).

"Jesus looking upon him loved him" (v. 21). This is the first indication of a movement from Jesus toward the rich man. Capable of doing everything that he sets out to do, and having the means to do it, he asks Jesus' advice on *what he must do* to attain eternal life (v. 17b). Jesus' love for him (v. 21a) leads to an attempt to wrest the initiative from the man. There is only one thing that he lacks. He must rid himself of his possessions and his habitual determination of his own life. He must first sell everything he has and give it to the poor. Reduced to a situation of need and dependence, he will have the opportunity to be *receptive* to the action of God in his life. He will not locate his treasure in this life, but with the only one who is good (see v. 18).

The invitation, "Come, follow me," links this account to the earlier vocation stories (see 1:16–20, 2:13–17, 3:13–19).[18] Those accounts highlighted the initiative and authority of Jesus, followed by the immediate, wordless obedience of those called. The first disciples left their nets, boats, hired servants, and their father (1:16–20), and Levi left his tax-house (2:13–15). But Jesus does not command them to sell everything and give it to the poor. Such a command is found only in this story. The earlier vocation stories show that a disciple must be receptive to the call of Jesus, manifesting unconditional trust in his person and word. "Jesus' demand is radical in character. He claims the man utterly and completely, and orders the removal of every other support which could interfere with an unconditional obedience."[19] The man fails, "for he had great possessions," and "went away" (*avph/lqen*) sorrowfully rejecting a vocation to discipleship (v. 22).[20] The theme of receptivity has been further developed by means of this story of a failed vocation to discipleship, and the everyday danger of allowing possessions to determine one's life. This is the reason for the man's failure to become a disciple. The link with the theme of discipleship, made clear in Jesus' calling him to follow in verse 21c, knits this episode into the wider context of 9:30–10:31.[21]

Jesus addresses the disciples, commenting on the difficulty people with many possessions will have entering the kingdom of God (v. 23). The countercultural nature of Jesus' remarks is highlighted by the amazement of the disciples (v. 24a: *evqambou,nto*). They lived in a world where wealth and possessions determined everything, from religion to politics, and everything in between.[22] Hard on the heels of a discussion over marriage and divorce (vv. 1–12), a second practical indication of what it means to serve and be receptive leaves the disciples stunned. Jesus draws away from the case of the rich man. He speaks of the difficulty for anyone to enter the kingdom of God (v. 24).[23] Jesus compares the difficulties the rich have entering the kingdom with a camel passing through the eye of a needle (v. 25). This statement means what it says: it is impossible.[24] From the *difficulty* (*dusko,lwj*) those having possessions might have (v. 23), Jesus moves to an *impossibility* (v. 25. See v. 27: *avdu,naton*). The disciples are overwhelmed by his words on the impossibility experienced by the rich (v. 25. See v. 26a: "exceedingly astonished [*perissw/j evxeplh,ssanto*]). If for everyone it is difficult and for the rich impossible, the disciples' question makes sense: "Then who can be saved?" (v. 26b). "The disciples understood Jesus correctly. The application of this saying is not limited to the case of this rich man but is relevant for everyone."[25]

The use of the passive voice in this question (*ti,j du,netai swqh/nai;*) shows that the disciples do not lack understanding. They recognize that people are saved by the action of God. It is not something that human beings are able to do by virtue of their possessions, strength, wisdom, or authority. God's ways are unlike human ways. All human effort to enter the kingdom is like trying to get a camel through the eye of a needle. It cannot be done. For human beings, entry into the kingdom is absolutely impossible, but all things (*pa,nta*) are possible with God (v. 27). The "all things" must be taken seriously. Both the rich man who has gone away sorrowful (v. 22) and the disciples who sink into misunderstanding and fear (vv. 25–26) can enter the kingdom of God. God can make the impossible possible![26] What is asked of them, as the example of the restoration of God's order in love and marriage (vv. 1–12) and the rich man's inability to accept a vocation to discipleship have shown (vv. 17–31), is *receptivity* to the countercultural ways of God, made evident in the person and teaching of Jesus (vv. 13–16).

Peter looks back to the beginnings of the Gospel story (see 1:16–20, 2:14) and recalls that—in contrast with the man of vv. 17–22—the disciples left everything, and unquestioningly followed Jesus (v. 28). Opening with a solemn "amen," Jesus praises and makes promises to those who have responded to the Gospel. Jesus lists the many possessions regarded as essential in the disciples' contemporary culture which they have put at risk: home, brothers and sisters, mother and father, children and lands.

Jesus' call to lose life for his sake and for the sake of the Gospel (see 8:35) has received a response. Peter's words (10:28) recall that this has already happened to people in the story, but 10:29–31 indicates that it has taken place in the lives of some who are readers of the story (10:29). They will be blessed abundantly even now, with the houses, the brothers and sisters, and the mothers, children, and land that come with belonging to a Christian community. They will lose nothing in their new family.[27] The Markan community experiences persecutions. This must be accepted as part of "this time" (v. 30a: *nu/n evn tw|/ kairw|/*). Still addressing the community, but looking beyond it, disciples will be blessed with entry into the eternal life promised by the kingdom (v. 30b: *evn tw|/ aivw/ni tw|/ evrcome,nw|/*).[28] The agenda of Jesus turns the world upside down. A vocation to service and recep-tivity, now indicated as the only way to enter the kingdom (vv. 24–27), is a vocation to a reversal of values (v. 31), even the culturally accepted values that surround marriage and wealth.

The reception of Jesus' demand that the man sell everything he has and give it to the poor as a prerequisite to following Jesus has long been a "thorn in the side" for the Christian churches.[29] This has been made even more complex by the almost total lack of interest in Mark 10:17–22, given the dominant use of the Gospel of Matthew in the tradition, and Matthew's condition: "If you wish to be perfect" (19:21).[30]

In the early centuries, despite Clement of Alexandria's contrary view, Origen, John Chrysostom, and Basil insisted that Jesus' command (Mark 10:21; Matt. 19:21) applied to everyone. One who retains anything more than what is needed for the necessities of life disobeys this commandment. The patristic period also developed allegorical readings of the text, in order to ease its severity (e.g., to be "rich" meant owning many evils), and this extended into the medieval period. On the basis of the Matthean "if you wish to be perfect" (19:21), the Catholic tradition has regarded the vow of poverty within the monastic and religious life as an "evangelical counsel," creating a two-tiered response to Jesus: the "perfect" and the rest.[31]

The edge has been taken off the radical nature of Jesus' call. The Protestant tradition rightly rejected the vowed life as a superior vocation within the universal call to holiness. But it tended to adopt what Ulrich Luz describes as "Protestant middle-class domesticity."[32] Christian life within a financially secure and relatively comfortable social situation tends to regard this word of Jesus as hardly relevant. We have "thrown out the baby with the bathwater." Mark 10:17–22 does not direct all seeking discipleship to divest themselves of their possessions. Wealth and possessions were *this man's problem*. They stood between him and an unconditional self-gift to following the way of Jesus. This is the universal message that comes from Jesus' encounter with the rich man. In God's established order, wealth and possessions have their place, but they regularly obstruct a Christian's unconditional acceptance of the word and person of Jesus. Ulrich Luz insists that we need to take this problem seriously: "It is my opinion that any concrete suggestion that does not lead to changes in both personal and ecclesiastical finances simply ignores the text. . . . Any present understanding of a biblical text must include practical application—that, in other words, a mere verbal, abstract understanding that excludes one's existence from the claims of the text is no genuine understanding."[33]

Across Mark 9:31–50, Jesus instructs failing disciples (9:32–34) on receptivity and service (vv. 35–50). Mark 10:1–31 tolls the same bell. But in this literary centerpiece of the Markan journey to Jerusalem (8:22–10:52), Jesus not only teaches *principles*. He points to God's right order in the lived reality of marriage and wealth. Jesus will shortly indicate that he asks them to follow a Son of Man who serves and lays down his life (10:45). Jesus' story challenges Christians to a reversal of the absolutes of "this world." The Christian reception of Mark 10:1–31 indicates that this "word of God" remains "living and active, a two-edged sword, piercing to the division of soul and spirit, of joints and marrow, and discerning the thoughts and intentions of the heart" (Heb. 4:12).

Notes

1. The development of a more juridically structured Western church owes much to the reforms of Pope Gregory VII (1073–85), during a period of intense conflict between secular and religious authority. The authority of the pope over the secular princes was dramatically acted out in the submission of Henry VII (Holy Roman Emperor) to Gregory VII at Canossa in 1077. For a summary of this period and its effects on the Catholic Church's self-understanding, see Francis J. Moloney, *Reading the New Testament in the Church: A Primer for Pastors, Religious Educators, and Believers* (Grand Rapids, MI: Baker Academic, 2015), 5–7. For a stimulating reflection on the role of Gregory VII in European and Catholic history, see Eamon Duffy, *Ten Popes who Shook the World* (New Haven, CT: Yale University Press, 2011), 59–69.

2. See Morna D. Hooker, *The Gospel according to St. Mark*, Black's New Testament Commentary (London: A. & C. Black, 1991), 235: "It is significant that Mark does not suggest here that Jesus contradicted the Torah, but rather that he pointed to its true fulfilment." See further, Joel Marcus, *Mark*, Anchor Yale Bible 27–27A (New York: Doubleday; New Haven, CT: Yale University Press, 2000–2009), 2:710–11.

3. See, e.g., Adela Y. Collins, *Mark*, Hermeneia (Minneapolis: Fortress, 2007), 469–70.

4. For a helpful survey, see David Instone-Brewer, *Divorce and Remarriage in the Bible: The Social and Literary Context* (Grand Rapids, MI: Eerdmans, 2002), 238–67.

5. For a recent fully documented study of this question, see Francis J. Moloney, *A Body Broken for a Broken People: Divorce, Remarriage, and the Eucharist* (New York: Paulist Press, 2015), 205–18.

6. The Eastern Orthodox traditions equally defend the indissolubility of what they regard as a "sacramental marriage." But they allow "separation" and subsequent remarriage in situations where the relationship has broken down completely, accompanied by a confession of sinfulness, and the imposition of an appropriate penance.

7. See Frederick W. Danker, *A Greek-English Dictionary of the New Testament and Other Early Christian Literature*, 3rd ed. (Chicago: University of Chicago Press, 2000), 854, s.v. *pornei,a.*

8. Ulrich Luz, *Matthew*, 3 vols., trans. James E. Crouch (Minneapolis: Fortress, 2001–7), 2:496.

9. Ibid., 2:496.

10. As Marcus, *Mark*, 2:710 puts it: "Jesus and the Markan Christians are people who rejoice in the dawning light of the new age—which is also the recaptured radiance of Eden."

11. See Moloney, *Body Broken*, 218–37.

12. Commentators regularly point out the appropriateness of the passage from marriage (vv. 1–12) to children (vv. 13–16). See, for example, Marcus, *Mark*, 2:713. Collins, *Mark*, 471, rightly points to the close link between the children who have nothing but respond to the opportunity of entering the kingdom (vv. 13–16) and the rich man who has everything (vv. 17–31) and does not respond positively.

13. William L. Lane, *Commentary on the Gospel of Mark*, New International Commentary on the New Testament (Grand Rapids, MI: Eerdmans, 1974), 360.

14. On the background to the "relatively low state of children," see Collins, *Mark*, 472, and the further indications there.

15. Hooker, *St. Mark*, 238. See also Marcus, *Mark*, 2:719.

16. The list given does not follow the biblical order of what is commonly called the "second table," probably determined by the context: a rich man is likely to defraud.

17. The passage reflects the early Christian belief that, however valuable Torah was to find God's ways, following Jesus and his teaching went further.

18. See Collins, *Mark*, 480.

19. Lane, *Mark*, 368.

20. Rather than following (*avkolou,qei mou*. See v. 21), he went away (*avph/lqen*).

21. The tragic nature of this failure is shown by the narrator's comment that the man went away "sorrowful" (*lupou,menoς*).

22. Among many, see Lane, *Mark*, 369: "In Judaism it was inconceivable that riches should be a barrier to the kingdom."

23. See the discussion of the attempts of early copyists to soften what Jesus says in Bruce M. Metzger, *A Textual Commentary on the Greek New Testament* (Stuttgart: Deutsche Bibelgesellschaft, 1994), 90. For a survey of exegetical attempts to do the same, see Marcus, *Mark*, 2:730–32.

24. It is misleading to regard Jesus' words as "hyperbole." Jesus means exactly what he says. As Denis E. Nineham, *The Gospel of St Mark*, Pelican New Testament Commentaries (Harmondsworth: Penguin Books, 1963), 275, comments: "It would be a mistake to ignore the utterly serious truth it expresses."

25. Eduard Schweizer, *The Good News according to Mark*, trans. Donald H. Madvik (London: SPCK, 1971), 214.

26. As Marcus, *Mark*, 2:736, puts it: "the divine grace that transforms the impossible into the possible by creating a new people of God out of hopeless human material."

27. See Marcus, *Mark*, 737–40.

28. The contrast between "this time" and "the time to come" is widespread in apocalyptic thought, but this is the only place where Mark uses it. See the valuable commentary in Collins, *Mark*, 482–83.

29. For much of what follows, see Luz, *Matthew*, 3:518–23.

30. Regarded as an abbreviation of Matthew, no commentary on Mark appeared till the turn of the sixth century. See Brenda D. Schildgen, *Power and Prejudice: The Reception of the Gospel of Mark* (Detroit, MI: Wayne State University Press, 1999).

31. The Matthean notion of "perfection" has been added to Mark 10:21. See Luz, *Matthew*, 3:513–14.

32. Ibid., 3:520. Luz rightly repeats the Protestant rejection of the idea of "evangelical counsels" and the creation of a two-tiered Church. Citing *The Catechism of the Catholic Church*, 2052–54, he describes this as "Catholic doctrine" (p. 522). He misunderstands Catholic doctrine and the role of *The Catechism of the Catholic Church*. For a Catholic rejection of a two-tiered Church, see, among many, Francis J. Moloney, *Disciples and Prophets: A Biblical Model for the Religious Life* (London: Darton, Longman & Todd, 1980), 3–15. On the universal call to evangelical poverty, see idem, *A Life of Promise: Poverty-Chastity-Obedience* (Wilmington, DE: Michael Glazier, 1984), 18–73. Even more extensively, see idem, *Reflections on Evangelical Consecration: Celebrating a Bicentenary* (Bolton: Don Bosco Publications, 2015), 185–241.

33. Luz, *Matthew*, 3:522.

FEMINIST PERSPECTIVES

Woman and Her Clothing in the Service of God

An African Feminist Reading of 1 Corinthians 11:2–16

Chantal Nsongisa Kimesa

Although parity between men and women is recognized and accepted in many contexts and cultures in theory, it is hard to bring it about in practical life. Women are deprived of their rights in favor of men. The text of 1 Corinthians 11:2–16 demonstrates this well. To adequately fulfill their role in society, women are expected to take up a certain responsibility. This essay pays particular attention to African men's attitude toward the dress of African women at the service of God, specifically African religious women.

The work is structured in three parts. The first presents the preliminary issues of the subject, the second deals with the exegesis of 1 Corinthians 11:2–16, and the third presents the attitude of African men with regard to the dress of African religious women, and relates this to the attitude of Paul in Corinth.

Preliminary Issues

Woman—Biblical Conception

Biblical history is marked by many civilizations from 1500 BCE to 100 CE. Women's identity and social roles are differently understood according to these civilizations during the time of the Old and New Testaments.

In the Old Testament, woman is subordinate to her husband and considered his property. She is under the guardianship of males for her entire life: her father before marriage (cf. 1 Sam. 18:17), her husband in marriage, and her eldest son at the death of her husband.[1] Women, however, can participate in public activities (cf. Deut. 12:12; 2 Sam. 6:19; Judg. 21:21; 1 Sam. 1:4) and can assume responsibilities in the sanctuary (Exod. 38:8).[2] Women's equal rights to men are recognized, because they are both created in the image of God and are to reign over creation

161

(Gen. 1:25–28), but these equal rights have not been respected throughout history until the coming of Christ.

In the NT, Jesus regards women as equal to men (John 4:7ff.; Mark 5:23ff.; 7:24ff.; Luke 10:38–42), making a woman one of his disciples (Luke 8:2; Mark 15:40–41) and the first witness of the Resurrection (Mark 16:1; John 20:1–17). In the early church, a woman is a deaconess (Rom. 16:1), an elder (Titus 2:3–5), a widow who spends much time in supplications and prayers (1 Tim. 5:5), one who has received the gift of prophecy (Acts 21:9). Paul affirms her equality with man in Christ (Gal. 3:28) and her subordination to man given the decorum rules of the cultural contexts of the addressees (1 Cor. 11:5–6, 14:34; 1 Tim. 2:11).

In the present state of things, the subordination of women stems from sin (cf. Gen. 3:16), which has perverted the man-woman relationship. Thus the authority of the husband became a dominion, and the submission of woman a total abandonment of her own will.[3]

Philosophical Conception

Philosophical moralists of Aristotle's time used to advise their readers on how to direct the members of their households. These counsels developed into the family codes. They established three categories subordinate to the man: the woman, the child, and the slave.[4] According to them, their subordination was related to the natural dimension of their being. It is primarily a natural fact before becoming a cultural one.[5]

Some thinkers issued discriminatory judgments about women, which conditioned their treatment in society.[6] For them, women are evil by nature (cf. Sir. 42:12–14), and thus laws that advocated their submission really sought their own good.[7] Others found them less intelligent—except a few women who had intellectually become men[8]—and exhorted them to learn philosophy from their husbands.[9]

Furthermore, all attempts by religious groups to consider women as equal to men were fought, especially in the first and second centuries CE. The old society structures were fighting against that.[10]

Use of a Veil

A cultural history of clothing shows that there is no same way of dressing from the origins of humanity until today. We rather notice diversity and specific evolution in every period and every culture. The veil of the woman was part of her clothing in some cultures, in particular in the Syro-Hittite world, during the Greek period.[11]

The veil was still a cultural practice in Paul's day. Men and women of different cultures covered their heads for specific reasons such as bereavement, feelings of shame, and so on.[12] In Corinth, the practice was important in the Christian communities, probably because of the presence of immigrants from the East who were in the city.

The use of a veil is an issue related to the culture of ancient Mediterranean society. A woman's veil hid her hair, which was a fundamental object of attraction for men.[13] Married women expressed fidelity to their husbands by wearing the veil. Virgins and prostitutes were unveiled, as a signal that they were looking for men.[14]

There is also the ritual use of a veil by both men and women in the pagan world.[15] They wore it during prayer and sacrifice as a sign of devotion. The veil meant the consecration of a person to deities.

Wearing the veil was also part of the Roman marriage customs, where the fiancée was traditionally veiled. Christianity has kept this usage both for consecrated virgins and for the fiancée. The veil meant for virgins the consecration of the person to God, and for the fiancée a mark of submission to her fiancé. She wears it until before the wedding. This is the time of initiation to the domestic worship of her husband.

Close Reading of 1 Corinthians 11:2–16

The text I want to analyze in these pages belongs to the section 8:1–11:34 where Paul deals with the theme of pagan and Christian banquets. Through this theme, he gives the community guidelines and advice for performing the worship of the Lord in an appropriate manner.

The text is divided into two parts: verse 2 and verses 3–16. The first sets out the compliments of the Apostle toward his converts for their loyalty both to the person of Paul and to the tradition that the same Paul handed down to them (v. 2). He bequeathed to them the tradition he received from the first apostles (Acts 9:26–30).[16] He gets ready to educate them about a practice peculiar to their society and its relation to their celebration of divine worship. In the second part, the Apostle expresses his wish through several arguments urging the addressees to respect family values (vv. 3–6), the order of creation (vv. 7–12), the order of nature (vv. 13–15), and Christian custom (v. 16).

This essay will follow the argumentative organization of the text.

Family Values

Paul highlights three categories of interdependent entities and shows on whom each depends as follows: the head of the man is *ho Christos* / "the Christ"; the head of the woman is *ho aner* / "man"; and the head of Christ is *ho Theos* / "God."

The term *aner* / "man, husband" differs of course from the word *anthropos* / "a human being," which indicates humankind: man and woman. The word *kephalē* / "head" can mean either "authority," which comes from the Hebrew word *rōš* / "head"[17] or "source."[18] The two meanings are present in the Septuagint, the Greek translation of the Hebrew Bible. Thus, in this work, the two meanings of the term *kephalē* / "head," "source" and "authority," are considered. However, in view of space limitations and also because the article is about women, I focus only on the sense of the affirmation about women: "the husband is the head of the woman."

At first glance, Paul's statement seems restrictive with regard to women compared to men. The head of the woman is her husband, and her husband's head is Christ. Referring to the meaning of "head," Paul says that it is not Christ who is the source and authority for the woman but her husband. Indeed, man as the source or origin of the woman refers to the creation story, which describes the origin of the woman from the rib of man by God (see Gen. 2:22). Certainly, Gen. 2:22 says that the man is the origin of the woman; however, the divine intervention of the Trinity (one of whose persons became man in Christ) is obvious. This implies that the man and his wife both come from God (1 Cor. 11:12). Concerning the meaning *kephalē* / "head" as "authority," this indicates that a married woman must obey or submit to her husband, because he is her authority. The hypothesis could be explained from the Pauline texts Ephesians 5:22–33, Colossians 3:18, 1 Timothy 5:14, Titus 2:4–5, and the Roman culture.

Ephesians 5:22–33, in particular, illustrates the meaning of the affirmation. The husband has authority over his wife, and thus she is called to submit to him. However, Paul here speaks of mutual submission between believers in a well-defined context: the one of the fear of the Lord (Eph. 5:21). He shows that it is not only the wife who must submit (Eph. 5:22–24), but also the husband. The latter will do so following the way Christ acted for the church (Eph. 5:25–28). The Christian novelty is that the man's authority is redefined because of his own submission to Christ in Ephesians 5:23.[19] And the subordination of women follows the model of the church's relation to Christ. In short, the mutual submission that Paul recommends decreases the negative aspect of the term "submission." Its meaning comes close to that of the term "respect" (Eph. 5:33).[20]

There is a problem, however, in reconciling Paul's teaching of gender equality in Christ (cf. Gal. 3:28; 1 Cor. 12:13; and Rom. 16:3–15 as well) with the wife's subordination to her husband. On the exegetical level, this question could easily support the view that, in the Pauline corpus, the authentic writings would support gender parity and the nonauthentic writings would show the woman's submission to her husband.[21] However, the text of 1 Corinthians 11:2–16 opposes this position, because the text is an extract from one of the authentic Pauline letters and yet contains the teaching on the subordination of women. Thus, it is clear that the question of the submission of women does not relate to the Pauline authorship of such and such a letter of the Pauline corpus, but to the question of the Greco-Roman cultural context of Paul's day.[22]

In his work of evangelization Paul takes into account the culture of the people[23] to whom he is sent and he brings to that culture the newness of the Gospel. From this, we understand that the proclamation of the Gospel must not do away with a people's culture, especially what is positive in it for human development. Evangelization brings added light to the culture. This is the whole task of inculturation, which is basic to the missionary activity of Paul, and which allows the Good News to take root in a culture and thus bring forth its fruits there.[24]

Another element that justifies the assumption of man as "head" of the woman, in the sense of being an "authority" for her, is the cultural order of Paul's day.[25] The culture of that time enormously contributed to the submission of women. More-over, the teachings of Jewish writers testify to it. Some of these writers seem to have thought that women are wicked by nature (Sir. 42.12–14).[26] Josephus supports the subordination of women by saying that the laws that prescribed their subor-dination sought the good of women themselves.[27] Philo focuses on the intellectual dimension of women who, according to him, have only a limited intelligence.[28] Plutarch recommends that women be educated in philosophy by their husbands.[29] Thus, in his capacity of *paterfamilias* / "father of the family," man had authority over woman.[30] Aristotle speaks of women's submission as an issue inherent in their nature and not merely a cultural fact.[31] Furthermore, women's subordination was considered a normal behavior, especially since it represented one of their greatest virtues in Greco-Roman society (Sir. 26:14–16).

What Paul desires of the Corinthians here also has to do with the question of covering or uncovering one's hair during divine worship. The Apostle defines a Christian practice by taking up some elements from the surrounding culture (v. 4), where men were accustomed to pray or prophesy with uncovered heads. In doing so, he honors Christ. However, the fact that the verb "pray" is related to the verb "prophesy" here would indicate that the reference is to actions that take place in groups, that is, in public, in a place of worship. In fact, prophets foretold and announced what will happen to others.

The practice of covering one's head was current in various cultures of ancient society, precisely in the time of the Apostle of the Gentiles. It involved both men (Gen. 24:65)[32] and women, especially in bereavement or during some humiliating event or situation.[33] Paul certainly knew this custom, but he rejects it for the Chris-tian married men of Corinth during public worship, because by so doing they would not honor their head, Christ. This is all the more so in the context of 1 Corinthians 11, where the act of covering the head is a sign of subordination to another person. The husband cannot submit to anyone; if he does so, he does not honor Christ. The prohibition of the Apostle here means that his Corinthian community will not follow the Jewish custom, according to which men did cover their heads during public worship; one can compare the case of the practice of circumcision, which was excluded for Gentile believers in the letter to the Galatians.[34]

On the other hand, a woman must cover her head when she prays or proph-esies in an assembly (v. 5). The statement contains a novelty with respect to Jewish custom: the woman can pray or prophesy during the divine worship. In this, Paul accepted the customs of the Roman and Greek pagan world, where the active participation of women in worship and women's use of a veil as a sign of submission to the deity are realities.[35] Moreover, we note that as regards the man, the break with custom is clear—he does not cover his head when praying or prophesying—but as regards the woman, there is no break with the culture: she is required to follow the usual custom in order to honor her husband.

The cultural use of head covering recommended in 1 Corinthians 11:5 by Paul for married women certainly stands in tension with his theology of gender equality (Gal. 3:27–28), of equality among the baptized (cf. 1 Cor. 12:13), and of freedom from the customs of the world (Gal. 4:3–5). Yet at the same time, it expresses certain values for the woman of that time. Since her hair was an essential and decisive aspect of male attraction to her,[36] she must, as a married woman, cover her head, otherwise she would be considered unfaithful to her husband. However, virgins and prostitutes who were seeking men were not held to this custom. Thus, to honor her husband and avoid distractions to other men present at worship, Paul urges women to put on the veil. In this way, the internal moral order of the community is protected and gender equality theology applies in serenity.

If, however, Paul applies the equality of all the baptized in Christ in a morally disordered context, the equality of all in Christ will not be perceived. Therefore, it is imperative to consider the culture of each people in the application of the Gospel message.[37]

Order of Creation

Paul justifies his exhortation on the clothing question by appealing to the origins of man and woman (v. 7) when he affirms that the man is the image and glory of God, while the woman is man's glory.

It seems that Paul does not consider Genesis 1:27, which presents man and woman together as the image of God,[38] but rather refers to another narrative of creation in Genesis 2:21–23. The latter describes the joyous emotion of man once he saw the woman God had created in shaping her from the rib he had taken from him (cf. v. 23). The man is at the peak of glory in seeing the woman. If in Genesis 2:7 God created the male human being according to his good pleasure, in Genesis 2:21 he created the female in order to satisfy the male's need to find among the creatures one like him. In addition, wisdom literature describes the perfect woman as "the joy of her husband" (Sir. 26:1–4; Prov. 11:16, 12:4, 31:23).[39]

Paul declares that the use of the veil is well founded (v. 10). Although the head covering expresses the submission of the wife to her husband, it also protects her dignity in relation to herself and also to her husband.[40] It allows her to assert her own dignity and thus prevent distractions to men during worship.

There is an undeniable difficulty in understanding the thought of the Apostle about gender equality and freedom from the customs of the surrounding society. The woman has to bear the burden of custom and the created order by the fact that she is obliged to adapt her conduct in order to prevent the man from falling into the lust of the flesh. Because of that, she is required to comply with the custom of the veil. Consequently, she must hide what brings out her beauty. In fact, against the opinion of Rosine Lambin, wearing the veil for worship (as Paul recommends to women here) does not relate to God, as was the case for the consecrated virgins or the Roman Vestals of pagan worship, but to human beings.[41] Indeed, the angels mentioned in verse 10—as another reason for a woman to cover her head—would be those who had sinned and been expelled from heaven and then desired human women (Gen. 6:2; also Jude 6), or those present in a cult who would be offended because of a violation of appropriate behavior,[42] or those who governed nations and whom Christians will judge (cf. 1 Cor. 6:3).

Order of Nature

Paul qualifies his statement at verse 11. He shows that both man and woman are interdependent in the Lord. The reciprocal relationship that unites them is anchored in the Lord.[43] On the one hand, we find here the Pauline theology of equality between men and women in Galatians 3:28, whose inspiration comes from Genesis 1:26–27, and on the other hand, we have Genesis 2:24. The coexistence of both sexes is based on the Lord Jesus, who by his incarnation has restored fallen creation, which had been disturbed by sin (Matt. 19:4).

Following André-Marie Dubarle, we affirm that this coexistence permanently manifests itself in procreation—in this sense, man is born of woman (1 Cor. 11:12). Paul shows an indisputable parity between men and women. He affirms two important realities of their lives: the woman comes from man (Gen. 2:21–23) and man is born of woman (Gen. 4:1).[44]

The Apostle leaves the cultural and scriptural aspects of Gen. 2:21–23 and takes up the Christian and scriptural aspects of Galatians 3:28. He clearly shows that there is parity between men and women. If the account of creation reveals a certain inferiority of women with regard to men, nevertheless, nature in the procreative order presents their equality and mutual importance (vv. 11–12). Moreover, both come from God.

In verse 13, Paul returned to the problem mentioned in verse 4 about a woman's use of a veil when she prays or prophesies. In verse 5, he appealed to the judgment of the Corinthians by asking them to consider whether it is advisable for the woman to pray with uncovered head. In verse 13, he also appeals to their judgment but only mentions the time of prayer and not that of prophecy, during which the woman must cover her head. Paul rightly expects an affirmative answer, given the knowledge of the Corinthians of what nature and culture recommend.

The question of wearing the veil for the woman when she prays or prophesies is a social and cultural issue. It is human society that establishes conventions recognized as appropriate for various situations. Paul uses these conventions to define the question of dress during worship.[45] This problem has to do with the pagan culture of the Mediterranean in Paul's day.[46] God, in contrast, is interested in the internal dimension of the person. However, it is up to humans to find the right external conditions that promote the contact of humans with God.

Stoic philosophical influence, according to which "nature does things well and one must follow its teaching,"[47] can be perceived in Pauline thought when he suggests that nature does not want to see a man with long hair (v. 14).[48] A man with long hair goes against nature and loses respect in the opinion of others, because he looks like a woman with long hair that was given to her as a veil (v. 5).

Paul recognizes that long hair honors women (v. 15). However, he seems to contradict this with his affirmation of 1 Corinthians 11:5–6. If the hair is given to women as a veil, why does she still need an artificial veil? And why should she cut her hair if she has it for a veil?

Christian Custom

Paul closes his speech by saying that the arguments of the contentious people are not in line with his custom or with that of the churches of God (v. 16). This discussion is about the use of a veil by women. There would have been in the community those who argued for the veil and others who were against it.[49] Paul would have encouraged those who supported the use of the veil, and these were probably in the majority. In addition, he congratulated them because they remembered him and kept the traditions that he passed on to them (1 Cor. 11:3). However, a minority in the community was against the use of the veil and contested it. To end the dispute, Paul invited the Corinthians to maintain the customs of the churches of God and to do away with an attitude of protest.

In conclusion, the use of a veil that Paul recommends to the women of the community of Corinth is a cultural fact. Therefore, it should not be a universal law. It is suitable for people who were already familiar with this practice. Yet this stance of Paul at first sight seems to put in question his thinking on gender equality and on the freedom of Christians with regard to pagan customs. Indeed, the idea of the equality of all in Christ would have its impact on the members only if the internal moral order of the community is established. Nonetheless, it follows from this teaching that a decent dress for divine worship is recommended. This Christian principle is suitable for all peoples of all times once the customs of the specific sociocultural milieu and its time are taken into account. What then about African society?

The Implication of the Message of 1 Corinthians 11:2–16 in the African Context

The following analysis focuses on the dress of African women in the service of God in the Catholic Church in particular, specifically African religious. African societies, predominantly Catholic, recognize the religious through her dress such as the church has established: a dress with a veil, or a loincloth costume with a scarf, that is an African specificity under the inspiration of the clothing of African women.

Africa, a continent of many nations, includes a diversity of cultures. It would be impossible to discuss the behavior of each African people in this article because of the limited number of pages. However, I will strive to present an element that is characteristic of this area globally—namely, respect for tradition—and how this affects the attitude of Congolese men to the dress of Congolese women in public.

Regarding the traditional dress of women in Congolese culture (DRC), in connection with Paul's statement in 1 Corinthians 11:2–16, women were always clothed from the waist down. And at the chest (breast), she dressed in a piece of cloth made of raffia or other bark. This was to avoid attracting the lust of men. Breasts, according to Congolese tradition, were an erogenous zone. On her head, women did not wear a veil, but they braided their hair. It is difficult to say exactly what was the reason for this hair braiding, but it was probably for aesthetic reasons. However, having the head covered brought a touch of royalty to a woman's bearing. For centuries, in Congolese culture, a woman regarded as "well dressed" for our society has become a source of self-respect and honor for the family. A woman does not dress any which way. She is the mirror of society. The loincloth, which replaces the tree bark, and the braided hair are the marks of a genuine woman; wearing a veil adds a touch not only of elegance but also of a certain royalty. The trousers that a Congolese woman might wear depend on circumstances and should not be treated as ordinary or usual clothing. Whereas in Europe this garment has the function of protecting against the cold, for African women it is to protect themselves against rape.

Thus, for the majority of Congolese men, a worthy and respectable Congolese woman should dress in loincloths and blouse, with braided hair and a head scarf. That is the way she should appear in public places and also at religious services. Religious women in the service of God in the Catholic Church ordinarily dress in loincloth costume and wear a veil.

In general, African people value and respect what is already established and has been transmitted to them. They are closely attached to tradition and do not think highly of change, even when postmodernity and climate change would call for innovation in people's behavior. In order to respect tradition, many Africans are seen as ready to castigate and punish any form of change.

The change of climate especially has an effect on human behavior that leads people to adapt their clothing, their food, their houses (air-conditioned house), and so on to protect themselves. With regard to the clothing of African women, change is readily accepted as long as a woman does not appear conspicuously unconventional in society. It is even encouraged or appreciated. Problems arise when a woman occupies an elite position, because African men want to see her dressed as culture and tradition established according to the function she performs. If she does this, she shows respect and consideration for herself and for African men.

African men, however, tend to be intransigent with regard to changes in the dress of African religious women. Certainly, a minority admits that the religious can modify her clothing provided that it is decent. This minority is open to dialogue when the dress does not reflect her religious identity and will note this with delicacy. The majority, however, definitely want African religious women to wear the canonical dress. By so doing, she is not only recognized and respected in African society but is less disturbed by men, because she does not unduly distract them. We say "unduly" because it can be said that woman attracts man by nature, but this attraction will not arrive at its normal outcome because of her dress, which reflects her total and exclusive belonging to God.

These conservative Africans do not hesitate to castigate and punish if the dress of a religious woman is inappropriate in the sense that it makes her look like a married African woman. They will humiliate her when the opportunity arises. These are attitudes which, in this author's opinion, reflect the respect of African tradition. And the punishment is in most cases imposed without prior dialogue. The religious finds herself overwhelmed by reproaches and a victim sometimes even of immoral acts. In my opinion, while respecting the African value of taking tradition into account, I believe that dialogue is important before considering any punitive treatment for a religious woman who might be dressed inappropriately.

In this regard, the Apostle Paul showed foresight. He saved the Corinthian women from the dishonor that would result from having their hair in a condition unsuitable for worship. Since their hair would be an object of seduction and distraction to the men of that time, the Apostle recommends that women wear the veil during prayer. Despite its restrictive aspect for women, this recommendation plays a significant role. It helps to maintain the moral order in the community and thus to live properly the Good News.

Moreover, one sees that women must do what they can to ensure their own safety and security before relying on the contribution of men. A woman needs to adopt a certain way of behavior, especially when she has to exercise a ministry in public. Indeed, she is partly the guarantor of the good or bad behavior of men. If she behaves inappropriately, in this case by dressing very badly, she may drag a whole group adrift. For their own good, the female elite of Africa are called to behave with reserve even though postmodern developments offer scope for change; they must go forward with restraint because the price to pay is very high and risks putting in question all that they are and all that they have achieved.

Notes

1. Herrade Mehl-Kœhnlein, "Femme," *Vocabulaire Biblique* (Paris: Cerf), 103.

2. Exod. 15:20; Judg. 4–5; 2 Chron. 34:22ff.; Josh. 2:9; Ruth 1–4; 1 Kings 17:12; 2 Kings 4:8ff.; etc.

3. Mehl-Kœhnlein, "Femme," *Vocabulaire Biblique*, 104; Xavier Léon-Dufour, Jean Duplacy, Augustin George, and Pierre Grelot, "Femme," *Vocabulaire Théologique* (Paris: Cerf), 438–39.

4. Aristotle, *Pol.* 1.2.1, 1253b.

5. Aristotle, *Pol.* 1.2.12, 1254b.

6. Ngimbi Nseka, "La femme zaïroise et son identité culturelle," *Revue Philosophique de Kinshasa* 7 (1993): 59–60.

7. Josephus, *Against Apion* 2.24 §200–201.

8. Philo, *Omn. Prob. Lib.* 117.

9. Plutarch, *Bride and Groom*, 48; id., *Mor. 145 DE*.

10. Tacitus, *Ann.* 2.85; Josephus, *Ant.* 18.3.4 §§64–80; Craig S. Keener, "Man and Woman," *Dictionary of Paul and His Letters*, Gerald Hawthorne, ed. (Downers Grove, IL: Intervarsity Press, 1993), 584–85.

11. Louis Monloubou and Michel du Buit, *Dictionnaire Biblique* (Paris: Desclée, 1984), 759.

12. Keener, "Man and Woman," 585.

13. Apuleius, *Met.* 2.8–9; *Sifre, Num.* 11.2.3; Keener, "Man and Woman," 585.

14. Mishna, *Ket.* 7, 6; Keener, "Man and Woman," 585.

15. Rosine Lambin, "Paul et le voile des femmes," *Clio* 2 (1995). https://clio.revues.org/488.

16. Ibid.

17. Wayne Grudem, "Does Kephale ('Head') Mean 'Source' or 'Authority Over' in Greek Literature?" *Trinity Journal* 6 (1985): 38–59; Joseph Fitzmyer, "Another Look at Kephale in 1 Corinthians 11.3." *New Testament Studies* 35 (1989): 503–11.

18. R. Scroggs, "Paul and the Eschatological Woman," JAAR 40 (1972): 283–303; A. Mickelsen, "What Does Kephale mean in the New Testament?" A. Mickelsen, ed. Women, Authority and the Bible (Downers Grove, IL: Intervarsity Press, 1986), 97–117.

19. Donald Guthrie, J. Alec Motyer, Alan Stibbs, and Donald J. Wiseman, *Nouveau commentaire biblique* (St.-Légier, Switzerland: Emmaüs, 2002), 1115.

20. Keener, "Man and Woman," 589.

21. Ibid., 587–88.

22. Ibid., 588.

23. André-Marie Dubarle, "Paul et l'antiféminisme," *Revue des sciences philosophique et théologiques* 60 (1976): 261–80, at 271.

24. Commission Biblique Pontificale, *L'interprétation dela Bible dans L'Eglise* (15 April 1993), 107.

25. Keener, "Man and Woman," 587.

26. *m. Abot* 2, 7.

27. Josephus, *Ag. Ap.* 2.24 §§200–201.

28. Philo, *Omn. Prob. Lib.* 117.

29. Plutarch, *Bride and Groom,* 48; id., *Mor.* 145 DE.

30. Aristotle, *Pol.* 1.2.1, 1253b.

31. Aristotle, *Pol.* 1.2.12, 1254b.

32. Guthrie et al., *Nouveau commentaire biblique,* 1115.

33. Keener, "Man and Woman," 585.

34. Lambin, "Paul et le voile des femmes."

35. Ibid.

36. Apuleius, *Metamorphoses* 2.8–9; Sifre, *Num.* 11.2.3; Keener, "Man and Woman," 585.

37. Guthrie et al., *Nouveau commentaire bilbique,* 1115.

38. Dubarle, "Paul et l'antiféminisme," 275.

39. Ibid., 275.

40. Ibid.; Guthrie et al., *Nouveau commentaire biblique,* 1115.

41. Lambin, "Paul et le voile des femmes."

42. Geza Vermes, *The Dead Sea Scrolls* (New York: Penguin Books, 1962); Guthrie et al., *Nouveau commentaire biblique,* 1115.

43. Guthrie et al., *Nouveau commentaire biblique,* 1115.

44. Dubarle, "Paul et l'antiféminisme," 273.

45. Guthrie et al., *Nouveau commentaire biblique,* 1115.

46. Dubarle, "Paul et l'antiféminisme," 273; Lambin, "Le voile des femmes."

47. Lambin, "Le voile des femmes."

48. Epictetus, 50, 125–30.

49. Dubarle, "Paul et l'antiféminisme," 273.

LIFE IN ABUNDANCE

Johannine Ethics from an Indian Feminist Perspective

Rekha M. Chennattu, RA

This essay begins with the presupposition of what it means to reflect on Johannine ethics from an Indian feminist perspective. Using the lens of Indian women's experiences and concerns, I explore various Johannine theological motifs in order to glean from them the elements of Johannine ethics and their implications for the global world.

Presupposition: An Indian Feminist Perspective

India is blessed with a great diversity of religions, traditions, languages, and cultures. Some great religions—Hinduism, Buddhism, Jainism, and Sikhism—originated in India and some others—Christianity and Islam—were brought to India and lived side by side peacefully for many centuries. The present moment in Indian history, however, gives witness to violence and hatred in the name of religious faith and its traditions. Among other things, Indian society also suffers from massive poverty, human rights violations, economic injustice, and political corruption. Indian society is, moreover, divided by inequalities of class, caste, race, color, disability, and gender discrimination—the subjugation of women and girls. But probably the most cruel, dehumanizing, and destructive as well as most comprehensive and pervasive of all inequalities is gender inequality—the socially and culturally imposed differences between women and men, boys and girls. The dominant means deployed in India by men and boys to reduce women and girls to fear and subjugation is rape. Daily, our newspapers show that sexual harassment, rape, and murder are the destiny of many women today.

It is in this context that we understand Indian feminism, which not only tries to create an awareness of the atrocities committed against women and the discrimination exercised against women in society, in the church, at work, or within the family but also tries to change these dehumanizing situations. Indian feminism envisages a culture that promotes relationships of mutuality and fosters cooperation and interdependence between men and women. Many people in India still prefer to shy away from being called feminist as it is a much misunderstood and misinterpreted concept. The conventions such as "being submissive" or "cultivating a capacity to endure suffering and humiliation" still reflect in many ways what Indian women were taught (and still believe) as the most natural, normal, and noble way of behaving in society. What, therefore, is the unique and distinct way in which Indian women respond to the present situation of cultural alienation, religious depriva-tion, and male domination? What seems appropriate in handling these issues is the strategy of constructive dialogue in view of challenging and changing the gender stereotypes in the church and in society. On the one hand, this strategy is sensitive to the deepest aspirations of Indian women, who try to integrate both mind and heart or reason and emotion. On the other hand, it enables Indian women to create a new culture that respects the dignity of every human person (male and female) and promotes interdependence in relationships.

The Johannine Ethics of Giving Life in Abundance

Using the lens of the Indian context in general and the experiences of Indian women in particular, I now turn to the Gospel of John to explore its moral vision and ethical paradigm for the global church. Specific ethical instructions and admoni-tions seem absent in John's Gospel because of the absence of the teachings on specific issues such as marriage and divorce, war and violence, and wealth and poverty. As Wayne A. Meeks observes: "It [John's Gospel] offers no explicit moral instruction."[1] Even though there are repeated appeals to keep Jesus' commandments, the content of these commandments is not always explicitly spelled out in the Gospel. Moreover, the Law of Moses in John's Gospel has a Christological function, is used in Christological debates (5:19–47), and is presented as prefiguring Jesus; and it does not offer any moral vision of the Johannine Jesus. However, as Richard Hays argues, "The ethical significance of the New Testament narratives cannot be restricted to their didactic content. John, even more pointedly than the other Gospels, shows that a fuller reading of the story is necessary in order to grasp its implications for shaping the life of the Christian community."[2] As D. Moody Smith aptly observes, "The Johannine Jesus gives us fundamental direction, but not a prescription for constructive action in complex situations."[3] We have in John's Gospel a rich and symbolic narrative of the divine word (*logos*) entering human history and that of the universe, in and through the person of Jesus, transcending the boundaries of culture, religions, and gender in order to give life in abundance to all.[4] The purpose of Jesus' coming into the universe was to give life, life in abundance (10:10). This is indeed the most powerful good news for Indian women and girls whose life from womb to tomb is threatened in India today. As an Indian woman reading John's Gospel, I cannot but use John 10:10 as the key to the ethical vision of the Johannine Jesus. I shall now explore some impor-tant theological motifs as presented by the narratives of John's Gospel in order to grasp the ethical vision of giving life in abundance.

An Ethic of Communion and Integration

John's incarnational Christology—the Word became flesh and pitched its tent among us (1:14)—presents Jesus as both divine and human as well as heavenly and earthly, and makes John's apparent dualism (meaning to say, God and world,

divine and human, from above and below) insignificant.[5] Jesus is the personifica-
tion of the eternal, preexistent Word which participated in the creative work of
God (John 1:1–5) as described in the Old Testament ("Then God said, 'Let there
be light'; and there was light" [Gen. 1:3]; "By the word of the Lord the heavens
were made, and all their host by the breath of his mouth" [Ps. 33:6]). The Word
pitched its tent *among* us (1:14) unlike the tent of the old covenant placed *outside*
the camp (Exod. 33:7–11). What came into existence through the Word was
creation (1:3–5), and what we received from Jesus was grace and truth or the fullness of the life and love of God (1:17). Jesus is presented as the only Son who has
seen the Father (1:18, 6:46) and is thus capable of revealing the Father or interpreting the will of the Father (1:18). Not only is Jesus the definitive manifestation
of God in human form in the universe (1:14), but he is also the definitive interpretation of the will of God for humans in the history of the universe (1:18). John's
prologue not only declares the Word as the agent of creation and the source of life
for the entire creation including human beings, but also affirms that the light of
the Word overcomes (and shines in) the darkness (1:5). The Word from heaven is
thus both the creator and the savior of human beings and of the entire universe (see
also 6:51, 12:47). John's portrait of Jesus underlines the intimate relationship and
communion between God, Jesus, human beings, and the entire creation and also
holds creation and salvation (redemption) together. John presents the mystery of
the Incarnation as a boundary-breaking moment when the divine encountered the
human, the heavens touched the earth, and the sacred penetrated the secular. So
the Incarnation is indeed God's way of integrating the divine and the human, the
heavens and the earth, the sacred and the secular, and creation and salvation.

An Ethic of Well-being/ Wholeness and Social/Economic Justice

The beneficiaries of the life-giving mission of Jesus include people from all
walks of life in manifold life situations, and with a preferential option for the poor
and the marginalized. A careful reader can glean from the Gospel Jesus' radical
social concern, which provides the basis for critiquing social norms that exclude or
exploit the less privileged ones in society. The Johannine Jesus begins his ministry
by responding to the humiliation of a poor family who could not afford enough
wine for their guests at their wedding celebration (2:1–11). Jesus reacts with indignation to the money changers and those selling the doves in the temple and rebukes
them for making the temple a profit-making marketplace of the privileged and the
powerful (2:13–22). Jesus challenges the narrow mentality of Nicodemus and prods
him to go beyond the closed boundaries of Jewish traditions (3:1–21). The Sabbath
controversies in chapters 5–10 are powerful critiques of Jewish religious norms and
practices that do not enhance life. Jesus brings healing and wholeness to the para-
lyzed man at the sheep-pool in Jerusalem who had "no one to put him into the pool
when the water was stirred up" (5:1–18). The compassion of Jesus feeds a hungry

crowd in the mountains of Galilee (6:1–15). Jesus rejects the marginalization of the man born blind as a social anomaly or sin (9:1–3). Jesus presents himself as the good shepherd who lays down his life for the sheep, which has significant religious and political implications for the first readers of the Gospel of John (10:1–18).[6] Jesus weeps at the death of his friend, Lazarus, and raises him to life (11:1–44). We have a graphic illustration of Jesus' love in action in the foot-washing event. Jesus overthrows the inequality that naturally existed among them and inaugurates a new covenant community of equals by washing the feet of his disciples and by serving them as his friends (13:1–20). Jesus' love for his disciples as his friends is spelled out in terms of self-giving to the point of death (15:13–14). During the dialogue between Jesus and Pilate at Jesus' trial, Jesus subordinates the imperial power of the Romans to the authority of God (19:1–16). The Johannine Jesus reaches out to all who are in need and on the margins, and brings them wholeness and fullness of life.

The only command or ethical rule given by the Johannine Jesus to his disciples is the reciprocal love modeled after Jesus' love—"love one another as I have loved you" (15:12). Only one passage, the imperative—love one another—expresses explicitly what it implies (13:34). After washing the feet of his disciples as his friends, thus establishing an equal partnership in his mission, Jesus invites the disciples to do as Jesus has done to them—to wash the feet of one another ("I have set you an example, that you also should do as I have done to you") (13:15).[7] The mutual love of the disciples is more than a mere emotional feeling of affection, and has something to do with a public, committed action in favor of God's choices. The Gospel presents this mutual love as the sign of their discipleship: "By this everyone will know that you are my disciples, if you have love for one another" (13:35). The disciples are to love one another, just as Jesus has loved them; and this love is the identity mark of Jesus' disciples (13:34–35).

Although the practical implications of the love command of Jesus are not explicitly developed at length in the Gospel, the admonition of the First Letter of John (1 John 3:18)—"to love in truth and action, and not in word or speech"—in the context of the financial needs of some members suggests that the Johannine ethic of love definitely entails sharing of material goods within the community ("How does God's love abide in anyone who has the world's goods and sees a brother or sister in need and yet refuses help?" [1 John 3:17]). The author of the letters of John presents this mutual love as a manifestation of their love for God (2:15, 4:20), and makes an explicit link between this mutual love and committed action in favor of God's choices (3:11–18). For example, the first letter talks about, on the one hand, "the loveless-ness" of the disciples (4:8), and, on the other, exhorts them to "obey his word" (2:5), "do what is right" (3:10), "obey his commandments and do what pleases him" (3:22) as manifestations of their brotherly/sisterly love for one another. The sharing of "material goods" or "economic justice" is understood as a practical implication of abiding in God's love and loving one another. From the perspective of First John, economic justice is definitely one way of making the disciples' love concrete, and thus the disciples are guilty of being liars when they withhold "the world's goods" from those of the community in need. In sum, establishing social and economic justice and sustaining a just and inclusive community are imperative for all disciples of Jesus.

An Ethic of Gender Equality and Radical Inclusiveness

The Gospel presents both women and men as ideal disciples and apostles. The first part of Jesus' ministry from Cana and back to Cana (in chapters 2–4) presents two women (the mother of Jesus and the Samaritan woman) as well as two men (John the Baptist and the royal officer) as true disciples who placed their complete trust in the power of Jesus. Here we have a perfect paradigm of both women and men as well as a radical inclusion of Jews, Samaritans, and Gentiles. John's Gospel upholds the full humanity and sacredness of women as God's beloved daughters who play important leadership roles in the community. As women leaders and committed disciples, we have the mother of Jesus (2:1–11, 19:25–27), the Samaritan woman (4:1–42), the Jewish sisters, Martha and Mary, and Mary Magdalene (20:1–18). Martha is placed on par with Peter when she makes the Christological confession of faith in Jesus as the Messiah (11:27), and Mary Magdalene is the first recipient of the appearance of the risen Jesus and is presented as an "apostle to the apostles" sent by the risen Lord to announce the good news of the resurrection to the disciples (20:17–18).

Based on Jesus' love commandment, "love one another," John's Gospel is often interpreted as promoting "exclusive sectarianism"—"loving only one another," and thus the Johannine community is seen as an "inward-looking community" with a hostile attitude to the world outside.[8] A careful reading of the Gospel, however, reveals a radical inclusivism from the very outset of Jesus' ministry. The beginning of Jesus' ministry takes place among a broad social mixture of people: Jews (2:1–3:36), Samaritans (4:1–42), and Gentiles (4:43–54). Jesus moves from the Jewish world to the Gentile world through the world of the Samaritans (chapters 2–4).[9] At the beginning of the Samaritan story, the narrator informs the readers that there existed no dealings between the Jews and the Samaritans (4:9), but at the end of the episode, the Samaritans become members of the new covenant community (4:42). Jesus' exchange with the Samaritan woman, representing people despised for their mixed descent and impurity in general, and women in particular, challenges prejudices against gender and ethnicity (John 4:1–42).[10] This episode thus projects a breaking down of all barriers—gender, religious, and racial—that will bring about a radical egalitarian understanding of Christian community. Moreover, among the disciples of Jesus as members of the Johannine community, the Gospel witnesses to a radical inclusion of other marginalized groups such as socially and religiously outcast sick people, the paralytic at the Sheep-Gate of Jerusalem (5:1–18), and the man born blind who dared to stand up for Jesus against the Jewish authorities who were afraid of being expelled from the synagogues (9:1–42), and of a religiously/morally outcast prostitute—the woman caught in adultery (7:53–8:11).

In addition, the Johannine understanding of the church does not promote any sort of hierarchy when it refers to the disciples as equal branches attached to the Vine of Jesus. The only way one can make a distinction is the branch bearing fruit and the one that does not bear fruit (15:8). The Johannine community is therefore best described as a new covenant community of egalitarian fellowship without distinctions of rank or gender or position.[11] A radical openness to include everyone as God's beloved child as well as to respect and accept everyone as an equal covenant partner in the community of Jesus would signal the hallmark of Johannine ethics.

An Ethic of Care for Creation

The Gospel in general and the Johannine prologue in particular (1:1–18) manifest a strong ecological bent. The world (*cosmos*), in the Johannine vocabulary, has at least four shades of meaning: (1) the universe—the material world and human beings in general (1:9, 10a–10b); (2) the material world, excluding human beings (17:5, 24); (3) human beings in general, excluding the material world ("I declare to the world [human beings] what I have heard from him" [8:26]); and (4) the nonbelievers. When Jesus talks about the world hating him and his followers, it is clearly a reference to this fourth category, namely, those who do not believe in Jesus (15:18–20). In many instances it probably has the first reference—the universe which includes both creation and humanity together (1:9–10, 3:16, 4:42). The Word is coming into this world, meaning to say, coming into the universe (1:9–10); God loved the world in 3:16, meaning to say, God loved the universe— the material creation as well as human beings. Other examples include Jesus' being called "the savior of the world" by the Samaritans (4:42), Jesus' giving up his life for the "life of the world" (6:51), and Jesus' coming in order to "save the world" (12:47). John's Gospel depicts the world or the material universe as created by God through the Word (1:3–5), and the Word made the universe its dwelling place by pitching its tent among us (1:14), and the whole of the physical and material universe is sanctified, saved by his death (6:51, 12:47). It is therefore an integral part of the mission of the disciples of Jesus to protect and keep creation (or the material universe) worthy to be the dwelling place of God. The care for creation can be considered an important aspect of Johannine ethics.

An Ethic of Doing the Will of God

Each Gospel presents a different portrait of Jesus, and consequently each has a different interpretation of what it means to be a follower of Jesus. The purpose of the Incarnation, according to John's Gospel, was to give to those who received Jesus, and believed in him, the power to become children of God (1:12). Being a disciple means taking one's place among the children of God. The believers or the disciples are those who are born of God and thus called to share in the life of God as God's children (1:13). The disciples share in the life of God—which has its origin from

God (5:26); which cannot be destroyed by death (11:26) but can be destroyed by sin (1 John 3:15). Elsewhere John's Gospel endorses abiding in Jesus' word (8:31–38) and doing the will of the Father as quintessential characteristics of the children of God (8:39–47). The experience of abiding in Jesus' word makes the disciples free to be engaged in the work of God.

The fourth evangelist conceives of discipleship as the fruit of a relationship with Jesus and with God initiated by a personal encounter. This intimate relationship is explained by different metaphors, such as the Shepherd and sheep or the Vine and branches. The Good Shepherd knows his own and his own know him (10:14); Jesus is the Vine and his disciples are the branches (15:5); Jesus abides in the disciples and they in him, and this relationship bears fruit (15:4) and glorifies the Father (15:8). The metaphor of the Vine and the branches defines discipleship in terms of an abiding covenant relationship with Jesus as well as a participation in Jesus' mission; the disciples, in bearing fruit, glorify the Father (15:1–8).[12] Bearing fruit is another term for performing the "works of God" (6:28). Jesus presents himself as the mediator through which human beings live in a relationship with God, which enables them to perform the works of God (6:27–28). As Jesus explained to Nicodemus, "Those who do what is true come to the light, so that it may be clearly seen that their deeds have been done in God" (3:21). The Johannine Jesus can do nothing on his own; he does only what he sees the Father doing (5:19), and is so committed to the will of the Father that Jesus refers to it as his food (4:34); he proclaims publicly that he has come not to do his will but the will of the one sending him (6:38). As Jesus was sent by the Father, Jesus in his turn sends the disciples into the world to do the will of Jesus who is sending them (20:21). This mutual love takes its visible form in their commitment to the will of God. In the light of the Good Shepherd discourse, which distinguishes the good from the false shepherds, we can say that God's radical concern for social and economic justice and the integrity of creation articulates God's will. We are called to uphold the same concern of God through our life and commitment. The life-giving and self-sacrificing attitude of the Good Shepherd inspires us to promote life and the well-being of all living beings.

A Spirit-guided Ethic and Discernment

The understanding of the Spirit as the Paraclete—the counselor or advocate—is unique to the Gospel of John (14:16). John 14 is rich in close parallels between the covenant promises of Yahweh to Israel and those of Jesus to his disciples.[13] As in the Old Testament, what is being affirmed here is the indwelling presence of God in the community. The Johannine Jesus promises that he would send the Paraclete who will guide the members of the community in his absence to do the will of God or to do what is right as it "declares to them what belongs to Christ" (16:14). The mission of the Spirit is to "teach them everything" and "to remind them of what Jesus has taught them" (14:26). There seems to be, therefore, a strong notion of an ongoing revelation of God's will in and through the presence and work of the Paraclete in the community. This has significant ethical implications. As Russell Pregeant aptly points out, "The notion of a Spirit-guided ethics necessarily implies a process of discernment. Thus, while love provides the broad principle on which ethical action is founded, there remains an irreducible open-endedness to ethical reflection: the community must count on the Spirit not only to guide it into deeper understanding of the truth but also to inspire and empower it in the process of discerning the good."[14] In every new situation, empowered by the Spirit, the disciples of Jesus are called to discern the appropriate action, which makes present the love and life that proceeds from the Father, and was revealed by the Son in his life, mission, death, and resurrection, and which ensures life for all.

The Johannine Ethics and Its Implications

The open-ended, liberating, and spirit-guided ethic of mutual love is at the service of life to the extent of laying down one's life for others. We are called to apply this ethical vision to individual moral issues in a manner that will enhance the life of all concerned by the issues. We do this by discerning the expected human behavior in the light of the teachings of the Johannine Jesus. Johannine ethics is the result of an experience of God, a religious experience of awakening, which evokes a religious response and manifests itself in a pattern of human behaviors that enhances the life of all—women and men; rich and poor; the sick and the healthy; learned and illiterate; high caste and low caste. It emerges from a praxis-oriented spirituality that takes seriously both personal conversion and social transformation. It is rooted in a faith conviction that equips the believers to become partners in God's life-giving and saving mission, transcending the boundaries of gender, conventional roles in society, religious traditions, and cultures. Johannine ethics is all about our relationship with God, with one another, and with the entire creation, which determines who we are and how we act. Our relationship with God enables us to have an optimistic worldview, which inspires courage to take risks always in favor of God's life-giving choices.

The vision of humanity as God's family challenges our lack of respect for human persons, challenges all discrimination based on class, caste, color, creed, and race. It calls us to participate in the ongoing struggle against all sorts of discrimination and injustice, against all that impedes our quest for truth and wholeness. Following the model of the Johannine Jesus, we need to use dialogue as the means to befriend the other and build up human communities of love, peace, justice, and harmony. We are called to join hands with people of other religions who will commit themselves to the promotion of justice in favor of the poor and to the care of creation, making visible the life-giving presence of God here and now in our human and cosmic history.

From the perspective of the Johannine ethics of life in abundance, the existence of destitution and deprivation is a measure of the failure of discipleship. We have produced "designer foods" and increased the yield a hundredfold, but we fail to silence the rumblings of hunger in the starving millions. We have created technologies of instant global communications, but live as strangers to our next-door neighbors. In the words of George Soares-Prabhu, "Rich (and greedy) Christians in a hungry world is a towering scandal which no amount of private devotions or much publicized almsgiving can take way."[15] In the context of India, where many girl children go missing every day due to female feticide and ever-increasing crimes against women, the Johannine ethic of giving life calls for a radical commitment to eradicate all forms of violence against women that devalue and dehumanize their personhood. It invites all human beings to participate in women's struggle for the right to life, and for justice, dignity, and wholeness.

In the context of global warming and environmental distress, which generate anxiety over the future of our planet, Johannine ethics challenges us to make bridges and integrate the secular and sacred dimensions of our life and existence. We are called to look for a sustainable development that takes care of creation and preserves it for future generations. We witness today disrupted weather patterns, and climate change has grown to be a key global issue. Cement production, deforestation, the burning of fossil fuels, the setting up of nuclear/thermal power plants, the driving of cars and other vehicles, and flying aircrafts—all emit carbon dioxide. All of us, participants of the ecosystem, are called to do our bit to make the mission of protecting the universe successful. In the context of the 2015 UN Climate Change Conference in Paris, Johannine ethics calls us to mobilize the resources of humanity, engaging all facets of society, to create and advocate policy, conduct and scrutinize research, and design standards to reduce CO_2 emissions.[16] We are called to respond to the problems of climate change and protect our planet, the dwelling place of God and humanity.

In conclusion, when we read the Gospel of John from a feminist perspective, being sensitive to the specific context of India, the ethical paradigm emerging from the Gospel is an ethic of giving life in abundance. Following the Johannine story of Jesus, one can affirm that the Johannine ethic of giving life in abundance presupposes a principle of radical equality and inclusiveness and a process of dialogue at all levels. It makes doing the will of God, loving one another, fostering communion, laying down one's life for the common good, working for economic and social justice, being inclusive, promoting gender equality, entering into a process of discernment, and caring for creation imperatives for all disciples of Jesus.

Notes

1. Wayne A. Meeks, "The Ethics of the Fourth Evangelist," in *Exploring the Gospel of John*, ed. R. Alan Culpepper and C. Clifton Black (Louisville, KY: Westminster John Knox, 1996), 318.

2. Richard B. Hays, *The Moral Vision of the New Testament: Community, Cross, and New Creation: A Contemporary Introduction to New Testament Ethics* (San Francisco: HarperSanFrancisco, 1996), 140.

3. D. Moody Smith, "Ethics and the Interpretation of the Fourth Gospel," in *Word, Theology, and Community in John*, ed. John Painter, R. Alan Culpepper, and Fernando F. Segovia (St. Louis, MO: Chalice Press, 2002), 120–21.

4. See also George Mlakuzhyil, *Path to Abundant Life in the Gospel of John* (Delhi: Media House, 2005); John R. Donahue, ed., *Life in Abundance: Studies of John's Gospel in Tribute to Raymond E. Brown* (Collegeville: Liturgical Press, 2005).

5. For a detailed discussion, see Rekha M. Chennattu, "The Word Became Flesh (John 1:1–18): A Cross-cultural/religious Expression of the Divine," in *Cross-cultural Encounter: Experience and Expression of the Divine*, ed. Mohan Doss and Andreas Vonach (Innsbruck: Innsbruck University Press, 2009), 43–51.

6. See Rekha Chennattu, "The Good Shepherd (Jn 10): A Political Perspective," *Jnanadeepa: Pune Journal of Religious Studies* 1, no. 1 (1998): 93–105.

7. See Sandra M. Schneiders, "The Foot Washing (John 13:1–20): An Experiment in Hermeneutics," *Catholic Biblical Quarterly* 43 (1981): 76–92.

8. See the comment of Barnabas Lindars, "The Johannine church is a beleaguered sect, alienated from the local society, intensely loyal internally, but hostile to those outside" (*The Gospel of John* [London: Marshall, Morgan & Scott, 1972], 58–59).

9. See the insightful work of Francis J. Moloney, *Belief in the Word: Reading John 1–4* (Minneapolis: Fortress, 1993).

10. For a detailed discussion, see Rekha Chennattu, "Women in Mission: An Interpretation of John 4," *Dharma Deepika: A South Asian Journal of Missiological Research* 21, no. 9 (2005): 23–32.

11. See, for example, David Rensberger, *Overcoming the World: Politics and Community in the Gospel of John* (Philadelphia: Westminster, 1988; London: SPCK, 1989), 148; Paul N. Anderson, *The Fourth Gospel and Quest for Jesus: Modern Foundations Reconsidered*, LNTS 321 (London: T&T Clark, 2006), 166.

12. Rekha M. Chennattu, "'The Covenant Motif: A Key to the Interpretation of John 15–16," in *Transcending Boundaries: Contemporary Readings of the New Testament*, ed. Rekha M. Chennattu and Mary Coloe (Rome: LAS, 2005), 141–59.

13. Rekha M. Chennattu, *Johannine Discipleship as a Covenant Relationship* (Peabody, MA: Hendrickson Publishers, 2006), 101–11.

14. Russell Pregeant, *Knowing Truth, Doing Good: Engaging New Testament Ethics* (Minneapolis: Fortress, 2007), 209.

15. George M. Soares-Prabhu, "'Good News to the Poor': The Social Implications of the Message of Jesus," *Biblebhashyam* 4 (1978): 212.

16. Don Tapscott, "Governing the Climate? States Can't Solve the Problem of Climate Change: It's Time for a New Strategy," *Huffington Post*, February 12, 2015.

LIBERATION THEOLOGY

Appropriating the Bible as "Memory of the Poor"

Jaime Vidaurrázaga

In this essay, I propose a narrative showing how a morally motivated renewal of the praxis and organization of the postconciliar Latin American church led to the discovery of the Bible as "memory of the poor," and that such a discovery and the corollaries that followed from it have shaped the way in which theological ethics has developed in the continent over the last five decades. I start by contrasting the way in which Vatican II was received in Latin America with the way it was received in the developed West, with special attention to the emergence of ecclesial base communities (*comunidades eclesiales de base*—CEBs) and of a theology of liberation, regarding both as the fruits of a moral choice taken by the church to stand on the side of the poor and vulnerable. As the CEBs engaged the biblical text in their lives of faith, they discovered that the story of the Bible is their story too—the story of an oppressed people yearning for authentic liberation. This insight led the Latin American church to respond to urgent moral problems in the continent with biblical language and prophetic courage. When this response was eventually codified in a theological ethical discourse, this discourse was heavily influenced by the Bible and by the prophetic mission of the church in Latin America.

Reception of Vatican II in the Latin American Reality

Many of the essays in this volume take the Second Vatican Council as a historical point of reference, which should surprise no one considering the momentous transformation that the council effected on the life of the church and on the practice of theological reflection. By the time the council took place, the biblical movement was decades old. In the field of moral theology, attempts to move beyond the moral manuals had been made since at least the 1930s.[1] However, efforts to renew these disciplines only directly affected the lives of the majority of Catholics around the world after the council issued official teaching in support of this process.

Although Vatican II did not produce a specific document addressing moral theology, the council's call to meet modern men and women where they are, and to address their "joy and hope, [their] grief and anxiety,"[2] dramatically boosted the renewal of moral theology among Catholics. The dry objectivism of the moral manuals was gradually replaced by a new emphasis on the primacy of conscience, on autonomy, and on interpersonal relations. Additionally, the council mandated the revision of seminary formation to make theological education more explicitly centered on the mystery of Christ,[3] and the teaching of moral theology more thoroughly informed by biblical sources.[4] Revising the seminary curriculum made possible the development of a moral theology more appealing to modern men and women.

In Europe, as well as in most of the developed world, the renewal of Catholic moral theology focused on autonomy and freedom as a way to reach out to modern men and women. This was an era of increased optimism due to the widespread experience of prosperity and expanding freedoms among the peoples of the developed world. The "person" became the central category of this renewal of moral theology to the point that in many circles this renewed system of understanding morality came to be known as "Personalism."

Because of the vast differences in Latin America's social, economic, and political context, Vatican II was received in a very different manner there. Different too was the way in which the renewal of moral theology took shape on this continent. The modern men and women, whose joy and hope, grief and anxiety the council wanted the church to embrace, were in this continent poor and marginalized peoples and not merely an abstract category used by scholars. In the midst of societies marked by a huge gap between the rich and the poor, those charged with implementing the reforms of Vatican II made the moral choice of siding with the poor and oppressed. The central category of this version of the renewal of theology in general and of moral theology in particular was the "non-person,"[5] the oppressed and almost obliterated subject struggling to survive in the midst of constant threats. The focus of this alternative way of addressing the renewal of moral theology was not autonomy as something mostly conquered already, but rather liberation from oppression and abuse.

The ethical choice to stand on the side of the poor and oppressed led to a two-pronged strategy for the implementation of Vatican II in Latin America. From a practical standpoint, the depth of suffering and oppression determined an urgent call to action, to engage in the praxis of liberation. As Gustavo Gutiérrez so aptly described it, a commitment to the cause of liberation was the first (and we may add the most urgent) step here. The theoretical side of this strategy, a new form of theological reflection, was to be a second step following the praxis of liberation.[6] The order of these two steps is a logical order of priorities and not necessarily a chronological one, but it nevertheless offers an ordering principle for the narrative that follows.

Latin American theologians and bishops returning from Vatican II, as well as other church leaders who learned about the work of the council through the documents issued by it, were motivated to take a fresh look at the reality faced by the people in their own continent. What they discovered was not only extreme need but also a budding historical movement of social, economic, and political transformation in which the poor themselves were the historical subjects fighting for their own rights and for a new society where all could share the same human dignity together. The "irruption of the poor"[7] in Latin American society had not been orchestrated or engineered by church activists, but Vatican II–minded church leaders could not let the opportunity to effect meaningful change in favor of the poor pass by during such an upsurge of activism. In many cases, religious communities of men and women, groups of motivated priests, and also some bishops physically moved their residences to poor shantytowns or far-removed and isolated villages in a process called "*insersión*," which included their engagement in social and political organization, as well as their participation in local customs and celebrations. The renewal of parish life through promotion of lay ministries was hardly distinguishable from the formation of committees of neighborhood improvement as a means to develop political leadership among the neighbors. Literacy campaigns, often designed as a means to increase awareness of rights as well as political participation and debate among the population, often were the place where new "*catequistas*" (also known in some regions as "delegates of the word") were effectively recruited. This was the context in which the first ecclesial base communities (CEBs) emerged.[8]

A church that had "rolled up its sleeves" and joined the work of fighting injustice and bringing about a more just society had to rethink and reformulate its discourse about God, Christ, salvation, its own organization and mission as a church, and more. This new theological reflection, which followed the work for liberation as a "second step," came to be known as a theology of liberation. This theology's emphasis on the primacy of praxis and on what eventually would be formulated as the "preferential option for the poor" has heavily influenced all innovative theological reflection in Latin America since the 1960s, including biblical exegesis and moral theology.

Morally Motivated Exegesis and Biblically Shaped Morality

New methodological approaches to biblical exegesis as well as a renewed theological approach to urgent moral issues developed under the methodological umbrella provided by the nascent theology of liberation. Novel approaches to both disciplines were also grounded on the experience and reflection generated by flourishing CEBs. The confluence between the theology of liberation and the work of the CEBs provided a unique space where biblical exegesis and theological ethics could fruitfully influence one another. This was a stark contrast to the previous religious environment in Latin America, which had impeded a mutually enriching interaction between these two disciplines, as I shall examine presently.

Christian missionaries arrived in Latin America on the same ships as the Spanish and Portuguese conquistadors, and the "evangelizing" labor of these missionaries provided religious justification for abusive practices like the encomiendas, the extirpation of idolatries, and so on. Leaving the few but significant exceptions of Bartolomé de Las Casas, Guamán Poma de Ayala, and others aside, the work of Christian missionaries provided a thin religious veneer that covered the brutality of European colonialist expansion. The "conquest" of Latin America by Europeans was experienced by the natives as political domination, economic exploitation, and almost complete cultural obliteration.[9] Since the struggle of independence was largely led by "criollo" elites (the American-born descendants of Spanish and Portuguese conquistadors), independence from colonial rule in the early 1800s did little to ameliorate the situation of the descendants of the native populations and of the Africans brought to the continent as slaves. The unchecked process of concentrating the ownership of land and other means of production in the hands of a few families in each region, as well as the increased presence of multinational companies interested almost exclusively in the extraction of raw materials, left a large percentage of criollo and mestizo populations impoverished and relatively disenfranchised.

Until the eve of the council, the official version of Christianity (apart from the many syncretic forms in which it had been appropriated by natives, mestizos, and Blacks into their communal lives) continued to be a religion imported from Europe together with many other forms of cultural imperialism. This approach to Christianity regarded the church as a divinely established institution housing an aggregate of individuals. Each Christian individual was obsessed with avoiding eternal damnation by focusing on the development of individual faith as an antidote to individual sin. Because of its lack of attention to the social dimension of sin and of salvation, this understanding of Christianity prevented individuals from challenging the status quo in any meaningful way. Latin American Christianity until the time of the council was a prime example of the Marxist description of religion as "opium of the people." Catholics' knowledge of the Bible was reduced to secondhand knowledge of a series of stories showing God's omnipotence and of a limited array of exemplars of individual faith and obedience to God's explicit design for their lives as individuals. Understanding of Christian morality was also reduced to the legalistic objectivism of the manuals, and once again to the pursuit of individual righteousness, often by attending the sacrament of confession and Mass regularly, to avoid eternal damnation.

Bringing biblical literacy to large groups of previously disenfranchised Christians now gathered in CEBs was not just an expedient way to achieve pastoral efficacy; it was a moral choice, the choice to provide the tools required by these Christian communities to have access to what Leonardo Boff would later call the "means of religious production."[10] Yet bringing biblical literacy to the masses often required the more elementary task of bringing basic literacy to them. The poor had been deprived of access to the Bible not only by a clerical church that feared the pluralistic thrust of Protestant "*sola Scriptura*," but also by an exploitative economic and social system that kept poor peasants and other manual workers illiterate and uneducated and thus easier to exploit.

As soon as they gained access to larger portions of the Bible and to rudimentary tools of biblical exegesis and basic knowledge of Israel's history, the poor and disenfranchised started to see themselves and their current struggles reflected in the stories told in the Bible. Time and time again, they became aware that the common experiences shared by ancient Israel and the early church mirrored their own current experiences. This discovery led these barely literate peasants and underemployed manual workers to gradually embrace the Bible as the memory of a continued historical struggle by the poor and oppressed whom God loves preferentially. This is how the Bible came to be embraced as the "historical memory of the poor" among the CEBs and among Latin American theologians.[11]

Members of the CEBs did not approach the Bible as a source of curious or exotic information. Their approach to the Bible was neither the aseptic approach of the scientist nor that of the armchair biblical scholar. The methodology of *ver, juzgar y actuar* (see, judge, and act) guiding the procedures in a CEB meeting led them to adopt a particular approach to the Bible. Such an approach departed from concrete questions and challenges discovered in the analysis of the economic, political, and social context in which the CEB lived. Their approach to the Bible searched for the proper moral stance with regard to those challenges and for a broader narrative of salvation into which the local CEB could contextualize the community's current struggle. Such an approach to the Bible led those in the community to commit themselves to the action required to transform their reality in the direction of more justice for all and hope for the possibility of a better future. It is not surprising that when the general assemblies of the Latin American Catholic Bishops in Medellín (1968) and Puebla (1979) embraced this same methodology, the positions adopted in their final documents (1) called for a church committed to the liberation of the poor from economic exploitation and political oppression,[12] (2) praised the labor of the CEBs,[13] and (3) gave strong backing to the developing intellectual endeavor called "theology of liberation," especially to the "preferential option for the poor."[14]

Prolific and innovative biblical scholars in Latin America at the time, both Catholic and Protestant, did not see themselves simply as members of academia. Rather, they realized that their work facilitated this process that came to be known as the popular reading of the Bible. They saw their own scholarship about the Bible as part of this reflective "second step" following their direct work with CEBs in the periphery of the cities where they lived. Native as well as adoptive Latin American biblical scholars, Catholic and Protestant authors alike, published innovative works systematizing the findings of their study of biblical passages and formulating appropriate methodologies for interpreting the Bible within CEB meetings. Such articles and books were often conceived as tools to further deepen the CEBs' use of the Bible in their continuous deliberations.[15]

Given that the CEBs' constantly used the Bible to evaluate ("judge") the data emerging from the social analysis of the reality surrounding them ("see"), it is not surprising that the CEBs and their theological advisers adopted biblical categories, and biblical language in general, to describe the urgency to address flagrant injustice and to formulate strategies and priorities for the praxis of liberation ("act"). For example, Latin American theologians engaged in discourse about God and faith warned their audiences that the threat to faith in their continent was idolatry, not atheism, as was the case in post-Christian Europe. Latin American idolatry presented itself in one of two ways: either worshiping the true God in falsifying ways (individualistic religiosity imported from Europe as described above), or worshiping the false gods of wealth or the national security state instead of the one true and living God. In either case, the idols of death hindered a true encounter with the God of life, whose life-giving preferential love for the poor was thoroughly described on the basis of biblical data from both the Hebrew Bible and the New Testament.[16] In addition, professional theologians as well as pastoral agents at all levels, including among the most prominent Dom Hélder Câmara and Monseñor Oscar Romero, emphasized the idea that the prophetic mission of the church requires *anuncio y denuncia* (to announce and to denounce) at the same time. A prophetic church could not announce the coming of God's reign as Good News without at the same time denouncing how far from the values of God's reign the present reality was because of the choices made by those in power, both in their own countries and in the international economic and political order.[17] Finally, the very concept of liberation carried with it strong echoes of the biblical experience of the Exodus from Egypt, of the return from the Exile in Babylon, of the people's yearning to be freed from Roman occupation in the times of Jesus, and of the New Testament's description of Jesus' mission as ultimate delivery from sin and death.

However, the influence of the Bible on the Latin American church's struggle for justice and peace was not limited to the use of a specific language. Biblical language was backed by courageous actions worthy of the bravest among the prophets of ancient Israel and among the apostles. Monseñor Romero became the emblematic representative of thousands of martyrs of the Latin American church. After calling the rank and file of the Salvadorian military forces to disobey unjust orders to kill innocent people, Romero delivered the last line of his last broadcast Sunday sermon, speaking as a true prophet: "In the name of God, and in the name of this suffering people, whose laments rise to heaven each day more tumultuous, I beg you, I beseech you, I order you in the name of God: stop the repression!"[18] He did not only use biblical language when he talked about the people's laments rising up to heaven; when he spoke he foresaw that he would pay with his life for this prophetic utterance.

The achievements of pioneers and heroes were assimilated into the institutional life of the church as the general assemblies of the Latin American episcopate in Medellín (1968) and Puebla (1979), later on in Santo Domingo (1992), and more recently Aparecida (2007) addressed a multitude of moral issues,[19] albeit from a mainly pastoral rather than a theoretical perspective. Despite attempts by powerful and well-connected bishops who opposed liberation theology to challenge the use of the *ver, juzgar y actuar* (see, judge, and act) method for running the assemblies following Medellín, the bishops nevertheless utilized the model in Puebla and Santo Domingo—although with some discussion about the inclusion of *orar* ("pray") as an extra step. The use of "see, judge, and act" by the assembly in Aparecida is especially important given that Cardinal Jorge Bergoglio, who would later become Pope Francis, was one of the leading voices and presided over the committee redacting the assembly's conclusions. These four assemblies also provided the space in which the preferential option for the poor found its initial official validation as a principle of Catholic moral reasoning and pastoral planning,[20] before it was later adopted by Pope John Paul II into his social encyclicals,[21] and finally incorporated into the store of principles of Catholic social teaching.[22]

In his recently issued first encyclical, *Laudato Si'*, Pope Francis addresses the current ecological crisis in a distinctly Latin American way. The pope writes as someone who understands and is empathetic to the concerns of the poor and the marginalized, especially to the ways in which they are most severely affected by the degradation of the environment. He also organizes the content of the encyclical in a sequence of steps roughly following the methodology of *ver, juzgar y actuar*.[23] Pope Francis also brings to the world stage the perspective of countries which have not benefited from the industrialization that precipitated this crisis, but are equally if not more affected by its deleterious effects. One telling example of this can be found in the way in which Pope Francis echoes the indignation expressed by Latin American bishops in Aparecida when they discussed proposals to "internationalize" sovereignty over the Amazon region.[24]

Latin American Theological Ethics Today

By their own admission, professional moral theologians in Latin America were late to join the rest of their colleagues in producing a systematic account of what a moral theology of liberation could look like.[25] But as Latin American professional moral theologians continue to systematize the multifaceted ways in which urgent moral problems had been addressed by their theological colleagues, they do so in a way that is thoroughly formed by biblical narratives and closely attuned to the needs of the poor.[26]

Mirroring the methodology of the CEBs, Latin American theological ethicists today start their work by analyzing Latin American societal reality. Because of the influence of the Bible in their work, Latin Americans often structure their theological ethics around the ultimate goal of God's reign and its values, and their ethics is thoroughly infused with the preferential option for the poor. Finally, at least in the case of works about applied ethics, their publications are intent on offering constructive proposals for effective action to make an impact on the moral improvement of Latin American society today.

Because of the primacy of praxis over dogma, and of the thorough use of biblical categories in moral evaluation of societal problems, Latin American theological ethics and biblical exegesis are notably ecumenical. Both in biblical studies and in moral theology, Catholics and many Protestants share a common language, are in constant dialogue with one another, and often participate in common projects of pastoral formation, planning, and evaluation.[27]

Moral theology used to be the exclusive dominion of priests in Latin America, as in most of the Catholic world before Vatican II. Even today, the number of women, lay Christians, and Christians from ethnic and other minorities among professional moral theologians is very limited.[28] However, in the model followed by the CEBs, everyone's opinion counts. Theological ethics emerging from the church of the poor is not the restricted dominion of a select group of experts, but rather the concern of the vast majority of Christians, all of whom are required to take, both individually and communally, a moral stance with regard to the issues at hand. Social workers, social scientists, environmentalists, and other professionals who happen to be Catholic are thus engaged in theologically driven ethical reflection and activism today.[29] Their participation in the theological conversation about ethical issues motivates Latin American theological ethics to address problems that had been unjustifiably neglected for decades, such as machismo, domestic violence, racism, abuses against indigenous peoples, destruction of the environment, discrimination against homosexuals, misconceptions about AIDS, and more.

Theological ethics coming out of Latin America is well positioned to participate in an enriching dialogue with theological ethics emerging from other corners of the world. Latin American theologians, as well as theologians from other parts of the "Third World," can teach their counterparts in the developed world about the way in which the large moral issues of the day, from environmental devastation to the treatment of pandemics, from the economic world order to the rise of violent fundamentalism, affect the poorest in the most devastating way. Together with post–Vatican II moralists from the world over, Latin American theologians share a biblically informed interest in Jesus as a moral exemplar and in God's reign as ultimate telos of Christian morality. Latin American theological ethicists can learn from their European and North American counterparts, a group that includes a larger proportion of women and lay professional ethicists, to challenge themselves to embrace new perspectives and to address the new topics mentioned above. Through the formation of regional and transcontinental networks of coordination and mutual enrichment, Latin American moralists hope to effect meaningful progress in tackling the most urgent moral problems that we face in an increasingly globalized and interconnected world today.

Notes

1. See James F. Keenan, *A History of Catholic Moral Theology in the Twentieth Century: From Confessing Sins to Liberating Consciences* (New York: Continuum, 2010).

2. Second Vatican Ecumenical Council, Pastoral Constitution *Gaudium et Spes* (1965), 1.

3. Second Vatican Ecumenical Council, Decree *Optatam Totius* (1965), 14, 16.

4. *Optatam Totius* 16.

5. Francisco Moreno Rejón, "Fundamental Moral Theory in the Theology of Liberation," in *Mysterium Liberationis: Fundamental Concepts of Liberation Theology*, ed. Ignacio Ellacuría, and Jon Sobrino (Maryknoll, NY: Orbis Books, 1993), 215. See also Jon Sobrino, "The Crucified Peoples: Yahweh's Suffering Servant Today," in *The Principle of Mercy: Taking the Crucified People from the Cross* (Maryknoll, NY: Orbis Books, 1994), 49–57.

6. See Gustavo Gutiérrez, *A Theology of Liberation: History, Politics and Salvation*, trans. and ed. Sister Caridad Inda and John Eagleson (Maryknoll, NY: Orbis Books, 1988), 5–12.

7. See ibid., xx–xxi.

8. See Marcello de C. Azevedo, "Basic Ecclesial Communities," in *Mysterium Liberationis*, 640–43; Leonardo Boff, *Church: Charism & Power*, trans. John W. Dierckmeier (New York: Crossroad, 1985), 125–30.

9. See Jon Sobrino, "Five Hundred Years: Structural Sin and Structural Grace," in *The Principle of Mercy*, 69–82.

10. See Boff, *Church: Charism & Power*, 112.

11. See Pablo Richard, "Bíblia, Memória Histórica dos Pobres," *Estudos Bíblicos* 1 (1984): 143–50; Gilberto da Silva Gorgulho, "Biblical Hermenutics," in *Mysterium Liberationis: Fundamental Concepts of Liberation Theology*, 124–28.

12. CELAM II (Medellín, 1968), "La Justicia", 12–23; "La Paz," 16–19; CELAM III (Puebla, 1979), 1159–65.

13. CELAM III (Puebla, 1979), 629, 648.

14. Ibid., 1134–65.

15. See Carlos Mesters, "The Use of the Bible in Christian Communities of the Common People (1981)," in *Liberation Theology: A Documentary History*, ed. Alfred T. Hennelly (Maryknoll, NY: Orbis Books, 1990), 14–28; Carlos Mesters, *Defenseless Flower: A New Reading of the Bible*, trans. Francis McDonagh (Maryknoll, NY: Orbis Books, 1989); Elsa Támez, "La Biblia y Sus Lectores en América Latina y el Caribe," *Pasos* 128 (2006): 1–5.

16. See Pablo Richard et al., *The Idols of Death and the God of Life: A Theology*, trans. Barbara E. Campbell and Bonnie Shepard (Maryknoll, NY: Orbis Books, 1983); Pablo Richard, *Fuerza etica y espiritual de la teología de la liberación en el contexto actual de la globalización* (La Habana: Caminos, 2004), 88–90.

17. See Gutiérrez, *Theology of Liberation*, 150–56.

18. Oscar Romero, "The Church in the Service of Personal, Community, and Transcendent Liberation" (homily delivered and broadcasted on March 23, 1980).

19. In Medellín and Puebla, the main concern was with economic and political justice. In Santo Domingo, there was explicit mention of human rights, ecology, and respect for local and indigenous cultures. In Aparecida, the bishops also addressed the challenges posed by globalization, governmental corruption, and environmental devastation, among others.

20. See CELAM III (Puebla, 1979), 1134–65; CELAM IV (Santo Domingo, 1992), 178; CELAM V (Aparecida, 2007), 501, 550.

21. See Pope John Paul II, Encyclical *Sollicitudo Rei Socialis* (1987), 42; Encyclical *Centesimus Annus* (1991), 57.

22. See Pontifical Council for Justice and Peace, *Compendium of the Social Doctrine of the Church* (2004), 182–84; Pope Francis, Apostolic Exhortation *Evangelii Gaudium* (2013), 199; Encyclical *Laudato Si'* (2015), 158.

23. See Pope Francis, Encyclical *Laudato Si'* (2015), 15. Pope Francis starts by reviewing the data emerging from diverse studies about the problem. He then evaluates this data on the basis of principles taken from the Bible, of an analysis of the "deepest causes" of the present situation, and of a focus on "our unique place as human beings." All of this enables him to offer "some broader proposals for dialogue and action" and "some inspired guidelines for human development."

24. See Pope Francis, Encyclical *Laudato Si'* (2015), 38. Cf. CELAM V (Aparecida, 2007), 86.

25. See Moreno Rejón, "Fundamental Moral Theory," 210; Antonio Moser and Bernardino Leers, *Moral Theology: Dead Ends and Alternatives*, trans. Paul Burns (Maryknoll, NY: Orbis, 1990), 59.

26. See, for example, Toni Mifsud, *Moral de discernimiento*, 2nd ed. (Santiago: Paulinas-CIDE, 1988), 1:64 ff.; Ronaldo Zacharias, "Dreaming of a New Moral Theology for Brazil," in *Catholic Theological Ethics in the World Church: The Plenary Papers from the First Cross-cultural Conference on Catholic Theological Ethics*, ed. James F. Keenan (New York: Continuum, 2007), 116–23.

27. Two interesting examples in this regard are the work of Pablo Richard Elsa Támez in the Departamento Ecuménico de Investigación (DEI) in San José, Costa Rica, and the work of José Severino Croatto in the Instituto Superior Evangélico de Estudios Teológicos (ISEDET) in Buenos Aires, Argentina. See Richard, *Fuerza etica y espiritual de la teología de la liberación*, 57–65; José Severino Croatto, *Los caminos inexhauribles de la Palabra* (Buenos Aires: Lumen-ISEDET, 2000).

28. See, for example, Neiva Furlin, "Teologia e gênero: A docência feminina em instituições católicas," *Revista Eclesiástica Brasileira* 71 (2011): 880–910.

29. A quick review of the articles published in the *Revista Eclesiástica Brasileira* in the last decade shows the diversity of topics addressed by Latin American theological ethicists (bioethics, ecological crisis, human trafficking, human rights), and how their articles share many of the elements discussed in this essay. See Rogério Jolins Martins and Márcio Fabri dos Anjos, "O princípio misericórdia: Uma contribuição à questão dos princípios em bioética," *Revista Eclesiástica Brasileira* 68 (2008): 350–70; Leo Pessini, "Bioética na América Latina: Algumas questões desafiantes para o presente e o futuro," *REB* 69 (2009): 314–28; Agenor Brighenti, "Gritos da Amazônia: A propósito do III Fórum Mundial de Teologia e Libertação," *REB* 69 (2009):596–617; Guillermo Kerber, "Justiça climática," *REB* 70 (2010): 22–38; Roberto Marinucci, "Da vendabilidade do ser humano: Alguns desafios da Campanha da Fraternidade 2014 sobre Tráfico Humano," *REB* 74 (2014): 7–32; Alvori Ahlert, "Ética e Direitos Humanos: Bases fundamentais para uma Sociedade Democrática," *REB* 74 (2014): 549–63.

Reading in a Revolution

Activist Catholics' Use of Scripture during the Last Decades of Apartheid, 1974–1994

Anthony Egan, SJ

There has never been a strong tradition of Catholic biblical ethics in South Africa, or a strong tradition of Catholic biblical scholarship, or even a strong Catholic theological tradition. Despite this inauspicious beginning to this essay, I shall argue that in the context of the anti-apartheid struggle there emerged at every level a moral discourse of resistance that drew—particularly at the grassroots level—on the (almost inevitably selective) use of the Bible as a resource. The focus in this essay is on the last twenty-five years of apartheid, particularly the decades of the 1970s and 1980s. Central to this were two key factors: ecumenism and a popular hermeneutics of liberation, which were embraced particularly by grassroots Catholic organizations (youth, students, workers, justice and peace committees) supported by a core group of activist clergy and theologians who served as the "organic intellectuals"[1] of these movements.

Such a stark opening statement or thesis demands a closer preliminary analysis to highlight the genuine complexity of the situation in which the theology to be examined is to be read. First, with regard to the lack of a strong local Catholic theological tradition, it should be noted that the Catholic Church in South Africa had for centuries (from Dutch colonization in 1652 until the 1830s) been suppressed in southern Africa.[2] When it was allowed to function, the church was essentially a foreign-supported mission for well over a century: almost all its clergy and bishops were from European religious congregations. The few local vocations, black and white, were trained in Europe until nearly the mid-twentieth century. When seminaries were set up locally, they were staffed almost exclusively by foreign clergy using the set *ratio studiorum* of the church. In addition, few locally trained priests were sent for graduate study: the bishops who would form the Southern African Catholic Bishops Conference (SACBC) in 1951 stressed training local pastors and saw little need for scholarship, assuming (wrongly as it turned out) that a steady stream of professors and formators would be available from the global North. Although the church created an impressive network of schools, it similarly did not consider higher education a priority—and the notion of lay Catholic theologians was not even on the ecclesial radar. The result was that by the 1970s, apart from a handful of South African clergy (mostly religious) who *had* studied abroad, there were very few Catholic academic theologians in any discipline, let alone in such esoteric subspecializations as biblical ethics.[3]

Second, because of deep-rooted and fairly open anti-Catholic sentiments within the country, the church was deeply uneasy about taking strong stands against segregation. This hostility intensified after the 1948 victory of the National Party, with its roots in an ultraconservative form of Calvinism, white Afrikaner nationalism, and commitment to rigid and systematic segregation, apartheid. Vatican representatives (there was no nunciature until the 1990s) counseled the SACBC to caution: there was a real fear of suppression. Despite this, a number of visionary bishops led by the South African archbishop of Durban, Denis Hurley, OMI, dragged the church from the 1950s onward into opposition to apartheid, often against the will of many white Catholics.[4] From cautious beginnings the SACBC became a powerful voice of resistance, moving from calls for gradualist political reform to demands for full democratic rights for all citizens.

While SACBC discourse was frequently highly generalized and philosophical in its tone (Hurley being primarily an expert in Thomistic theology and Catholic Social Teaching [CST]), its strength lay in encouraging—particularly after Vatican II—the development of largely lay-led movements within the church. Guided by mainly progressive-minded South African clergy, such groups as the Young Christian Workers (YCW), Young Christian Students (YCS), the National Catholic Federation of Students (NCFS), Catholic Students Association (CASA), and local justice and peace commissions (J&P) took new directions. All were ecumenical in their sympathies; many in fact became de facto ecumenical movements. While still using CST, they also drew heavily on the Bible for their inspiration, much of which resonated with the growing political crisis in South Africa. Similarly, although they often took more radical stances than the SACBC, they maintained a close if occasionally tense relationship with the bishops, with the result—my third key clarification—that both sectors of the church mutually influenced each other. These groups came into their own in the 1970s, and by the 1980s, some (notably YCS and YCW) were integral parts of the broader internal resistance that would contribute to the liberation that would culminate in the election of the first really democratic government of South Africa in 1994.

Starting to Read in a Revolution: Catholics and the Bible in the 1970s

With the state having crushed almost all political resistance by the early 1960s, opposition to apartheid largely rested with the churches and the Liberal Party. While religious opposition came mainly from European-founded Protestant churches, together with groups tied to the Christian Institute of dissident Calvinist theologian Beyers Naude and a handful of Catholics like Denis Hurley, Vatican II's reforms spurred progressive Catholics to engage more openly in the struggle. YCW and YCS grew, particularly in the late 1960s, and included the participation of increasing numbers of black laity. Groups like NCFS maintained and strengthened their long-held ties with the secular and politically liberal National Union of South African Students (NUSAS). In the late 1960s, J&P was set up at parish, diocesan, and national levels. All these group were heavily CST-oriented in their moral tone and drew heavily on the See-Judge-Act method of Joseph Cardijn and YCW/YCS.

Vatican II's "rediscovery" of Scripture (thoroughly encouraged by Hurley among others), growing ecumenical cooperation, and the emergence of Black Consciousness (BC) (led by Anglican lay student Steve Biko) started to shift the discourse. Catholics began to read the Bible more thoroughly; ecumenical contact forced many to reread it through a less dogmatic lens than before. In a society where theological study was limited and resources even more so, Scripture was for most South Africans the only source (apart from basic catechisms) for such reflection. With its biblical emphasis, the religious offshoot of BC, black theology (read through the twin lenses of African culture and political oppression), further inspired black Catholics, including many seminarians.

The catalyst for the little revolution in biblical ethics (Catholic and ecumenical) of the 1970s was a crisis in the student movement and wider church. In 1969, black students withdrew from NUSAS and formed the BC-oriented South African Students' Organization (SASO), arguing that though well-intentioned, NUSAS was white-dominated (it was), and though liberal politically it could not really meet the desires of blacks for liberation. The same happened in NCFS: black Catholic students would later form CASA. The divorce was shocking for both organizations, but ultimately liberating.

Both NUSAS and NCFS came to conclude that they had to embrace a more radical politics. Initially in the early 1970s, both groups, together with YCW, worked closely in training and setting up new black trade unions, starting from Durban in 1973. Dialoguing with BC and drawing on the New Left ideas of the philosopher Rick Turner (a friend of Biko who would, like Biko, be assassinated later in the decade), this secular response caused tension within NCFS, some of whose members embraced the charismatic renewal. At this point, biblical ethics came in to save NCFS and other Catholic groups from what was once called the split between the "God Squad" (charismatics) and the "Action Faction" (the trade unionists).[5]

The SACBC had created a school of African languages for missionaries in the 1950s. In the 1970s, this school—Lumko—moved from the rural Eastern Cape to Johannesburg and started developing lay leadership programs, both as a means to empower the laity internally and to generate theological reflection on daily life.[6] Parallel to this, a South African laywoman, Anne Hope, studied the *conscientizacion* method of Brazilian educationist Paulo Freire and applied it to black parishes, BC groups, and students within South Africa until she was forced into exile in Kenya. These tools, collected into the three-volume *Training for Transformation* manual (one of the most widely circulated albeit banned texts in South Africa during the 1980s), combined Marxist social analysis, Africanist and BC ideas, and simple (exegetically simplistic) biblical readings to inspire and encourage grassroots activism.[7] Lumko's texts, though less left-wing in tone, also drew on a liberating reading of the Bible, notably the prophetic books like Amos, and were widely used mainly in poorly resourced black township J&P and Bible study groups over the next two decades.[8] They would also gain traction in parts of Asia, notably India and the Philippines.

Liberation theology came to South Africa through two sources. First, the BC movement's theological wing (many BC members were clergy or seminarians) drew on 1960s North American black theology, adapted to its new context.[9] For mainly white groups like NCFS, and arguably for the wider Catholic community, black theology was hard to adapt. The second movement, one that later dominated the contextual theology movements of the 1980s, emerged out of lectures given by NCFS National Chaplain Albert Nolan, OP, in the wake of his discovery of liberation theology at a chaplains' conference of the International Movement of Catholic Students in Lima, Peru, in 1974.

Nolan edited his talks at successive NCFS conferences into the book *Jesus before Christianity* (hereafter *JBC*) published locally in 1976,[10] and subsequently globally into many languages, making it the best-selling South African theology text, as well as Orbis Books' second-best seller of all time. Nolan, who had a doctorate in Christology from Rome, has never called himself a biblical scholar, but *JBC* is essentially a distillation of modern (mainly German) biblical Christology read through an unashamedly radical political ethics that owes as much to the thought of Biko and Turner as it does to the Bible.[11]

Two images dominate the book: the person of Jesus as a first-century political activist and his central message of the kingdom of God. Seen as one of the earliest works of "Historical Jesus Research" in South Africa, one that acknowledged the historical constructedness of the Gospel sources but avoided theorizing about textual origins in favor of an ethical, almost nonreligious, reading of the person and ministry of Jesus,[12] Nolan explicitly stated that the book was intended for persons of any faith or none. Stressing Jesus' preaching and practice over "dogmatic" themes such as incarnation or resurrection, he homed in on the kingdom of God as central to understanding the historical Jesus.

Nolan's Jesus understood the kingdom as "a future state of affairs *on earth* when the poor would no longer be poor, the hungry would be satisfied, and the oppressed would no longer be miserable,"[13] a human community where Satan (the symbol of evil, personified by those who reigned unjustly) did not rule: a community of solidarity and equals, who shared wealth, and rejected power, status, and prestige. Such a kingdom, which called disciples to struggle against oppression and inequality, demanded faith understood as belief that

> goodness is more powerful than evil and truth is stronger than falsehood. To believe in God is to believe that in the end goodness and truth will triumph over evil and falsehood and that God will conquer Satan. Anyone who thinks that evil will have the last word or that good and evil have a fifty-fifty chance is an atheist.[14]

Faith in Jesus and faith in the resurrection was, for Nolan, primarily faith in Jesus' kingdom project, which his disciples had pursued after the crucifixion (and before it became an official religion of the Roman Empire!). True believers in the present day (1970s) were those who shared faith in the kingdom and worked to see it fulfilled:

> Jesus was experienced as *the* breakthrough in the history of [humanity]. . . . His word was God's word. His Spirit was God's Spirit. His feelings were God's feelings. . . . To believe in Jesus today is to agree with this assessment of him. We do not need to use the same words, the same concepts or the same titles. We do not need to use titles at all. . . . Either you accept the kingdom as Jesus understood it or you don't. You cannot serve two masters. . . . To believe that Jesus is divine is to choose to make him and what he stands for your God.[15]

Although largely derivative of German and a few Latin American scholars (many of whom themselves drew on Germans)[16] for its exegetical content, despite its "low Christology," and even though at times it skirted close to the "secular Christianity" of theologians like Harvey Cox and Paul van Buren of the 1960s, *JBC* was never condemned either by the SACBC or by the Congregation for the Doctrine of the Faith—largely because Nolan was himself an important theological adviser to South Africa's bishops and because the book proved immensely popular.

At the level of reader response, it struck a chord with successive generations of mostly young white South African Catholics (and many Protestant contemporaries) who could not identify with the "Black Christ" of black theology or the apolitical figure of charismatic Christianity. Readers saw in the "biblical" figure of Nolan's Jesus an ethical model that broke with both an exclusively black savior and a politically impotent faith, and offered an imperative for action. By offering a radical figure who was at once recognizable in Scripture and public life, couched in moral terms that transcended the specifically South African context, the book rapidly became a best seller throughout not only the English-speaking world (US, Britain, Philippines, and India) but through translations in Francophone, Spanish, Lusophone, and even Korean contexts where young activists of Christian background struggled to keep a semblance of faith in revolutionary circumstances. Although rapidly dated in terms of its scholarship, it was a prescribed work in progressive seminaries and theology faculties from South Africa and the Philippines to Harvard.

Within lay South African activist Christian circles, *JBC* remained the single most read book throughout the late 1970s until 1994. In addition, it gave a much-needed theological content (however simplistic) to the Catholic-based grassroots Christian organizations of South Africa (NCFS, CASA, YCS, YCW, and J&P), even those most heavily secularized in the 1980s (like YCS and YCW) or those deeply influenced by black theology. With regard to the latter, it offered a bridge between the black theology of the 1970s and the new contextual theology of the

1980s and early 1990s, particularly in the wake of the virtual collapse of the Black Consciousness movement brought about by the murder of Steve Biko in 1977 and the subsequent suppression of the movement.

Reading a Revolution:
The Bible as a Way of Understanding
(and Engaging in) a Revolution, 1980–1994

At the end of the 1970s, a strongly biblical ethics of resistance rooted in the person and vision of Jesus had permeated Catholic grassroots organizations in South Africa. These groups had thoroughly imbibed a liberationist hermeneutic from black theology, liberation theology, and the homegrown variants typified in Catholic circles by Nolan's *JBC* and subsequent writings. Though classical Thomist ethics and CST continued to be the theological mainstay of the SACBC, the Catholic grassroots approach had taken on a more biblical direction, a direction that some elements of the SACBC would soon follow. The battle to create a theology for the struggle against apartheid, for reading the Bible in what was increasingly acknowledged as a national democratic revolution, had been won. In the 1980s the task turned to reading the revolution as an epic of biblical proportions—and the church as itself a "site" of that struggle. Under the circumstances, ecumenism became the norm—most Christians, including Catholics, often self-identified as part of either the "church of/for liberation" or the status quo.

The Catholic movements discussed above, in part because they had rediscovered the Bible, had also by the 1980s to a large degree become ecumenical in fact if not in name. Though some—mainly those rooted in parishes or dioceses (like J&P) or in mostly white middle-class circles (NCFS)—retained a strongly Catholic character; others (like YCS and YCW) were overtly ecumenical, occasionally interfaith (and sometimes welcoming explicitly nonreligious members), while enjoying the institutional protection of the SACBC. These groups were by the mid-1980s openly working with broad internal anti-apartheid resistance movements like the ANC-sympathetic United Democratic Front (UDF) and trade unions. By the democratic election of 1994—the end of what I would describe as the "long 1980s"—some were openly aligned to the ANC and South African Communist Party, both parties enjoying widespread lay Catholic support.

The ecumenical Institute for Contextual Theology (ICT)[17] was founded in 1981 out of the remnant of BC-aligned black theology (including pastors like the Reformed theologian Allan Boesak, and professors such as Itumeleng Mosala, Takatso Mofokeng, John de Gruchy, and Charles Villa-Vicencio) and the new local liberation theologies pioneered by activist-scholars such as the Redemptorist Larry Kaufmann and Albert Nolan—the latter giving up the opportunity to become Master General of the Dominican Order in 1982 to continue his work with ICT. Drawing together such talents with a variety of Catholic, Protestant, Pentecostal, and African Initiated Church ministers and laity in South African townships, ICT's program focused on the See-Judge-Act/Training for Transformation methods of social analysis and on biblical liberation exegesis that shifted the focus to developing a way of reflecting theologically on the dynamics of resistance. It produced materials easily accessible to lay Christian activists within church and the community and trade union organizations. In the late 1980s, a smaller group called the Theology Exchange Programme (TEP) ran "exchange programs" with similar movements in the Philippines and Latin America. Professional academic theologians (centered in the universities of Natal, Cape Town, and Western Cape) added specialist expertise to ICT, as did prominent preachers whose sermons and talks—including to secular movement gatherings—were reproduced by ICT.

The climax of ICT's work was the publication in 1985 of the *Kairos Document*,[18] a challenge to the churches to decisively get off the political fence and definitely embrace the struggle for liberation. Noting, and dismissing as literally demonic, the apartheid state's use of theology to promote the status quo in the name of anticommunism and personal piety, the document—drafted by an ecumenical committee based on workshops with township clergy in South Africa's main cities—also condemned the "official" theologies of churches that talked of nonviolence and reconciliation (taken, by this stage mistakenly, as moral compromise and gradualism). Drawing on classic biblical liberation motifs—exodus, the prophets, and Jesus' uncompromising challenge to the status quo—*Kairos* called explicitly for a prophetic theology of resistance, identification with the struggle, and the use of the churches' preaching, liturgical, and pastoral resources to overthrow apartheid. What unsettled many churches, including the Catholic Church, was its refusal to equate the violence of the state and the violence of liberation movements.

In September 1985, the semi-official Theological Advisory Commission (hereafter TAC) of the SACBC published an extensive report called *The Things That Make for Peace*.[19] Though produced in parallel with (and not in response to) the *Kairos Document*, it presented a more nuanced theological analysis of the political situation and drew on the work of three Catholic biblical scholars (Jabulani Nxumalo, OMI, John Maneschg, MCCJ, and Paul Decock, OMI).[20] Rejecting "ready-made" fundamentalist answers from Scripture, the authors highlighted the ethical ambiguity of violence and tried to balance appeals to the God of battles with the prophetic call to shalom and the covenant of peace rooted in justice. They revisited Jesus' image of the kingdom of God (*pace* Nolan) but included in it love of enemies. They echoed Pauline themes of struggle against principalities and powers and the need for Christians to stand for truth peacefully:

In exercising patience and forbearance under affliction and persecution, the believer is not giving in to a fatalism that nothing will ever be done to overcome evil. Rather, their restraint is an expression of hope in God's power that will finally rectify matters, punishing the wicked and rewarding the just. . . . Not only does this hope sustain one through failure and disappointment, but relieves one of the burden of absolutizing one's struggles as though one had to rectify the whole of history oneself.[21]

What this implied (and what the SACBC implemented) was a program of commitment to comprehensive justice (drawing on Psalm 72) that would redeem everyone. Critical of revolutionary violence while thoroughly condemning state repression, they advocated a way of mercy and compassion. Echoing Isaiah (especially chapter 54) and Hosea, they saw liberation as an act of God in which all were called to contribute, but rooted in compassion that demanded mercy, even for enemies: "Since God has not cut one's enemy off from his sustaining mercy, so as a condition for sharing his love neither shall we."[22]

The book was widely read and used by J&P groups and in some youth organizations more closely linked to the church (like NCFS), but it was not the church's final word. Throughout the 1980s, the SACBC issued a range of statements, mostly condemning repression but also grassroots/guerrilla atrocities (e.g., killing of civilians, necklacing, etc.). The SACBC cautiously welcomed the *Kairos Document* but criticized its misinterpretation of reconciliation. Significantly, as the 1980s drew to its bloody conclusion, shortly before the state conceded and started negotiating a transition to democracy, the SACBC went so far as to acknowledge that the ANC's decision to use force was "understandable" given the circumstances while maintaining its unease with violence itself.

Not all Catholic grassroots movements shared the SACBC's view. Though none openly embraced armed resistance, many felt that any attempt at moderation was compromise. Some, like YCS and CASA, endorsed the ANC and UDF interpretation of the situation. This can be illustrated by YCS (and former NCFS) National Chaplain Albert Nolan's explicit use of the ANC's theory of internal colonialism (called "colonialism of a special type"): South Africa was a mirror of the imperial world system, with the white minority (the metropolis) ruling over the black majority, the latter colonial subjects in their own country.[23]

Nolan's position was stated in his book *God in South Africa* (hereafter *GISA*), written while he was in hiding avoiding detention without trial during the 1985–1990 national state of emergency, in which the state declared martial law to crush growing internal resistance. The book became for the 1980s what *JBC* had been in the 1970s: the most clearly articulated theology of liberation for activist Catholics, though it showed a number of theological and political developments.

While *JBC* focused on an activist Jesus using historical-critical scholarship, at times anticipating in tone the Jesus Seminar group, *GISA* was much closer to what Thomas Schubeck and William Spohn have called "liberation ethics."[24] While *JBC* made almost no reference to South Africa, *GISA* was thoroughly embedded in South African 1980s reality. Indeed, one might argue that whereas *JBC* sought to call readers to radical discipleship by reading Jesus in a political sense, the locus of *GISA* was the struggle itself, reading the struggle through an appropriation of

Christian doctrine and Scripture (something the *Kairos Document*, in which Nolan had had a hand, had demanded).

Starting with the Gospel, Nolan argued that the "Gospel for us today is *shaped* by what the Bible says about God but its *content* is the latest news about the wonderful works of God in South Africa today. . . . The Gospel message today must take the shape of good news for the poor ... a prophetic message for our times"[25] The life and message of Jesus (i.e., salvation and the rule of God), rooted in his conflict with authorities that led to his death, "refer to all these things and we use them as [the struggle's] norms and guiding principles but they will not be the contents of the good news for us today" because having the mind of Christ meant "tackling the problems of our times in the spirit in which he tackled the problems of his times."[26]

Biblical themes of personal and social sin and evil had to be read into the sin and suffering of South Africa's crucified people under apartheid oppression. Even the cross had to be thus understood:

> Jesus was crucified some two thousand years ago but the Gospel we preach today is not only about that past event. The Gospel is about Christ being crucified today. It is about the crucifixion of the people of South Africa. This does not mean we are simply *comparing* the suffering of our people with the crucifixion of Jesus Christ. The crucifixion of God in Jesus Christ *is*, for us, the crucifixion of the oppressed people in our country.[27]

Salvation, from sin in all its dimensions, was primarily the salvation that comes with political liberation in South Africa. The practice of Jesus and the prophets demanded total commitment to liberation from structural sin in the name of God's reign. Christian hope for salvation had to be read through the secular signs of political hope—grassroots movements, the ANC, trade unions, protest actions, and ongoing resistance. The idea of people's power—a political strategy to seize de facto control of parts of the country and establish parallel government—was a sign of such hope: "The power of the people that is manifested in the struggle is indeed the power of God. . . . People's power like the power of God is invincible. Nowhere is this more apparent than in the power of people who are willing to suffer and die for the liberation of others. Nothing can destroy such power."[28]

Even revolutionary violence had to be read carefully: although violence was always morally problematic because it caused suffering, "the fundamental question is who is the aggressor and who is the defender."[29] The controlled use of force by the ANC and others could be seen as understandable and prevented "undisciplined and mindless violence."[30] Though nonviolence, the actual practice of Jesus, was obviously better—and the actual practice of 90 percent of the 1980s struggle—it could not be made a moral absolute.[31]

In short, what Nolan concluded to be a thoroughly biblical understanding was that the Christian task in 1980s South Africa was commitment to the abolition of apartheid through multifaceted but relentless resistance. Many scholars faulted his use of Scripture, tradition, and moral reasoning, but few rejected him outright: to do so would have been to align themselves with an obnoxious state and its theological apologists, including many conservative white Catholics. It is a measure perhaps of the zeitgeist of struggle that neither of his books was ever formally condemned by the hierarchy.

Bible, Ethics, and Struggle

When democracy came to South Africa in 1994, the grassroots Catholic activist groups largely collapsed. Whereas their secular counterparts like the UDF were subsumed into the victorious ANC, the movements dissipated into the Catholic mainstream or (as in the case of YCS and YCW) de facto ceased to exist. Some of the latter moved into the ANC itself, with many of its members cutting formal ties to the church. NCFS and CASA re-amalgamated into the Association of Catholic Tertiary Students (ACTS), and largely ceased to have a political voice, let alone a distinctive political theology. The networks of J&P groups dwindled in their significance, eclipsed by a highly professional SACBC Catholic Parliamentary Liaison Office lobby that engaged (mainly drawing on CST) directly with Parliament. By the early 2000s even Lumko was defunct. With these movements' demise the tradition of radical grassroots biblical ethics almost completely disappeared. The now-elderly Albert Nolan, who was awarded a decoration by the government for his intellectual contribution to liberation, largely retired from public life.

What can one say about the *Catholic* biblical ethics that the era under discussion produced? First, it was the product of a small group of activist Catholics whose voice was far louder than its numbers. Second, it was spearheaded by a handful of theologians, Albert Nolan being the most important, who were neither professional exegetes nor professional moral theologians. The result was that it lacked the sophistication of the Latin American moral exegetes like Carlos Mesters or even Gustavo Gutiérrez. South African Protestants (like Allan Boesak, Itumuleng Mosala, and Gunther Wittenberg) were better exegetes, and the Catholics were frequently happy to adapt (often simplifying in the process) their thinking. Catholic thinking frequently drew explicitly or implicitly on other sources like CST and just-war theory, augmented by simple biblical analogy. Quite often, too, context predominated, as did ideology (notably Marxism, BC, and ANC political thought). I would argue that the reason for this was not intellectual laziness as much as the paucity of trained Catholic theologians.

Finally, despite such limitations, the theology that emerged had the effect of bringing Catholics into the struggle for liberation in South Africa, keeping many believers in the church during turbulent times—even if we became in many cases "God-fearing Marxists," as a Muslim colleague once put it. It also created a context for those, however few in number, who continue the tradition of publicly engaged moral theology addressing the problems of post-apartheid democratic South Africa.

Notes

1. The Italian Marxist Antonio Gramsci's idea was very influential in South African activist circles during the 1980s, including among religious people.

2. For this history, see William E. Brown, *The Catholic Church in South Africa, from Its Origin to Present Day* (London: Burns & Oates, 1960); Garth Abraham, *The Catholic Church and Apartheid: The Response of the Catholic Church in South Africa to the First Decade of National Party Rule, 1948–1957* (Johannesburg: Ravan, 1989); Joy Brain and Philippe Denis, eds., *The Catholic Church in Contemporary Southern Africa* (Pietermaritzburg: Cluster, 1999).

3. Susan Rakoczy, "Catholic Theology in South Africa: An Evolving Tapestry," *Journal of Theology for Southern* Africa 122 (July 2005): 84–106; Anthony Egan, "Catholic Intellectuals," in *The Catholic Church in Contemporary Southern Africa*, ed. Joy Brain and Philippe Denis (Pietermaritzburg: Cluster, 1999), 314–48.

4. Paddy Kearney, *Guardian of the Light: Denis Hurley: Renewing the Church, Opposing Apartheid* (New York: Continuum, 2009).

5. Anthony Egan, *The Politics of a South African Catholic Student Movement, 1960–1987* (Cape Town: UCT Centre for African Studies, 1991), esp. 39–88.

6. Lumko, "History" (2015) at: http://lumko.org.

7. Anne Hope and Sally Timmel, *Training for Transformation* (Gweru, Zimbabwe: Mambo, 1984); background: http://www.populareducation.co.za and http://www.grail-programmes.org.za.

8. For example, see Oswald Hirmer, *The Pastoral Use of the Bible (Gospel Sharing Methods)* (Germiston: Lumko Institute, 1994); Gabriel Afegbagee and Chrysostome Kiyala, "The Amos Programme—Reading the Bible in the Context of Modern Life," *Bulletin Dei Verbum* 84/85 (2008): 40–43.

9. The key text of black theology is Basil Moore, ed., *Black Theology: The South African Voice* (London: C. Hurst, 1973). Cf. Daniel R. Magaziner, *The Law and the Prophets: Black Consciousness in South Africa, 1968–1977* (Johannesburg: Jacana Media, 2010).

10. Albert Nolan, *Jesus before Christianity*, 2nd ed. (Cape Town: David Philip, 1986).

11. Neither are mentioned or discussed, however, perhaps because by 1976 both were under house arrest and could not be quoted in South Africa. Both would be murdered: Biko in police custody on September 12, 1977, and Turner killed by "unknown" assassin/s on January 8, 1978.

12. Pieter J. J. Botha, "'Historical Jesus Research and Relevance in South Africa," *HTS Teologiese Studies/Theological Studies* 65, no. 1 (1999): Art. no. 154, 11 pages.

13. Nolan, *Jesus before Christianity*, 46.

14. Ibid., 85.

15. Ibid., 135–36.

16. As one sees in the earlier writings of Leonardo Boff, Jon Sobrino, and even Gustavo Gutiérrez.

17. For an account see Lawrence T. Kaufmann, "Contextual Theology in South Africa: An Analysis of the Institute for Contextual Theology, 1981–1994," PhD thesis, Academia Alfonsiana (Rome, 1997).

18. Kairos Theologians, *Challenge to the Church: The Kairos Document* (Johannesburg: Institute for Contextual Theology/Skotaville, 1985).

19. Theological Advisory Commission, *The Things That Make for Peace* (Springs: Order of Preachers, 1985). This title will be abbreviated throughout as *TTMP*.

20. The latter, the most widely published scripture scholar in South Africa, has included in his output both "technical" essays and more overtly political "pastoral" articles. See Paul B. Decock, "On Biblical Trajectories," *Grace & Truth* 7, no. 4 (1986): 175–83; idem, "A 'This-Worldly' or an 'Other-Worldly' Salvation," *Grace & Truth* 8, no. 4 (1988): 168–80; idem, "Inculturation and 'Communism' in Luke-Acts," *Grace & Truth* 9, no. 2 (1989): 54–64.

21. *TTMP*, 61.

22. Ibid., 139.

23. Albert Nolan, *God in South Africa: The Challenge of the Gospel* (Cape Town: David Philip, 1988), 70–74. This title will be abbreviated *GISA*. While drawn from ANC and South African Communist Party theorists, "CST," as it was called, echoes the "world systems theory" of Marxist political analyst Immanuel Wallerstein.

24. Thomas L. Schubeck, *Liberation Ethics: Sources, Models, and Norms* (Minneapolis: Fortress, 1993), esp. 129–73; William C. Spohn, *What Are They Saying about Scripture and Ethics?* (New York: Paulist Press, 1984), 54–69.

25. Nolan, *GISA*, 16, 17.

26. Ibid, 18.

27. Ibid, 66–67.

28. Ibid., 166.

29. Ibid., 170.

30. Ibid., 171.

31. This contrasts dramatically with Richard Hays's position. See Hays, *The Moral Vision of the New Testament* [San Francisco: HarperCollins, 1996], and Hays, "Narrate and Embody: A Response to Nigel Biggar, 'Specify and Distinguish,'" *Studies in Christian Ethics* 22, no. 2 [2009]: 185–98 but is closer to the just-war position of Hays's critic, Nigel Biggar (see Biggar, "Specify and Distinguish! Interpreting the New Testament and 'Non-violence,'" *Studies in Christian Ethics* 22, no. 2 [2009]: 164–84).

CONFUCIANISM

The Role of Cultural Context in Reading the Bible

The Chinese Case

Louis Gendron

Many Chinese intellectuals have a sense, even the certitude, that they own a very old and rich cultural tradition, which should be sufficient to nourish them for a lifetime, at least in the areas of meaning, wisdom, and morality. As a matter of fact, China was for many centuries isolated from other wisdom traditions and was prosperous and feeling quite well. When Buddhism came to China, it did not displace the original culture. Rather, it was eventually very much absorbed into the main culture, while also affecting the culture to a certain degree.

After the arrival of Western missionaries in the seventeenth century, the Chinese people were happy to learn about many Western scientific and technical discoveries. Some insightful missionaries were excited to learn about Chinese traditional moral wisdom, which had been handed down century after century since long before the beginning of the Christian era. There is something in the Chinese culture that sounded very healthy and deeply in accord with the Christian moral heritage. Those missionaries were also impressed by the fact that the Chinese saw their ancestors as very much alive and even revered them with great respect. Most traditional Judeo-Christian moral virtues were well known to the Chinese, and some were even developed to a higher degree, in particular filial piety. The traditional fourth commandment, "Honor your father and mother," seemed to have been understood by the Chinese in a way that was deeper and more wide-ranging than anything in the Judeo-Christian tradition.

In today's China (including Taiwan, which has kept more of the traditional culture) one gets the impression that most people who belong to the new generations have only a superficial knowledge of their millenary cultural roots. What they do know has come through small bits of ancient texts that have been included in school textbooks. Most of their study time has had to do with mathematics, chemistry, English, geography, and so on. And most of their free time is spent on activities that have very little to do with their cultural tradition. As a result, although traditional Chinese ethics are still known, their impact on personal character, on family organization, and on social institutions has become limited and is competing (often unfavorably) with new sets of values.

Those few Christians who go into biblical studies belong to the same new generations who know little about their own cultural tradition. In the Catholic Church, those preparing for the priesthood have to spend two years doing philosophical studies. If philosophical studies are done in their own country, they effectively spend part of their time in the study of Chinese philosophy, and they thus become more cognizant of their cultural roots.

It may be interesting here to look into the lived experience of an elderly Chinese scholar, for whom the traditional cultural context is still alive, and who at the same time is a biblical scholar who has spent his life studying and researching the Word of God, always looking for wisdom. What follows is a summary of an interview conducted with Mark Fang Chih-jung, SJ,[1] and a presentation of a few key concepts to be found in his Chinese writings.

Reflections from an Elderly China and Biblical Scholar

Mark Fang Chih-jung, SJ, was born in 1926. He was the first Chinese to earn a Doctorate in Sacred Scripture at the Pontifical Biblical Institute in Rome. For fifty years he has been teaching Scripture and doing research at the Fu Jen Faculty of Theology of St. Robert Bellarmine in Taiwan. Among other achievements, Mark Fang and a Protestant scholar have worked for twenty years on a new ecumenical Chinese translation of the four Gospels just published in 2014.[2]

Over the years Mark Fang has always kept a great interest in the study of Chinese classics, in particular the Four Books.[3] He has also spent several years explaining the Christian faith to the main administrators of Fu Jen Catholic University, a majority of whom are not Christian. One focus of his lectures has been the great harmony between the Chinese classics and the Christian Scriptures. He has also produced a still unpublished commentary of the Four Books titled "East and West Classics: Looking at Them Together."[4]

Mark Fang's doctoral thesis was on the Wisdom literature, which he found particularly close to the Chinese classical literature. Anyone who has been in contact with Mark Fang over the years has observed a double phenomenon: first, a real love for the Chinese moral tradition as inspiration for life and, second, a deep belief that there is always something new and inspiring to be found in the Word of God.

One question often comes back in Mark Fang's conversation: Does the Bible provide something that one cannot find in Chinese culture?

Mark Fang believes that this is indeed the case. For instance, the clearest instance of the newness of the biblical message compared with Chinese culture can be found in the first eleven chapters of Genesis, in particular chapters 1–4. Here one can understand the rapport between God and the world. The same is repeated in the New Testament with the opening of John's Gospel: at the beginning, the Word.

The "revelation" of God in Scripture is something that one does not find in Chinese culture, and it includes the deepest meaning of the human family and of the world. From Scripture, we get to know where we are coming from and where we are going. The result is a great peace of mind, a peace that gets deeper as one becomes older.

Once we know revelation and have accepted it, then we begin perceiving new meanings in many aspects of Chinese writings, meanings that are far from obvious without the help of revelation. For instance, one finds some hints about the Trinity. Confucius explains the Chinese character for "king" (王): One perpendicular line traversing three horizontal lines, and so we have a king, image of the three-in-one (Trinitarian) God.

Chinese classics give great importance to ethics, moral life. This is expressed by the harmony between heaven, earth, man/woman, kin, and teacher. It is also expressed by harmony in the five major relations: king/citizen, father/son, husband/wife, brothers/sisters, and among friends. With revelation, we realize that the relation between God and man/woman is more important than all the other relations. Jesus is the one who taught it most clearly, and without revelation we would really miss what is the most important.

In the Four Books one finds the best of the Chinese cultural heritage, but at the end there is no real answer to the most basic question: Finally, where are we coming from? Of course, we know that all Chinese people will be taken care of, but only the New Testament comes with a clear response to this basic question, especially through the resurrection of Jesus, resurrection of flesh and spirit. How else could we know?

The Four Books are full of wise moral teachings, particularly the last chapters of the book of *Mencius*,[5] in which justice, for instance, is treated extremely well. But at the end, nothing is as clear as in the New Testament.

Let us take for example the *Analects*[6] of Confucius, which are an ongoing dialogue between Confucius and his disciples, in many ways similar to what we find in the Gospels, but five hundred years before Jesus' time. In the *Analects* we find some remarkable passages. These are eye-opening sayings full of wisdom about human life. At age seventy-three, Confucius was really wise. For instance, we find three interesting statements by Confucius in Chapter 37 of Book 14 of the Analects:

不怨天，不尤人，下學而上達，知我者其天乎。

This is a very compact statement written in classical Chinese. We can translate it as follows: "I never complain about heaven nor blame men. I learn human affairs from here below so that I can know the mandate of heaven above. Probably only Heaven knows me."[7]

In this passage, one can see that Confucius accepts his human condition peacefully, learns from human experience, and believes that what he learns conforms to the order of things. His conscience is clear and he feels at one with Heaven (whatever he understands by "Heaven": whether a personal God or not).

A Look at the *Analects*: On Filial Piety

To appreciate what Christian revelation brings to Confucian culture we can look at what Confucius says concerning filial piety and how it compares to the Word of God. We quote four brief chapters along with the explanatory comments of Robert Hsu, the translator and editor of the *Analects* of Confucius (book 2, chapters 5–8):[8]

> Meng Yi Zi, a marquis of Lu,[9] asked Confucius about filial piety. Confucius answered, "Filial piety is not to violate the rules of propriety." Later, when Fan Chi was driving for Confucius, Confucius told him, "Meng Sun asked me about filial piety, and I answered him, saying, 'Filial piety is not to violate the rules of propriety.'" Fan Chi then asked, "What does it mean?" Confucius said, "When the parents are still alive, one serves them following the rules of propriety; when the parents pass away, one buries them following the rules of propriety and one performs ancestral rites following the rules of propriety." (Ch. 5)
>
> Meng Wu Bo[10] asked Confucius about filial piety. Confucius answered, "Parents worry most when their children are sick." (Ch. 6)
>
> [When children are doing fine in all matters, the only thing their parents can be worried about is the health of the children. Consequently, when children are taking good care of their health, they are showing filial piety.][11]
>
> Zi You asked Confucius about filial piety. Confucius answered, "Nowadays, filial piety is meant to be able to feed parents. However, people feed their dogs and horses as well. Without respect, what is the difference between feeding one's parents and feeding one's dogs and horses?" (Ch. 7)
>
> [This man was forty-five years younger than Confucius and was a literary man with high social position and wide influence. But maybe because of that, he neglected filial piety and is here admonished by Confucius.]
>
> Zi Xia asked Confucius about filial piety. Confucius answered, "When one is serving one's parents, to assume an appropriate attitude is the most difficult thing to do. When it comes to daily labors, the children take the toil of them. When it comes to food and wine, the parents enjoy them first. Do you think filial piety is to fulfill only these two duties?" (Ch. 8)

[Here Confucius goes further in explaining what he means by showing respect to one's parents. "To assume an appropriate attitude" is to assume "a peaceful, happy look" or to assume "a smiling attitude."]

What comes to mind after reading these sayings from Confucius is the fourth commandment in the Bible: "Honor your father and mother so that you may live long in the land that Yahweh your God is giving you" (Exod. 20:12). Concerning the commandments which have to do with relationships among people, the fourth commandment is the first on the list, showing its importance in the Bible. It is also the only commandment to which is appended a promise: "so that you may live long." Saint Paul also mentions this point in Ephesians 6:1–3: "Children, be obedient to your parents in the Lord—that is what uprightness demands. The first commandment that has a promise attached to it is: Honor your father and your mother, and the promise is: so that you may have long life and prosper in the land."

Jesus himself gives importance to filial piety. He once said to the Pharisees and scribes:

How ingeniously you get round the commandment of God in order to preserve your own tradition! For Moses said: Honor your father and your mother, and, Anyone who curses father or mother must be put to death. But you say, 'If a man says to his father or mother: Anything I have that I might have used to help you is Korban (that is, dedicated to God),' then he is forbidden from that moment to do anything for his father or mother. In this way you make God's word ineffective for the sake of your tradition which you have handed down. And you do many other things like this" (Mark 7:9–13).

Jesus talks to the Jews in a way that is more direct than Confucius talking to Marquis Meng and son![12]

The Confucian Concept of
Heaven and the Biblical Notion of God

If we go deep into the Chinese culture's understanding of the ground of being, we once again find a close affinity with the biblical world. This is clear when we look at the very notion of God.[13]

In many ancient cultures, like Egypt, Babylon, Syria, and so on, there was a great variety of gods, created by human imagination. By contrast, in the ancient Confucian culture, although not much was written about the spiritual world, a process of conscientization had led to the wise affirmation of a personal Heaven (God).

God, as revealed in Scripture, is creator and savior. God, in a way that nobody would have imagined, has entered history and walked with humankind, responding with mercy to repeated human sinfulness. God has also shown a very special love for and attention to the poor, the weak, and the abandoned.

In the New Testament, God has shown love to the fullest, sent his Son to reveal everything about God. Jesus was a teacher who "walked the talk," the same as Confucius did. But Jesus sacrificed himself unto death and rose again to new life, sharing his new life with us. The new life, together with the new commandment of love (love for God and love for all), keeps us in union with God.

Union between Heaven and humankind is precisely at the center of Chinese culture. The biblical culture and the Chinese culture have evolved separately for thousands of years before encountering each other. In the Chinese ancient texts, we find the equivalent of the different types of biblical literature—Law, Prophets, Wisdom—as if they were blood-related. Union between Heaven and humankind is also the biblical ideal, first realized in Jesus and then opened to all people. The Chinese used to say "Everyone can become Yao and Shun" (the most revered ancestors of the Chinese) and now "Everyone can become Jesus."

The Heaven of Chinese culture and the God of Scripture do not conflict at all. They should actually be integrated. In the last centuries East and West have interacted a lot, but at the level of spiritual life the interaction has been minimal, without much communion. Mark Fang believes: "If the Chinese people, on the firm basis of their belief in Heaven, would also believe in the biblical God and accept God's messenger Jesus, then not only the Chinese people would become more blessed, Chinese culture would be more brilliant and the whole of humanity would be enriched."[14]

Confucius and the other Chinese sages have been helping generations to understand human life and how to live ethically and wisely. Their wisdom is often comparable to what we find in the Bible. But it seems that in the end something is missing in the body of Chinese wisdom literature. This "something" is precisely what someone like Paul Xu Guangqi (1562–1633) a scientist and scholar who became one of China's first Catholics after meeting with Matteo Ricci, finally found. It fulfilled his search for ultimate meaning and enriched his understanding of his own cultural tradition.

Notes

1. The section titled "Reflections from an Elderly China and Biblical Scholar" is based on an interview with Mark Fang, conducted in August 2015. Mark Fang Chih-jung, SJ, was born in the Anhui Province of China. He was baptized as a child together with his mother, became a seminarian at age nineteen, was sent to Rome at twenty-one to continue studies of philosophy and theology, entered the Society of Jesus in Spain in 1952, and was ordained a priest in 1955. He studied Holy Scripture in Rome and Germany beginning in 1958 and completed the Doctorate in Sacred Scripture in 1963. He has been teaching the Old Testament since 1964, starting in Baguio, Philippines, and then moving in 1967 to the Fu Jen Faculty of Theology of St. Robert Bellarmine. He was Provincial of the China Province

(1978–84) and Dean of the Faculty of Theology (1984–93). Although now retired from teaching, he has not stopped doing research and publishing numerous books and articles in Chinese, mostly about Holy Scripture, often in dialogue with Chinese culture.

2. *The Four Gospels: Interconfessional Version* (Taipei: Bible Society in Taiwan, 2014).

3. The Four Books (Chinese pinyin: Sìshū) are Chinese classic texts illustrating the core value and belief systems in Confucianism. They were selected by Zhu Xi in the Song dynasty to serve as a general introduction to Confucian thought, and they were, in the Ming and Qing dynasties, made the core of the official curriculum for the civil service examinations. They are: *Great Learning*; *Doctrine of the Mean*; *Analects;* and *Mencius*.

4. Mark Fang, "East and West Classics: Looking at Them Together" (unpublished manuscript, 110 pages).

5. A collection of conversations of the scholar Mencius with kings of his time. In contrast to the sayings of Confucius, which are short and self-contained, the *Mencius* consists of long dialogues with extensive prose.

6. The speeches of Confucius and his disciples, as well as the discussions they held. Since Confucius, the *Analects* has heavily influenced China and later other East Asian countries as well. The imperial examinations, started in the Jin dynasty and eventually abolished at the founding of the Republic of China, emphasized Confucian studies and expected candidates to use the words of Confucius in their essays.

7. Translation taken from Robert Hsu, *Translating the Analects into Modern Chinese and English* (Tainan: Catholic Window Press, 2013), 393. With a foreword by Mark Fang.

8. Ibid., 27–30.

9. Marquis Meng had been sent by his parents to Confucius to learn rules of propriety.

10. This is the son of Marquis Meng.

11. Translation and explanation from Hsu, *Translating the Analects into Modern Chinese and English*.

12. The above comments are adapted from Mark Fang's (unpublished) book "East and West Classics: Looking at Them Together."

13. This section is a brief summary of an early writing of Mark Fang's: "A Comparison between the Confucian Concept of Heaven and the Biblical Notion of God," *Collectanea Theologica Universitatis Fujen*, no. 31 (Spring 1977): 15–41 (written in Chinese).

14. Ibid., 39.

Part III

The Bible and Contemporary Ethical Issues

SOCIAL ISSUES

"WHAT SHALL WE DO THEN?"

Engaging Ethical Issues in India/Asia with the Bible

Mathew Illathuparampil

Asia, including India, is a land of indigenous sacred texts that carry religious stories, faith confessions, mystic contemplations, and ethical codes. They belong to Hinduism, Buddhism, Jainism, Sikhism, Zoroastrianism, Gnostic religions, Confucianism, Shintoism, and more. Such texts have constituted to a large extent the cultural ethos of the region called Asia. But the Bible is considered by many an imported religious scripture in Asia, even though it is a product of West Asia. In fact, Asia enjoys a peculiar relationship with the Bible.

When the Bible reached East and South Asia in the third century CE, it carried mention of Asian commodities and traces of Indian moral stories. In China, the Bible merged with the teachings of Buddha and Lao Tzu to produce the Jesus Sutras. The missionaries, imperialists, nationalists, reformers, and exegetes used biblical texts in order to influence religion, politics, society, and daily life. The Bible has also served to promote the welfare of women, social outcasts, and untouchables in Asian countries.[1] However, the Bible remains practically a marginal text in Asia in its huge sociocultural and political ambit. For example, in India it is the sacred scripture of two minority religions, Judaism and Christianity, whose adherents make up less than 3 percent of the total population of the country. While recognizing that it is the scripture of only a small population in Asia, this essay seeks to explore how the Bible can address multifaceted ethical issues faced by Asian/Indian people in its largely non-Christian context.

Enabling a contextualized exposition of the theme, I focus on the Indian situation without losing its representative nature of the Asian perspective. As a preliminary step, I mention a few methodological issues in dealing with this theme. Subsequently, out of a variety of ethical problems facing contemporary India/Asia, this essay attends to three issues: shocking poverty amid the sagas of development, the caste system, and religious pluralism. Taken in themselves, these social realities may not always represent ethical issues. But in real life situations of Asia/India, they pose hard ethical issues. They are issues arising out of the economic and socioreligious context constitutive of this region/nation. I shall briefly examine which values or visions the Bible has to offer in addressing the chosen issues.

Methodological Questions

The task of engaging ethical issues in Asia/India with the Bible represents a move from the text to the context. Naturally it raises certain methodological questions. I mention three such questions, implicating the text (Bible), the discipline (ethics), and the context (Asia/India) without really trying to address them for want of space in this work. Recognizing those questions would help us admit the limitations of this exercise.

First, is there an Indian interpretation of the Bible that can legitimize applying the Bible to a largely "pagan" cultural context? Indian interpretation of the Bible, in George M. Soares-Prabhu's view, "results from the cross fertilization of modern methods of New Testament exegesis with contributions from Indian exegetical tradition, coming to flower in the stormy climate of the socio-cultural reality of India Today."[2] Surveying the Indian situation, Soares-Prabhu writes:

> Most exegetes in India still follow the historical criticism they learned in the Western biblical schools in which they were trained. Some have tried (with some success) to adapt Latin American liberation hermeneutics to the Indian situation. A few others have attempted to apply traditional Indian methods of interpretation to the Bible, or to interpret it in the light of classical Hindu teaching. . . . The gap between the "liberationists" who explore the relevance of the Bible for the social aspirations of India's poor and outcast, and the "ashramites" who are trying to relate the message of the Bible to the religious traditions of India, is yet to be bridged.[3]

The views of Soares-Prabhu deserve critical review.[4] However, it needs to be noted that we are condemned to engage the ethical issues in India with the Bible without the backing of a much-wanted Indian interpretation of the Bible.[5]

Second, how far can we apply the Bible to ethical questions written with a multicultural script? Is the Bible an outdated text in view of contemporary moral issues? Where is the moral authority of the Bible for contemporary men and women? Does the Bible, despite its vast variety of materials, offer any coherent idea of moral virtue and obligation?[6] Some of the apparent moral prescriptions in the Bible look culture-bound. For instance, the morality of eating food offered to idols, prohibiting a freed slave from keeping his slave-woman wife, and so on. These are much-debated issues.[7] Therefore, what should be the typology of approaching ethical directives found in the Bible?[8] Stanley Hauerwas holds that "the moral significance of Scripture . . . lies exactly in its power to help us remember the stories of God for the continual guidance of our community and individual lives."[9] But in a multicultural context, stories of biblical God will clash with stories of "pagan" Gods, thus diffusing the moral authority of the Bible.

Third, can we ever adequately identify or categorize ethical issues in a vast land called Asia/India? It is very difficult. Ethical issues are rooted in their social, religious, political, medical, business, and cultural contexts. Ethical values are at risk or in mutual conflict in all these areas in different ways. Hence, any attempt is doomed to be selective.

While recognizing the unresolved methodological questions, in this attempt I will focus on three characteristic features of Asia/India that engender a wide array of ethical issues. They are poverty, the caste system, and religious pluralism. My task is to suggest how the Bible provides a certain value orientation to engage them meaningfully.

Poverty

India is one of the fastest-growing economies in the present world. Despite its affluent upper layer, nearly 300 million people live in extreme poverty in India, according to a recent UN report, and face deprivation in terms of access to basic services, including education, health, water, sanitation, and electricity.[10] In 2000, India, along with 189 member countries of the UN, charted out an ambitious agenda, the Millennium Development Goals, to free millions of people from poverty and hunger by the end of 2015. But its success has proved limited.[11]

Poverty is a multifaceted reality. It is measured in different ways. Hunger is perhaps the gruesome face of it. In India 275 million people live below the poverty line or have income of less than $1.25 a day. India remains home to one-fourth of the world's poor and more than one-third of all malnourished children. Poverty is also responsible for the large numbers of children who remain out of school and fail to complete primary education.

Poverty hits women worst. India tries to achieve gender parity at the primary-education level. Women need empowerment in economic, political, and social spheres. Many women remain non-earning members working on household chores. There is a high infant mortality rate in the country. India was to have reduced the maternal mortality rate to 140 per 100,000 live births by the end of 2015.

Poverty is biting when it comes to areas of health, sanitation, and medical care. India has effectively controlled the spread of diseases such as HIV/AIDS, tuberculosis, malaria, and polio. The prevalence of HIV among pregnant women between the ages of fifteen and twenty-four declined to 0.39 percent in 2010 from 0.89 percent in 2005. The mortality rate due to tuberculosis has fallen to 24 per 100,000 people in 2011 from 38 per 100,000 in 1990. However, medical treatment has become very costly, increasingly making it affordable only to the rich. India faces a massive open-defecation problem. According to the UN report, which was based on a government survey, 59.4 percent of households in rural India and 8.8 percent in urban India had no toilet facilities.[12]

Other figures might show the index of poverty in relation to environmental protection, deforestation, food security, and so on. Distributive justice, right to life and survival, human dignity, inequality, work policy, allocation of resources, responsibility for the other, and so on are ethical values that are blatantly violated through persistent poverty of the masses.[13]

The Bible on Poverty

In a largely religious land like India, the relevant biblical vision in view of poverty might be this: economic security is a benefaction from God; this blessing has to be gained within a supportive community and through one's own efforts. In other words, poverty cannot be condoned, glorified, ignored, or considered part of one's destiny or the result of one's past deeds (*karmaphala*).

Financial security is a benefaction from God. Genesis teaches us that God provides for our survival and welfare with generosity (Gen. 2:8–15). Furthermore, right from Israel's election, God promised a land. The life and destiny of this people are centered on the land. It served as a pledge of God's election of this people and the special bond with God. Land provided for their survival, wealth, and power. It empowered them to discharge their cultic, military, and juridic duties.[14] The gift of economic security can be inferred also from the Sabbath (Deut. 5:12–15), the Sabbatical-related law of the fallow (Exod. 23:10–12; Lev. 25:1–7, 18–24), and the Jubilee (Lev. 25). What God glorifies are sabbatical rests, releases, and feasts where there are no class divisions between master and slaves, rich and poor, aliens and natives. God provides far more than enough for such relaxation from labor. Jesus sees too that human needs are met to the point of abundance (Matt. 14:13–21; Mark 6:34–44; Luke 9:12–17; John 2:1–11, 6:1–15). These miracle stories have their theological significance while they refer to spiritual and material abundance. The Bible does not allow us to glorify poverty, holding that God has preferential love for the poor. Material prosperity actually is a gift and a task for deeper participation in God's providence and righteousness. The biblical God is not an otherworldly, distant figure.

Economic security promised by God is fulfilled only to the extent that we take responsibility for the other. It is a conditional promise. There must be mutual financial assistance so that no one shall be in want. Israelites were supposed to lend money for food in hard times (Deut. 15:7–10; Lev. 25:35–37) but without charging interest (Exod. 22:25; Deut. 23:19–20; Lev. 25:36–37). They were to stop working and celebrate feasts as equals (Exod. 23:10–12; Lev. 25:1–7, 18–24). Every fifty years must mark a Jubilee where land has to be returned to the original owner, slaves released, and debts written off (Lev. 25). Widows, orphans, and strangers were to be treated as God's preferred ones. Israelites were to tithe from their bounty and produce (Deut. 14:22–29).[15] A country becomes a land "flowing with milk and honey" only when God's ordinances are observed (Deut. 4:1, 5:31, 6:1–3, 11:8, 31, 12:1). The New Testament also upholds our responsibility for others' economic security (Luke 16:19–31). It becomes a norm of the final judgment (Matt. 25:31–46). The early church was a living example of such sharing with the consequence that no one was in want (Acts 4:32–37).

Community assistance is not meant to keep a segment of the society lazy and unproductive. It is to help each household do what it can for economic prosperity. How the land was allocated and divided among Israelites (Josh. 18:1–10, 26:52–56) shows how much importance is given to economic independence and financial viability of each family. They considered the size of the household and the fertility of the land. The need for personal efforts is well stressed by Saint Paul. He rebukes those who have forsaken hard work in view of the much anticipated immediate parousia (2 Thess. 3:6–12). He was an example of such toil, in spite of his provisions to earn support from the churches he was serving. Saint Paul never gives an impression of voluntary dispossession as it was practiced in the Jerusalem church. In his vision, the faithful are supposed to maintain dedicated application to work. They shall not go for any liquidation of capital. Saint Paul does not even suggest common ownership or pooling of resources.[16] According to the biblical vision, to redeem the poor in the country, India has to talk more in terms of social justice and solidarity, rather than capitalist ethos.

The Caste System

The caste system is a sociocultural reality observed in India with a sort of religious rigor. It informs various dimensions of Indian society. It is not restricted to any particular religion, although it is thought by many as something intrinsic to Hinduism.[17] The foundational castes are the Brahmins (priests), Kshatriyas (warriors, nobility), Vaishyas (farmers, traders, and artisans), and Sudras (tenant farmers and servants). Those born outside the caste system are considered the untouchables. The caste system is a reality that cuts across all religions and social groups in India. In general, Indian Christianity and Islam are not free from caste-infused divisions.

Despite the long endurance of the caste system, there are signs of the gradual collapse of conventional caste boundaries in India. Political awareness, movements in support of the *dalits*,[18] increasing urbanization, and greater democratic process contribute to this trend. However, despite all the countermovements and the prohibition of the practice of untouchability by constitutional measures, the caste system still prevails with all its disvalues.

The caste system is not as innocent as it may sound with regard to division of labor. It basically implies exclusivity in terms of marriage relations, meals, and religious worship. It consists of class structure with an exceptional rigidity. Therefore, the caste system allows marriages only to people from within the same caste. Exclusivity could regulate transactions of food grain and other household articles. The lower-caste people are not allowed to take water from the same source used by the upper-caste people in villages.

The caste system is an issue that affects a great number of people in India. The human dignity of the low-caste people is denigrated. It results in caste-discrimination in the workplace, social space, political fortunes, and religious practices, including access to burial places.

The Bible on the Caste System

The Bible upholds the basic ethical concept of human dignity against a caste-ridden society. The term *dignity* is not original to the Scriptures. It was borrowed from Greco-Roman usage by the early Christian writers.[19] Genesis 1:26–27, which describes the role and glory of the human person in creation, serves as an introduction to the formulation of the Christian concept of human dignity. In Genesis 1:26–27 the worth and nature conferred by God upon the human person is marked by the expression *imago Dei*. However, the Bible, according to James Luther Mays, does not predicate explicitly anywhere the expression "human dignity." But human capacities such as reason, free will, and knowledge, and human attributes such as righteousness and happiness, which can justify human dignity, could reasonably be found in the Bible. According to Mays, *imago Dei* shows the primacy of the human person's relationship to God.[20] No person endowed with inalienable human dignity can be denigrated and discriminated against in the caste system.

Biblical hospitality is the antidote to overcoming a caste system. According to Paul, all are one in Christ irrespective of caste, creed, or gender (Gal. 3:28). The Bible shows numerous examples of the acts of hospitality. They include welcoming strangers for food, lodging, and protection (Gen. 18:28, 19:1–8; Job 31:16–23, 31:31–32); permitting the strangers to harvest the corners of one's fields (Lev. 19:9–10; Deut. 24:19–22; Ruth 2:2–17); clothing the naked (Isa. 58:7; Ezek. 18:7, 18:16); tithing food for the needy (Deut. 14:28–29, 26:1–11); and including the alien in religious celebrations (Exod. 12:48–49; Deut. 16:10–14).

According to Luke, Jesus was himself killed because of the way he ate. He ate with sinners and announced the coming of the reign of God in the symbolism of banquets.[21] Given the political and historical sensibilities of Palestine in Jesus' time, we can sense that by linking meals with the reign of God, Jesus was triggering a confounding of set boundaries and a silent revolution. While meals were supposed to be part of household hospitality, Jesus linked food with the reign of God. Agriculture, trade, taxation, and land were issues thought to be the domain of the reign of God (or the king in secular context). But Jesus transgressed this pattern by the simple symbol of meals. It was offensive to many, for it amounted to a certain reversal of sociopolitical and religious powers. Briefly, acts, messages, and symbols of hospitality were not merely part of friendly social living for Jesus.[22] The Bible challenges the caste-led Indian society with hospitality cutting across caste and color divisions.

Religious Pluralism

Indian society in particular and Asian societies in general are notable for their cultural, linguistic, and religious diversity. It is a constitutive factor of these societies. In India, eight world religious communities coexist, namely, the Hindus (82 percent), Muslims (12.12 percent), Christians (2.6 percent), Sikhs (2 percent), Buddhists (0.7 percent), Jains (0.4 percent), Parsis (0.3 percent), and Jews (0.1 percent). Apart from the indigenous religions, the immigrant communities also brought their own religious faiths, customs, and cultures. The cultural and social similarities among different religious faiths and their mutual interaction and accommodation over a long period resulted in the concept and practice of religious tolerance and national secularism.

Religious pluralism becomes an ethical issue when it breeds hatred of the religious other. It has become the foundation of what we call "communalism." Many people have been brutally killed over the years by communal forces in India and other countries. Religious pluralism gives way to religious fanaticism. It has begun to creep into all aspects of life such as politics, social life, and cultural expressions, and so on. Thus the other religious faiths are viewed suspiciously. The other becomes an object of conversion or conquest. There are threats against religious freedom. However, the biggest challenge posed by religious pluralism is the religiously couched differing ethical views. Despite commonly shared values among different religions in India, there emerge mutually conflicting ethical views regarding the value of life, respect of others, peace, social justice, and so on.

The Bible on Religious Pluralism

The biblical approach to religious pluralism is complex. At least three caveats are in order. First, religious pluralism demands that we make an integral reading of the Scriptures. We need a careful reading of the text and the context of the Bible to decipher the fabric of communal tendencies and universalist attitudes in the Scriptures. Yves Congar, for example, insists that Israel was not chosen over and against others, but for other peoples. "Israel was chosen *as a people* because God's purpose is to unite all men in a single spiritual people, the Church, to save them and lead them to communion with Him, not in isolation but as a community. Israel was thus chosen for and on behalf of all, *pars pro toto*."[23] Universalist outlook is not lacking in the Old Testament.[24] Similarly, the openness and universality of Jesus in the New Testament cannot be overlooked. In the eschatological expectation, there is no vengeance on the Gentiles, which was characteristic of Jewish apocalyptic thought during Jesus' time.[25] The Gentiles also have a share in Jesus' invitation to salvation.

Second, biblical monotheism naturally presupposes exclusivism. The Bible understands wickedness and sin not just in terms of moral and ethical conduct. It is worried as much about the purity of religion as with moral virtues. The fundamental sin is idol worship.

Third, the biblical approach to religious diversity has two layers: diversity within the Christian communities, which can become even heretical; the other is the approach to people of other religious faiths. John Hick observes that "neither Old nor New Testament writers knew of any of the great world faiths beyond Judaism and Christianity. And therefore no application of biblical statements to Islam, Hinduism, Buddhism, etc. can possibly claim to represent the original meaning of the text [1 Tim. 2:4–6]."[26] Consequently, we are dealing with issues that did not directly come within the purview of the authors of the biblical texts.

As a biblically founded approach to mutually differing ethical views supported by various religious ideologies, we may offer interfaith ethical dialogue and intra-faith criticism. First, in interfaith ethical dialogue, one has to bring different religious narratives into mutual conversation and encounter. It will eventually expose the underlying ethical approaches in mutual conversation. Religious stories, epics, and narratives reach the believers' minds and hearts and thus make the irresistible options open to them by calling on the moral imagination of the believers. They project a world that captures the readers and makes their ethical claims and demands in an attractive way, but mostly not in the form of propositions. What is required is not a comparative study of different religious narratives citing different ethical questions but exposure of how stories are told on relevant themes. For want of space, I do not try an exercise of confronting various religious narratives here.[27]

Obviously there are irreconcilable differences between different religious narratives. Therefore, it is quite natural that the ensuing ethical conclusions also will be different from one another. The conflicts may occur in terms of the nature and the number of the gods; or the nature of the transcendent projected by each religion or the values that should guide us morally.[28] However, many authors tend to think that conflicts among religious narratives are only apparent and that deeper theological analysis will make them very thin or even null and void.[29] This is indeed a debatable opinion.

Let me take one example. Narratives of the Hindu Bhagavad Gita, the Buddhist Sutras, and the Christian Gospels about violence are not the same. For example, Lord Krishna recommends to Arjuna an attitude of renunciation without regard for the action at stake. The implication is that under the right circumstances, violence is permitted, provided the warrior engages in it without desire (*kama*). The narrative context of this advice was the battle between Kauravas and Pandavas.[30] Buddha has the following advice against harming others: "Seeking one's own happiness, he, who harms other pleasure-seeking sentient beings with a rod, will not experience hereafter. Seeking one's own happiness, he who does not harm other pleasure-seeking sentient beings with a rod, will experience happiness hereafter" (Dhammapada vv. 131–32).[31] He gave this piece of advice when the Buddha witnessed some children injuring a snake with sticks.[32] But the Gospels, especially in the Sermon on the Mount, deplore all sorts of violence (Matt. 5:38–42). The obvious implications are for total pacifism and the love of one's enemy. However, there are fewer pacific Catholics than those who think that use of violence may be justified as the last resort to protect oneself from an unjust aggressor.

Second, intra-faith criticism will have to begin with religious scriptures. For instance, Jesus criticizes Jewish rites and rituals, including mores of purity, Sabbath, and authority (Mark 7:1–23, 10:2ff., 12:13ff.), as well as antagonism to the Temple and the concept of "chosen people" (Mark 11:15; Matt. 3:9). For Christians, the Old Testament will have to be read in view of the New Testament in a prognostic way. The New Testament will have to be read in view of the Kingdom of God promised and inaugurated by Jesus. But if one focuses on one aspect of the whole story, it may not do it justice. For example, one can find in the Bible a number of stories in which God is pictured as violent, abusive jealous, narcissistic, and so on.[33] Such texts are to be compared to and criticized by other texts.

The process of encountering the religious narratives shall not be restricted to narratives found in sacred literature, but religions are to confront their own narratives of the recent past also. They need not be written documents; they could be events experienced by people. For example, the narratives of the Holocaust; narratives of Hindu-Muslim conflict in India; narratives of the struggles between Catholics and Protestants in Northern Ireland. Why should we subject the recent narratives to intra-faith critique? In view of Muslim-Hindu relations in India, Riffat Hassan writes: "Knowing what we did or did not do does not alter the history of the past, but this knowledge—if accepted with courage and honesty—can lead to a different kind of future."[34]

When John the Baptist preached about Jesus, the future believers asked him, "What shall we do then?" (Luke 3:10). He explained to them the ethical norms that they were to follow. Seeking to engage ethical issues in India with the Bible would look similar to this event. Unlike John the Baptist, what the Bible can offer is to give a value-orientation rather than any solution to particular problems. However, even that is not an easy task. For many, reading or using the Bible for ethical guidance may seem a dicey venture at best. To make it effective, we need to have resolved the methodological issues that we have already raised. Until that is achieved, any attempt like ours, though promising in itself, is condemned to be unfinished and truncated.

Notes

1. R.S. Sugirtharajah, *The Bible and Asia: From the Pre-Christian Era to the Postcolonial Age* (Cambridge, MA: Harvard University Press, 2013).

2. George M. Soares-Prabhu, *Collected Writings of George M. Soares-Prabhu,* ed. Francis X. D'Sa, Scaria Kuthirakkattel, and Isaac Padinjarekuttu (Pune: Jnana-Deepa Vidyapeeth, 1999–2003), 2:29.

3. George M. Soares-Prabhu, "Interpreting the Bible in India Today," in *Collected Writings of George M. Soares-Prabhu,* ed. Francis X. D'Sa, Scaria Kuthirakkattel, and Isaac Padinjarekuttu (Pune: Jnana-Deepa Vidyapeeth, 2003), 4:17.

4. For one such attempt see Martin Sebastian Kallungal, "Cross-Religious Reading of the Bible in India: George M. Soares-Prabhu's Unfinished Project," in *Provoked to Speech: Biblical Hermeneutics as Conversation*, ed. R. Bieringer, R. Burggraeve, E. Nathan, and M. Steegen (Leuven: Peeters, 2014), 249–74.

5. For an example see Augustine Thottakara, ed., *Indian Interpretation of the Bible* (Bangalore: Dharmaram Publications, 2000).

6. Allen Verhey, "The Use of Scripture in Ethics," *Religious Studies Review* 4 (1978): 28–37.

7. James M. Gustafson, "The Place of Scripture in Christian Ethics: A Methodological Study," *Interpretation* 24 (1970): 430–55; Thomas W. Ogletree, *The Use of the Bible in Christian Ethics: A Constructive Essay* (Philadelphia: Fortress, 1983); Richard B. Hays, "Scripture-Shaped Community: The Problem of Method in New Testament Ethics," *Interpretation* 44 (1990): 42–55.

8. Certain models are examined by John Brunt and Gerald Winslow. John Brunt and Gerald Winslow, "The Bible's Role in Christian Ethics," *Andrews University Seminary Studies* 20, no. 1 (1982): 3–21.

9. Stanley Hauerwas, "The Moral Authority of Scripture: The Politics and Ethics of Remembering," *Interpretation* 34, no. 4 (1980): 365.

10. UN Economic and Social Commission for India and the Pacific, *India and the MGDs: Towards a Sustainable Future for All* (New York: UN, 2015), 4.

11. See "India's Progress Towards Achieving the Millennium Development Goals," http://www.in.undp.org/content/india/en/home/post-2015/mdgoverview.html.

12. Ibid., 11.

13. William Aiken and Hugh LaFollette, eds., *World Hunger and Morality*, 2nd ed. (Upper Saddle River, NJ: Prentice Hall, 1996); William A. Galston and Peter H. Hoffenberg, eds., *Poverty and Morality: Religious and Secular Perspectives* (Cambridge: Cambridge University Press, 2010).

14. Albino Barrera, *Economic Compulsion and Christian Ethics* (Cambridge: Cambridge University Press, 2005), 78–80.

15. Ibid, 82.

16. Ibid, 91.

17. Talcott Parsons, *The Structure of Social Action: A Study in Social Theory with Special Reference to a Group of Recent European Writers* (Toronto: Collier-Macmillan, 1966), 557.

18. Rajni Kothari, "Rise of the Dalits and the Renewed Debate on Caste," *Economic and Political Weekly* 29, no. 26 (1994): 1589–94.

19. R. Kendall Soulen and Linda Woodhead, "Introduction: Contextualizing Human Dignity," in *God and Human Dignity*, ed. R. Kendall Soulen and Linda Woodhead (Grand Rapids, MI: William B. Eerdmans, 2006), 3.

20. James Luther Mays, "The Self in the Psalms and the Image of God," in *God and Human Dignity*, ed. R. Kendall Soulen and Linda Woodhead (Grand Rapids, MI: William B. Eerdmans, 2006), 35.

21. Robert J. Karris, *Eating Your Way through Luke's Gospel* (Collegeville, MN: Liturgical Press, 2006), 97.

22. Mathew Illathuparampil, "Generous Imaginings: Theology of Hospitality," *Jeevadhara* 40, no. 240 (2010): 425–36.

23. Yves Congar, *The Catholic Church and the Race Question* (Paris: Unesco, 1953), 28.

24. See Isaiah 11:9, 14:1–2, 19:19–25; Zech. 11:11–13, 8:20–23, 14:20–21; Joel 3:1–2; Mal. 1:11.

25. Joachim Jeremias, *Jesus' Promise to the Nations* (London: SCM, 1967), 41–46.

26. John Hick, *The Second Christianity* (London: SCM, 1983), 77. 1 Tim. 2:4–6 reads: "God . . . desires all humans to be saved and to come to the knowledge of the truth. For there is one God, and there is one mediator between God and humanity, the human being Christ Jesus, who gave himself as a ransom for all, the testimony to which was borne at the proper time."

27. Anchoring on various themes such as war, peace, cosmos, and liberation, the following work makes an instructive attempt in confronting Christian, Hindu, Islamic, and Buddhist religious narratives. As part of religious narratives, it brings in contemporary figures such as Mahatma Gandhi and Martin Luther King Jr. (Darrel J. Fasching and Dell Dechant, *Comparative Religious Ethics: A Narrative Approach* [Oxford: Blackwell, 2001]).

28. Gary L. Comstock, "The Truth of Religious Narratives," *Philosophy of Religion* 34 (1993): 135.

29. Ibid., 136.

30. The spirit of detachment which is rendered in a rich way in Sanskrit as *nishkamakarma* in Bhagavad Gita could be placed against the ideal of "active indifference" found in the Spiritual Exercises of Ignatius. A highly activist culture that lacks inner depth may find meaning in these ideals. Pavulraj Michael, "*Nishkama Karma* and Active Indifference," *Studies in Interreligious Dialogue* 23, no. 2 (2013): 207–25.

31. Mahinda Deegalle, "Theravada Attitudes towards Violence," *Journal of Buddhist Ethics* 10 (2003): 82–93.

32. Though among many religions Buddhism is the least associated with violence, there is a history of Buddhist-related violence such as torture, wars, and suicides. Within the monastic traditions alone, there are centuries of Buddhist violence in Asia. Michael Jerryson and Mark Juergensmeyer, *Buddhist Warfare* (Oxford: Oxford University Press, 2010), 226.

33. For such an account see Jeremy Young, *The Violence of God and the War on Terror* (London: Darton, Longman & Todd, 2007).

34. Riffat Hassan, "The Basis for a Hindu-Muslim Dialogue and Steps in That Direction from a Muslim Perspective," in *Religious Liberty and Human Rights in Nations and Religions*, ed. Leonard Swidler (Philadelphia: Ecumenical Press, 1986), 131.

The Bible and Contemporary Social Issues in Light of the Brazilian/ Latin American Context

Maria Inês de Castro Millen

Since the promulgation of the documents of Vatican II, Brazil has interpreted the significance of the council in a variety of ways, using different interpretive lenses of ecclesial communities and the academy. Some important insights are put forth as guideposts for today. Among these insights, this essay will take up the concept of reading the signs of the times by affirming the importance of recognizing Sacred Scripture as the heart and soul of all theology, and pointing out the need for greater efforts on the part of everyone to produce good fruits by means of charity and justice in order to sustain life in the world.

Increasingly, it has become more evident that the task of doing theology is in urgent need of a truthful discernment of the signs of the present time, a discernment that should be guided by the method proposed by Pope John XXIII: to consider first those aspects of the current reality that are good and positive, and only after that to consider the negative aspects, so as to be in a position to address them and transform them. This method of engaging reality points to a hope that has been entrusted to humanity, a hope that it has been able to cultivate until now, contrary to the prophecies of doom and disaster and the pronouncements of unending scandals and evils.

In an effort to better understand the methodology of Pope John XXIII, it is helpful and instructive to review some of his writings. In the Apostolic Constitution *Humanae Salutis* (1961), John XXIII states in paragraph 4:

> While distrustful souls see nothing but darkness falling upon the face of the earth, we prefer to restate our confidence in our Savior, who has not left the world he redeemed. Indeed, making our own Jesus' recommendation that we learn to discern "the signs of the times" (Matt. 16:4), it seems to us that we can make out, in the midst of so much darkness, more than a few indications that enable us to have hope for the fate of the Church and of humanity.[1]

In his encyclical letter *Mater et Magistra*, John XXIII focuses very heavily on new "signs of the times." In paragraph 3, he states: "Hence, although Holy Church has the special task of sanctifying souls and making them shares of heavenly bless-

226

ings, she is also solicitous for the requirements of men in their daily lives, not merely those relating to food and sustenance, but also to their comfort and advancement in various kinds of goods and in varying circumstances of times."[2]

In his 1962 address to members of the International Union for Prehistoric and Protohistoric Sciences, Pope John XXIII declared: "The Church, a friend of the Sciences, takes joy in all of the new achievements that are the result of your scholarly and unbiased research. With our paternal benevolence, we invoke upon all of you, upon your families and upon your work, an abundance of divine graces, with our Apostolic blessing."[3]

Speaking to participants in the training course for spiritual directors of seminaries in 1962, John XXIII exhorted them, saying: "Strive to prepare young people to know the world in which they are called to live and to work. Teach them to sanctify all that progress has to offer that is good, healthy and beautiful."[4]

The documents of Vatican II reflect the optimism and hope of John XXIII. In the Pastoral Constitution *Gaudium et Spes*, paragraph 4, the phrase "signs of the times" is used explicitly and presented in this way:

> To carry out such a task, the Church has always had the duty of scrutinizing the signs of the times and of interpreting them in the light of the Gospel. Thus, in language intelligible to each generation, she can respond to the perennial questions which men ask about this present life and the life to come, and about the relationship of the one to the other.[5]

This particular text points to another insight that is important to highlight: Sacred Scripture, especially the Gospel, is the light that should illuminate reality and assist us in interpreting it correctly. In the conciliar document *Dei Verbum*, paragraph 24, the Council Fathers declare: "The study of the sacred page is, as it were, the soul of sacred theology."[6] In *Optatam Totius*, paragraph 16, the following exhortations are found:

> The students are to be formed with particular care in the study of the Bible, which ought to be, as it were, the soul of all theology. . . . Special care must be given to the perfecting of moral theology. Its scientific exposition, nourished more on the teaching of the Bible, should shed light on the loftiness of the calling of the faithful in Christ and the obligation that is theirs of bearing fruit in charity for the life of the world.[7]

Here, another insight is articulated: "to produce fruit in charity, for the life of the world."

Thus, discerning the signs of the times, interpreting them in the light of God's Word and seeking out new ways of being Christian in the world became a deeply valued method that was captured in the expression "see, judge, and act." With regard to the reception of the council, this method was well understood and applied throughout Latin America, as reflected in the work of the Episcopal Conference of Latin America and the proceedings of its meetings in Medellín, Puebla, Santo Domingo, and, more recently, in Aparecida.

The Signs of the Times in Brazil and Latin America

Looking at the current reality, it is necessary to recognize not only the great achievements of our time, but also the enormous disparities that are readily verified when seen in the light of the teachings of Sacred Scripture. Latin America possesses abundant riches that are clearly evident, but which succumb to a persistent affliction caused by the social, economic, cultural, and political disturbances that have had a devastating impact on the majority of people, who have been cruelly subjected to a precarious situation of poverty and vulnerability.

In the context of globalization, a convergence of the signs of the times is in evidence, revealing the realities of the current situation. In one way or another, the entire world participates in the same reality. This contemporaneity, referred to as post- or hypermodernity, is present everywhere, manifesting itself in rapid changes that revolutionize concepts of time and space, and the very manner in which we inhabit the world. There is, however, a certain shared sense of awareness that the present time is characterized not only by an era of profound and rapid changes in every aspect of life but also by an epoch of true and real change. This means that we are not simply undergoing extensive transformations, but radical changes in our vision of life, of the values that pertain to life, and the criteria used to determine the small and significant decisions that inform our commitments. A new, complex, and challenging world is revolutionizing everything. As it emerges, it summons from us a response. Some characteristics of this new moment in time should be noted. In the first place, great progress has been made in the fields of science and technology. This progress has been truly revolutionary and has benefited many different sectors, including health care, communications, and transportation. As noted in the documents of Aparecida, it has affected every area of social engagement: culture, economics, politics, the arts and sciences, education, sports, and religion.[8] As a consequence, we are experiencing something absolutely new in terms of our relationships among ourselves as well as our relationship to space, time, the environment, and with God.

It is necessary, therefore, to recognize that this new context brings with it many challenges that need to be understood and faced, given the vast horizon of countless transformations that are taking place. Given our "disposable" culture, the trivializing of evil, the experiences of fragmentation, the pervasiveness of individualism, utilitarianism, consumerism, and so many other "isms," it is evident that these realities are contributing factors to the crisis of meaning that disrupts and disheartens people and institutions, resulting in fatigue when it comes to pursuing the good as well as an intolerable sense of isolation that erodes all hope and even the desire to live.

In Brazil, and in almost all of Latin America, some more specific problems can be substantiated. The neoliberal economic system, which seeks profit at any price, has led to pervasive forms of corruption, the politics of patronage, the misuse of public resources, a lack of concern for the common good, the obstruction of justice, social inequalities, an ever-growing increase in violence especially among young people, little importance given to education, and the exclusion of the weakest and most vulnerable from the advantages made possible through progress. These situations affect life negatively, especially the lives of the poorest, undermining the values of happiness, solidarity, and hospitality that are characteristic of the Brazilian people. The indifference of the powerful toward the needs of the weakest and most fragile members of society is considered standard behavior. It is commonplace for those who live in misery to be viewed as belonging to another world and to be treated by the system as though they were invisible, relegated to the margins of a society in which their interests are never taken into account.

In a number of his writings, Gustavo Gutiérrez addresses the complex world of the poor by examining the multidimensional aspects of poverty. Many people are excluded from society as a consequence of their fundamental economic needs, the color of their skin, for the simple fact of being a woman, because of their sexual orientation, their age or their cultural background. According to Gutiérrez, "The poor constitute the 'other' of a society that builds itself up by ignoring or denying their most basic rights, oblivious to their lives and their values."[9] Here, it still must be noted that simply taking account of this reality is not enough. The root causes that contribute to the crushing devastation of an important part of humanity need to be studied, properly understood, and truthfully revealed so that an alternative history may be written.

In the face of this situation, which leads to changes in the very ethos of diverse peoples and requires a new set of rules for coexistence and harmonious living, theological ethics turns to Sacred Scripture, the very foundation of Christianity in its most original and particular form, in order to offer the world possible pathways to reconciliation and peace.

Sacred Scripture Illuminates Life

In our efforts to better understand contemporary reality in the light of biblical revelation, we must first consider the background of the texts and the intentionality of their writers. In recounting the story of universal salvation, starting from the experience of the people of Israel, Sacred Scripture gradually discloses who God is by placing us in the midst of the profound mystery of the Divine, while simultaneously revealing who the human person is in relationship with this God and with all of God's creation.

Without denying the vast and varied significance of the religious message of the Sacred Scriptures, it can be said that the Bible may be viewed as a remarkable compendium of social ethics. That is to say that, from the very beginning, the biblical text presents the human person as essentially a relational being, and, for this reason, all human actions, ways of living and inhabiting the world, have positive and negative repercussions that affect the whole of social existence.

While we should remain cognizant of the impossibility of summarizing all of the biblical sources that are foundational for social ethics, there is merit in at least providing a synthesis of some specific foundations considered to be pertinent for the purpose of this reflection. Beginning with the book of Genesis, we receive the revelation that God is the creator and savior of all things (Gen. 1–2). Everything that exists was created by the Lord, and it is this creative action that saves the world from primordial chaos and the possibility of nonexistence. Human beings, both men and women, are created in the image and likeness of God, and called to participate in God's creative work. Made from the earth, they are creatures like all other creatures, but when God breathes life into their nostrils, they become destined for the adventure of being human. Together with all other human beings, they are endowed with the freedom to discover their most original essence, their best reasons for living, and the most profound meaning of their ultimate end.

From the very beginning, the dignity of human beings is guaranteed, and no person or thing can take this from them. Through the relationship that they cultivate with God, they become capable of recognizing the gift of life that God graciously offers them and understanding that God has called them into being, in fidelity, responsible freedom, and creativity, to be the guardians of all life and of all creatures, just as God is for them.

The creation narratives emerge from the historical experience of the relationship of the people of Israel with God and with the people with whom they share their daily lives. The central event of this story is found in the book of Exodus and reveals a God who is concerned about God's people, and who, drawing near to the people with graciousness, freely offers salvation/deliverance and the promise of life: "Then the Lord said: I have witnessed the affliction of my people in Egypt and have heard their cry against their taskmasters, so I know well what they are suffering. Therefore I have come down to rescue them from the power of the Egyptians and lead them up from that land into a good and spacious land, a land flowing with milk and honey" (Exod. 3:7–8).

The promise of a new land reflects the efficaciousness of God's love for the people, as realized over the long course of history through sealed and established covenants, summarized in the following declaration: "Ever present in your midst, I will be your God, and you will be my people" (Lev. 26:12). In this context of freedom and covenant, the people receive specific directives to guide their behavior, so that they may live in freedom and happiness, and never again have need of Pharaoh. The Decalogue, as it is understood, presents rules which, if observed, promote just and loyal relationships among the people, guaranteeing the dignity of everyone as well as the good life that each one desires, always living in the light of the relationship they have made with God (Deut. 5). As Bernhard Häring observes,

"The Decalogue is the identification card of the covenant,"[10] and points to an ethos of the Decalogue, a realized commitment to our common humanity, an ethos that must be reaffirmed constantly, and an ethos that is a manifestation of our yes to the God of the Covenant. A precise description of the ethos of the Decalogue is presented by the prophet Micah: "You have been told, o mortal, what is good, and what the Lord requires of you: Only to do justice and to love goodness, and to walk humbly with your God" (Mic. 6:8).

So the covenant, which is always being renewed, illuminates history and offers direction regarding the pathways to be followed. However, over the course of this same history, people make mistakes and errors in judgment, and little by little, they distance themselves from the covenant they made with God and from the commandments that guaranteed their freedom and sustained the lives of everyone. With the creation of new laws and disregard for the common humanity that bound them together, with the seduction of prosperity, and the quest for new kings who would give them prestige and power over other peoples, and overly confident in the wisdom of their own schemes, the Israelites end up in exile once again, subject to the domination of another nation. While in exile they remember the covenant and seek forgiveness. And so, this history continues to repeat itself over and over again, even after the new and definitive covenant is established between God and humanity in the fullness of time (Gal. 4:4).

In the light of all of this, the Old Testament reveals that God raises up prophets and entrusts them with an ethical mission of reminding the people, through proclamations and admonitions, of the essence of the Law of the Covenant, which consists of maintaining a special relationship with God, that will result in the observance of justice and of righteousness so as to provide a guarantee for life, especially for the poor and the needy.[11] The presence of the poor and the impoverished among the people, along with the neglect of orphans, widows, strangers, and Levites, signaled a breaking of the Covenant. "There shall be no one of you in need" (Deut. 15:4). "If one of your kindred is in need in any community in the land which the Lord, your God, is giving you, you shall not harden your heart nor close your hand against your kin who is in need" (Deut. 15:7). The existence of a needy person in the midst of the people, even only one, signified the need for an appeal to do a better job of living out the covenant.[12]

The poor are at the center of Sacred Scripture. From the beginning, they warranted the special attention of God. The election of the people of Israel points to this:

> The Lord, your God, has chosen you from all the peoples on the face of the earth to be a people specially his own. . . . It was not because you are more numerous than all the peoples that the Lord set his heart on you and chose you; for you are really the smallest of all peoples. It was because the Lord loved you and because of his fidelity to the oath he had sworn to your ancestors. (Deut. 7:6b–8a)

The sacred text lists, in many circumstances, the merciful and loving gaze of God, his preferential attention toward the poorest of the poor and the disabled, for the weakest, and those most in need. Due to the fact that they have no one to care for them, God takes them into his arms and rescues them, offering special comfort and consolation to those who are sorrowful and oppressed.

The prophetic mission to denounce evil and announce the love of God is based on a twofold experience as God's people and as the people of God. Thus, they become the memory of the people and insist on saying that to forget the poor is to forget God, and that this means that they have forgotten truth about their own identity.[13] Forgetting that, before God, all of us are creatures, equal in dignity, we embrace a way of life that increases the number of poor people and further oppresses those who are already poor. Thus fraternity crumbles, life is diminished, the essential is lost, and people's relationships with God and with others are characterized by superficiality. On September 29, 2013, Pope Francis, in a homily to catechists, reflected on the loss of our memory of God:

> How does something like this happen? How do some people, perhaps ourselves included, end up becoming self-absorbed and finding security in material things which ultimately rob us of our face, our human face? This is what happens . . . when we no longer remember God. . . . If we don't think about God, everything ends up flat, everything ends up being about "me" and my own comfort. Life, the world, other people, all of these become unreal, they no longer matter, everything boils down to one thing: having.[14]

The prophets of Israel realize this reality and denounce a religion that takes refuge in the externals of cult ritual so as not to commit itself in any authentic way with real people. So says the Prophet Isaiah:

> What do I care for the multitude of your sacrifices? says the Lord. I have had enough of whole-burnt rams and fat of fatlings; in the blood of calves, lambs, and goats I find no pleasure. . . . When you spread out your hands, I will close my eyes to you; though you pray the more, I will not listen. Your hands are full of blood! Wash yourselves clean! Put away your misdeeds from before my eyes; cease doing evil; learn to do good. Make justice your aim: redress the wronged, hear the orphan's plea, and defend the widow. Come now, let us set things right, says the Lord: Though your sins be like scarlet, they may become white as snow; though they be red like crimson, they may become white as wool. (Isa. 1:11, 15–18)

The quest for law and justice is a constant in the words of the prophets of Israel. Frequently they rebuke those who, through their abuse of power, oppress the people. Once again the Prophet Isaiah voices his concern: "Is this not, rather, the fast that I choose: releasing those bound unjustly, untying the thongs of the yoke; setting free the oppressed, breaking off every yoke? Is it not sharing your bread with the hungry, bringing the afflicted and the homeless into your house; clothing the naked when you see them, and not turning your back on your own flesh?" (Isa. 58:6–7).

The prophet Jeremiah addresses the king of Judah using similar words: "Thus says the Lord: Do what is right and just. Rescue the victims from the hand of their oppressors. Do not wrong or oppress the resident alien, the orphan, or the widow, and do not shed innocent blood in this place" (Jer. 22:3).

Speaking to the princes of Israel, the prophet Ezekiel is no less incisive: "Thus says the Lord God: Enough, you princes of Israel! Put away violence and oppression, and do what is just and right! Stop evicting my people!—oracle of the Lord God" (Ezek. 45:9).

Offering advice to King Nebuchadnezzar, the prophet Daniel says: "Therefore, O king, may my advice be acceptable to you; atone for your sins by good deeds, and for your misdeeds by kindness to the poor; then your contentment will be long-lasting" (Dan. 4:24).

So too the prophet Amos admonishes the religious leaders of his time, saying: "I hate, I despise your feasts, I take no pleasure in your solemnities. . . . Rather let justice surge like waters, and righteousness like an unfailing stream" (Amos 5:21–24).

It can be said, then, that the prophets sought the way of justice in order to change oppressive structures and transform the society. They sought the way of solidarity in order to change people's modes of relating and renew the community. They sought the way of the mystic in order to change the manner of thinking and raise consciousness. Three ways to a single goal.[15]

Together with Pope Francis, it is useful for us to remember the qualities of a person who is truly a prophet: He or she is a person of three times: a person who does not forget the past, who contemplates the present, and courageously points the way to the future. "This is the prophet: a person with a penetrating vision who listens to God's words and proclaims them; who knows the present realities and goes toward into the future. But first, the prophet listened to God's Word."[16]

Jesus of Nazareth was moved by the same logic as that of the prophets before him. Jesus, the Word incarnate, inaugurates a new moment in time, yet he does not distance himself from the prophets of Israel. He recognizes himself as a prophet when he says: "A prophet is not without honor except in his native place and in his own house" (Matt. 13:57). The people also viewed him as a prophet: "And when he entered Jerusalem the whole city was shaken and asked, 'Who is this?' And the crowds replied, 'This is Jesus the prophet, from Nazareth in Galilee'" (Matt. 21:10–11).

This prophet is the Word made flesh. He is the one who came to establish the new and everlasting covenant between God and people. He is the Way, the Truth and the Life. He is the one who fully reveals God and the human being who is in relationship with God. For this reason, it is not possible to speak about Christian

social ethics without allowing ourselves to be guided by the life, works, and words
of Jesus Christ.

José M. Castillo, when speaking to the representatives of the church in Spain,
made a very strong statement that should disturb and unsettle every one of us: "To
justify privilege, people use philosophy, history, and international rights. They rarely
point to the example of Jesus or use the Gospel as their starting point."[17]

Perhaps this is because in Jesus, God manifested once again his preference for
the little ones. He chose a stable as the place for his birth and Nazareth of Galilee
as the city in which he would live his early years. Jesus is born poor, in the midst of
the poor, and to fulfill his mission he does not go to the capital city of Jerusalem,
nor does he call upon the influential people of his time. Surrounded by simple peasants and fishermen, disreputable people and sinners, he becomes an itinerant "with
nowhere to lay his head" (Matt. 8:20), and so, he establishes the kingdom of God
on earth. His manner of life and his actions give credibility to his words and model
for us the ethical perspectives that we ought to consider.

Beginning his public ministry, after an enlightening experience in the desert,
Jesus returned to Galilee "with the power of the Spirit" (Luke 4:14). In Nazareth,
he entered the synagogue, read out loud from the prophet Isaiah (Isa. 61) and said:
"Today this scripture is fulfilled in your hearing" (Luke 4:21). His mission was
explained in a few words: consecrated to announce the Good News to the poor, to
proclaim liberty to the captives, recovery of sight to the blind, to let the oppressed
go free, and to announce a year of favor from the Lord.

The Gospels, in describing the encounter of Jesus with the poor of his time,
make use of a Greek expression, the verb *splagchnizomai*, which means: to be
moved, as in to move one's bowels. This signifies a "visceral reaction, one of the
most intimate and human sensations that a person can experience. . . . Jesus reacted
viscerally to the poor people before him as they fainted from hunger (Mic. 6:34,
8:2)."[18] We need to understand, therefore, that Jesus could not bear to see people
in need; he could not stand to see people in pain. This sensitivity to the suffering of
others took him out of his comfort zone and moved him to act in such a way that
he directly confronted the situation before him.

This is how he lived, and this is why he died. He was persecuted and rejected,
like the prophets who came before him, but he redeemed us through love, and, as
God who became human, he entrusted to us an unquestionable legacy. The love that
Jesus proclaims and lives is the axis upon which the reign of God turns, a love that is
offered, gratuitously and without reservation, a love that is always ready and able to
forgive and to gather into the same communion of life even those who are enemies.
This is the synthesis of the old Law, paradoxically summarized and expanded.

By virtue of the love that he offers, Jesus cuts through the vicious circle of institutionalized violence, overcoming it without creating more victims, and also taking
with him to the final victory those who do not deserve it, those who faltered and
those who failed to be faithful until the end. This logic of the love of God, even
if it is understood, has yet to be lived out fully by those of us who call ourselves

Christians. How well we know the difficulties that prevent us from fully embracing this project. Mindful of our creatureliness, which brings to light our limitations, our internal contradictions, and our sins, still God shows us the way, and for those of us who are Christians, it is the only way. God knows our fragility; still God calls us forth to overcome it. "Be perfect, therefore, as your heavenly Father is perfect" (Matt. 5:48).

Therefore, it is possible to say that the ethics of Jesus is a revolutionary ethics that seeks the transparency of love, that always desires the happiness of others, their well-being, their pleasure, their joy, their freedom, without ever seeking to dominate them or diminish them in any way, and no matter what the reason, to never ask them for anything in return. In this manner, Jesus shows us that the way to encounter God does not involve the negation of our humanity, but rather, he tells us that the more fully human we are, the closer we will be to God. As the First Letter of John declares: "Those who say 'I love God' and hate their brothers and sisters are liars; for those who do not love a brother or sister whom they have seen, cannot love God whom they have not seen" (1 John 4:20). Christian spirituality, in many instances and for diverse reasons, has taken us down several pathways. In order for us to draw near to God, we should sacrifice many things that are part of our human condition. A real encounter with another person, with all of the difficulties that it may involve as well as all of the joys and pleasures that may arise from the experience, cannot be rejected in the name of an ethic proposed by Jesus. The other is always the criterion of our adherence to Jesus' plan. In the other's hour of need, he or she should be our absolute priority when it comes to taking action. For this reason, we always should be prepared to respond to the needs of others and willing to set aside our own immediate interests and concerns. The parable of the Good Samaritan, as recounted by Jesus, illustrates this imperative with great clarity. As Pope Francis states in *Evangelii Gaudium*, "Going out to others in order to reach the fringes of humanity does not mean rushing out aimlessly into the world. Often it is better simply to slow down, to put aside our eagerness in order to see and listen to others, to stop rushing from one thing to another and to remain with someone who has faltered along the way."[19]

The Gospels tell us that the other to whom we must be attentive in a preferential way is the one who is poor, the one who is in need, the one who is excluded, the one who is unable to repay us (Luke 14:14). As Pope Francis says in *Evangelii Gaudium*: "There can be no room for doubt or for explanations which weaken so clear a message. Today and always, 'the poor are the privileged recipients of the Gospel,' and the fact that it is freely preached to them is a sign of the kingdom that Jesus came to establish."[20]

Returning to the Bible as the foundation for social ethics, we experience along the way a certain sense that a change in direction is needed with regard to our manner of being and acting in human history. In order to be more faithful to our Christian experience, we must understand its rootedness in the original foundations of Christianity. In doing so, we can deduce certain ethical imperatives that can be summarized as follows: service instead of power, gracious giving instead of exchange, generous sharing in place of overconsumption, focusing on the other instead of one's self, replacing grandiosity with modesty, appealing to the good instead of cold and callous legalism, proposing instead of imposing, replacing indifference and hatred with love, dispelling bitter and resentful sadness with hopeful joy.

Only in this way will we become seeds of a new world, producing delicious and desirable fruits, capable of bringing consolation to many people and giving meaning to their lives.

Translated by Margaret Eletta Guider, OSF

Notes

1. Pope John XXIII, Apostolic Constitution *Humanae Salutis* (December 25, 1961). www.vatican.va.

2. Pope John XXIII, "Encyclical Letter *Mater et Magistra*. On Christianity and Social Progress" (May 15, 1961), in *Catholic Social Thought: The Documentary Heritage,* ed. David L. O'Brien and Thomas A. Shannon (Maryknoll, NY: Orbis Books, 2002).

3. Pope John XXIII, *Discurso del Santo Padre a los participantes en el VI Congreso Internacional de Ciencias Pre-históricas y Proto-históricas* (Castelgandolfo, September 1, 1962). www.vatican.va.

4. Pope John XXIII, *Discorso del Santo Padre ai partecipanti al corso di aggiornamento pedagógico per i direttori spiritual dei seminari d'Italia* (Rome, September 9, 1962). www. vatican.va.

5. Vatican Council II. "Pastoral Constitution on the Church in the Modern World," *Gaudium et Spes,* December 7, 1965, no. 4, in *Documents of the Vatican II,* ed. Austin P. Flannery (Grand Rapids, MI: Eerdmans, 1975).

6. Vatican Council II. "Dogmatic Constitution on Divine Revelation," *Dei Verbum,* November 18, 1965, n. 24, in *Documents of the Vatican II,* ed. Austin P. Flannery (Grand Rapids, MI: Eerdmans, 1975).

7. Vatican Council II, "Decree on the Training of Priests," *Optatam Totius,* October 28, 1965, no. 16, in *Documents of the Vatican II,* ed. Austin P. Flannery (Grand Rapids, MI: Eerdmans, 1975), 720.

8. CELAM, *Documento de Aparecida,* 2007, Texto conclusivo da V Conferência Geral do Episcopado Latino-Americano e do Caribe (Brasília/São Paulo: Edições CNBB/Paulus/ Paulinas, 2007), no. 35.

9. Gustavo Gutiérrez, "Situação e tarefas da Teologia da Libertação," in *Ao lado dos pobres,* by Gerhard Ludwig Müller and Gustavo Gutiérrez (São Paulo: Paulinas, 2014), 73.

10. Bernhard Häring, *Teologia moral para o terceiro milênio* (São Paulo: Paulinas, 1991), 126.

11. See Armindo dos Santos Vaz, "O específico da justiça na Bíblia hebraica," *Cultura* 30 (2012): 63–75. www.cultura.revues.org.

12. Conferência dos Religiosos do Brasil, *A leitura profética da história* (São Paulo: CRB, Loyola, 1992).

13. Fred Kammer, *Fé-justiça em ação. Uma introdução ao pensamento social católico* (São Paulo: Loyola, 2009).

14. Pope Francis, Holy Mass on the Occasion of the "Day for Catechists" during the Year of Faith (Rome, September 29, 2013). www.vatican.va.

15. Conferência dos Religiosos do Brasil. *A leitura profética da história.*

16. Pope Francis, Holy Mass on Santa Marta (Rome, December 16, 2013). *Homem de olhar penetrante.* www.osservatoreromano.va.

17. José Maria Castillo, *A ética de Cristo* (São Paulo: Loyola, 2010), 13.

18. Ibid., 94.

19. Pope Francis, Apostolic Exhortation on the Proclamation of the Gospel in Today's World, *Evangelii Gaudium* (November 24, 2013), no. 46. www.vatican.va.

20. Ibid., no. 48.

The Kingdom Proclamation of Jesus in the Gospels

Context and Challenge to North America

John R. Donahue

A church that does not provoke any crisis, preach a Gospel that does not
unsettle, proclaim a word of God that does not get under anyone's skin or
a word of God that does not touch the real sin of the society in which it is
being proclaimed: what kind of Gospel is that?

> —*Archbishop Oscar Romero, The Violence of Love*

After relative neglect in the early years of modern biblical criticism, recent
decades have witnessed a virtual cornucopia of works on New Testament ethics.[1]
A constant theme is that Jesus' proclamation of the kingdom (reign) of God is the
foundation of not only his life and ministry but also shapes the theology of the
synoptic Gospels.[2] This proclamation also presents a fundamental challenge to
values that are pervasive in the life and culture of North America, especially the
United States. Given both the scope of the topic and the vast amount of literature,
I can only highlight major themes and present bibliography so that readers may
themselves explore and be enriched by insights of others who have been and are still
engaging this startling proclamation of Jesus.

The Gospel of Mark: Power Subverted and Redefined

In a very helpful article, Robert J. Brawley surveys the various approaches to the
ethics of Mark: (1) extracting norms for judging people and events; (2) determining
bases for evaluating motivations, purposes, and objectives; (3) cultivating virtues;
(4) discovering Jesus' ethical teachings; (5) finding critiques of people, systems,
and structures that perpetuate injustice and envisioning justice; (6) locating ethics
in God's will for humanity and the world; and (7) living in response to God.[3]
Although these clearly overlap, they all grow out of the fundamental proclamation
of Jesus: "The time is fulfilled, and the kingdom of God has come near; repent, and
believe in the good news" (1:14–15).

Though the phrase "kingdom of God" rarely appears in the Old Testament, it
obviously reflects the OT idea of Yahweh ruling as a king (Exod. 15:18; Isa. 24:23,

52:7; Ezek. 20:33; Mic. 4:7; Pss. 93:1, 97:1, 146:10).[4] In the OT the phrase expresses "an eschatological hope for a period when God's salvation would be realized, when his dominion over the minds and lives of human beings would be accomplished, and they would be withdrawn from subjection to danger, evil, and sin."[5] In the New Testament, the phrase becomes a cipher for the Christ event: the entry of Jesus of Nazareth into history by "his ministry, passion, death, and resurrection. As the Christ and the risen Lord, he is the Father's special anointed agent for the preaching and establishment of this dominion henceforth among human beings."[6]

Yet the kingdom of God itself is multivalent and there is no one-to-one correspondence with the kingdom of God and any concept or expression. It evokes a host of associations rooted in the Old Testament understandings and in the New Testament summarized by three terms, *reign(ing)*, the power of God active in creation and history; *realm*, not simply a spiritual power but also a "home" or situation where this power is exercised and recognized, so much so that people can "enter" it; and *rule*, the guidelines for a way of life according to its proclamation and presence. J. Dominic Crossan states that kingdom "judges all human rule," which provides the focus for the present discussion of Mark's understanding of the kingdom of God, which subverts dominating power and summons to a radical discipleship.[7] The first words of Mark are a clarion call: "The beginning of the good news of Jesus, Messiah, Son of God," rooted in the great prophets of Israel and first heralded by John's summons to "prepare the way" for a stronger one who will come after him (1:1–8). After his adoption as son by the Father and testing in the wilderness, as noted above, the first words of Jesus set the stage for the whole Gospel. Jesus arrives in Galilee proclaiming the good news: "The time is fulfilled, and the kingdom of God has come near; repent, and believe in the good news" (1:14–15). Each phrase is pregnant with meaning. With the good news rooted in the proclamation of Isaiah, by the arrival of Jesus heralded by the preaching of John, and through the messianic preparation of Jesus (baptism and testing), the decisive time (*kairos*) for the good news has arrived in the action of God in Jesus. Yet it contains a "not yet" since while the message is offered, it has not yet been accepted.[8] It requires *metanoia*, not simply "repentance," in the sense of sorrow for sin, but rather "think again," or "reconsider," and belief in the good news, which is an act of trust in the story of Jesus that will unfold. The proclamation is both gift and demand.

But the Gospel is not simply a story of Jesus but of what it means to respond to him and follow his teaching (discipleship). In a brief, iconic narrative, the first act of Jesus is to begin to form such a community, but the calm of the Galilean seaside is immediately shattered by a demoniac shouting: "What have you come to do with us, Jesus of Nazareth? Have you come to destroy us?" (1:24). A power struggle surfaces: Jesus rebukes the demon, silences him, and in extraordinarily vivid language— "convulsing with a loud cry"—leaves the man. The bystanders are awestruck and exclaim, "What is this?" A new teaching with authority (*exousia*, also power), a term used in the LXX and intertestamental literature especially of God and God's works, representatives and emissaries.[9] Conflict on earth in the apocalyptic horizon of Mark mirrors the heavenly battle between the power of God and the power of evil. The power of God manifest in Jesus is power over evil spirits and illness, *on behalf of* suffering people, while rejecting the powers of the "anti-kingdom": misuse of religious authority, brutality of political power, the desire for prestige, and ultimately the power to kill. The life and teaching of Jesus subverts such power and offers an alternate vision of true power, which liberates people from illness and demonic power, "restores people to God and community, calls for generosity to the poor, challenges oppressors, fosters mutual service, counsels cessation of force, and much more."[10] Three aspects of Mark illustrate the powers of "anti-kingdom."

Misuse of Religious Authority

Jesus' activity on behalf of the sick and marginal evokes violent opposition from religious leaders, primarily the scribal and priestly authorities in Jerusalem. After he heals a man on the Sabbath, Pharisees and Herodians conspire on how to destroy him (3:6, also in 11:18, 12:12, 14:1), and when the crowds follow Jesus not only from Galilee but from Jerusalem and surrounding territories, "scribes from Jerusalem" accuse him of being possessed by Beelzebul (3:22). As Jesus draws near Jerusalem and compares the leaders to the unfaithful vineyard tenants of Isaiah (12:1–11; Isa. 5:1–10) and castigates the scribes for devouring the houses of widows (12:40), the opposition heightens, culminating in Jesus' arrest, hearing before the Sanhedrin, and death on the cross. Although the historical reasons for the death of Jesus are disputed, contemporary research focuses on the alliance between the priestly aristocracy and the Roman governor who saw the actions of Jesus as a threat to their power and authority.[11]

Brutality of Political Power

Even before the opening scene of the ministry of Jesus, violence overshadows the narrative with the arrest (literally "handing over") of John the Baptizer, whose fate will be revealed at the macabre birthday party of Herod [Antipas] (6:14–29), attended by a collection of royal retainers, military leaders, and aristocrats (6:21). Mark's readers are given a glimpse of a world that governs their lives, but is fundamentally corrupt. A young woman dances and pleases (with sexual overtones) Herod and the reclining guests, so much so that Herod promises her by oath to give whatever she asks. Though surrounded by the accoutrements of power, Herod is ultimately weak, and, though sorry for his promise, orders John's execution, which foreshadows the death of Jesus.

Desire for Power and Prestige

The desire for prestige and power over others hardens the hearts of the chosen disciples and blocks their response to follow Jesus on the way of the cross. In the great middle section of the Gospel (8:27–10:52), three times Jesus predicts that he will suffer and die in Jerusalem, and the disciples progressively rebuff him (8:33–38) and in two instances bicker about positions of prestige in the community (9:31–32, 10:32–45). The final instance occurs just before Jesus enters Jerusalem, when Jesus rejects their attitudes in vivid and stark terms: "supposed" gentile rulers lord it over their subjects, the great ones (important people) flaunt their power (*exousia*), but "it shall not be so among you." In contrast, "whoever wishes to become great among you must be your servant, and whoever wishes to be first among you must be slave of all," and the foundation of servant leadership is that the "Son of Man came not to be served but to serve, and to give his life as ransom for many" (10:45).

"Son of Man" evokes the figure from Daniel 7, where the seer, after viewing a sequence of powerful kingdoms destroyed one after the other, has a vision of a heavenly judgment scene where the ancient of days gives "dominion and glory and kingship" to "one like a son of man coming with the clouds of heaven" (7:13–14). Although the reference to the one like the son of man is disputed, clearly the scene is one of radical reversal of dominating power in favor of "the holy ones," most likely the Jewish martyrs under Antiochus IV Epiphanes (215–164 BCE). Jesus as the suffering son and, later, exalted son of man (14:61–62), is the servant leader and martyr, whose life, given for others, will be ransom (price paid for freeing a slave) for a suffering people. This is the example of true power for his followers.

The Gospel of Matthew:
A Community Formed by Mercy and Justice

In plotting the trajectory of the kingdom proclamation of Jesus, Matthew takes pride of place, "with fifty references to the kingdom of God/heaven, thirty-two of which are peculiar to him."[12] While repeating Mark's emphasis on the power of God's reign, by his portrayal of Jesus as a teacher, Matthew enhances the ethical demands of the kingdom and "in line with the traditional Jewish interpretation of the term, gives it a metaphorical and spatial characteristic [realm] by imaging it as a place to which people can gain entrance, refuse to enter, or place obstacles in the way of others entering (5:20, 7:13, 7:21, 18:3, 18:9, 19:23, 21:31, 23:13)."[13] Only Matthew uses the phrase "Gospel of the kingdom" (4:23, 9:35, 24:14), and a theme of the whole work is "seek first the kingdom of God, and his justice" (6:33).[14]

As a scribe who brings from his household things old and things new (13:36), Matthew continues his Jewish heritage of God's power that shapes communities, and it became "the best suited to the manifold needs of the later church, the most cited by the church fathers, the most used in the liturgy, and the most serviceable for catechetical purposes."[15] The Sermon on the Mount (chaps. 5–7), the first of five major discourses of Jesus, begins with the paradoxical proclamation of blessings on marginal and suffering people, the poor, the meek, mourners, and those who hunger for justice, along with those who strive for peace, show mercy, and will suffer for the sake of justice (5:1–12), and is followed by a complex of the teachings of Jesus that have defined and challenged Christianity through the ages—for example, marital fidelity, reconciliation of conflict, shocking forgiveness, no violence in the face of evil, love of enemies, and the Golden Rule: to love others as one's self, "for this is the law and the prophets."[16]

Later, when citing the dual command to love God (Deut. 6:4) and neighbor (Lev. 19:18), Matthew adds to the Markan text (Mark 12:28–34) that the law and prophets "hang on" ["are dependent on"] these two commands (22:40), so that the love command is at the heart of both Judaism and the teaching of Jesus. The sermon then concludes with the mandate that true discipleship is not found in one who does mighty works in the name of Jesus but "who does the will of my Father in heaven" (7:21–23).

Not only does Matthew enhance the teaching of Jesus, but offers the most complete picture of Jesus as the "servant of the Lord" by citing the full text of the second servant song of Isaiah (12:18–21 = Isa. 42:1–4), where the chosen servant "will proclaim justice to the Gentiles," and "will not break a bruised reed, or quench a smoldering wick until he brings justice to victory."

This citation has been called "the hermeneutical key" for Matthew's entire Gospel[17] and many scholars link it to the earlier citation of Isaiah 53:4, in Matthew 8:17: he "cured all the sick, to fulfill what had been said by Isaiah the prophet: 'He took away our infirmities and bore our diseases.'" The action of the servant will be gentle and healing, and when the servant brings justice to victory, the Gentiles (*ethnē*) will hope in his name, which foreshadows the mission of the disciples to make disciples of all nations (*ethnē*) (28:16–20). This mission of the servant is a work of justice in its fullest sense: concern for those who are suffering, but now extending beyond the people of Israel (see also Isa. 51:4–6). The servant who will not break the bruised reed recalls the values of the beatitudes and of Jesus who is "gentle and humble of heart" (11:28–29). The work of the servant here— understood as saving help and liberating people from various infirmities—is a foreshadowing of the grand scenario of the final judgment in Matthew 25:31–46.

Before his birth, Jesus is called king by the wise men from the East, who are seeking "the child who is born King of the Jews" (2:2); in his ministry, in the quotation from Isaiah at the entry to Jerusalem: "Your king is coming to you, humble, and mounted on a donkey" (21:5, see Isa. 62:11); in the mocking during the crucifixion and on the inscription on the cross: "This is Jesus, the King of the Jews" (27:37).

In the parable of the last judgment (25:31–46), Jesus appears as king when, as exalted son of man on a throne, he judges the nations and separates the sheep from the goats on the basis of how they responded to the needs of "the least of his brothers and sisters." Matthew's pageant of the last judgment has become the "Gospel within the Gospel," for people dedicated to works of mercy and justice for the multitudes today suffering hunger, thirst, horrible illness, and imprisonment, but with varying interpretations of who are "the least" and who are judged on the basis of their care for them.

The "classic" interpretation is that "in the final judgment the standard by which Christians are measured is the works of compassion that they have or have not done toward their poor and needy Christian brothers and sisters."[18] A "universalistic" interpretation has become commonplace: anyone (Christian or non-Christian) who does such works of mercy to any suffering person will be welcomed into eternal life, which, however, is scarcely the meaning of Matthew. Another variation is a "missionary" reading. The least of Jesus' brothers and sisters are his followers now hidden in those sent to proclaim the good news to the whole world (Matt. 28:16–20), who suffer things similar to early Christian missionaries and Paul (2 Cor. 11:22–32), and those judged are "nations" who welcome or reject them.

Whatever the interpretation of who is judged, the parable reveals that justice is constituted by acts of loving-kindness and mercy to those in need; the world will be made "right" or "just" when the way the least are treated becomes the norm of action. For all interpretations, Christ is present in the marginal and suffering of the world, and they are the true bearers of Jesus' presence and are a continuing challenge to the world's myopia.

The sufferings borne by the least of the brothers and sisters of the son of man summon the church to be an authentic and faithful witness of the Gospel. The church cannot preach acts of loving-kindness to the hungry, the thirsty, the imprisoned, and the naked unless it too is a church in mission which bears these same sufferings. No Gospel is harsher than Matthew on an ethics of words without deeds. The church too often suffers from a massive credibility gap, and the values which it proposes *to the nations* must be those that the church itself witnesses *in the midst* of the nations.[19]

The Gospel of Luke:
"The kingdom of God is among you" (17:21)

The Danger of Wealth

Kingdom in Luke follows the traditions of Mark and Matthew, but with significant alterations and additions. The annunciation to Mary contains the promise that "He will reign over the house of Jacob forever, and of his kingdom there will be no end" (1:33). In Luke, Jesus is "the kingdom-preacher par excellence," since, unlike Matthew 3:2, John the Baptist does not announce the kingdom, and Jesus announces the good news of the kingdom only after he assumes the role of the anointed prophet of Isaiah, who comes "to bring good news to the poor, to proclaim release to the captives and recovery of sight to the blind, to let the oppressed go free" (4:18; Isa. 61:1, 58:6), which links the kingdom to concern for the marginalized.[20] Only in Luke does Jesus speak of the kingdom in his presence and activity: "The kingdom of God is among you" (17:21), which led Origen to describe Jesus as *autobasileia* (himself, the kingdom).[21] Jesus' Sermon on the Plain is addressed to disciples as the real poor, hungry, grief-stricken, and outcasts of the world, who are declared happy because the kingdom of God is "yours," [or on behalf of you] but is followed by woes on a different audience: "You who are rich who have received their consolation" (6:20–24). We will focus on the stark contrast between rich and poor along with the danger of wealth and call attention to Luke's Samaritan stories as crossing social and religious barriers.

Luke's distinctive concerns with the rich and the poor and with possessions emerge most strongly in material unique to his Gospel. The early chapters provide an overture to the whole Gospel. The infancy narratives show special concern for the ʿanawîm, people without money and power. In her Magnificat, Mary praises a God who puts down the mighty from their thrones, fills the hungry with good things, and sends the rich away empty-handed (Luke 1:52–53). Mary and Joseph cannot find lodging in an inn, and the first proclamation of Jesus' birth is to people on the margin of society ("shepherds," 2:8–14).

Luke's warning against the dangers of wealth and his concern for the marginalized appear mainly in significant parables: The Rich Fool (12:13–31) and The Rich Man and Lazarus (19:16–31).[22]

The Parable of the Rich Fool (Luke 12:13–21)

Luke begins with an all too familiar fight over an inheritance that Jesus is asked to adjudicate.[23] Jesus refuses, but warns against greed by recounting a parable that illustrates that one's life does not consist of possessions. Greed (lit., Greek, *pleonexia*, grasping for more) is one of the most pilloried vices in antiquity, called "the metropolis of all evil" by Diodorus Siculus.[24] Paul calls it idolatry, since the desire for wealth begins to take over one's life (Col. 3:5).

In the parable, a rich man's land produces a bountiful harvest—usually a sign of God's blessing. He attempts to secure this future by building bigger barns, storing the grain and other goods, so he can sit back and say, "You have many good things stored up for years—rest, eat, drink, and be merry." Suddenly the voice of God thunders, "fool" (using language forbidden to humans, Matt. 5:21–22), "this night your life will be demanded of you" (lit., "They are demanding your soul from you"). The word "demand" (*apaitousin*) is commonly used for collecting a loan. The rich man did not realize that the fruits of his harvest were "on loan" from God and not to be used for his own gratification. He forgets the most basic event of his religious heritage by not observing the law that gleanings from the harvest are to be left for the poor and the alien, which Deuteronomy twice roots in the nature of God, who freed the people from slavery (Lev. 19:9, 23:22; Deut. 24:21).

In an ominous warning that provides an *inclusio* to the initial warning against greed (12:13), Jesus says, "So it is with those who store up treasures for themselves but are not rich toward God" (12:20). The following verses describe a lifestyle of trust in God without "anxiety" over material needs, since "it is the nations of the world that strive after all these things, and your Father knows that you need them. Instead, strive for his kingdom, and these things will be given to you as well" (12:30–31).

The Rich Man and Lazarus (16:19–31)

The parable begins with vivid contrasts: designation of status (rich) versus poor; dressed in purple garments of fine linen (both very costly in the ancient world) versus being clothed in ulcerous sores; sumptuous daily meals, most likely with other rich dinner guests, versus scavenging for food with dogs as his only companions.[25] The poor man dies, and angels carry him to the bosom of Abraham, but with a surprising reversal of fate: the rich man in torment in the underworld first *sees* the very Lazarus who lay at his gate with Abraham. Abraham, as the guardian of the covenant fidelity of the people, assumes the role of teacher, disclosing to the rich man the dire fate that awaits him. The key to understanding this harsh punishment is that the rich man first *sees* the very Lazarus who lay at his gate when the chasm between them is eternally fixed. During his lifetime, his wealth created a gulf that made him *blind* to the sufferings of the poor man; now he can gaze on him only when it is too late.

The rich man then begs Abraham to send Lazarus to warn his brothers, who apparently lived the same lavish lifestyle. Abraham replies that they have the same opportunities he had, the law and the prophets, a reference to the injunctions of the Torah to care for the poor and the needy, and the warnings of the prophets, like those of Amos. Abraham again states that without listening to the law and the prophets, the brothers will not be converted, even if someone should rise from the dead.

The abiding validity of "the law and the prophets" must always form Christian conscience. Belief in the risen Jesus is a hallmark of Christian faith, and perhaps some in Luke's community felt that this was enough; they no longer had to take seriously the Jewish tradition of justice and compassion for the weak. But the one risen from the dead who offers salvation today is the same Jesus who listened to the voice of Moses and the prophets and offered love and acceptance to the marginalized of his day, while uttering sober warnings to the proud and prosperous.

Crossing Social and Religious Barriers

In the Gospel, Jesus breaks through social and religious barriers by frequent meals with "tax collectors and sinners," by his close association with women followers, and above all by his favorable portrayal of the hated Samaritans. This hatred arose from the all too familiar claim of different groups to define a religious tradition, joined to a history of interreligious violence. When Jesus praises a lawyer who quotes the command to love God and neighbor as the way to eternal life, the lawyer then asks, "Who is my neighbor?" Jesus responds with the familiar parable of the "Good Samaritan," which describes what it means to be "neighbor." A man is robbed, beaten, and left for dead along the Jericho road. After a priest and a Levite pass, a Samaritan sees him, has compassion, stops, binds up his wounds, and brings him to an inn. Throughout history this story serves as a paradigm for coming to the aid of a suffering person, but the real shock of the parable is that a "Samaritan" does this—the hated outsider becomes the one who showed mercy (saving help).[26]

The second Samaritan narrative occurs when Jesus, traveling on the boundary between Samaria and Galilee, heals ten lepers who cry out, "Jesus, Master, have mercy upon us." The great shock of the narrative, then, is that the one who returns "glorifying God in a loud voice" and who gives thanks to God is a Samaritan whom Jesus calls "a foreigner" (the Greek literally means "a person of a different kind or nature"). This positive view of the Samaritan should be joined with the other major Samaritan incident, the parable of the Good Samaritan.[27] These two Samaritan stories provide an arch from the initial stages of Jesus' long journey to Jerusalem to near its conclusion. Taken together, the two narratives provide exemplars of the greatest commandments: to love God with one's whole heart and soul and to love one's neighbor as one's self, and to glorify God by praise and thanksgiving (Luke 17:15, 18). In our world today where suspicion of "the other" and violence toward "the other" are rampant, these Samaritan stories should shape Christian practice today as it did for the missionary church in the Acts of the Apostles that continued to break through religious and ethnic barriers, and brought the good news to the Samaritans and all the nations of the world.

The Kingdom Proclamation of Jesus: Context and Challenge

The works in this series address the world context of Catholic theological ethics, but from locally determined perspectives. Stephen Bevans describes this approach as "a way of doing theology in which one takes into account: the spirit and message of the Gospel; the tradition of the Christian people; the culture in which one is theologizing; and social change in that culture."[28] The present essay is an attempt to join reflection on the "kingdom proclamation" of Jesus in the synoptic Gospels with suggestions of how it challenges aspects of the culture of the United States during the second decade of the twenty-first century.

Jesus in the Gospel of Mark challenges a worldview that exalts power and prestige, which are hallmarks of contemporary values and public rhetoric. From "American exceptionalism," to near riots over admission of children to prestige kindergartens, there is pathology to be "the best" and for the maintenance of power. These values, like the air we breathe (also often polluted), "are embodied in, and exercise their power through, societal institutions and structures: economics, politics, culture, race, religion."[29] Mark's Gospel offers a countervision where power now functions as liberating service for others and when Jesus "came into conflict with those who held power. Clerical circles and civil authorities collaborated; he was put on trial. He was sentenced to death. But the reason for his speaking and acting remained in the memory of the people."[30] Death could not conquer him or silence his teaching.

Matthew's legacy to Catholic ethics is a compendium of the fundamental values of the teaching of Jesus, which are to be translated into action with the warning "that everyone who hears these words of mine and does not act on them will be like a foolish man who built his house on sand" (7:26). For Matthew, to be a church is to experience community,[31] and today, in contrast to the strong individualism of religious belonging in the United States, "a communal sensibility remains central to Catholic identity."[32] Neither Matthew's community nor the church today is to neglect "the weightier matters of the law: justice and mercy and faith" (23:23), which unfold in special care for the least of the brothers and sisters of Jesus.

More perhaps than any NT document, the Gospel of Luke speaks to the current context of church and society. We have emphasized the evil of greed and the danger of wealth, which coincides with an avalanche of contemporary studies on the evil effects of greed and on the gap in income and wealth between rich and poor—and the vast majority of people. Likewise, Luke's vivid Samaritan narratives overturn people's conception of "the others" as marginal and threatening, and embody the true meaning of love of God and neighbor. These sections of Luke speak to what remains as the most destructive element in US society, the abiding presence of covert and overt racism.[33] The Gospel of Luke summons the whole church in the United States to a profound conversion of the imagination that may open doors to a more demanding and profound transformation of values and practices.[34]

The kingdom proclamation of Jesus opens many doors for Catholic ethics in the twenty-first century; who will enter?

Notes

1. Some examples would be Daniel Harrington, SJ, and James Keenan, SJ, *Jesus and Virtue Ethics: Building Bridges between New Testament Studies and Moral Theology* (Lanham, MD: Sheed and Ward, 2002); Richard B. Hays, *The Moral Vision of the New Testament: Community, Cross, New Creation: A Contemporary Introduction to New Testament Ethics* (San Francisco: HarperSanFrancisco, 1996); Frank J. Matera, *New Testament Ethics: The Legacies of Jesus and Paul* (Louisville, KY: Westminster John Knox Press, 1996); and Alan Verhey, *Remembering Jesus: Christian Community, Scripture and the Moral Life* (Grand Rapids, MI: Eerdmans, 2002).

2. See especially Brian K. Blount, *Go Preach! Mark's Kingdom Message and the Black Church Today* (Maryknoll, NY: Orbis Books, 1998), and *Then the Whisper Put on Flesh: New Testament Ethics in an African American Context* (Nashville, TN: Abingdon Press, 2001), 91. Blount notes that the kingdom is "the foundational cornerstone for the ethical presentations" in the synoptic Gospels; Bruce Chilton and J. H. McDonald, *Jesus and the Ethics of the Kingdom* (Grand Rapids, MI: Eerdmans, 1987); William R. Herzog II, *Jesus, Justice and the Reign of God: A Ministry of Liberation* (Louisville, KY: Westminster John Knox Press, 1999); Gerhard Lohfink, *Jesus of Nazareth: What He Wanted, Who He Was* (Collegeville, MN: Liturgical Press, 2012); and Norman Perrin, *Jesus and the Language of the Kingdom* (Philadelphia: Fortress Press, 1976).

3. Robert J. Brawley, "Mark," in *Dictionary of Scripture and Ethics*, ed. Joel B. Green (Grand Rapids, MI: Baker Academic, 2011), 506. Brawley's list of approaches would apply also to the other Gospels.

4. See also 1 Sam. 12:12; Isa. 6:5, 33:22, 43:15; Jer. 8:19; Mic. 2:13; Zeph. 3:15; Zech. 14:9, 14:16; Ps. 47:3, 47:8) on the kingship and royal authority that are ascribed to him; (Obad. 21; Pss. 103:19; 145:11–13) on his ruling as king.

5. Joseph A. Fitzmyer, *The Gospel according to Luke, I—IX*, Anchor Bible, 28 (Garden City, NY: Doubleday, 1981), 155.

6. Ibid.

7. John Dominic Crossan states that "the kingdom of God is people under divine rule, and that, as ideal, transcends and judges all human rule" (*The Historical Jesus: The Life of a Mediterranean Jewish Peasant* [San Francisco: HarperSanFrancisco, 1991], 126).

8. Lohfink, *Jesus of Nazareth*, 33.

9. James Edwards, "The Authority of Jesus in the Gospel of Mark," *Journal of the Evangelical Theological Society* 37 (1994): 219.

10. Cheryl S. Pero, *Liberation from Empire: Demonic Possession and Exorcism in the Gospel of Mark*, Studies in Biblical Literature, 150 (New York: Peter Lang, 2013), 41.

11. The most comprehensive treatment of the issues involved is found in Raymond E. Brown, *The Death of the Messiah: From Gethsemane to the Grave, A Commentary on the Passion Narratives in the Four Gospels*, 2 vols. (New York: Doubleday, 1994). His discussion of the "Jewish Trial" (328–97) is itself a virtual monograph complete with extensive bibliographies (315–27).

12. Matera, *New Testament Ethics,* 36.

13. Margaret A. Hannan, *The Nature and Demands of the Sovereign Rule of God in the Gospel of Matthew* (London: T & T Clark, 2006), ix–x.

14. See W. D. Davies and Dale C. Allison. *A Critical and Exegetical Commentary on the Gospel according to Saint Matthew*, ICC, 3 vols. (Edinburgh: T. & T. Clark, 1988–97), 1:102: "So to seek the kingdom is to seek righteousness, which is its precondition, and to seek righteousness is to seek the kingdom, to which it leads."

15. Raymond E. Brown, *The Churches the Apostles Left Behind* (New York: Paulist Press, 1984), 124.

16. See esp. Yiu Sing Lúcás Chan, *The Ten Commandments and the Beatitudes: Biblical Studies for Real Life* (Lanham, MD: Rowman and Littlefield, 2010).

17. Craig S. Keener, *The Gospel of Matthew: A Socio-Rhetorical Commentary* (Grand Rapids, MI: Eerdmans, 2009), 360.

18. Ulrich Luz, *Matthew 21–28: A Commentary*, Hermeneia (Minneapolis: Fortress, 2005), 272.

19. John R. Donahue, "The 'Parable' of the Sheep and the Goats: A Challenge to Christian Ethics," *Theological Studies* 47 (1986): 3–31.

20. Fitzmyer, *Luke I–IX,* 154.

21. *autobasileia*, Origen, *In Mt. Hom.* 14:7, Migne, *Patrologia Graeca* 13, 1198.

22. For a survey of discussion of wealth and poverty see John R. Donahue, "Two Decades of Research on the Rich and the Poor in Luke-Acts," in *Justice and the Holy: Essays in Honor of Walter Harrelson*, ed. Douglas A. Knight and Peter Paris (Atlanta, GA: Scholars Press, 1989).

23. Donahue, *Seek Justice That You May Live: Reflections and Resources on the Bible and Social Justice* (Mahwah: Paulist Press, 2014), 209–11.

24. They call it "the metropolis of all evil deeds" (Diodorus Siculus) or "the greatest source of evil" (Dio Chrysostom), examples taken from *A Greek-English Lexicon of the New Testament and Other Early Christian Literature*, rev. and ed. Frederick Danker (Chicago: University of Chicago Press, 2000), 824.

25. Donahue, *Seek Justice,* 212–16.

26. Mercy is most often thought to be "compassion or forbearance shown especially to an offender or to one subject to one's power" (*Merriam-Webster*). In the Bible it is a more comprehensive term described as "compassion and saving help" (Luke 10:37) or "the willingness to enter into the chaos of another" (James F. Keenan, SJ, *The Works of Mercy* [Lanham, MD: Rowan and Littlefield, 2005], 3).

27. John R. Donahue, "Who Is My Enemy? The Parable of the Good Samaritan and Love of Enemies," in *The Love of Enemy and Nonretaliation in the New Testament*, ed. Willard Swartley (Louisville, KY: Westminster/John Knox, 1992), 137–56.

28. Stephen Bevans, *Models of Contextual Theology* (Maryknoll, NY: Orbis Books, 1992), 1, esp. n. 2.

29. James P. M. Walsh, *The Mighty from Their Thrones: Power in the Biblical Tradition* (Philadelphia: Fortress Press, 1987), 153.

30. Dorothee Soelle, "The Role of Political Theology in the Liberation of Men," in *Religion and the Humanizing of Man*, ed. James M. Robinson (Council on the Study of Religion, 1972), 131–32.

31. Ulrich Luz, *The Theology of the Gospel of Matthew* (Cambridge: Cambridge University Press, 1993), 158.

32. Jerome P. Baggett, *Sense of the Faithful: How American Catholics Live Their Faith* (New York: Oxford University Press, 2009), 126.

33. I wrote these reflections as the virus of racism, ever dormant in US society, has again claimed innocent lives, especially at the Emanuel African Methodist Episcopal Church in Charleston, South Carolina. For powerful descriptions of such deep-seated racism, see Ta-Neshi Coates, *Between the World and Me* (New York: Spiegel and Grau, 2015) and Joe Feagin, *The White Racial Frame: Centuries of Racial Framing and Counter Framing* (New York: Routledge, 2010). Feagin, a sociologist and a leading researcher on racism in the United States for more than forty years, is the author of more than sixty books, including *How Blacks Built America: Labor, Culture, Freedom, and Democracy* (New York: Routledge, 2016).

34. I use imagination in the sense described by William Lynch, as "all the resources of man, all his faculties, his whole history, his whole life, and his whole heritage, all brought to bear upon the concrete world inside and outside of himself, to form images of the world and thus to find it, cope with it, shape it even make it" (*Christ and Prometheus* [Notre Dame, IN: University of Notre Dame Press, 1970], 23).

GENDER AND SEXUALITY ISSUES

GENDER ISSUES IN BIBLICAL ETHICS

On the Reception of Old Testament Texts for a Sexual Ethics in Gender-Democratic Societies

Irmtraud Fischer

The view that the Bible no longer has any relevance to contemporary questions of ethics and morality is a view that one encounters more and more frequently in German-speaking Catholic circles. The Bible is regarded as a historical document from a distant age and culture, with nothing meaningful to say about central existential questions such as right conduct and the good life.

Nonetheless, it seems that in recent years, under the inspiration of the Second Vatican Council, there has developed a field of research in so-called "virtue ethics"[1] for which the Bible is a central foundation of theological[2] ethics. When scholars speak of biblical ethics, they mostly (and often exclusively) refer to the New Testament. The Old Testament is scarcely ever regarded as exemplary,[3] or at most, only in very specific problem areas.

Old Testament scholars themselves have doubtless their own share in this deplorable situation. One whose work is not theological in the strict sense can no longer simply assert that he or she is doing theology. In the paradigm of the historical-critical method, investigations have a more strongly philological, archaeological, or comparative legal interest. In investigations oriented to literary criticism, the interest lies more frequently in the demonstration of "narratological" or "poetological" characteristics. The perspectives from which some exegetes approach the text are sociological or psychological, rather than theological. The theological questions are then often treated as an appendix, or are simply left to those who work in practical theology. Is it then surprising that exegetical studies are scarcely received by systematic theologians nowadays?

The Contextualization of German-Language Scholarship

In my own German language, Central European context, the question posed in the present essay has its roots in the last third of the twentieth century. The question links biblical anthropology[4] with central topics of feminist theological research, which has increasingly developed into gender studies from the 1990s onward. Research into Old Testament ethics[5] had tended earlier on to be neglected in the German-language area, but now there are numerous studies, especially social-historical and feminist investigations, that take up individual questions in this field. One has the impression that the field of biblical ethics is attracting considerable interest today.[6] And a new dynamic is emerging in recent years in the field of research into Old Testament anthropology, which is closely linked to basic questions of ethics.[7]

Even though there have as yet been only a few German-language publications in Old Testament ethics and gender research,[8] ethical questions are inherent in this field, just as they are in social history, for wherever groups in society are discriminated against, it is necessary to take an ethical position.

The Contextualization of Biblical Texts
in Ancient Near Eastern Societies

Ancient Near Eastern societies have a patriarchal structure. From the early 1980s onward, feminist theology has not simply defined patriarchy as dominion by men;[9] using the criteria applied today to the phenomenon of intersectionality, it has also defined patriarchy as a social-hierarchical societal form in which female members of one social stratum are lower in rank than the men who belong to the same social stratum. But the most serious societally effective difference between persons in the Ancient East was not their gender, but rather the citizenship status of the free and the unfree, since this was the criterion on which the decisive question depended: Did someone have the rights of a person, or did these rights belong among the property rights of the slave owners?

Criteria for the definition of social status in patriachal socities		
Criterion	positive	negative
Legal status	free	unfree
Gender	male	female
Age in free persons	old	young
Age in unfree persons	young	old
Economic status	rich	poor
Ethnicity	native	foreign
Religion	dominant	foreign/deviant
Psychophysical status	healthy	sick, handicapped

Ethnicity, religion, and psychophysical status were probably just as important in biblical times as they are in many societies today, but the economic status was—like today—a weightier matter in that period, because where the appropriate resources are available, one can relativize in almost every historical period the discriminatory effect of almost all the criteria. (In ancient Israel, however, enslaved persons were not capable of holding property.)

The Contextualization of Biblical Statements about Gender in the Customs and Ethos of Ancient Israel

For an ethical evaluation of gender relationships, it is not enough to bear in mind the intersectionality of all these criteria. The fundamental regulations of customs and ethos with regard to the biographical course of life are also relevant,[10] and especially the conception of patrilocal marriage, where young people are married soon after reaching sexual maturity, and live in the (extended) family group of the husband. For the woman, living in a virilocal marriage means that she must leave her family of origin, thereby losing the immediate and everyday support of her relatives when conflicts arise. The consequence for her parental house is not only the loss of a worker (the dowry is doubtless to be understood as compensation for this), but above all the fact that her parents will be taken care of, not by the daughter, but by the son—and by his wife. In ancient Israel, therefore, having sons meant societal security both for men and for women. This security was not given through daughters, since they left the house when they got married, and were therefore unavailable to look after their own parents in time of illness or old age. When we today evaluate the preference given to the male gender, we must bear in mind these solid social-historical background factors, which no longer exist in Western societies.

Another premise for ethical judgments with regard to sexuality[11] is the possibility of polygyny. Although in normal instances people lived monogamously, the possibility for men of being married simultaneously to several women determines the legal construction of adultery: a man only ever commits adultery against someone else's marriage, but a woman always commits adultery against her own marriage. This unequal treatment of the genders is determined by the patrilineal succession that is usual in patriarchal societies. In historical periods without genetic or DNA tests, this succession made it necessary to be certain about paternity, since men wanted to be absolutely sure, when the inheritance of the father was handed on, that they were giving it to their own biological sons. This means that marital fidelity is an absolute value only for women. For married men, it is only the wives of another man who are taboo. Sexual relations with unfree women will scarcely have been regarded as a competition to a marriage, since it was only a marriage that could produce legitimate children.

Although, in the ideal case, a marriage can be based on love,[12] or love can appear in the course of time in arranged marriages, marriage does not mean a life partnership based on emotions, so much as the transition into the status of adult existence, with all its societal consequences and honors.

Conceptions of the Relationship between the
Genders in Biblical Creation Texts

It is above all in the creation narratives that we encounter ancient Israel's reflections on what the human being is and on how his or her relationship to God is to
be defined.[13]

Genesis 1 understands the human being as male and female like the animals,
but created in the image of God. The Priestly Source, which is close to the Ancient
Eastern *Listenwissenschaft,* emphasizes by means of the formulation זכר ונקבה
("male and female," 1:27)[14] exclusively the biological sexual difference between
human beings, which is to be seen as the presupposition for the ensuing command
to "be fruitful and multiply." This choice of wording allows the text to avoid any
indication of societal differences between human beings.[15]

Genesis 2, in contrast,[16] emphasizes that man and woman are created as a
"help" for each other. This second, less ancient[17] creation narrative places the accent,
not on the reproductive aspect of binary sexuality, but on the aspect of the *vita
communis*: man and woman are created for each other, so that they may help each
other (עזר: Gen. 2:18, 18:20).[18] The so-called "cheer of the bridegroom" at 2:23–24
confirms the total suitability of the woman (cf. Gen. 29:14) and thus points to the
priority of the relationship between genders over against the relationship to one's
parents, since the patrilocal form of marriage, which was customary in the Ancient
East, is reversed here (2:24).[19]

Genesis 3 then offers an etiological explanation of the difference between the
societal situation that exists in reality and the divine plan of creation. Genesis 3:16
speaks of a relationship between the man and woman that is marked by dominance[20] and submission. The text sees this, not as a divine ordering, but as the result
of human transgression of God's command. From then onward, "hard toil" (עצב)
characterizes the life of both genders.

The Normativity of Heterosexuality in the
Creation Texts and Its Societal Context

All three texts presuppose heterosexuality as a norm that is not called into question,
and as the only sexual relationship between humans. This focus is explained by the fact
that in many epochs of ancient Israel, a couple had to have several children, in order
that at least one of them would reach reproductive adulthood. In a demographically
precarious society, children are thus generally seen as a sign of blessing (cf. Gen. 1:28;
Deut. 28:4). Young people were given in marriage immediately after they reached sexual
maturity, in order to make full use of the fertile phase of life, which usually did not last
for even three or four decades, thanks to the mortality risk to women in giving birth and
in childbed, as well as to malnourishment and a lack of medical care.

In societies in which having children is regarded as a societal necessity, young
people got married and became parents even before the possibility of a different

sexual orientation could be considered. It is thus not by chance that the very rare references in the narrative texts of the Bible to same-sex relationships always occur in the case of characters who are presented as married.[21] The likely explanation of the negative evaluation of homosexuality in the Holiness Code (Lev. 18:22, 20:13),[22] or of transvestitism in Deuteronomy 22:5, is that the public acting-out of these sexual orientations[23] was regarded as a threat to the family that already existed at the biographical point in time of a person's coming out.[24] Besides this, where people's thinking and their lives follow the concepts of the subordination of the female gender to the male, a man who "makes himself a woman" must expect societal ostracism.

Hermeneutical Bridges between
Biblical Texts and the Reality of People's Lives Today

Both ethicists and biblical scholars agree today that one cannot simply translate "what is in the Bible" into ethical principles. Fundamentalist positions that want to impose this by force (and precisely in the context of sexual ethics) overlook the fact that one must also select the relevant texts: one does not pluck out one's own eye if it seduces one into doing wrong (cf. Matt. 5:27–32). The Bible has authority, but one cannot employ it in an authoritarian manner in order to arrive at ethical decisions.[25]

This is why the path of application via analogy has often been taken. The *imitatio Christi* can also be seen as a classic bridge between the text and ethical deductions.[26] For the actualization of the text, Allen Verhey employs the concept of "Scripture as scripted script," requiring performance, that goes back to Nicholas Lash.[27] But the ancient writers were already well aware that all biblical literature must be actualized. In regard to the application of ethical norms of sacred scripture, this means that they must be adapted to contemporary situations and to changed times.

Virtue ethics[28] tends to look, not so much at good individual actions, as at a person's good attitude toward life and how the person is formed in view of a goal. One could draw an analogy to the function of Torah here, since this is not to be believed, but to be *done*. One must, however, bear in mind that the Old Testament does not lend any support to an individualistic ethics ("What ought *I* to do?"). It sees the people in the center, and is thus to be defined primarily as a social ethics ("What ought *we* to do?").

Reception

There are many concepts of how one takes the path from the Bible to moral-ethical decisions; let us add to these the concept of reception.[29] Reception, as a hermeneutical process, presupposes that the Bible has normative importance for ethical decisions, as the reference text that is to be received. It also takes into account the existential context of those who enact the reception. This undergoes change in the course of history and is also differentiated in terms of region and cultural tradition and (as I have shown in detail above) in terms of the potential ability to act on the basis of a person's societal position. One who appeals to the Bible today cannot simply assert that one is doing this in a neutral manner, although this is in fact frequently done, with the nineteenth-century conception of ethics and piety and the premises established by the rejection of the Enlightenment, which found its overt expression in the *Syllabus Errorum* of 1863. To which texts does one appeal, and why are these mostly chosen exclusively from the New Testament, although the Old Testament would be much richer (for example, sapiential literature as ethical instruction, narratives as narrative ethics, legal texts, directives, and teachings)?[30]

Scholarly exegesis finds the idea of a canon in the canon extremely disputable, but it is probably unavoidable for the ethical application, since not all the attempts to describe God's action in an inculturated manner still make sense today.[31] Nevertheless, the entire Bible must remain sacred scripture, not only because it contains the Word of God for believers, but also for practical reasons: different times and contexts have different access routes, and one can also learn from negative examples. The hermeneutical approach of reception has its starting point not only in the Bible or only from today's needs. It can thus give the appropriate space both for the text and for its addressees and recipients. It is also possible to pay due heed to the fact that the long chain of various receptions is also at work as tradition. This concept can better grasp the diversity of the biblical affirmations, as well as the fact that not every text has the same resonance in every person.

Examples of Old Testament hermeneutical centers for the deduction of ethical decisions could be justice, which essentially takes the option against paternalism, or the "formula of mercy," which points to the disproportionate effectiveness of good behavior. It does not lose sight of the perpetrators, but it speaks at the same time against clan liability (cf. Exod. 34:6–7). Similarly, one could define the exodus paradigm as a hermeneutical center, with liberation at its heart—in Deuteronomy, this liberation is accompanied by the gift of Torah as a guideline for life in the promised land. Another such center would be the love of God, which is incomplete without the love of neighbor (cf. Lev. 19:18), which has, unfortunately, very often been interpreted paternalistically throughout history.

Intersectionality as the
Hermeneutical Premise of Ethical Decisions

In the course of Western history, moral-ethical guidelines were usually defined with white, free men as the standard. But a "common good" that deserves this name cannot use criteria of discrimination to exclude groups of persons. This is why we must always investigate both the biblical text that is to be received and the ethical decision to which it gives rise, asking the following questions: Who formulates the text? Whom does a decision benefit? Whom does it harm? What interests lie behind ethical imperatives, and what goal do they serve? What "collateral damage" is taken into account here, and what collateral damage is simply not seen, although it is certainly present? Who has the power to let one specific reception become the official tradition? What circumstances determine this, and what circumstances make it impossible? In this process, who consigns other receptions to oblivion, and what motivates this action?

One could extend the list of these "control questions" at will. They take seriously the fact that there is no objective, universally valid guideline for the evaluation of ethical decisions. One who has no power to put up effective resistance to the actions of others and to extricate oneself from decisions that are imposed on one cannot be held accountable in the same way as a person who has the power not only to formulate guidelines, but also to enforce them—or to act against them without being prevented from doing so. I mention only one example, the human right to sexual self-determination, which democratic countries acknowledge as something self-evident. At the same time, however, they take no genuinely effective action against the trafficking of women for prostitution, thus depriving those concerned with the possibility of laying claim to this right. Until recently, the churches too evaluated prostitution in the sense of "blaming the victim," and this must be denounced as incurring guilt in relation to women who all too often had no other possibility of feeding and supporting their families.

The Bible as an
Ethical Guideline for Gender-Democracies?

Democracies of the Western kind have raised the equality of the genders before and in the law to constitutional status, although this has not yet been realized de facto in every secular sphere of life. The discussion of the acceptance of other forms of living than heterosexuality has not yet been concluded in the individual European countries, although the tendency as a whole points to the dismantling of discrimination.

In my church, the Roman Catholic church, women do not have the same legal status.[32] The pope, as the highest authority, has confirmed once again that they cannot be ordained, and this entails their exclusion from all the positions in which the most important decisions are taken. It is virtually impossible nowadays to explain this plausibly in gender-democracies, and it is becoming ever more clearly a question on which the survival of the big European churches depends. The subordination of "the woman" under "the man," which is expressed in the exclusion of women from every competence to take the ultimate decisions within the church, must be called a blind spot in the ethical consciousness.

The reception of the etiological narrative of Genesis 3 cannot be recommended in gender-democracies for an ethics of the shared life of the two genders or for a sexual ethics, since what must be explained today is not the patriarchy, but rather the equality of the genders. It therefore seems clear that we should begin with the creation texts, which see an equal partnership of the two genders as willed by God. Receptions within the Bible itself, such as the Song of Songs, large sections of which are set in a paradisiac garden, employ metaphors that sing of the successful attainment of an egalitarian relationship between the genders. This shows that even in patriarchal societies, it was possible to draw a generous fence around the sexual life.

Prosperous Western societies with a high life expectancy, low mortality rates among infants and in childbed, as well as an optimal nutritional situation and medicinal care, no longer need to ensure the survival of society by bringing as many children as possible into the world. Accordingly, the original constellation of arguments that justified the normativity of heterosexuality is no longer compelling. An actualized reception of the Genesis texts could affirm that sexual relationships of every structure and every orientation that exists in God's good creation ought to be lived in such a way that people in their sexuality become a "help" to each other in the construction of a good and appropriate life. It goes without saying that "falls" are possible, and very probable, in other forms of living than heterosexual relationships. But the human being should not get resigned to the broken order of creation: the Song of Songs teaches that it is precisely the erotic of a relationship between two persons that can lead them back into the paradise willed by God, where there is no superiority and subordination between human beings, and a respectful way of dealing with the creation is a matter of course, because the human being understands himself or herself as the image of God in the world.

This concrete example shows that the concept of reception integrates each specific context and is thus able to bring about a necessary widening of the Catholic concept of tradition—because one can inquire into the power relationships that were involved in the emergence, the selection, and the normative handing-on of this tradition. This contextualization makes it possible to apply biblical affirmations in a variety of ways here and now, and doubtless also at varying speeds. Europe is not therefore becoming godless.

All that those who live in tolerant gender-democracies expect of their churches is that they should respect basic ethical decisions of the secular society and inculturate these. This is not in the least a plea for an arbitrariness in ethics. On the contrary, we must struggle on equal terms, in a variety of forms of living, to arrive at ethical decisions that make a good life possible for everyone, not only older, Christian, healthy, and mostly white, free men.

Translated by Brian McNeil

Notes

1. In this field of research, we should mention above all James Keenan (see, e.g., "Proposing Cardinal Virtues," *Theological Studies* 56, no. 4 [1995]: 709–29); see also the discussion in Bernard Hoose, ed., *Christian Ethics: An Introduction* (Collegeville, MN: Liturgical Press, 1998). The Bible is regarded here as important, not so much for concrete ethical discourses, but for the formation of the character.

2. What would deserve the name "theological ethics" more exactly than an ethics that is based on the foundations of the faith—which (in the Catholic understanding) are to be quarried, not indeed only from scripture, but also from scripture?

3. This is unfortunately also true of Lúcás Chan, *Biblical Ethics in the 21st Century: Developments, Emerging Consensus, and Future Directions* (New York: Paulist Press, 2013), 111. The only Old Testament example he gives, from the book of Ruth, is problematic. It depicts Boaz as a hero to be imitated, although—despite having the financial means—he initially fails to take care of the two widows when they arrive (Ruth 1). He then gives Ruth his paternalistic permission to work. Finally, he takes care of the women on a permanent basis only when he is challenged to do so.

4. In the German-language area, biblical theology even today remains deeply marked by the monumental work of Hans-Walter Wolff, which was reprinted in 2010 with two appendixes by Bernd Janowski (Hans-Walter Wolff, *Anthropologie des Alten Testaments* (Munich: Chr. Kaiser, 1973). See also the comprehensive collection of essays edited by Bernd Janowski and Kathrin Liess, *Der Mensch im alten Israel: Neue Forschungen zur alttestamentlichen Anthropologie,* HBS 59 (Freiburg i.Br.: Herder, 2009), or the book by Silvia Schroer and Thomas Staubli, *Die Körpersymbolik der Bibel,* 2nd ed. (Gütersloh: Gütersloher Verlagshaus, 2005).

5. See Eckart Otto's *Theologische Ethik des Alten Testaments* (Stuttgart: Kohlhammer, 1994), which is primarily concerned with legal texts. One exception that should be mentioned here is the work of the ethicist Marianne Heimbach-Steins and her husband, the Old Testament scholar Georg Steins. See, for example, Marianne Heimbach-Steins and Georg Steins, eds., *Bibelhermeneutik und Christliche Sozialethik* (Stuttgart: Kohlhammer, 2012). In the English-language sphere, see, e.g., John Barton, *Understanding Old Testament Ethics* (Louisville, KY: Westminster John Knox Press, 2003), and Katharine Dell, ed., *Ethical and Unethical in the Old Testament: God and Humans in Dialog,* Library of Hebrew Bible/ OT Studies 428 (New York: T & T Clark, 2010).

6. In 2014, the annual assembly of the AGAT ("Arbeitsgemeinschaft der Katholischen Alttestamentlerinnen und Alttestamentler des deutschen Sprachraums") took as its topic "Old Testament ethics": see Christian Frevel, ed., *Nur Zehn Worte? Zur Bedeutung des Alten Testaments in ethischen Fragen,* QD 273 (Freiburg i.Br.: Herder, 2015), which includes a bibliography of the most recent German-language secondary literature and an overview of current research.

7. In 2013, a project group under the leadership of Jürgen van Oorschot was founded with the aim of meeting once a year for conversations and the presentation of recent studies. The first meeting on the topic "Anthropology/Anthropologies of the Old Testament" took place in Wittenberg from May 22 to May 24, 2014. Its papers are published: Jürgen van Oorschot and Andreas Wagner, eds., *Anthropologie(n) des Alten Testaments,* WGTh (Leipzig: Evangelische Verlagsanstalt, 2015), with bibliographical references to the most recent German-language publications.

8. See, e.g., the dissertation by Kerstin Rödiger, *Der Sprung in die Wirklichkeit ...: Impulse aus dem rhetorischen Ansatz Elisabeth Schüssler Fiorenzas für die Rezeption biblischer Texte in narrativer Sozialethik,* Ethik im theologischen Diskurs/Ethics in Theological Discourse 18 (Vienna: LIT, 2009). Another scholar who builds on Schüssler Fiorenza's approach is Sharon D. Welch, "Biblical Interpretation in Christian Feminist Ethics," *Studia Theologica* 51 (1997): 40–43. See also Ina Praetorius, *Handeln aus der Fülle: Postpatriarchale Ethik in biblischer Tradition* (Gütersloh: Gütersloher Verlagshaus, 2005).

9. Following the definition by Elisabeth Schüssler Fiorenza, *In Memory of Her: A Feminist Theological Reconstruction of Christian Origins* (New York: Crossroad, 1983), 29–30. See the table in Jorunn Økland et al., "Introduction: Women, Bible and Reception History: An International Project in Theology and Gender Studies," in *The Bible and Women*, ed. Irmtraud Fischer and Mercedes Navarro Puerto with Andrea Taschl-Erber (Atlanta: SBL Press, 2011), 9–10.

10. For a more detailed discussion, see Irmtraud Fischer, *Die Erzeltern Israels: Feministisch-theologische Studien zu Gen 12–36*, BZAW 222 (Berlin: de Gruyter, 1994), and eadem, *Women Who Wrestled with God: Biblical Stories of Israel's Beginnings* (Collegeville, MN: Liturgical Press, 2005; published in 2015 as an e-book).

11. On the sexual laws in the Old Testament, see Hilary B. Lipka, *Sexual Transgression in the Hebrew Bible,* Hebrew Bible Monographs 7 (Sheffield: Sheffield Phoenix Press, 2006).

12. We can infer the possibility of love marriages from texts such as Genesis 29:9–29 (Rachel and Jacob) or the Song of Songs, although the latter does not speak of marriage.

13. For more detail, see Irmtraud Fischer, "Egalitär entworfen—hierarchisch gelebt: Zur Problematik des Geschlechterverhältnisses und einer genderfairen Anthropologie im Alten Testament," in *Der Mensch im alten Israel: Neue Forschungen zur alttestamentlichen Anthropologie,* ed. Bernd Janowski and Kathrin Liess, HBS 59 (Freiburg i.Br.: Herder, 2009), 265–98.

14. The Primordial History employs this designation not only in the case of the human being (see also 5:2), but also in relation to the animals (6:19, 7:3, 7:9, 7:16).

15. Catholic doctrine bases on this text the formulation "equal in value but different," which it uses to establish the unequal rights of the two genders; on this, see Norbert Lüdecke, "Mehr Geschlecht als Recht? Zur Stellung der Frau nach Lehre und Recht der römisch-katholischen Kirche," in *". . . männlich und weiblich schuf er sie . . ." (Gen 1:27): Zur Brisanz der Geschlechterfrage in Religion und Gesellschaft,* ed. Sigrid Eder and Irmtraud Fischer, Theologie im kulturellen Dialog 16 (Innsbruck: Tyrolia, 2009), 183–216.

16. The church fathers already underlined the contrast between the two protologies. Thanks to the Platonic understanding of "image," they saw in Genesis 1 the creation of the spiritual human being, and in Genesis 2 the creation of the bodily human being. On this, see Kari Elisabeth Børresen and Emanuela Prinzivalli, eds., *Le Donne nello sguardo degli antichi autori cristiani: L'uso dei testi biblici nella costruzione dei modelli femminili e la riflessione teologica dal I al VII secolo,* La bibbia e le donne 5.1 (Trapani: Il Pozzo di Giacobbe, 2013).

17. On the late dating, see the following two monographs: Michael Unger, *Die Paradieseserzählung Gen 2/3: Eine exegetische Untersuchung* (diss., Graz, 1994, also online), and Trygve N. D. Mettinger, *The Eden Narrative: A Literary and Religio-historical Study of Genesis 2–3* (Winona Lake, IN: Eisenbrauns, 2007).

18. On this, see already Walter Vogels, "It Is Not Good That the 'Mensch' Should Be Alone; I Will Make Him/Her a Helper Fit for Him/Her (Gen 2:18)," *Église et Théologie* 9 (1978): 9–35, and the creative interpretations by Phyllis Trible, *God and the Rhetoric of Sexuality* (Philadelphia: Fortress Press, 1978).

19. This affirmation should not be misunderstood as a reference to a matriarchal remnant in this text, which was usually dated early and assigned to the "Jahwist."

20. The Vulgate translation is the first to employ legally relevant terms here; from then onward, it was possible to appeal to the Bible in support of the dependent legal position of "the woman": see Ciriaca Morano Rodríguez, "Cambiamenti sociali ed evoluzione dell'immagine della donna nel cristianesimo primitivo: Approccio filologico alle traduzioni

bibliche latine e alla relativa esegesi," in *Le Donne nello sguardo degli antichi autori cristiani: L'uso dei testi biblici nella costruzione dei modelli femminili e la riflessione teologica dal I al VII secolo,* ed. Kari Elisabeth Børresen and Emanuela Prinzivalli, La bibbia e le donne 5.1 (Trapani: Il Pozzo di Giacobbe, 2013), 175–89.

21. This can be seen in the relationship of David, who is otherwise characterized as a womanizer, in 1 Samuel 20:17 and 2 Samuel 1:26; or in Ruth, whose primary relationship to Naomi (Ruth 1:14–17) is interpreted in an echo of Genesis 2:23, but who finally brings a child into the world with Boaz—but a child whom she bears for her mother-in-law (4:14–17). For more detail, see Irmtraud Fischer, *Rut,* HThK, 2nd ed. (Freiburg i.Br.: Herder, 2005), *ad loc.*

22. It is noteworthy that the two great collections of laws, the Covenant Code and the Deuteronomic law, contain no such prohibitions. The essay by Robert K. Gnuse, "Seven Gay Texts: Biblical Passages Used to Condemn Homosexuality," *Biblical Theology Bulletin* 45, no. 2 (2015): 68–87, sees no evidence that these two legal texts deal with homosexuality as a freely chosen relationship between two adults. On these topics, see the standard work by Martti Nissinen, *Homoeroticism in the Biblical World: A Historical Perspective* (Minneapolis: Fortress Press, 1998).

23. This applies, of course, to all Lesbian-Gay-Bi-Trans-Inter-Queer and other orientations (LGBTIQ+).

24. Despite the formulations of the legal texts, which regard this conduct as deserving death, their evaluation is still mild in relation to Ancient Eastern legal collections.

25. This point is already made by Kenneth Himes, "Scripture and Ethics: A Review Essay," *Biblical Theology Bulletin* 15, 2 (1985): 71: "To say that the Bible is authoritative is, of course, not the same as understanding its function in an authoritarian manner."

26. Chan, *Biblical Ethics*, 104, gets to the heart of the matter: "All biblical literature—including biblical rules and principles—promotes analogical reflection" (with a reference to Richard Burridge, "Imitating Jesus: Reading the Eternal Word Response," *Scottish Journal of Theology* 63, no. 3 [2010]: 336–52).

27. See Allen Verhey, "Scripture as Script and as Scripted: The Beatitudes," in *Character Ethics and the New Testament: Moral Dimensions of Scripture*, ed. Robert L. Brawley (Louisville, KY: Westminster John Knox Press, 2007), 19–34.

28. Chan, *Biblical Ethics*, 85, emphasizes four aspects of virtue ethics: "(1) dispositions and character formation; (2) practices and habits; (3) exemplar; and (4) community and communal identity."

29. On the theoretical foundations, see Irmtraud Fischer, "Forschungsgeschichte als Rezeptionsgeschichte in nuce," in *Congress Volume Munich 2013,* ed. Christl M. Maier, VT.S 163 (Leiden: Brill, 2014), 182–216.

30. The decisive questions here have already been posed by William C. Spohn, *What Are They Saying about Scripture and Ethics?,* rev. and exp. ed. (New York: Paulist Press, 1995), 5–20.

31. For example, in biblical times, a revenging God meant hope for the oppressed, but there are great reservations in modern Western cultures with regard to this image of God.

32. The formulation of the Code of Canon Law, "equal in value but different," is not to be understood as an indicator of equal rights, but as the contrary: the dignity of "the woman" consists precisely in her subordination, which also makes her incapable of representing Christ. On this, see the article by Lüdecke, "Mehr Geschlecht als Recht?"

The Inevitability of Scandal

A Moral and Biblical Analysis of Firing Gay Teachers and Ministers to Avoid Scandal

Christopher P. Vogt

In September 2014, Jamie Moore was forced to resign as choir director at St. Victoria parish in Victoria, Minnesota, after Archbishop John Nienstedt learned that Mr. Moore had entered into a civil same-sex marriage with his long-time partner.[1] Archbishop Nienstedt stated that he was empowered to demand the dismissal of church workers who engage in public conduct that is in conflict with official church teaching. In a similar incident, Colleen Simon was fired from her position as Director of Social Ministry at St. Francis Xavier parish in Kansas City, Missouri, after her civil marriage to a woman became public in a local magazine article.[2] These are just two of many recent cases in which lay ministers and teachers have been fired for acting in ways that contradict official church teaching. Although a few have been fired for violating Catholic teaching on other issues (e.g., in-vitro fertilization or pregnancy out of wedlock) the majority of dismissals have been related to sexual orientation and same-sex relationships. New Ways Ministry has documented over forty cases of LGBT-related dismissals from Catholic institutions since 2012.[3] About nineteen people were fired for marrying a person of the same sex; eight were fired for publicly supporting same-sex marriage or civil unions (typically on social media); and eight were fired when school or parish officials became aware that they were involved in a sexual relationship with a person of the same sex.

The number of dismissals is likely to grow. A number of Catholic dioceses and school systems have taken steps to make it easier to dismiss teachers for violating the church's moral teaching. For example, San Francisco's Archbishop Salvatore J. Cordileone has taken steps to add new morality clauses to the faculty handbook that governs the conduct of teachers within his jurisdiction.[4] The new language specifies that teachers are forbidden from publicly challenging the church's teaching on homosexual acts, artificial contraception, and embryonic stem-cell research. Similar clauses have been added or strengthened in Oakland, Miami, Los Angeles, Cleveland, and Cincinnati.[5] The scope of what constitutes a public challenge to church teaching can be quite wide. For example, in response to a reporter's question about whether it would be a violation of the archdiocese's new morality clauses for

a teacher to post photos of her gay son's wedding on Facebook, Archbishop Cordileone responded, "If someone was upset and reported it . . . the person with the
Facebook page would have to be talked to."[6]

Catholic Moral Tradition on Avoiding Scandal

Although school and church officials have not often used this language, a desire
to avoid scandal is the objective underlying their decisions to tighten morality
clauses and to fire personnel. Here scandal is understood in multiple ways simultaneously. One the one hand, it is an effort to avoid what Angela Senander has
termed "sociological scandal": significant and sustained negative public reaction to
an action performed by a person employed by a school or parish that runs contrary
to social expectations, law, or morality.[7] On the other hand, church and school officials are seeking to avoid scandal in a theological sense as well; they are seeking to
suppress behavior that would serve as a stumbling block for the faithful or lead
some people away from the faith altogether. Thus when Cleveland's Bishop Richard
Lennon stated that a crucial purpose of morality clauses in teachers' contracts is to
avoid "confusion about what it means to live an authentically Catholic life" among
the faithful, he is drawing on the moral tradition of avoiding theological scandal.
The underlying concern is not bad publicity, but rather that ordinary Catholics will
be drawn into erroneous belief or engage in morally wrong actions as a result of the
scandalous behavior of others.[8]

The current *Catechism of the Catholic Church* frames avoiding scandal as a
moral imperative that grows out of respect for the dignity of all people. It defines
scandal as "an attitude or behavior which leads another to do evil," adding that
"anyone who uses the power at his disposal in such a way that it leads others to do
wrong becomes guilty of scandal and responsible for the evil that he has directly
or indirectly encouraged."[9] The *Catechism* warns that it is especially serious when
scandal is given by teachers or anyone with responsibility for educating others.[10]

There are significant similarities between the catechism's treatment of
scandal and what we find in the *Summa Theologiae,* but the latter includes more
complexity.[11] Aquinas highlights the importance of intentionality by distinguishing
more serious instances of direct (intentional) scandal from those caused acciden-
tally (indirect). He also notes that a scandal does not necessarily indicate sinfulness
on the part of the one causing scandal because sometimes a morally indifferent or
good act can precipitate scandal if others perceive that act to be wrong.[12]

Saint Thomas also highlights the importance of moral agency among those
who are scandalized by arguing that the actions of one person can never cause
another person to sin. Instead, at most we can say that an act that might cause
scandal provides an occasion for another person to lose his or her way. Aquinas
insists that the would-be victims of scandal retain some degree of freedom to
avoid their own downfall.[13] In response to the very same potentially "scandalous"
behavior, one person may stay on the spiritual high road while another may stumble

and fall into sin. Hence, the primary cause of scandal sometimes lies in the weakness of the one scandalized. Even so, Christians have a responsibility to take care that their actions do not cause someone else to falter, even inadvertently.

Aquinas notes that there is more than one way to prevent scandalizing the weak. The best remedy would be to avoid actions that might unnecessarily cause confusion. If that is not feasible, scandal should be avoided by "admonition." In other words, a person should be proactive in terms of explaining why his or her actions are not morally objectionable and why others should not be scandalized by those actions.[14] Aquinas recognized that it might not be possible to sway a person from being scandalized by means of education or admonition. In those cases, the appropriate response depends largely on the nature and importance of the act that would cause scandal. If the act is wrong, one should refrain from it. If it is indifferent and you could refrain from the act without doing yourself spiritual harm, it would be better to avoid the activity. However, if the activity is crucial for one's own spiritual well-being, one can proceed. When faced with a choice of hiding the truth or avoiding scandal, Aquinas strongly recommends telling the truth.[15]

Finally, Aquinas makes the important observation that scandal sometimes can be caused by the malice of the scandalized. Using the example of the Pharisees who were scandalized at the teaching of Christ, Aquinas suggests that sometimes people invoke the threat of scandal in order to stir up trouble. He suggests that if earnest efforts at explanation and admonition fail, one should consider the likelihood that such scandal arises from malice. At that point, one should proceed with the pursuit of a spiritual good even if it would cause scandal.[16]

Analyzing Recent Cases
through the Lens of Theological Scandal

In seeking to apply the Catholic moral tradition on scandal to the issue at hand, we face at least two significant challenges. First, the discussion of scandal we find in the tradition is oriented toward an individual's discernment regarding whether he or she personally should engage in an act that might cause scandal. The proper response of those in authority when another person might cause scandal is not addressed at length. More significantly, the controversial nature of homosexuality and same-sex relationships in church and society today make any straightforward application of the traditional concept of scandal very difficult. Aquinas and the more recent moral manuals maintain that it might be morally legitimate to engage in a good or morally indifferent activity that we foresee will cause scandal, but they would not ever condone a morally wrong action. There is no ambiguity in the literature about whether a person should refrain from wrongdoing, especially when it would cause the further harm of scandal.[17] Thus it could be argued that there is no need to go any further with our inquiry about scandal. Teachers and ministers are engaged in wrong behavior that is contrary to the faith that might lead children and others astray. Their behavior must be condemned and their professional service to the church must end.

A closer examination of the situation reveals more complexity. Part of the reason there is such intense controversy about these cases is that there is strong disagreement in the church about whether gay and lesbian relationships are morally legitimate. Without question, in the past few decades there have been several emphatic statements from magisterial authorities declaring unequivocally that same-sex marriage is wrong, and sexual intimacy between two men or two women is contrary to revelation and the natural law.[18] At the same time there is reason to doubt whether that teaching has been received by the faithful, especially in the United States, where these controversies are unfolding. The number of Roman Catholics in the United States who support same-sex marriage has been rising (from 40 percent in 2001 to 57 percent in 2015).[19] There is considerable disagreement in theological circles about the moral legitimacy of gay and lesbian relationships and same-sex unions.[20] Even among members of the hierarchy there has been evidence of a divergence of opinion regarding the morality of same-sex relationships and how to interact with gay couples pastorally.[21] Thus it would be wrong to suggest that there is no need for further moral and pastoral reflection on these matters.

Recent work by Angela Senander and Lisa Fullam on scandal can offer some useful insights. Fullam points out that scandal can be double-edged. Sometimes, church efforts to prevent scandal can end up causing what she calls "opposite scandal."[22] An unrelenting focus on clarity of teaching can blind church leaders to the fact that their attempts to prevent scandal may themselves be perceived as scandalous. For example, many church leaders refused to condone the use of condoms to reduce the spread of HIV/AIDS because they feared it might cause confusion about church teaching on artificial contraception. That action caused a case of "opposite scandal" because some people interpreted their failure to advocate condom use as a sign that church officials cared more about condemning artificial contraception than preventing the spread of a deadly disease. Fullam's point is not that church officials were acting maliciously but that "opposite scandal is still scandal—it still leads people into a misunderstanding of moral truth, generally by refusing to grant moral weight to the real complexity of our lives individually and socially."[23]

Efforts to prevent scandal by firing teachers and lay pastoral ministers provide an excellent illustration of the dangers of "opposite scandal." In many cases, the reaction to the forced removal of gay and lesbian teachers or lay ministers has been strongly negative. After Bishop William Murphy of Rockville Centre, New York, took steps to remove Nicholas Coppola from his role as a religious education instructor and minister to the homebound in his parish, over 18,000 Catholics signed a petition of protest.[24] Elsewhere, over 70,000 signatures were gathered online, and $3,600 was raised to protest the dismissal of Barb Webb from her position as a chemistry teacher at Marian High School in Bloomfield Hills, Michigan. Webb was fired when school officials learned that she had become pregnant by in-vitro fertilization and was planning to raise her baby with another woman to whom Webb is married.[25]

There is evidence that these firings cause scandal in the sense of confusing the faithful as well. Even while denouncing same-sex unions and insisting that homosexual acts are contrary to natural law, the Catholic Church has affirmed that the "intrinsic dignity of each person must always be respected in word, in action, and in law."[26] Firing men and women for seeking state recognition of their gay partnership or for being in an openly gay relationship can easily be interpreted as calling into question the church's affirmation of the intrinsic worth and dignity of gay men and women. A guidance counselor at Charlotte Catholic High School in North Carolina reported that after a teacher was fired at the school for announcing his intention to marry his longtime partner, a student asked whether he was at risk of being expelled from school for being gay.[27] Some men and women who have been fired for being in gay relationships have reported that they do not feel respected as persons, with one adding that "it's very difficult for me to go into church and find the peace to worship."[28]

A very specific understanding of the nature of faith underlies efforts to protect the faithful by firing gay teachers. Angela Senander traces it back to Vatican Council I, where there was a strong emphasis on continuity of teaching and a fixed understanding of doctrine. Under that model, revelation in Christ is primarily propositional. Faith is an affirmation of those propositions and to dissent from them is to fall into error and to cause scandal.[29] That view of faith stands in sharp contrast to other models, which emphasize faith's dynamic qualities. For example, Karl Rahner defined faith as a response to the mystery that grounds all that is—a response to an encounter with God.[30] Although God's self-revelation in the life, death, and resurrection of Jesus Christ as recorded in Scripture is always central and normative, Christian faith is also a relationship with a living God who is encountered anew in prayer and in one's life in community and in the world. This view holds that our understanding of the fullness of God and of the implications of revelation is not yet complete.[31] Mark Jordan has argued that church officials have used the notion of scandal as a weapon to enforce silence in order to avoid facing the reality of disagreement within the church about sexual morality.[32] Senander has similar concerns, but puts the matter more theologically: "When faith is reduced to teaching, and when dissent from any teaching becomes a scandal, one will miss the invitation of the Holy Spirit to communicate God's reign in new ways."[33] Turning to Scripture will help us recover a broader theological understanding of scandal.

Christ and His Preaching as Scandalous

Although there are passages in the New Testament that speak to the issue of scandal in the sense of some Christians causing others to falter by their behavior (Matt. 18:6; Mark 9:42; Rom. 14:13; 1 Cor. 8:9), it is more typical to read of Jesus' teaching or the cross or Jesus Christ himself as scandal (Matt. 13:57; Mark 6:3; 1

Cor. 1:23; Gal. 5:11; 1 Pet. 2:8; Rom. 9:32–33). His life, his preaching, and his humiliating death on a cross all upset expectations, offended sensibilities, and challenged everyone, including his disciples. All who encountered Jesus personally and all those who later heard the Gospel encountered a message that at once challenged them and called them to new faith and understanding. In response, some were moved to faith, while others were "put to shame" in the sense of being judged by God.[34] Thus as we look closely at the New Testament, we find that there is a certain inseparability of scandal (in the sense of the possibility of offense) and the possibility of faith.[35] The same Christ is experienced by some as a stumbling block but as a sanctuary by others.[36]

To say that Jesus Christ caused scandal is to say more than that he put forward a challenging call or message; it is to say that Jesus and his disciples engaged in behavior that many people regarded as morally offensive and wrong. Scandalous behavior runs contrary to social conventions and often against the law and accepted norms of morality as well.[37] Jesus became an offense or scandal by challenging individuals' most cherished beliefs and violating their assumptions about the way the world should be.[38] One of the most significant ways in which Jesus caused scandal was by eating with people who were "unclean" or who were guilty of associating with the pagan Roman Empire by working as tax collectors (Matt. 9:11). Table fellowship with sinners was scandalous in itself, but what the Pharisees perceived to be even more offensive was the fact that Jesus called these people to be his disciples.[39] To call such people to discipleship was to show offensive disregard for order and the Law. Similarly, Jesus and his disciples caused scandal by harvesting food on the Sabbath (Matt. 12:1–2). Their actions were offensive in that they violated custom and religious law. In both cases, Jesus responded to the Pharisees who criticized his behavior by alluding to Hosea 6:6: "Go and learn the meaning of the words, 'I desire mercy, not sacrifice'" (Matt. 9:13), and "If you knew what this meant, 'I desire mercy, not sacrifice,' you would not have condemned these innocent men" (Matt. 12:7). Jeremiah Alberg notes, "Jesus' behavior appears scandalous to them *because* they have read the Hebrew Scriptures, so now they need to reread them in order to find a new meaning. They thought they knew what those Scriptures meant; Jesus is telling them that they were mistaken."[40] They did not know the meaning of mercy or what God truly desires. Sometimes, it was by giving offense and causing scandal that Jesus revealed God's kingdom.

Just as the behavior of Jesus and his disciples was sometimes seen to be scandalous, so too can many of the parables he told. An excellent example of a parable that scandalizes in order to bring about conversion is the parable of the laborers in the vineyard (Matt. 20:1–16). In this familiar story, a landowner goes out and hires laborers to work in his vineyard, hiring a different group at dawn, nine, noon, three, and five o'clock. At the end of the day, he asks his foreman to pay the laborers the same daily wage, beginning with the last ones hired. The workers who labored longer than the rest protest (or murmur, a reference to Exod. 16:3–8) at what they perceived to be the unfairness of not being paid more for working longer in the scorching sun.[41] In response, the landowner reminds them that he has paid each what he promised to pay and he directs them to "take what is yours and go" (Matt. 13–14).[42] The parable characterizes the owner's actions as an instance of freedom and generosity and concludes with a familiar formulation of reversal: "thus the last will be first and the first will be last."

We can see scandal at work in this parable on a number of levels. First, the characters in the story itself are scandalized. They see the landowner's actions as unjust and they begin to grumble. Second, the hearer of the parable is scandalized. It is easy to sympathize with those who have worked a long day without receiving any additional reward. The claim that the first shall be last is a reversal not only of expectations, but of conventional wisdom regarding equity. The hearer is thrown off balance and faced with a choice in hearing this story that highlights God's generosity and special love for "the least of these." Will the hearer be scandalized and turn away, or will he or she be drawn to faith through a reexamination of his or her understanding of justice? The parable works because the hearer can see the possibility of scandal but instead allows the encounter with the story to be an opportunity to grow in faith.[43]

In contrast to some modern approaches to parable criticism that attempt to boil down parables to one clear point, it can be fruitful to see the parable as an occasion for reexamination and response by the reader. The parable is not a container of meaning that is received, but as John Dominic Crossan suggested, it is "a metaphor or normalcy which intends to create participation in its referent."[44] The meaning is not limited to the parable itself, but includes the response of the reader.[45] A parable is a moment to encounter the kingdom of God and the different sort of living that the kingdom requires. Parables introduce a way of thinking that is strange and disorienting. To use Paul Ricoeur's language, parables of the kingdom of God disorient in order to reorient us toward a new way.[46] This dynamic of disorientation and reorientation is impossible without the disruption that scandal provides.

Let us take one more example of how scandal can provide an opportunity for conversion by turning to the parable of the Good Samaritan (Luke 10:25–42). The familiar parable is told by Jesus in the context of an encounter with a scholar of the law who seeks to test Jesus "and to justify himself" by asking "And who is my neighbor?" (v. 29). The story Jesus tells in response shifts the focus from who counts as one's neighbor to the question of what sort of behavior is incumbent upon a member of God's chosen people.[47] Scandal is essential to the story in at least three ways. First, the man who fell victim to robbers proves to be scandal (stumbling block) to the priest and the Levite who encountered him. They were faced with a challenge and did not respond well. Second, the parable is meant to scandalize the lawyer. The fact that the protagonist of the story is a despised Samaritan is disorienting and challenging for him. David McCracken captures this well:

> The lawyer is challenged to look and to perceive, to listen and understand. If he does so . . . his world truly will be turned upside down. Instead of

testing or tempting itinerant teachers, instead of justifying himself, instead of providing correct answers that he does not enact, he will have to "do" in the manner of the formerly hated Samaritan; he will have to live by loving God and loving neighbor, and this will mean living in something other than the established and respectable world of priests and Levites.[48]

Third, Luke's readers are personally confronted by the challenge to "go and do likewise" (v. 37). The reader is not meant to judge the lawyer's response, but to respond personally. Both the lawyer and the reader are faced with the choice of scandal or faith. Will they take offense at the imperative of Jesus to remove any limit to the scope of who counts as neighbor? Will they scoff at the notion that an untouchable could have something to teach them about how to live well and to inherit eternal life? Will they stumble at the realization that God requires them to act with mercy and love rather than to debate the finer points of law and ethics? Or will they be led to conversion by their encounter with this parable that disrupts the neat boundaries dividing those who are good from those who are evil?

Practical and Pastoral Implications

The Pharisees were scandalized by the message of Christ. Their sense of certainty regarding the Law and what constituted holy living and sinfulness made it impossible for them to respond to God's invitation in Christ. One can see similarities between the mistakes of the Pharisees of Jesus' time and some responses to contemporary controversies about gay marriage.[49] To see faith as a settled container of truth that has been passed on to us by Jesus and the apostles puts one at risk of taming the faith to the point that one loses sight of the need for ongoing conversion.

Many in the church today see "the world" and popular culture as profoundly corrupt, dangerous, and inimical to the faith. There certainly is evil and moral corruption in our world today, but this fact has led some to an unqualified negative stance toward the world. Growing tolerance for or acceptance of homosexuality and same-sex marriage has been viewed through that lens of corruption and decline. The church is seen as a defender of morality against a corrupt, immoral, secular society. Many decades ago, Enda McDonagh warned that "undiscerning or blind self-indulgent and self-protective non-conformity in face of a particular civilisation is no more an act of faith than an undiscerning self-indulgent conformity. At the theological and pastoral level the work of listening to and responding to the true call of God as embodied in the world in which we live must continue unremittingly."[50] The present controversy requires ongoing discernment of whether shifts in understandings about gay relationships and gay marriage are a sign of the times that are calling the church to reexamine its teaching on sexuality and to reexamine the question of whether it is wise or just to cast people out for living in committed same-sex relationships. An understanding of scandal more fully informed by the New Testament should lead us to ask whether the phenomenon of gay men and women promising loving, lifelong commitment to each other should be an occasion for Christians to be scandalized in the very different sense of seeing long-held certainties unexpectedly overturned by the living God. This is not a call to retreat into moral relativism. It is a suggestion that punitive actions against gay men and women by principals, pastors, and bishops are inconsistent with Christian charity, are likely to cause "opposite scandal," and do not reflect the fact that we are at a moment that requires prayerful discernment.

The response of the Church to same-sex marriage and the reality that there are many gay men and women who have lived their entire lives as committed Catholics inevitably will cause scandal. If church and school officials take a tolerant stance or offer a tentative blessing in response to these realities, some Christians will be scandalized. If church officials continue to condemn these relationships and fire teachers and ministers for being gay or getting married, others will be scandalized. One of these responses is a scandal of human weakness—a failure to live the Gospel. The other is joined to the scandal of Christ who calls the church to give scandal by adhering to the path of the Gospel rather than the established order of things. It is important not to allow self-righteous cries of "scandal" to short-circuit the vitally important process of discernment in which the whole of the church should engage today as it decides which scandal is which.

Notes

1. Paul Blume, "Archbishop Forces Music Director's Resignation after Marriage," KMSP-TV, September 23, 2014. www.myfoxtwincities.com.

2. Francis DeBernardo, "As Another Lesbian Church Employee Is Fired, Catholicism Continues to Diminish," May 16, 2014. New Ways Ministry, newwaysministryblog.wordpress.com.

3. "Catholicism, Employment, and LGBT Issues," May 19, 2016. newwaysministryblog.wordpress.com.

4. Carol Pogash, "Morals Clause in Catholic Schools Roils Bay Area," *New York Times*, February 26, 2015.

5. David Gibson, "Miami Catholic Archbishop Tells Employees If They Support Gay Marriage, They Could Be Fired," *Religion News Service*, January 7, 2015. www.cruxnow.com; "Unwed Catholic School Teacher Fired over Pregnancy," Associated Press, February 4, 2014; Audie Cornish, "Morals Clauses Prove Controversial for Catholic School Teachers," *National Public Radio* (transcript), July 15, 2014. www.npr.org; "Archdiocese of Cincinnati Expands Morals Clause in Teacher Contracts," WLWT News 5, Cincinnati. www.wlwt.com.

6. Pogash, "Morals Clause."

7. Angela Senander, *Scandal: The Catholic Church and Public Life* (Collegeville, MN: Liturgical Press, 2012), 7–8.

8. "Cleveland Diocese Expands Moral Clause to High School Teachers: Bans Sterilization, Cohabitation, Gay 'Marriage,'" April 10, 2015. *Life Site News*. https://www.lifesitenews.com.

9. *Catechism of the Catholic Church*, 2nd ed. (Vatican City: Libreria Editrice Vaticana), no. 2284 and no. 2287.

10. Ibid., no. 2285.

11. St. Thomas Aquinas, *Summa Theologiae*, II-II, q. 43, online edition, trans. Kevin White. www.newadvent.org.

12. ST II-II, q. 43, a. 1 and ST II-II, q. 43, a. 3.

13. ST II-II, q. 43, a. 1, Reply to Obj. 3.

14. Twentieth-century moral manualists made the same recommendations. For example see Bernhard Häring, *The Law of Christ*, vol. 2, trans. Edwin G. Kaiser, CPPS (Westminster, MD: Newman Press, 1963), 480.

15. ST II-II, q. 43, a.7, *sed contra*.

16. ST II-II, q.43, a.7.

17. Henry Davis, *Moral and Pastoral Theology*, vol. 1, "Human Acts, Law, Sin, Virtue." 8th ed. (London: Sheed and Ward, 1959), 334–35.

18. Congregation for the Doctrine of the Faith, *Considerations Regarding Proposals to Give Legal Recognition to Unions Between Homosexual Persons*, June 3, 2003. On homosexual acts and the natural law see *Letter to the Bishops of the Catholic Church on the Pastoral Care of Homosexual Persons*, October 1, 1986. www.vatican.va.

19. Pew Research Forum, "Changing Attitudes on Gay Marriage," July 29, 2015. http://www.pewforum.org.

20. For a detailed, critical engagement of Catholic teaching on sexual ethics, including homosexuality, see Todd A. Salzman and Michael G. Lawler, *The Sexual Person: Toward a Renewed Catholic Anthropology* (Washington, DC: Georgetown University Press, 2008). The US Catholic Bishops' Committee on Doctrine issued a detailed critique of the book and declared that "neither the methodology of *The Sexual Person* nor the conclusions that depart from authoritative Church teaching constitute authentic expressions of Catholic theology." USCCB, "Bishops' Doctrine Committee Says Book by Creighton University Professors Conflicts with Catholic Teaching on Sexuality," September 22, 2010, www.usccb.org.

21. John A. Dick, "Belgian Bishop Advocates Church Recognition of Gay Relationships," *National Catholic Reporter*, December 30, 2014. www.ncronline.org. Luke Hansen, "Cardinal Marx on Francis, the Synod, Women in the Church and Gay Relationships," *America*, January 22, 2015. Bob Shine, "O'Malley: Trend of Workers Fired for LGBT Issues 'Needs To Be Rectified,'" *National Catholic Reporter*, September 25, 2015.

22. Lisa Fullam, "Giving Scandal," *America*, November 1, 2010.

23. Ibid.

24. David Gibson, "Catholic Bishop Returns Petitions to Ousted Gay Man," *Washington Post*, April 25, 2013.

25. "Backlash at Catholic High School over Firing of Pregnant Gay Teacher," *Guardian*, September 26, 2014.

26. Congregation for the Doctrine of the Faith, "Pastoral Care of Homosexual Persons," no. 10.

27. Matt Comer, "Charlotte Catholic Fires Gay Teacher for Saying He'll Marry Gay Partner," *Charlotte Observer*, January 12, 2015. www.charlotteobserver.com.

28. Ibid.

29. Senander, *Scandal*, 36.

30. Karl Rahner, *Foundations of Christian Faith: An Introduction to the Idea of Christianity*, trans. William V. Dych (New York: Crossroad), esp. 116–26.

31. Senander, *Scandal*, 29.

32. Mark Jordan, "Scandal and the Culture of Silence," *Gay and Lesbian Review*, July–August 2002, 15. For an extended treatment see Jordan's book *The Silence of Sodom: Homosexuality in Modern Catholicism* (Chicago: University of Chicago Press, 2000).

33. Senander, *Scandal*, 46.

34. David McCracken, *The Scandal of the Gospels: Jesus, Story, and Offense* (New York: Oxford University Press, 1994), 30.

35. Søren Kierkegaard, *Practice in Christianity*, ed. and trans. H. Hong and E. Hong (Princeton, NJ: Princeton University Press, 1991): 143–44.

36. McCracken, *Scandal of the Gospels*, 31.

37. Senander, *Scandal*, 8.

38. McKracken, *Scandal of the Gospels*, 7.

39. Jeremiah L. Alberg, *Beneath the Veil of Strange Verses: Reading Scandalous Texts* (East Lansing: Michigan State University Press, 2013), 75.

40. Ibid., 77.

41. Benedict T. Viviano, "The Gospel according to Matthew," ed. Raymond E. Brown, Joseph A. Fitzmyer, and Roland E. Murphy, *The New Jerome Biblical Commentary* (Upper Saddle River, NJ: Prentice Hall, 1990), 663.

42. Both are references to classic conceptions of justice: the fulfillment of a contractual obligation and "to give each according to his due." See ibid.

43. McCracken, *Scandal of the Gospels*, 78–79.

44. John Dominic Crossan, *In Parables: The Challenge of the Historical Jesus* (New York: Seabury, 1973): 15–16. Cited in McCracken, *Scandal of the Gospels*, 86.

45. This is a central claim of McCracken's approach to interpretation of scandal. For two key sources for this approach, see Mikhail Bakhtin, *The Dialogic Imagination*, ed. and trans. Michael Holquist and Caryl Emerson (Austin: University of Texas Press, 1981) and *Speech Gems and Other Late Essays*, trans. Vern W. McGee (Austin: University of Texas Press, 1986).

46. Paul Ricoeur, "Biblical Hermeneutics," *Semeia* 4 (1975): 121. See also "The 'Kingdom' in the Parables of Jesus," *Anglican Theological Review* 623 (1981): 168. C.f. McCracken, *Scandal of the Gospels*, 88.

47. Robert J. Karris, "The Gospel according to Luke," in Brown, Fitzmyer, and Murphy, *New Jerome Biblical Commentary*, 702.

48. McCracken, *Scandal of the Gospels*, 136.

49. Enda McDonagh, *Doing the Truth: The Quest for Moral Theology* (Notre Dame, IN: University of Notre Dame Press, 1979), 182.

50. Ibid.

SCRIPTURE AND SEXUAL ETHICS

From Absolute Trust and
Systematic Suspicion to a Hermeneutics of Appreciation

Ronaldo Zacharias

According to Vatican II, the scientific presentation of moral theology "should draw more fully on the teaching of the holy Scripture and should throw light upon the exalted vocation of the faithful in Christ and their obligation to bring forth fruit in charity for the life of the world."[1] For many people, this means "to go back to the Bible" in order to find the relevant texts and to see what they have to say. In other words, the Bible is assumed as a source, something to delve into. But the question that tends to be undervalued is what model of interpretation is used for those who operate on this assumption.[2]

The common point of departure does not necessarily mean common conclusions will be reached: fundamentalists will go back to the Bible to find appropriate proof texts to justify the literal application of what is quoted to everyday life; historical critics will go back to the Bible to better understand its historical conditioning character, and to weigh rationally whether it is applicable or not.[3] The risk is, according to Robin Scroggs: "Where the Bible agrees with those [contemporary] sensitivities, it is invoked to support what one already knows to be correct. Where the Bible disagrees, it is relegated to its historical context and becomes something we have overcome in our struggle for the truth."[4]

Some questions arise: Isn't the Bible more than a source to be analyzed for enforcing this or that behavior? Isn't it more than an archaeological site to dig into for revelatory propositions? Should not the Bible be read within a process of community formation and mission? Should not the community read the text in ways that are transforming and life-giving?[5]

Rather than dedicating these reflections to a critical exegesis of the biblical texts, my aim is to show that it is important—and possible—to change the tint of the glasses through which we approach and read the Bible. In doing so, I hope it will be easier to understand what kind of helpful guidance we should expect from the Bible regarding sexuality.

Absolute Trust or Systematic Suspicion?

One of the risks of "going back to the Bible" is the tendency to select texts that we feel speak for or against our particular understanding of sexuality and use them as if they imparted a shared theological vision and a common attitude regarding sexuality. As Daniel Harrington reminds us, the Bible's moral teaching does not appear in only one literary form. The risk is to "take these teachings out of their narrative and historical frameworks and treat them as free-floating moral principles."[6] With much stronger criticism, Stephen Barton stresses that the text cannot become "captive to tribal interests of one kind or another, whether conservative fundamentalism, liberal biblical criticism, feminism, gay liberation or whatever," because "when this happens, the meaning of the text and even more the truth of the text tend to get confused with the question of whether or not the text can be used to support the identity and self-understanding of the group concerned."[7] The question is what are the criteria used to choose one text and give it authority? Are such criteria derived from the Bible itself? Or do they depend on who is reading it? If some text is selected because it fits the beliefs of the one who selects it, the authority of the text is compromised.[8]

For Scroggs, what is at stake is the authority of the Bible. He does not hesitate to assert that "what we need is a new understanding of the role of the Bible in the church today that acknowledges the actual reality of the situation—an understanding that takes the Bible as a foundational document but not as authoritative, that is, an understanding that does not assume that the Bible determines all that we are to think and do."[9] I agree with Scroggs. However, the fact that the Bible does not determine all that we are to think and do in present circumstances does not mean that it is without compelling arguments and value. In other words, we cannot avoid being in dialogue with the biblical texts, just as we cannot appeal to biblical assertions as the only correct ones just because they are in the Bible. Our dialogue with the text requires that we remain open to what the Bible has to say in a way that involves critical thinking. In the process of thinking critically, we come to realize that it is not difficult to deal with issues that pertain to culture-bound realities, but "to decide just what the legitimate parameters are and whether one's own views have forced one to stay outside those parameters."[10]

Should there be absolute trust or systematic suspicion when approaching the biblical text? The first attitude tends to identify the literal meaning of the text with its direct application. The second tends to establish the meaning of the text in order to apply it, or to disregard it as irrelevant. Both attitudes are problematic because they imply that the reader-interpreter of the text is its judge. As Walter Brueggemann rightly suggests, there should be a convergence of "obedient interpretation and interpretive obedience."[11] We cannot undervalue that "literary criticism helps us appreciate how the text speaks, but is mute when we come to ask, is what it says true?"[12] And this is so because this question goes beyond the realm of exegesis and becomes a theological, ecclesial, and practical question. The fact that the text "speaks" does not mean that it has only one meaning. How could we guarantee the meaning that we reach now is the same intended by the original author or the biblical communities? Even if it were, shouldn't we take into account that the text can have meanings that were not seen or anticipated by the original author or by the biblical communities?[13] Can we ignore that we are influenced by the history of the reception of the text by previous generations?[14]

Considering the preceding points, I want to clarify that I do not intend to give voice to specific texts in matters of sexuality.[15] But rather, I prefer to focus on the Bible as a whole, in order to see how it shaped people and communities that tried to reason morally and act accordingly.[16]

It is very hard to find an articulate and coherent treatment of sexuality in the Bible. If, on the one side, sexuality is considered as one of the blessings of creation, on the other, it can destroy social order if allowed free rein. At the same time that the ideal of monogamous marriage "conveys a positive place for sexuality within the social order . . . all wrongful behavior was seen through the metaphor of sexual activity."[17] It seems that sexuality was reduced to a question of social control: "who, with whom, and when," to quote Tikva Frymer-Kensky.[18] To better understand such an ambiguity, we need to take into consideration the following key points.[19]

First, as the Bible reflects a patriarchal culture, the God of Israel had to be male. But "he is only male by gender, not by sex."[20] Consequently, God does not behave in a sexual manner. It is interesting to note that, although an anthropomorphic language is used to describe God, God is always thought of "above the waist;" although God is the "husband" of Israel, there are no physical descriptions or erotic metaphors to express God's affection. For Israel, sexuality cannot be associated with God. As the Creator, God was the "Other," the one distinct from God's creation. Sexuality belongs to the realm of creatures. The archetypal sexual relationship was no longer divine but human; at the same time the prototypal couple was no longer portraying a God and God's consort, but two created beings. In other words, Israel separates the sexual and the sacred.[21]

Second, not being a sacred reality, "all hints of sexuality had to be kept far away from cultic life and religious experience."[22] The separation of sexuality and cultic life was also embedded in the purity provisions of the sacred laws. The essential divisions of human existence—holy and profane, life and death, male and female—were intended to be kept intact, and the Law played its part in that. Anything that blurs the established distinctions cannot be tolerated (within this perspective we must understand the biblical view of homosexuality, bestiality, adultery, and incest).[23]

Third, the proper sphere for dealing with sexuality was the Law.[24] Considering that the marital structure was the only structure established by God at the beginning of human existence, such a structure was assumed as the "legal" place for sexuality. Sexuality had a place in the social order because it bonded and created the family. The purpose of sexual laws was "to control sexual behavior by delineating the proper parameters of sexual activity, those relationships and time in which it is permissible."[25]

Fourth, for Israel, sexuality was a two-edged sword: "a force for bonding and a threat to the maintenance of boundaries."[26] It is through the Law that we can infer that there was in Israel a great concern about sex. In other words, it was through the Law that the anxieties of the people were revealed. However, the lack of alternative ways to discuss and express such anxieties and concerns reveals the vacuum in Israel's discussion on sex.[27]

Fifth, with reference to tradition and laws, the world of the New Testament differed little from the world of the Old Testament. Probably because of this we find relative silence about the argument in the world of Jesus of Nazareth, at least as expressed through the Gospels. What this may mean is difficult to surmise. On the other hand, it is not incorrect to affirm that Jesus interprets the Law and overcomes it by stressing the priority of interiority. Reaffirming the importance of faithful commitment and personal relationships in marriage, extending forgiveness to those who had committed sins of a sexual nature, and proposing celibacy "for the sake of the kingdom of heaven" as a way of life for his disciples, the Jesus of the Gospels saw sexuality not as something extraordinary; he saw the sins related to it, not as sins graver than others. Rather, for Jesus, sexuality was "simply one aspect of human existence for which man is responsible."[28] Finally, the relative silence in the Gospels on matters sexual was filled by the first-century Hellenistic—dualistic—philosophy. Sexuality, part of the physical principle of the person, should be dominated by reason, the spiritual principle. The goal of an ethical life becomes the controlling of passion. Sexuality and marriage were good, but an eschatological preference for the celibate state was better. Man and woman were equals in Christ, but not in the social sphere. The Word of God was proclaimed, but the *status quo* resisted change.[29]

Considering all the above points, what kind of helpful guidance should we expect from the Bible regarding sexuality? It is not a matter of being dismayed when we realize that we cannot expect too much. As William Countryman well states, "We should not ignore the fallibility of Scripture but should understand it as inevitable if God is to communicate with us in this created universe, where we are all bound to the limitations of time and space."[30] This does not mean that the Bible is less valuable to us. The fact is that, even if we cannot count on a great deal of help from the Bible, we are called to make decisions about issues of sexuality without any assurance that these decisions are sanctioned by the Spirit—and this is much more frightening.

Beyond Absolute Trust and Systematic Suspicion

Acknowledging that the Bible is a collection of books that are the result of specific historical circumstances, and that biblical moral teachings are presented in "various literary forms (commands, prohibitions, case laws, prophetic exhortations, wise sayings, and so forth) and frequently in the course of a narrative (as in Exodus through Deuteronomy and in the Gospels),"[31] we cannot expect anything other than a variety of interpretations on human sexuality as presented in the Bible. And these various perspectives, as has been noted already, must be interpreted within their narrative and historical frameworks.

I believe that one way of dealing with the lack of what the Bible directly says about sexuality is to take into consideration the "spirit" that characterizes the making of moral decisions in the Old and New Testaments. Although this "spirit" does not specifically refer to sexuality, it has important practical implications for sexual ethics. It is from this perspective that I wish to continue.[32]

If we take the Bible as a whole, we can infer that biblical ethics has a deep religious orientation: the ethics of Israel derives from the will of God, who offered to God's people the possibility of taking part in a covenant with God. The love of God is manifested in each event of a history that has its definitive reason in a free call. For example, the great deeds of God expressed in the Exodus and in the pilgrimage through the desert constitute the foundation of an obedience that Israel freely accepts.

The Decalogue was assumed by the people as their concrete way of replying to God's call. Interpreted within the context of the Covenant, the Decalogue becomes the word and revelation of God. The Decalogue, in being considered as an expression of God's will, manifests the way of life that God expects of God's people. To practice the commandments meant to accept the supreme power of God. Israel's ethical life consists in recognizing such a dependence as based on love, and submission to God's will as the only fair attitude toward God. In other words, to live according to the precepts of God becomes an attitude of absolute thankfulness to God's call. This is what we mean when we say that the ethics of Israel is grounded in their religion: Israel's faith is expressed through the practice of their moral life.[33]

For Israel, the most important thing was not the material observance of this or that law, but the meaning of it within the religious context in which it was practiced. It is "dialogue" that characterizes the moral dialogue between Israel and God.[34] It is important to consider that aside from the Decalogue, Israel had to deal with a great number of other moral laws. The spirit that animates Israel to observe the moral laws is the same as the spirit that animates it to embrace the Decalogue: those who love God practice the commandments as well as the precepts of the Law. Within such a perspective it is not difficult to understand why, for Israel, the Law was praised as a sacred reality, as a real sacrament of God's presence. Such a reality changes when the synagogues substitute the Temple, and the scribes become more important than the priests. The religious dimension of the moral life is converted into pure casuistry. What really matters is the observance of the precept and not the spirit that animates such an observance.[35]

Taking into account the religious dimension of Israel's practice of the Law, could we infer that biblical moral laws were revealed directly and immediately by God? Here it is important to distinguish something that is directly revealed by God from something that is presented within the context of revelation. It is within the second perspective that the Decalogue must be understood. A historical analysis of the commandments reveals that there is a great parallel between them and the laws of other people of the Near East.[36] When assumed by Israel, these laws—after a natural process of purification—were put within the context of revelation. On the one hand, Israel is open to the ethical values elaborated by men and women of a different culture to the point of assuming many of them, and on the other hand, when Israel incorporates these values into the sphere of the Covenant, it assumes them as a concrete "Word of God" for the people.[37]

What can we infer from this process of reception-depuration-assimilation-transformation? It means that what God expects from God's people is what the people discover that they must do. I do not mean to say that God accommodates Godself to the mentality of each era or culture. I only mean that God allows that we ourselves—autonomous and responsible people—discover the best ways to enter into a relationship with God and manifest to God our respect and friendship. If the "revealed" moral changes and developments took place during the history of the people, it is because, from the beginning, human intelligence did not fully understand what true values were. Therefore, some sort of imperfections and limitations are inherent in human judgment.

It is proper for the human condition to approach the truth with doubt and suspicion. The difficult path of discovering and understanding the truth is the result of a historical process. And God is the first to appreciate the effort that the human being makes to discover the truth, without requiring—at least at the beginning—more than the human being can imperfectly discover in a particular context and era. This means that God's word and will "become flesh" in the human yearning to discover and embrace the absolute "good." Our way of obeying God cannot be reduced to a mere observance of the Law. It is more than that: it is our openness and docility to God's call, which is manifested in many different ways other than through God's written Word.[38]

It is the possibility of responding to God's call that configures the biblical anthropology of the Old Testament, and, consequently, its biblical morality. Although the human being is defined in the Old Testament as the "image and likeness" of God, the concept of the transcendence of God from the Old Testament does not allow one to think of "image and likeness" as an imitation of God. It is only within the context of the New Testament—because of the influence of Hellenism—that the imitation of God will be possible.[39] As *eikon* of the Father, Jesus does not only reveal the Father but he also becomes a visible model for the faithful. With Jesus, biblical ethics will no longer be limited to obedience to a precept, but it will be characterized as an increasing conformity with a person.[40] As William Spohn asserts, "Jesus Christ is the paradigm for Christian moral life."[41] To imitate Jesus will be the fundamental practice of the Christians. It is such a likeness with Jesus that will identify all Christians as children of the Father. In other words, it will be the likeness with Jesus that will allow us to discern the traits that are characteristic of our way of life. As Harrington says, "New Testament ethics is oriented toward encountering God and doing God's will in the light of the Christ-event. It is concerned with God's redemptive action through Christ and how people of faith may participate in it."[42] For Wolfgang Schrage, New Testament ethics follows from God's saving act in Jesus Christ and reflects it. Moreover, it is implicit in it.[43]

If Jesus as the *eikon* is to be followed, are we then in a position to go to the New Testament to extract from it specific norms of conduct or concrete orientations to resolve our ethical dilemmas? As the historical-critical method of interpretation of the Bible reminds us, it is not possible to apply Jesus' teachings without a previous hermeneutic. More than a manual of morality, Jesus came to reveal a way of life completely rooted in love. If there is something definitive in the New Testament it is the fact that Jesus came for others. He knew how to make his life a permanent gift to God and for the others.[44] He freely accepted giving his life and, in so doing, transformed his own attitude into the supreme norm of our existence. In being so explicit and definitive, his attitude is, at the same time, so open and flexible that it could embody many ways of living and be assumed in new and different situations.[45] In the spirit of the New Testament, a moral life, more than being reduced to this or that practice, is the visible manifestation of an existence that at least tries to be ministry, gift, and love. In other words, Christian ethics is characterized by the effort to discern in each concrete historical moment and in each concrete situation the demands that derive from love.[46]

Within this perspective, what should we do with the concrete norms of behavior that appear in the New Testament? First, we should never accept them literally, but rather ask ourselves how to understand their meaning within the sociological and cultural context from which they emerged. As Schrage well asserts, "New Testament ethics is contextual ethics, ethics in the context of specific situations."[47] Trying to understand the meaning of the norms according to the intention of the author and of the biblical community and within its concrete historical context is not synonymous with discovering its message for our time through the hermeneutic process. Mere exegesis is something that has no resonance in our personal and communal lives. Consequently, we must distinguish between the message that these norms manifest—the value of which always remains—and its concrete incarnation in the context in which we live. What we read in the Bible is much more than what the text offers us. The mere reading of the text is not enough to discern and to realize the will of God. The most important thing is to realize the difficult effort involved in putting into practice the new and fundamental *ethos* of the Gospel. In other words: we are called to discover which ways of living best embody our option for love, service, and the gift of ourselves.

Taking into consideration the "spirit" that characterizes making moral decisions in the Old and New Testaments, how can we read the Bible as a guiding beacon for our sexual lives? Is it possible to reconcile such a "spirit" with the fact that, according to the Bible, sex is assumed to belong to heterosexual marriage, and, therefore, any kind of sexual relationship outside of such a context is not included in it?[48] To answer these questions, it is important to consider the following points: the fact that the Bible affirms sexual relations as pertaining to the context of heterosexual marriage does not permit us to infer that sexuality is meaningful "only" with respect to marriage; the fact that premarital and homosexual sex, for example, are not included in the ideal does not permit us to infer that nonmarital heterosexual unions cannot bear witness to grace and God's blessing; the fact that procreation is a blessing linked with sexual differentiation does not permit us to infer that it is essential to or primary for morally normative expressions of human sexuality; the fact that persons of a different sex are suitable partners does not permit us to infer that they are suitable partners "because" of their difference; the fact that sexuality is affirmed as a good in itself does not permit us to infer that it lies beyond the sphere of human responsibility; the fact that sexuality needs control does not permit us to infer that continence can be imposed; the fact that the Bible has rules does not permit us to infer that they are sufficient for us when it comes down to concrete decisions.

We need to be aware of the fact that the biblical authors, although they recognize the goodness of sexuality, do not deal with the question of "how" people ought to think and feel about themselves as sexual beings. It becomes evident that more than reconciling what was said thus far with the general parameters of a biblical sexual morality, we need a new kind of approach to the Bible in order to make it a guiding light for our sexual lives. I think that Lisa Cahill and William Spohn offer some interesting insights on this point.[49]

Cahill is interested in a social and communal approach to the Bible. She shifts the discussion from a norm-oriented approach to an approach that emphasizes the responsibility that Christian sexual ethics has in helping "to build up the unity of the Christian community." For her, it is important to go beyond the literal meaning of the text in order "to develop a sexual ethic that promotes Christian communities analogous in shape to those reflected by the New Testament materials on morality. The early Christian communities challenged their cultures by embodying, however haltingly and imperfectly, a new set of relationships characterized not by power, domination, and exclusion but by compassion, solidarity, and inclusion."[50]

Spohn, in linking the adequate interpretation of biblical text with the personal generosity that allows the reader to enter the world of the text, shifts the discussion from the hermeneutics of suspicion to what he calls "the hermeneutics of appreciation." That is to say, what really counts in Christian life is not entering a text and its world, but "being welcomed into a mysterious and encompassing relation with God in Christ through the power of the Spirit."[51]

Taking into account all that has been said thus far, the task before us involves much more than appealing to Scripture for rules, guidelines, and principles. It also demands that we take into consideration the following insights.

There is an astonishing diversity in biblical reflections on the moral life and in the modes of discourse that inform our understanding. Only in God do we find the unity that we seek. The one God of Scripture "calls forth the creative reflection and faithful response of those who would be God's people."[52] The primary requirement for discerning God's will in changing moral contexts demands that we seek and strive to be shaped by our relationship with God. In other words, what we find in Scripture should "help us to shape our identity as people of faith and moral agents."[53] What matters most is not what this or that text says, but rather the attention given to the presence and activity of God in the here and now as well as the disposition that enables us to be shaped by God's Spirit who reveals to us that sanctity is plural. God's will and our openness to embrace it have a plurality of forms. What really matters is the substance!

When it comes to sex and sexuality, the Bible "remains relatively uninterested in the morality of sex per se."[54] What really matters is that God created us for relationships. Given our belief that the very being of God is essentially self-giving and relational, God could not *not* have imprinted in us God's essence. If God created us as we are, it is because God wanted to give us the capacity to discover our own essence precisely through relationships with others in which we must put forth an effort to give, receive, and share love. In other words, our human experiences of love "bear the trinitarian mark."[55] Because of this, "our thinking about sexuality . . . has to begin with God: the Christian vision of God as a Trinity of love, where the love between the Persons of the Trinity is characterized by desire for union with the other, a love characterized also by faithfulness, mutual indwelling, interdependence and trust, and flowing over in the creation and redemption of the world."[56] What really matters is love!

Translated by Margaret Eletta Guidry, ODF

Notes

1. Vatican Council II, "Decree on the Training of Priests," *Optatam Totius*, October 28, 1965, no. 16, in *Documents of the Vatican II*, ed. Austin P. Flannery (Grand Rapids, MI: Eerdmans, 1975), 720.

2. For an official Catholic view of the interpretation of the Bible, see Pontifical Biblical Commission, "The Interpretation of the Bible (April 15, 1993)," *Origins* 23 (1994): 497–524; Pontifical Biblical Commission, *The Bible and Morality: Biblical Roots of Christian Conduct* (Vatican City: Libreria Editrice Vaticana, 2008), 129–221. See also Charles H. Cosgrove, ed., *The Meanings We Choose: Hermeneutical Ethics, Indeterminacy and the Conflict of Interpretations* (London: T&T Clark, 2004); Charles H. Cosgrove, *Appealing to Scripture in Moral Debate: Five Hermeneutical Rules* (Grand Rapids, MI: Eerdmans, 2002), and the great work of Yiu Sing Lúcás Chan, *Biblical Ethics in the 21st Century: Developments, Emerging Consensus, and Future Directions* (New York: Paulist Press, 2013). Lúcás Chan advocates that a true biblical ethics needs to have the exegetical work of biblical theologians and the interpretive work of theological ethicists.

3. See Holger Szesnat, "Human Sexuality, History, and Culture: The Essentialist / Social Constructionist Controversy and the Methodological Problem of Studying 'Sexuality' in the New Testament and its World," *Scriptura* 62 (1997): 335–61.

4. Robin Scroggs, "The Bible as Foundational Document," *Interpretation* 49 (1995): 19.

5. See Stephen C. Barton, "Is the Bible Good News for Human Sexuality? Reflections on Method in Biblical Interpretation," *Theology and Sexuality* 1 (1994): 45.

6. Daniel J. Harrington, "Biblical Studies and Moral Theology," *Church* 13, no. 4 (1997): 16.

7. Barton, "Is the Bible," 47.

8. See the inspiring work of Carol Smith, "'It's in the Book': Using the Bible in Discussions of Human Sexuality," in *Religion and Sexuality*, ed. Michael A. Hayes, Wendy Porter, and David Tombs. Studies in Theology and Sexuality 2. Roehampton Institute London Papers 4 (Sheffield: Sheffield Academic Press, 1998), 125–34. For further discussion of the authority of the Bible, read the excellent Bruce C. Birch, "Scripture in Ethics," in *Dictionary of Scripture and Ethics*, Joel B. Green, general editor (Grand Rapids, MI: Baker Academic, 2011), 31–32.

9. Scroggs, "Bible," 19. By authority, Scroggs means "the view that the texts, both ethical and theological, are binding on believers of all times" (28n2), and by foundational document, he means "those documents that have elicited, set the basic agenda for and defined what Christianity means as a *historical reality*" (23). William Countryman seems to join Scroggs in asserting that the Bible is "not addressed directly to us, as if to provide us all these things here and now"; it offers us "*not one* identity (and so forth) *but many*, coupled with a certain distance in that all these were offered originally to someone else." According to Countryman, more than simply expressing authority for us in our own circumstances, the Bible "is rather like a historical record of the exercise of authority." See William Countryman, *Biblical Authority or Biblical Tyranny? Scripture and the Christian Pilgrimage*, rev. ed. (Valley Forge, PA: Trinity Press International; Boston: Cowley Publications, 1994), 38.

10. Scroggs, "Bible," 25.

11. For Walter Brueggemann, obedient interpretation seeks "to see how the Bible authorizes, evokes, and permits a world that is an alternative to the deathly world of our dominant value system," and interpretive obedience "is an act of imaginative construal to show how the nonnegotiable intentions of Yahweh are to be discerned and practiced in our situation." See Walter Brueggemann, *Interpretation and Obedience: From Faithful Reading to Faithful Living* (Minneapolis: Fortress, 1991), 1.

12. Barton, "Is the Bible," 51.

13. Harrington, "Biblical Studies," 16; Birch, "Scripture in Ethics," 30.

14. For the sake of the purpose of these reflections, I am not going to analyze the history of the difficult and ambiguous relations of Christianity to sexuality. Although I am aware of the impact that the tradition has had on the consciousness or the unconsciousness of Christians in our day, I will limit myself to referring to some comprehensive studies on this subject: Peter Brown, *The Body and Society: Men, Women, and Sexual Renunciation in Early Christianity* (New York: Columbia University Press, 1988); Wayne A. Meeks, *The Origins of Christian Morality: The First Two Centuries* (New Haven, CT: Yale University Press, 1993).

15. See the significant work done by Lisa Cahill as an attempt to give voice to some scriptural texts: Lisa S. Cahill, *Between the Sexes: Foundations for a Christian Sexual Ethics* (New York: Paulist Press, 1985); Thomas A. Shannon and Lisa S. Cahill, *Religion and Artificial Reproduction: An Inquiry into the Vatican "Instruction on Respect for Human Life in Its Origin and on the Dignity of Human Reproduction"* (New York: Crossroad, 1988), 21–53; Lisa S. Cahill, *Sex, Gender and Christian Ethics* (Cambridge: Cambridge University Press, 1996), 121–65.

16. Harrington characterizes this approach as historical-hermeneutical. See Harrington, "Biblical Studies," 15.

17. Tikva Frymer-Kensky, "Law and Philosophy: The Case of Sex in the Bible," *Semeia* 45 (1989): 98.

18. Ibid.

19. The context in which the views of Hebrews and Christians were formed cannot be ignored if we want to capture "the distinctiveness of insight into the significance of human sexuality conveyed by both the Old and the New Testaments." See Raymond Collins, "The Bible and Sexuality," *Biblical Theology Bulletin* 7 (1977): 149.

20. Frymer-Kensky, "Law and Philosophy," 90. See also Jackie A. Naudé, "Sexual Ordinances," in *New International Dictionary of Old Testament Theology and Exegesis,* vol. 4, ed. Willem A. VanGemeren (Grand Rapids, MI: Zondervan, 1997), 1201: "There is absence of sexuality from the divine sphere. God, usually envisioned as male in gender, is not phallic; he does not represent male virility. Although the prophets use a powerful marital metaphor for the relationship between God (husband) and Israel (wife), it is never described in erotic language. God neither models nor grants sexual potency or attraction."

21. It is important to note that Israel was surrounded by people who, by means of myths, projected their experience into the sphere of the gods. Myths of fertility, passion, destruction, and marriage—as described by Collins—were used to articulate the meaning of human sexuality. The variety of myths "indicate not only the polyvalence of human sexuality, but also a fragmentary view of human sexuality" among those people (Collins, "Bible," 150). Israel, on the contrary, develops its understanding on sexuality within a monotheistic context (149–52). There was no sexuality associated with God, no goddess at his side, and therefore no creation by divine begetting of offspring.

22. Frymer-Kensky, "Law and Philosophy," 91.

23. See Eric Fuchs, *Sexual Desire and Love: Origins and History of the Christian Ethic of Sexuality and Marriage* (New York: Seabury, 1983), 35–40.

24. Exceptions include the Song of Songs, a biblical book where sexuality is treated explicitly. According to Carey Ellen Walsh, "Sex is not exactly an aside, but it is mere prologue to the focus of narrative action. This is typical of biblical scenes; they tend to offer mere clauses on sex that provide background data for subsequent actions or peoples." See Walsh, *Exquisite Desire: Religion, the Erotic, and the Song of Songs* (Minneapolis: Fortress, 2000), 36.

25. Frymer-Kensky, "Law and Philosophy," 92. Any sexual relationship outside of marriage should be considered as a threat to the social order.

26. Ibid., 99.

27. Frymer-Kensky's work can be placed within the perspective that laws mirror philosophical principles of a given society.

28. Raymond F. Collins, "The Bible and Sexuality II," *Biblical Theology Bulletin* 8 (1978): 3.

29. Ibid., 10–17.

30. Countryman, *Biblical Authority*, 123–24.

31. Harrington, "Biblical Studies," 16.

32. Because I am not going to dedicate much attention to the relationship between the Bible and moral theology, I note the following works that address this topic: Thomas W. Ogletree, *The Use of the Bible in Christian Ethics: A Constructive Essay* (Philadelphia: Fortress, 1983); Charles Curran and Richard McCormick, eds., *The Use of Scripture in Moral Theology*. Readings in Moral Theology IV (New York: Paulist Press, 1984); William C. Spohn, *What Are They Saying about Scripture and Ethics?*, fully rev. and exp. ed. (New York:

Paulist Press, 1995); Jeffrey S. Siker, *Scripture and Ethics: Twentieth-Century Portraits* (New York: Oxford University Press, 1997); Kenneth R. Himes, "Scripture and Ethics: A Review Essay," *Biblical Theology Bulletin* 15 (1985): 65–73; Erin Dufault-Hunter, "Sex and Sexuality," in *Dictionary of Scripture and Ethics*, 718–20, 723–28; Christian Frevel, "Sexualidade," in *Dicionário de termos teológicos fundamentais do Antigo e do Novo Testamento*, ed. Angelika Berlejung and Christian Frevel (São Paulo: Paulus / Loyola, 2011), 429–32.

33.   Gerhard von Rad, *Old Testament Theology*, vol. 1, *The Theology of Israel's Historical Traditions*, trans. D. M. G. Stalker (New York: Harper and Brothers, 1962), 190–203.

34.   Romeo Cavedo, "Morale dell'Antico Testamento e del Giudaismo," in *Nuovo Dizionario di Teologia Morale*, ed. Francesco Compagnoni, Giannino Pianna, and Salvatore Privitera (Milan: Paoline, 1990), 785.

35.   Ceslas Spicq, *Théologie morale du Nouveau Testament* (Paris: Librairie Lecoffre, 1965), 1:17–60.

36.   Giuseppe Barbaglio, "Decalogo," in *Nuovo Dizionario di Teologia Morale*, ed. Francesco Compagnoni, Giannino Pianna, and Salvatore Privitera (Milan: Paoline, 1990), 204–18; Francesco Sole, "Raffronti della Legge Mosaica con altre legislazioni dell'Antico Medio Oriente e con la Morale Evangelica," *Euntes Docete* 26 (1973): 443–89.

37.   The same thing was done by Paul regarding his catalogues of virtues and vices: although from pagan origin, such catalogues became a source of valid orientation for Christian life. See Raymond O'Collins, "Scripture and the Christian Ethics," in *Proceedings of the Twenty-Ninth Annual Convention, Chicago, June 10–13, 1974*, by the Catholic Theological Society of America (New York: Ed. Offices, Manhattan College, 1974), 230–35; Victor Paul Furnish, *Theology and Ethics in Paul* (Nashville, TN: Abingdon Press, 1968), 86–89.

38.   It is worthwhile to highlight that the religious and human dimensions of ethics are two complementary dimensions of the same reality. It is human at the same time that the human being discovers it—through reason—in his or her own being. And it becomes religious when it is lived as a way of responding to God. In other words, human autonomy is not irreconcilable with faith, as openness to faith does not imply neglecting the human effort to seek the good.

39.   Spicq, *Théologie morale du Nouveau Testament*, 2:688–744.

40.   Although we know little about the sexual life of Jesus, his deeds and sayings indicate to us how he lived the values that Christians uphold with regard to sexuality. William E. Phipps has written an interesting work on the sexuality of Jesus and proposes ways that Christians should attempt to imitate Jesus. Even though I do not fully agree with his conclusions, his work is worth reading. See, for example, *The Sexuality of Jesus* (Cleveland: Pilgrim Press, 1996), esp. 191–206 and *The Sexuality of Jesus: Theological and Literary Perspectives* (New York: Harper and Row, 1973), esp. 133–50.

41.   William C. Spohn, *Go and Do Likewise: Jesus and Ethics* (New York: Continuum, 1999), 1.

42.   Harrington, "Biblical Studies," 13.

43.   Wolfgang Schrage, *The Ethics of the New Testament*, trans. David E. Green (Philadelphia: Fortress, 1988), 8.

44.   This is the centrality of the *kerygma* that constitutes the core of the New Testament. See Rinaldo Fabris, "Morale del Nuovo Testamento," in *Nuovo Dizionario di Teologia Morale*, ed. Francesco Compagnoni, Giannino Pianna, and Salvatore Privitera (Milan: Paoline, 1990), 788–92.

45. See, for example, the Pauline ethics: Fabris, "Morale de Nuovo Testamento," 793–98, and Spohn, *Go and Do Likewise*, 10–11.

46. For Spohn, "Christians should be faithful yet creative to the story of Jesus in applying it to their contexts." See Spohn, *Go and Do Likewise,* 4.

47. Schrage, *Ethics of the New Testament*, 5.

48. For Cahill, these are the "*general* parameters of a 'biblical' sexual morality [that] are not in great dispute." Lisa S. Cahill, "Sexual Ethics: A Feminist Biblical Perspective," *Interpretation* 49 (1995): 6.

49. I am aware that I should make room in my reflection for the role, function, gift, power, and claim of different voices regarding new approaches to the Bible, but given the purpose of these reflections, I will simply indicate some of them: Elisabeth Schüssler Fiorenza, *In Memory of Her: A Feminist Theological Reconstruction of Christian Origins* (New York: Crossroad, 1983); Michael Walzer, *Interpretation and Social Criticism* (Cambridge, MA: Harvard University Press, 1987); Carlos Mesters, *God, Where Are You? Rediscovering the Bible*, trans. John Drury and Francis McDonagh (Maryknoll, NY: Orbis Books, 1995); Carlos Mesters, *Defenseless Flower: A New Reading of the Bible*, trans. Francis McDonagh (Maryknoll, NY: Orbis Books; London: Catholic Institute for International Relations, 1989); Tom Hanks, *The Subversive Gospel: A New Testament Commentary of Liberation*, trans. John P. Doner (Cleveland: Pilgrim Press, 2000).

50. Cahill, "Sexual Ethics," 6.

51. Spohn, *Go and Do Likewise*, 5. I do not deny that the hermeneutics of suspicion has made a positive contribution that has led to important shifts in the realm of biblical, historical, and theological studies. The work done by many liberation and feminist theologians confirms this point.

52. Allen Verhey, "Ethics in Scripture", in *Dictionary of Scripture and Ethics*, Joel B. Green, general editor (Grand Rapids, MI: Baker Academic, 2011), 5.

53. Birch, "Scripture in Ethics," 31.

54. Dufault-Hunter, "Sexual Ethics," 719.

55. Sarah Coakley, "Living into the Mystery of the Holy Trinity: Trinity, Prayer, and Sexuality," *Anglican Theological Review* 80, no. 2 (1998): 230.

56. Stephen C. Barton, "'Glorify God in Your Body' (1 Corinthians 6.20): Thinking Theologically about Sexuality," in *Religion and Sexuality: Studies in Theology and Sexuality* 2, Roehampton Institute London Papers 4, ed. Michael A. Hayes, Wendy Porter, and David Tombs (Sheffield: Sheffield Academic Press, 1998), 372.

Contributors

Paul Béré, SJ, a member of the Society of Jesus, is from Burkina Faso. He received his doctorate from the Pontifical Biblical Institute in Rome. He teaches at the Jesuit Faculty of Theology in Africa and Madagascar (Abidjan), and at the Biblical Institute (Rome).

José Manuel Caamaño López holds a doctorate in theology and a master's degree in Scripture. He is a professor in the theology faculty of the Pontifical University Comillas (Madrid) where he teaches a variety of courses in moral theology and bioethics. He is also the director of the Chair of Science, Technology and Religion of La Escuela Técnica Superior de Ingeniería (ICAI) at the same university. Among his publications are the following books: *Autonomía moral: El ser y la identidad de la Teología moral* (Madrid: San Pablo-Upcomillas, 2013), *La eutanasia: Problemas éticos al final de la vida humana* (Madrid: San Pablo-Comillas, 2013), *Ante el dolor y la muerte: Paisajes de un viaje hacia el misterio* (Madrid: PPC, 2015), and *Moral fundamental: Bases teológicas del discernimiento ético*, in collaboration with J. Martínez (Santander: Sal Terrae, 2014).

Lisa Sowle Cahill, PhD, University of Chicago, is the Monan Professor of Theology at Boston College, and past president of the Catholic Theological Society of America and the Society of Christian Ethics. Her works include *Global Justice, Christology and Christian Ethics*; *Theological Bioethics; Family: A Christian Social Perspective;* and *Sex, Gender and Christian Ethics*.

Yiu Sing Lúcás Chan, SJ (1968–2015), STL, PhD, was a Jesuit priest and a gifted pioneer in the fields of biblical ethics and Asian theological ethics. In addition to envisioning and editing this book, he wrote *The Ten Commandments and the Beatitudes: Biblical Studies and Ethics for Real Life* (Rowman and Littlefield, 2012) and *Biblical Ethics in the Twenty-first Century: Developments, Emerging Consensus, and Future Directions* (Paulist Press, 2013) and edited *Doing Catholic Theological Ethics in a Cross-Cultural and Interreligious Asian Context* (Dharmaram, 2016). His writings have appeared in *America, Asian Christian Review, Asian Horizons, Budhi, Chinese Cross Currents, Colloquia Theologica,* and *Theological Studies*. He held fellowships at Yale University, Georgetown University, and Trinity College, Dublin, and teaching positions in Cambodia, Ireland, Macau, the United States, and his native Hong Kong. He was a board member and the Asian regional director of Catholic Theological Ethics in the World Church and an assistant professor at Marquette University.

Rekha M. Chennattu is a professor of New Testament at Jnana-Deepa Vidyapeeth, Pontifical Institute of Philosophy and Religion, Pune, India. She is the author of *Johannine Discipleship as a Covenant Relationship* (Hendrickson Publishers, 2006). She was a participant at the Synod of Bishops on New Evangelization in October 2012.

John R. Donahue, SJ, was born in Baltimore and has a PhD in New Testament studies from the University of Chicago. He is the Raymond E. Brown Distinguished Professor of New Testament Studies (Emeritus) at St. Mary's Seminary and University, Baltimore. He previously taught New Testament at the Vanderbilt Divinity School and at the Jesuit School of Theology in Berkeley, California. He has lectured widely on biblical topics throughout the United States, in Africa, and in the Philippines.

Anthony Egan, SJ, based at the Jesuit Institute South Africa in Johannesburg, lectures part-time in medical ethics at University of Witwatersrand Faculty of Health Sciences and teaches in the Fordham University Ubuntu student exchange program at Pretoria University. He has published three books, numerous book chapters, articles, and over 1,000 book reviews, serves as an international columnist for *America* magazine, and regularly offers commentary on South African radio and television.

Irmtraud Fischer is a professor of Old Testament at the University of Graz, Austria. She was vice rector at Graz from 2007 to 2011. From 1997 to 2004 she held the chair for Old Testament and Women's Studies at the University of Bonn, Germany, and she has been a guest professor in Marburg, Bamberg, Vienna, Jerusalem, and Rome.

Aristide Fumagalli, born in Italy in 1962 and ordained a diocesan priest in 1991, received his doctorate from the Pontifical Gregorian University in Rome. Today he is a professor of moral theology, specializing in fundamental morals and sexual ethics, at il Seminario Arcivescovile, la Facoltà Teologica dell'Italia Settentrionale e l'Istituto Superiore di Scienze Religiose di Milano.

Louis Gendron, a Canadian Jesuit, has been in Taiwan for fifty years and is currently president of the Fu Jen Faculty of Theology of St. Robert Bellarmine and professor at the same faculty, with specializations in moral theology and psychology. He has also taught professional ethics in Fu Jen Catholic University.

Mathew Illathuparampil is a professor of Christian ethics at the Pontifical Institute of Theology and Philosophy, Alwaye, India. He holds a PhD in Christian ethics from Catholic University Leuven, Belgium. Since 2003, he has also taught in various institutions of theological learning. His areas of interest include fundamental moral theology, social ethics, and business ethics. His recent publications include *Frozen Values: A Theology of Money* (co-editor, 2014), *Business Ethics and Corporate Governance* (2013), *Indian Ethos and Management Values* (2011), and *Technology and Ethical Ambiguity* (2009). He presently serves as the Rector of St. Joseph Pontifical Seminary, Mangalapuzha, Alwaye, India.

James F. Keenan, SJ, is Canisius Professor and Director of the Jesuit Institute at Boston College. He recently authored *University Ethics: How Colleges Can Build and Benefit from a Culture of Ethics* (Rowman and Littlefield, 2015) and edited with Yiu Sing Lúcás Chan and Shaji George Kochuthara, *Doing Catholic Theological Ethics in a Cross-Cultural and Interreligious Asian Context* (Dharmaram Press, 2016). He is presently writing *A Brief History of Catholic Ethics* (Paulist Press).

Marian Machinek, a Polish moral theologian, priest, and member of the Congregation of Missionaries of the Holy Family, is a professor and holder of the Chair for Moral Theology and Ethics in the Faculty of Theology at University of Warmia and Mazury in Olsztyn, Poland. Studies in Kazimierz Biskupi, Poland, Vienna, Austria, and Augsburg, Germany. His special interests include theological-moral anthropology, bioethicist questions at the beginning and the end of human life and biblical ethics. His publications include *Życie w dyspozycji człowieka: Wybrane problem etyczne u początku ludzkiego życia* (*Life at the Human Disposition*: *Selected Moral Problems at the Beginning of the Human Life*) (Olsztyn, 2004); *Śmierć w dyspozycji człowieka: Wybrane problem etyczne u kresu ludzkiego życia* (*Death at the Human Disposition: Selected Moral Problems at the End of the Human Life*) (Olsztyn, 2004); *Spór o status ludzkiego embrionu* (*Controversies surrounding the Status of the Human Embryo*) (Olsztyn, 2007).

Maria Inês de Castro Millen is a professor of moral theology at the Superior Education Center of Juiz de Fora (CES), in Brazil. She earned her doctorate from the Pontifical University of Rio de Janeiro, Brazil. She is president of the Brazilian Society of Moral Theology (SBTM). She publishes principally in the area of fundamental moral theology and bioethics.

Francis J. Moloney, SDB, was a member of the International Theological Commission to the Holy See (1984–2002), and is a member of the Order of Australia. Widely published, he has held major academic positions at Catholic Theological College (Melbourne), Australian Catholic University, and the Catholic University of America (Washington, DC). He is currently serving as a senior professor fellow of Catholic Theological College within the University of Divinity, Melbourne, Australia.

Chantal Nsongisa Kimesa is from the Democratic Republic of Congo. She is a sister from the congregation of the Daughters of Our Lady of the Sacred Heart, received her doctorate in biblical theology in 2009, and is a professor at Major Seminar Jean XXIII and at Saint Augustin University, both in Kinshasa.

Wilfrid Okambawa, SJ, from Benin Republic (West Africa), teaches New Testament and Greek at the Jesuit Institute of Theology in Abidjan (Côte d'Ivoire). His research fields are Pauline Literature and Hermeneutics of Interculturality.

Gina Hens-Piazza is a professor of biblical studies at the Jesuit School of Theology at Santa Clara University and the Graduate Theological Union, in

Berkeley, California. A national and international lecturer, she is the author of five books and numerous articles that address topics of biblical justice, especially in regard to women.

Thomas D. Stegman, SJ, a member of the US Midwest Province of the Society of Jesus, is dean and professor of New Testament at Boston College School of Theology and Ministry. Focusing his research on the Pauline writings, he is the author of *The Character of Jesus: The Linchpin to Paul's Argument in Second Corinthians* (Pontifical Biblical Institute, 2005); *Second Corinthians,* in the Catholic Commentary on Sacred Scripture series (Baker Academic, 2009); and *Opening the Door of Faith: Encountering Jesus and His Call to Discipleship* (Paulist, 2015). He is also a co-editor of the *Paulist Biblical Commentary* (forthcoming) for which he wrote the commentary on Romans.

Alain Thomasset, SJ, holds a doctorate in theology from the Catholic University of Leuven. He was on the staff of the Jesuit Social Center in Paris (CERAS) before becoming a professor of moral theology at the Centre Sèvres, the Jesuit faculties in Paris, where he is also the director of doctoral studies in theology. He is currently the chair of ATEM, an ecumenical and international association of francophone moral theologians, and is also a contributor to the journal *Recherches de Science Religieuse.* His most recent book is *Les vertus sociales: Justice, solidarité, compassion, hospitalité, espérance* (Lessius, 2015).

María Cristina (Tirsa) Ventura Campusano was born in the Dominican Republic. She studied chemical engineering and theology and lived in Brazil, where she completed her master's degree and doctorate in religious sudies with an emphasis in Old Testament. She received a PhD in education with a focus on educational mediation at the University De La Salle, Costa Rica, where she is a professor and researcher. She teaches ethics, epistemology, and philosophy of education, emphasizing a qualitative research methodology.

Jaime Vidaurrázaga was born in Peru, and has studied in Peru, Brazil, and the United States during his career. He holds a doctorate in theological ethics from Boston College and currently teaches theology at Emmanuel College in Boston, Massachusetts. His professional interests include fundamental moral theology, New Testament ethics, and liberation theology.

Christopher P. Vogt is an associate professor of theology and religious studies at St. John's University in New York City. His recent publications include essays on virtue ethics, moral formation, and social ethics.

Ronaldo Zacharias, SDB, earned his doctorate from the Weston Jesuit School of Theology in Cambridge, Massachusetts. He is a professor of moral theology at the Salesian University Center (UNISAL) in São Paulo, Brazil. He also is president of UNISAL and secretary of the Brazilian Society of Moral Theology (SBTM). He publishes principally in the areas of fundamental moral theology and sexual ethics.

Index